We Gather Our Family and Family of Friends to Share in Our Celebrations.

Everyone is Welcome to Our Table of Plenty.

Abbondanza !

aliment
ambrosia
antipasto
appetizers
barbeque
bite
board
bounty
bread
breakfast
break the fast
BRUNCH
buffet
chew
chomp
chow
chow-down
crumbs
collation
comestible
consume
cooking
CUISINE

devour
diet
DINE
dinner
eat
eatables
edibles
entree
fare
feast
feed
fill
fodder
food
food stuff
forage
goodies
graze
grit
groaning board
GROCERIES
grub
have a bite

hand-out
junk food
keep
larder
lunch
manna
meat
menu
mess
meal
movable feast
nibble
nosh
NOURISHMENT
nutriment
partake
pick
PICKINGS
picnic
pig out
PLENTY
potluck
provender

refreshments
regimen
repast
slop
smorgasbord
SNACK
spread
STORE
subsistence
sup
supper
support
sustenance
SWEETS
table
TAKE-OUT
three-square
tidbits
trough
viand
victuals
vittles

CONTENTS OF THIS TABLE

iv

INTRODUCTION

In 2004, when I had turned 72, I published my first menu cookbook, **MENU LOG: A Collection of Recipes as Coordinated Menus**. Three additional menu cookbooks, plus an address book of poetry and color photography (about dogs and a couple of cats) have followed in rapid succession. My four menu cookbooks comprise a catalog of hundreds of recipes, most of which are original recipes inspired by family, friends and my Italian heritage. Menus have been coordinated to marry Appetizer/Soup to Salad to Entrée to Dessert, in a seasonal ambiance ...and a "healthy" cuisine: less fat, less salt and sugar, more vegetables and fruits. I've been creating and documenting recipes since I was ten years old. My habit, then, as it is now, has been to maintain a diary of newly created recipes, readily accessible on the kitchen counter, my "lab table" for cooking experiments. My purpose has been to restore the Home-Cook to the simple pleasures of home-cooking.

MENU LOG: A Collection of Recipes as Coordinated Menus (408 pages) is a spectacular menu cookbook with an exciting and innovative format, which contains 52 menus and additional holiday menus with over 500 recipes. The coordinated menus are presented in easy-to-follow graphic detail, noting cooking and preparation times and advanced preparation. Additional sections include Brunches, Sandwiches, Buffet Selections, Hors d'oeuvres, Dressings, Sauces and Gravies and more Desserts. MENU LOG was written especially for the modern home cook who has little time to prepare daily "special" meals.

LUNCH IS IN THE BAG! A Celebration of the Midday Meal (203 pages) includes 52 coordinated luncheon menus in a seasonal ambiance, a bunch of Brunches, Sandwiches, Heroes-in-the-Making and *Lite*-Bites for Two, in addition to a section devoted to Dressings, Sauces and Gravies. A celebration of the midday meal, this cookbook sets the table for a special lunch; say, on a weekend, a "free day", a special get-together at home with family and friends – as well as suggestions for a picnic in the park.

Inspired by my Italian traditions and heritage, **FROM THE TABLE OF PLENTY, Food for the Body, Manna for the Soul** (426 pages) is my invitation to share in the bounty. This is an heirloom, inspirational menu cookbook in a seasonal ambiance, a collection of over 500 recipes, 100 menus, 75 reflections.

ALL ARE WELCOME TO THIS TABLE embraces my family and family of friends with our remembrances from my mother's and my own home-grown collection of recipe treasures; from a time when home-cooking was "in style", and when Mama used a wooden spoon and a rotary beater. We invite you to enjoy treats at Brunch; to celebrate Lunch with its many faces. You will find over three dozen complete Dinner Menus, arranged in a seasonal ambiance; and Casseroles/One-Pot Suppers, followed by more and varied Desserts. In addition, we present an expanded section on Cheese, Grilling, Dressings, Sauces and Gravies.

My family and I invite all of you to share and to taste our home-style recipes, written for you, the "home-cook", and your family and family of friends. Retrouvaille of the Home-Cook!

From my house to your house,

Abbondanza!

Marion O. Celenza

PREFACE

All Are Welcome To This Table

"A UNIVERSAL RECIPE"

Eat Healthy.

Share A Smile; Enjoy A Laugh.

Help Others.

Walk In The Sun.

Play With A Friend; Love Animals.

Remember Your Friends In Your Prayers;

Pray For The Not-So-Friendly.

Be Happy.

Feel Good!

A Family Thanksgiving.

COOKING BY NUMBERS

My Mother was gifted and talented in needlecrafts. She crocheted tablecloths, doilies, bedspreads. My favorite of her bedspread designs was the Rose of Sharon, three-dimensional 5-inch ivory roses, blooming over huge silky squares. For this project she had used an ivory Bucilla silk/cotton thread, number 30 crochet hook. She connected over 120, 9-inch three-dimensional crocheted squares, completing her work of art by hand-knotting a 5-inch fringe around 3 sides of the king-size coverlet. In my humble opinion, this bedspread could reside very comfortably, on a wall in the Louvre.

When I was in my early thirties, she had designed and crocheted in a pineapple stitch, a two-piece dress of ecru cotton, lined with silk. It has never lost its classic beauty. She had knitted sweaters, scarves and comforters for the entire family. She even designed and crocheted stuffed toy animals for all of the children in her life. Her needle embroidery designs were where her creative juices soared. Mama moved her splinter needles with their colorful threads, in and out, over and under, "painting" her "still life" cloth canvases, as gardens, filled with flowers and butterflies and bees. The most challenging of her works is "Sacred Heart of Mary", complete with a shimmering gold teardrop on Mary's cheek. She had "copied" this artwork from a picture in a religious periodical. One could call it her "painting by numbers". She followed her "instructions" perfectly: matching color for color, tone for tone, one section at a time.

ALL ARE WELCOME TO THIS TABLE, as in all of my cookbooks, presents "cooking by numbers". To create your own little culinary masterpieces, simply follow the directions, work the formulae.
1. *First of all, carefully read the entire recipe, from special notes under the recipe title to the list of ingredients, to the prepping and cooking directions.*
2. *List the basic ingredients to be used in the recipe.*
3. *List herbs, spices and condiments which are required.*
4. *Take note of the equipment you will use: pots, pans, utensils, cooking aids.*

Just before you assemble the recipe, ready all of the supplies. Rinse the vegetables; sift the flour; chop the tomatoes; grease the pan. Preheat the oven at least 15 minutes prior to using. (Be sure that your clean oven's thermostat is properly regulated and that the racks are centered.) Proceed with the recipe, step by step; observe correct measurements.

Read the recipe instructions. Follow the directions.
Enjoy the delicious results.

1

Tasty Accessories for Breakfast and Brunch

Doris and Michelle feed the youngsters.
Photos: L. Orlando Kloenne

2

PANNE DOLCE

1¾ cups low-fat milk

¾ cup granulated sugar

½ tsp. salt

½ cup butter or Smart Balance spread

¾ cup warm water (105°-115°)

2 pkg. fresh active dry yeast

7 cups unsifted all-purpose flour

2 tsp. fennel seeds

1 tsp. anise seeds

⅓ cup pignola nuts (pine nuts)

½ cup shelled pistachio nuts

½ cup candied lemon peel

½ cup candied citron

3 tbsp. grated orange peel

1½ cups golden raisins

3 tbsp. sweet wine, like Marsala or Madeira

GLAZE:

1 egg yolk or ¼ cup egg substitute   2 tbsp. water

Have ready: a floured board and a floured rolling pin; and a greased cookie sheet.

In a medium-size saucepan, heat milk just until bubbles form around edge of pot. Remove from heat. Stir in sugar, salt and butter (or Smart Balance), until butter is melted and sugar is dissolved. Cool to lukewarm (105°-115°).

In a large bowl, sprinkle yeast over warm water (105°-115°), stirring until dissolved. Stir in milk mixture and thoroughly blend. Add 4 cups flour; beat until smooth, about 2 minutes. Gradually, add rest of flour; beat until smooth, about 2 minutes. Add remainder of flour by hand, mixing the dough until it leaves sides of bowl. Turn onto a lightly floured board. Knead 5 minutes, or until smooth. Thoroughly rinse and dry the used large bowl.

Grease the same bowl. Shape dough into a ball and return it to the greased bowl. Turn the ball of dough in the greased bowl to coat on all sides. Cover the bowl with a clean linen towel; set aside in a warm place, free of drafts (85°) for 1 hour, or until dough has doubled in bulk.

Line dough board with a sheet of waxed paper. Scatter fennel and anise seeds over the waxed paper. With a rolling pin, crush fennel and anise seeds. In a medium-size bowl, combine raisins, nuts, seeds, lemon peel, citron, orange peel and Marsala. Blend thoroughly; allow to stand.
Turn dough onto a lightly floured board. Roll into a 14x14-inch square, ½-inch thick.

Sprinkle surface of dough with fruit mixture. With your hands, roll up dough, jelly-roll style. Then, with floured rolling pin, roll out filled dough to a 13x13-inch square. Cut in half and shape each half into a round 8-inches in diameter. Place 2 loaves on greased cookie sheet. Cover with a clean linen towel and allow to rise in a warm place (85°) for 1 hour or until doubled in bulk.

Preheat oven to 350°.

When loaves have doubled in bulk, with scissors, make 3 cuts on top of each loaf, to form a triangle. Brush tops of loaves with a mixture of egg yolk (or egg substitute) and water. Bake loaves for 50-60 minutes or until golden-brown. Cool completely on wire rack. If desired, wrap and freeze for later use. Makes 2 loaves.

CHOCOLATE-POPPY SEED BREAD

$\frac{1}{2}$ cup low-fat evaporated milk

$\frac{1}{4}$ cup butter or Smart Balance spread

$\frac{1}{4}$ cup granulated sugar

$\frac{1}{2}$ tsp. salt

1 pkg. fresh active dry yeast

$\frac{1}{4}$ cup warm water (about 105°-115°)

2 eggs or $\frac{1}{2}$ cup egg substitute

3 cups unsifted all-purpose flour

FILLING:

1 cup poppy seeds

2 cups boiling water

$\frac{1}{2}$ cup low-fat evaporated milk

$\frac{1}{2}$ cup honey

2 tbsp. butter or Smart Balance spread

$\frac{1}{2}$ cup finely chopped walnuts

$\frac{1}{2}$ cup each: mixed candied fruit, chopped, semi-sweet mini chocolate morsels

$\frac{1}{2}$ tsp. ground cinnamon

1 tsp. vanilla extract

1 egg, beaten, or $\frac{1}{4}$ cup egg substitute

GLAZE:
1 egg or $\frac{1}{4}$ cup egg substitute, beaten with 1 tbsp. cold water   2 tbsp. poppy seeds

Have ready: a floured board and a floured rolling pin; and a greased cookie sheet.

Place $\frac{1}{4}$ cup butter (or Smart Balance spread), sugar and salt in a medium-size bowl. Heat $\frac{1}{2}$ cup milk in a small saucepan until bubbles form around edge of pot. Pour milk over butter mixture; stir to melt butter. Cool to 105°-115°. Sprinkle yeast over $\frac{1}{4}$ cup warm water (105°-115°); stir to dissolve; add to milk mixture.

Stir in 2 eggs (or egg substitute) and $2\frac{1}{2}$ cups flour. Blend, then beat with a wooden spoon. Add remaining flour by hand . Mix until dough leaves sides of bowl. Turn dough out on floured board. Roll dough over on the board to coat all sides with flour. Knead dough by folding dough toward you.

Make the FILLING. Cover 1 cup poppy seeds with boiling water; soak seeds for 30 minutes; drain. Place in small saucepan; add $\frac{1}{2}$ cup milk, honey and butter (or Smart Balance spread). Stir over medium heat until thick, about 10 minutes. Remove from heat. Add nuts, chocolate morsels, fruit, cinnamon and vanilla. Cool the filling for 10 minutes; then, beat in 1 egg (or egg substitute).

Turn dough out onto lightly floured board. Grease a large cookie sheet. Roll dough into a 12x18-inch rectangle. Spread filling to 1-inch from edge of dough. Roll up lengthwise; pinch edges closed. Place loaf seam-side down on cookie sheet and shape loaf into a horseshoe **U**.

Cover with a clean linen towel; allow loaf to rise in a warm place (85°), free from drafts, until doubled in bulk, about 1 hour.

Preheat oven to 375°.

Brush surface of loaf with beaten egg (or egg substitute); sprinkle with poppy seeds. Bake in preheated oven at 375° for 25-30 minutes, or until golden. Remove from cookie sheet to wire rack. Delicious when served warm. About 20 slices.

4

ANISE EASTER EGG BREAD

Reprinted from: MENU LOG: A Collection of Recipes as Coordinated Menus by
Marion O. Celenza, page 284. (A traditional Easter egg twist which will delight all with its
decorative appearance and sweetly scented aroma and taste. Perhaps some will be left over for
tomorrow's breakfast. A soft-textured bread. May be prepared a couple of days in advance.)

1 cup unsifted all-purpose flour

$\frac{1}{2}$ cup granulated sugar

1 tsp. salt

1 pkg. active dry yeast

additional 3 cups flour (or more)

$\frac{1}{2}$ cup milk

$\frac{1}{2}$ cup water

$\frac{1}{2}$ cup (1 stick) butter or Smart Balance spread

3 eggs, room temperature
    or $\frac{3}{4}$ cup egg substitute

1 tbsp. anisette liqueur

$\frac{1}{4}$ tsp. nutmeg

$\frac{1}{2}$ cup raisins

1 tbsp. crushed anise seeds

5 raw eggs, colored

$\frac{1}{4}$ cup melted butter or
    Smart Balance spread

FROSTING:

1 cup confectioners' sugar   4-5 tbsp. anisette liqueur

(1) In a 6-quart mixing bowl, place 1 cup flour, sugar, salt and undissolved yeast. Stir to mix.
(2) In 1-quart saucepan, place water, milk and butter, cut into pieces. Heat on low until liquids
    are warm.
(3) Add liquid to dry ingredients, beating at medium speed for 2 minutes. Then, beat at high speed
    for 2 minutes.
(4) Add 3 eggs (or $\frac{3}{4}$ cup egg substitute), anisette, nutmeg and 1 cup flour or more to make a
    thick batter. Beat at high speed for 2 minutes.
(5) At this point work by hand- dough will be heavy. Add more flour to make a soft dough
    (about 2 cups). Add raisins and anise seeds.
(6) Turn dough onto floured board; knead for 8 to 10 minutes until smooth and elastic.
(7) Place dough in clean greased bowl, turning dough to grease all sides.
(8) Cover with clean cloth and let rise in warm place about $1\frac{1}{2}$ hours until doubled.
    (A good place to allow bread to rise is in a large oven which has been previously preheated
    to 150° then turned off.)
(9) Punch down dough and turn onto lightly floured board. Divide into 2 equal pieces.
(10) Roll each piece into a 24-inch rope and twist 2 ropes together loosely to form a ring on a greased
    9x15 baking sheet. Place raw colored eggs in centers of each twist. Brush ring with melted butter
    (or Smart Balance spread).
(11) Cover again with cloth and let rise in warm place for 1 hour until double.
(12) Heat oven to 350°. Bake ring 30 to 35 minutes. Remove from oven and cool on a rack.
(13) Frost with a mix of confectioners' sugar and anisette.

PUMPKIN BREAD

[A Cooking Hint: Use substitutes to fit health needs. Use low-fat or fat-free sour cream or yogurt instead of whole milk products.]

1 can (1 lb.) pure pumpkin

1 cup granulated sugar

¼ cup canola oil

1 cup low-fat plain Greek yogurt

1½ cups all-purpose flour

1½ cups whole wheat flour

2 tsp. baking powder

2 tsp. baking soda

2 tsp. cinnamon

½ tsp. salt

1 cup cranberry raisins

Preheat oven to 350°.

Have ready: 2 greased 9x5x3-inch loaf pans.

In a large mixing bowl, beat together, pumpkin, sugar, oil and yogurt. In a medium bowl, combine flours, baking powder, baking soda, cinnamon and salt. Add to pumpkin mixture, stirring until moistened. Stir in raisins.

Pour into 2 greased 9x5x3-inch pans and bake for 50-60 minutes. Cool cakes on wire rack for 10 minutes; remove from pans and cool completely. Makes 2 loaves; 8-10 servings each loaf.

PUMPKIN COFFEE CAKE

1½ cups brown sugar, packed

½ cup canola oil

1 can (1 lb.) pure pumpkin

2 tbsp. low-fat milk

6 egg whites, or 6 portions dried egg whites
(Sold in specialty food stores; follow
directions on container for reconstituting
egg whites.)

2 cups all-purpose flour

1½ cups oats

½ cup golden raisins

2 tsp. ground cinnamon

1 tbsp. baking powder

2 tsp. baking soda

¼ cup oats for sprinkling

Preheat oven to 350°.

Have ready: Grease a non-stick 10-inch tube or Bundt pan.

In a large bowl, beat sugar and oil until fluffy. Mix in pumpkin, egg whites and milk. Gradually, add flour, 1½ cup oats, raisins, baking powder, baking soda and cinnamon. Mix thoroughly. Spread the batter into a greased 10-inch tube or Bundt pan; sprinkle top of batter with remaining ¼ cup oats. Bake cake in preheated oven at 350° for 60-70 minutes or until inserted toothpick removes clean. Cool cake for 10 minutes; remove from pan. Serves 10-12.

6

OLD-FASHIONED TOMATO SOUP CAKE

Reprinted from: MENU LOG: A Collection of Recipes as Coordinated Menus
by Marion O. Celenza, page 53.
(When you taste this cake, childhood memories will be re-awakened. Prepare on the day before.)

CAKE:

2 cups flour

1 cup granulated sugar

1 tsp. baking powder

1 tsp. cinnamon

$\frac{1}{2}$ tsp. nutmeg

$\frac{1}{2}$ tsp. cloves

$\frac{1}{2}$ tsp. salt

1 can condensed tomato soup (do not add water)

1 tsp. baking soda

1 beaten egg or $\frac{1}{4}$ cup egg substitute

$\frac{1}{2}$ cup corn oil

1 cup chopped nuts

1 cup white raisins

CREAM CHEESE FROSTING:

$\frac{3}{4}$ cup confectioners' sugar

6 oz. cream cheese (low-fat)

2 tsp. grated lemon rind

2 tbsp. milk

Ralph and Ellie Mazza Breakfast in Southern California.
Photo: R. Mazza

Preheat oven to 350°.

Have ready: 8-inch tube pan or 5x7 loaf pan, greased and floured.

Prepare the CAKE. Sift together flour, sugar, baking powder, spices and salt into a large mixing bowl. Add tomato soup into which baking soda has been dissolved. Add 1 beaten egg, oil, nuts and raisins; mix well. Pour into a greased and floured 8-inch tube pan or 5x7 loaf pan. Bake for 45 minutes. Toothpick will come out clean. Cool.

Prepare the CREAM CHEESE FROSTING. Remove cake from pan when thoroughly cooled. Cream the cheese and gradually add sugar and milk. Beat well. Add rind and beat until fluffy. Spread frosting over cake. Serves 8-10.

CINNAMON CRUMB CAKE

[A Cooking Hint: Use substitutes to fit health needs. Use low-fat or fat-free milk or evaporated milk instead of whole milk products.]

1 cup butter or Smart Balance spread

1½ cups granulated sugar

½ tsp. salt

3 large eggs or ¾ cup egg substitute

1 tsp. vanilla extract

2 cups all-purpose flour

2 tbsp. low-fat milk

2 tbsp. ground cinnamon

CRUMB TOPPING:

⅔ cup all-purpose flour

¼ cup granulated sugar

¼ cup butter or Smart Balance spread

½ tsp. vanilla extract

¼ tsp. ground cinnamon

Preheat oven to 350°.
Have ready: a greased and floured 8-9 inch square or round pan.

Prepare TOPPING. In a medium bowl, with a pastry blender, combine all ingredients until blended and crumbly. With your hands, press crumbs together to form large crumbs. Set aside.

Prepare CAKE. In a large bowl, with electric mixer, beat butter (or Smart Balance spread), sugar and salt at medium-high speed until light and fluffy, about 5 minutes. Gradually, beat in eggs, one at a time (or egg substitute, a portion at a time), beating well after each addition. Beat in vanilla, scraping sides of bowl. On low speed, gradually beat in flour, then milk, until just blended. With spatula, gently fold in cinnamon until just marbled. Spoon batter into prepared pan. Evenly sprinkle crumb topping over cake, lightly pressing crumb mix into batter.

Bake in preheated oven at 350° for 30 minutes or until inserted toothpick removes clean. Cool cake on wire rack for 5 minutes. Carefully, remove from pan and serve warm, or cool completely. Serves 8-10.

RASPBERRY JAM COFFEE CAKE

1 pkg. (3 oz.) low-fat cream cheese

$\frac{1}{4}$ cup butter or Smart Balance spread

2 cups Bisquick

$\frac{1}{3}$ cup low-fat milk

1 cup raspberry preserves

ICING:

1 cup confectioners' sugar, sifted

1-2 tbsp. low-fat milk

$\frac{1}{2}$ tsp. vanilla extract

Preheat oven to 425°.

Have ready: A floured pastry board; grease a 9x15-inch baking pan.

Cut cream cheese and butter (or Smart Balance spread) into Bisquick until crumbly. Blend in milk. Turn dough onto floured board; knead 8 to 10 strokes and form into a ball.

Lay a sheet of waxed paper on board and roll out the dough to form a 8x12-inch rectangle. Turn rectangle onto the greased 9x15 baking sheet. Remove waxed paper from dough rectangle. Spoon and spread raspberry preserves in a strip down the center of dough. Make $2\frac{1}{2}$-inch cuts at 1-inch intervals on the vertical sides of the dough. Fold the $2\frac{1}{2}$-inch strips over the filling. Bake cake in preheated oven at 425° for 12-15 minutes. Remove from oven to cool.

Meanwhile, <u>Prepare ICING</u>. Combine confectioners' sugar, 1-2 tablespoons milk and vanilla; blend into a smooth icing. Drizzle icing on top of cooled cake. Serves 8-10.

PINEAPPLE BANANA BREAD
(A recipe contributed by Enid Lopes, inspired by her Virgin Islands heritage.
1 cup applesauce may be substituted for crushed pineapple.)

$3\frac{1}{3}$ cups sifted all-purpose flour

$1\frac{1}{2}$ cups granulated sugar

1 tsp. baking soda

1 tsp. salt

1 tsp. ground cinnamon

$1\frac{1}{4}$ cups corn oil

$1\frac{1}{2}$ tsp. vanilla extract

3 eggs

1 cup crushed pineapple, thoroughly drained

2 cups mashed ripe bananas

1 cup flaked coconut (optional)

Preheat oven to 350°.
Have ready: A 9-inch Bundt pan, greased and floured; or, coated with a baking spray like *Baker's Joy*.
Thoroughly mix all ingredients in a large bowl. Pour batter into prepared Bundt pan. Bake in preheated oven at 350° for 1 hour, 20 minutes; an inserted toothpick will remove clean. Serves 8.

BERRY GOOD MUFFINS

1 cup cooked oatmeal

$1\frac{1}{2}$ cups all-purpose flour

2 eggs or $\frac{1}{2}$ cup egg substitute

$1\frac{1}{2}$ tbsp. canola oil

$1\frac{1}{4}$ cups cranberry juice or white grape juice

1 cup unseasoned applesauce

$\frac{1}{4}$ cup granulated sugar

dash of salt

1 cup blueberries, rinsed, drained thoroughly

1 tbsp. grated orange zest

Preheat oven to 400°.

Have ready: muffins tins, $3\frac{1}{2}$ - 4-inch cups, greased.

Grease muffin tin cups. In a large bowl, combine all ingredients, mixing thoroughly. Spoon batter into greased muffin cups, $\frac{3}{4}$-filled. Bake muffins at 400° for 20-25 minutes, depending on size. Inserted toothpick will remove clean. Makes 6-8 large muffins.

PECAN RAISIN SOY MUFFINS

1 cup soy powder

1 cup whole wheat flour

$\frac{1}{4}$ cup uncooked oat bran

1 egg, beaten, or $\frac{1}{4}$ cup egg substitute

dash of salt

$1\frac{1}{4}$ cups low-fat or fat-free milk

$\frac{1}{4}$ cup honey

2 tbsp. canola oil

1 tbsp. baking powder

1 tsp. ground cinnamon

$\frac{1}{4}$ tsp. ground cloves

$\frac{1}{2}$ tsp. ground nutmeg

$\frac{1}{2}$ cup cranberry raisins

$\frac{1}{4}$ cup finely chopped pecans

Preheat oven to 350°.

Have ready: muffin tins, $2\frac{1}{2}$ - 3-inch cups, greased.

Grease muffin tin cups. In a large bowl, combine all ingredients, mixing thoroughly. Spoon batter into greased muffin cups, $\frac{3}{4}$-filled. Bake muffins at 350° for 30-35 minutes, depending on size. Inserted toothpick will remove clean. Makes 8-10 medium-sized muffins.

APPLE-BRAN MUFFINS

1 cup bran kernels cereal or grape nuts
    cereal kernels

1 cup low-fat or fat-free milk

1 cup whole wheat flour

3 tsp. baking powder

$\frac{1}{4}$ cup light brown sugar or $\frac{1}{4}$ cup molasses

1 egg or $\frac{1}{4}$ cup egg substitute

1 cup unseasoned applesauce

$2\frac{1}{2}$ tbsp. canola oil

dash of salt

$\frac{1}{2}$ cup golden raisins (optional), OR

$\frac{1}{2}$ cup chopped walnuts (optional), OR

$\frac{1}{2}$ cup dried blueberries or cherries (optional),
        (OR, a combination of the options)

Preheat oven to 400°.

Have ready: greased muffin tins with $2\frac{1}{2}$-3-inch cups.

Grease muffin tin cups. Soak cereal in milk for 5 minutes. Add and combine remainder of ingredients. Spoon batter into greased muffin cups, $\frac{3}{4}$ -filled. Bake muffins at 400° for 20-25 minutes, depending on size. Inserted toothpick will remove clean. Makes 6-8 medium-large-sized muffins.

OAT BRAN MUFFINS

$1\frac{1}{2}$ cups whole wheat flour

1 cup uncooked oat bran

$\frac{1}{2}$ cup honey (or $\frac{1}{4}$ cup brown sugar)

$\frac{1}{2}$ tsp. ground cinnamon

$\frac{1}{4}$ tsp. ground nutmeg

2 tsp. baking powder

dash of salt

1 cup low-fat or fat-free milk

1 egg, beaten or $\frac{1}{4}$ cup egg substitute

3 tbsp. canola oil

1 cup golden raisins OR 1 cup chopped apples
        OR 1 cup blueberries

Preheat oven to 400°.

Have ready: greased muffins tins with $2\frac{1}{2}$-3-inch cups.

Grease muffin tin cups. Combine all ingredients in a large bowl; blend thoroughly. Spoon batter into greased muffin cups, $\frac{3}{4}$-filled. Bake muffins at 400° for 15-25 minutes, depending on size. Inserted toothpick will remove clean Makes 6-8 medium-large muffins.

CRANBERRY PUMPKIN BRAN MUFFINS
[A Cooking Hint: Use substitutes to fit health needs: use honey instead of sugar.
1 cup honey = 1¼ cups sugar plus ¼ cup of liquid.]

1½ cups whole wheat flour

1 cup oat bran, uncooked

½ cup honey (or ¼ cup brown sugar)

½ tsp. cinnamon

¼ tsp. nutmeg, ¼ tsp. ground cloves

2 tsp. baking powder

dash of salt

1 cup low-fat or non-fat milk

1 egg beaten, or ¼ cup egg substitute

3 tbsp. canola oil

1 cup canned pure pumpkin

2 cups fresh cranberries, coarsely chopped in food processor

½ cup finely chopped almonds

1 cup tiny marshmallows

more cinnamon and brown sugar for sprinkling,
  as garnish

Preheat oven to 400°.

Have ready: greased muffin tins with 3½-inch cups.

Grease large muffin cups. In a large bowl, thoroughly mix all ingredients except: cranberries and almonds. Fold in cranberries and almonds. Spoon batter into greased muffin cups, ¾-filled. Scatter tiny marshmallows over muffins in tins; sprinkle tops of muffins with cinnamon and brown sugar. Bake muffins in preheated oven at 400° for 15-20 minutes. Inserted toothpick will remove clean. Cool slightly before removing them from pan. Yields about 6 large muffins.

4 PANCAKE RECIPES

(Pancakes freeze well up to a couple of months. You may want to prep an extra batch to freeze. Lay a large sheet of aluminum foil on a board about 18 inches long. Cut 5 or 6 sheets of waxed paper, about 12 inches long. Lay one sheet of waxed paper on top of foil. As you prepare pancakes, lay 2 of them side-by-side on foil/ waxed paper. Follow with a 12-inch sheet of waxed paper; then lay 2 more cooked pancakes on top of fresh wax paper and continue to make two stacks of pancakes (probably 10-12 pancakes). Top with another sheet of waxed paper and wrap the bundle of pancakes with the extensions of foil. Slide the entire package into a large plastic baggie and seal with tape. Freeze until needed; thaw in refrigerator for 1 day. Remove waxed paper between pancakes and bake pancakes on a baking sheet in stacks of 2-3. Loosely lay a sheet of foil on top of stacks and bake them in preheated oven at 300° for 12-15 minutes until heated through. Serve with maple syrup or honey or your favorite fruits and jams.)

APPLE-CHEDDAR PANCAKES

3 cups Bisquick low-fat flour mix

$1\frac{1}{2}$ cups low-fat or fat-free evaporated milk

2 eggs, beaten, or $\frac{1}{2}$ cup egg substitute

1 Granny Smith apple, pared, cored, finely chopped

$\frac{1}{2}$ cup Cheddar cheese, shredded

$\frac{1}{4}$ tsp each: ground nutmeg, ground cinnamon, ground cloves

canola oil for griddle or skillet

(thin slices Virginia ham or boiled ham; thin slices Cheddar cheese, optional)

(*A Tasty idea!* Lay 1 slice ham, 1 slice Cheddar between 2 pancakes; wrap in foil and
   warm in oven at 250° for a few minutes. Serve with pure maple syrup.)

Preheat greased griddle or skillet to 320°.

Beat milk and eggs (or egg substitute) into Bisquick. Stir in apple and cheese and spices. Mix thoroughly. If batter is too thick, add a few tablespoons of milk.

Grease griddle or skillet with canola oil and heat to 320°. Pour $\frac{1}{2}$ cup batter per pancake. When batter bubbles, turn pancake over with a thin spatula and cook other side for 1-2 minutes, until light golden brown. Grease skillet or griddle before cooking each batch of pancakes. Transfer pancakes in stacks of 2-3 to a warming tray. Lay a sheet of foil over pancakes to keep warm. Warm in a low oven, 200°. Serve with pure maple syrup or honey. Serves 3-4. Makes 10-12 (4-inch) pancakes.

CHOCOLATE PUMPKIN PANCAKES

3 cups Bisquick low-fat flour mix

1 can (1 lb.) pure pumpkin

$1\frac{1}{2}$ cups low-fat (or fat-free) evaporated milk

2 eggs or $\frac{1}{2}$ cup egg substitute, beaten

3 oz. semi-sweet chocolate morsels,
   melted over hot water

$\frac{1}{4}$ cup brown sugar

$\frac{1}{2}$ tsp. each: ground cinnamon, ground ginger

$\frac{1}{4}$ tsp. ground cloves

canola oil for griddle or skillet

   Preheat greased griddle or skillet to 320°.
   Beat milk and eggs (or egg substitute) into Bisquick. Blend 1 can pure pumpkin into batter. Stir in sugar, melted chocolate and spices. Mix thoroughly. Add a few tablespoons of milk if batter is too thick.
   Pour $\frac{1}{2}$ cup of batter (for each pancake) onto a preheated greased griddle or skillet. When surface bubbles, turn over pancakes with a thin spatula to cook the other side for 1-2 minutes, or until set. Grease griddle or skillet before cooking each batch of pancakes. Transfer pancakes to a warming tray in stacks of 2-3. Cover stacks of pancakes lightly with foil and keep them warm in oven at 200°. Makes 10-12 (4-inch) pancakes. Serves 3-4.

NUTTY CHOCOLATE CHIP PANCAKES

3 cups Bisquick low-fat flour mix

$1\frac{1}{2}$ cups low-fat or fat-free evaporated milk

2 eggs or $\frac{1}{2}$ cup egg substitute, beaten

1 cup unseasoned applesauce

$\frac{1}{4}$ cup brown sugar

1 cup semi-sweet chocolate morsels

1 tsp. vanilla extract

$\frac{1}{2}$ tsp. ground cinnamon

$\frac{1}{2}$ cup finely chopped walnuts

canola oil for griddle or skillet

   Preheat greased griddle or skillet to 320°.
   Beat milk and eggs (or egg substitute) into Bisquick. Blend applesauce into batter. Stir in sugar, chocolate morsels, nuts, vanilla and cinnamon. Mix thoroughly. Add a few tablespoons of milk if batter is too thick.
   Pour $\frac{1}{2}$ cup of batter (for each pancake) onto a preheated greased griddle or skillet. When surface bubbles, turn over pancakes with a thin spatula to cook the other side for 1-2 minutes, or until set. Grease griddle or skillet before cooking each batch of pancakes. Transfer pancakes to a warming tray in stacks of 2-3. Cover pancakes lightly with foil to keep warm in oven at 200°. Makes 10-12 (4-inch) pancakes. Serves 3-4.

BLUEBERRY-LIME PANCAKES

2 cups Bisquick low-fat flour mix

$1\frac{1}{2}$ cups low-fat or fat-free evaporated milk

2 eggs or $\frac{1}{2}$ cup egg substitute, beaten

$\frac{1}{4}$ cup fresh lime juice, 1 tsp. lime zest

1 pint fresh blueberries, rinsed, drained, patted dry with paper towels

canola oil for griddle or skillet

    Preheat greased griddle or skillet to 320°.

    Beat milk and eggs (or egg substitute) into Bisquick. Stir in lime juice, lime zest and blueberries and mix thoroughly. Add a few tablespoons of milk if batter is too thick.

Pour $\frac{1}{2}$ cup batter (for each pancake) onto a preheated greased griddle or skillet. When surface bubbles, turn over pancakes with a thin spatula to cook the other side for 1-2 minutes, or until set. Grease griddle or skillet before cooking each batch of pancakes.

    Transfer pancakes to a warming tray in stacks of 2-3. Cover pancakes lightly with foil and keep them warm in oven at 200°. Makes 10-12 (4-inch) pancakes. Serves 3-4.

SWEDISH PANCAKES

1 cup all-purpose sifted flour

1 tbsp. granulated sugar

3 large eggs or $\frac{3}{4}$ cup egg substitute

2 cups low-fat milk or evaporated milk

5 tbsp. canola oil

Blueberry, Strawberry, Raspberry Preserves and/or pure Maple Syrup at serving

    Preheat oven to 200°.

    Have ready: a heat-resistant serving platter.

    Mix flour and sugar into a 2-quart bowl. Beat eggs (or egg substitute) with milk. Pour this mixture into the dry ingredients and stir until smoothly blended. Stir in 4 tablespoons canola oil.

    Lightly brush a heavy skillet or griddle with remaining 1 tablespoon oil and heat pan to moderate. Drop the batter, 1 tablespoon at a time, onto the hot greased skillet. Cook for about 1 minute, or until tiny bubbles start to appear on surface of pancakes. Then, turn pancakes over and cook other side for about one minute. Do not overcook. Transfer tiny pancakes to a heat-resistant serving platter; lay a piece of foil over the platter. Keep pancakes warm in a preheated oven at 200° as you prepare rest of batter.

    Serve with Blueberry, Strawberry or Raspberry Preserves and/or pure Maple Syrup. Makes about 2 dozen $2\frac{1}{2}$-inch Swedish pancakes.

15

PARTY-TIME PANCAKES

$2\frac{1}{2}$ cups all-purpose flour

1 tbsp. baking powder

$\frac{1}{4}$ tsp. salt

1 cup (6 oz. pkg.) semi-sweet mini
    chocolate morsels

$1\frac{3}{4}$ cups low-fat milk (or evaporated milk)

$\frac{1}{3}$ cup canola oil

2 large eggs or $\frac{1}{2}$ cup egg substitute

$\frac{1}{3}$ cup brown sugar, packed

about 2-3 tbsp. canola oil for griddle or skillet

confectioners' sugar (optional)

    Have ready: griddle or large skillet, greased with canola oil.

    Combine flour, baking powder, salt and morsels in a large bowl. Combine milk, eggs, oil and brown sugar in a medium bowl. Add sugar mix to flour mixture; stir until just moistened. Batter will be lumpy. Heat griddle or skillet to medium; lightly brush with oil. Pour $\frac{1}{4}$ cup batter in a circle on hot, greased griddle/skillet (*NOTE: suggestion below). If the pan is large enough, you may be able to cook 2 pancakes at a time. Cook them until bubbles appear on surface of pancakes. Turn over pancakes and continue to cook other side about 1 minute longer, or until golden. Repeat the process with remaining batter, brushing the griddle with oil each time. Keep pancakes covered lightly in foil, in a warm oven as you prepare them.
Makes 15-16, 4-inch pancakes.

    *NOTE: You may wish to create pancake shapes by using large cookie cutters. Brush inside of large cookie cutters with oil; place them on greased griddle/skillet. Pour about $\frac{1}{4}$ cup batter into the cookie cutters and cook until bubbles are well-formed. Remove cookie cutters; turn pancake and continue to cook on other side for 1 minute.

SCRIPPELLE IMBUSSE ABRUZZESE
(These "stuffed pancakes" were my husband's faves.)

about $\frac{1}{4}$ cup olive oil to maintain the fry pan

4 eggs or 1 cup egg substitute, beaten

1 cup all-purpose flour

about $\frac{1}{4}$-$\frac{1}{2}$ cup water

$\frac{1}{2}$ cup Romano cheese, grated

4-6 thin slices prosciutto, minced
    (cut with scissors)

1 cup less-salt chicken broth
    (OR: see page 81 for
      Homemade Chicken Broth.)

    Preheat oven to 300°.

    Have ready: a 9-inch shallow baking dish; a 5-inch fry pan.

    Beat eggs (or egg substitute) in a bowl; gradually stir in flour. When mixture is smooth and creamy, add just enough water to make a thin flowing batter. Heat a 5-inch fry pan and grease it with olive oil. Pour in the pan, a serving spoon of batter (just enough to coat the bottom of the pan). And just enough to form a thin pancake. As soon as pancake bubbles, turn it over with a thin spatula and cook other side. Make pancakes, one at a time, greasing the pan each time. Lay pancakes on a board (or on sheet of aluminum foil). Sprinkle each pancake with grated cheese and a portion of minced prosciutto. Tightly roll up pancakes; place them, seam down, side-by-side, in a shallow 9-inch baking dish. Over rolled pancakes, pour enough boiling chicken broth to cover about one-third of depth. Cover dish; allow to rest in heated oven (heat turned OFF) for several minutes to allow broth to be absorbed. Makes 6-8 Scrippelle.

BASIC FRITTER BATTER

$1\frac{1}{2}$ cups all-purpose flour

$\frac{1}{2}$ tsp. salt

$\frac{1}{4}$ tsp. black pepper

3 tbsp. canola oil

2 large eggs or $\frac{1}{2}$ cup egg substitute

$\frac{1}{2}$ cup water

canola oil for pan

Have ready: griddle or large skillet, greased with canola oil.

Sift flour into a mixing bowl. Add oil, salt and pepper. Whisk in eggs (or egg substitute) one portion at a time. Gradually whisk in water until batter is thoroughly blended. SUGGESTIONS to add to the batter.

(A) Pumpkin Fritters
  1 lb. can pure pumpkin   1 tsp. pumpkin pie spice   1 tbsp. brown sugar
(B) Corn Fritters
  1 lb. can creamed corn   1 tbsp. fresh cilantro, minced   2 tbsp. onion, minced
(C) Shrimp Fritters (or Bay Scallops)
  1 cup tiny shrimp, peeled (or bay scallops, chopped)   1 tbsp. parsley, minced
(D) Ham 'n Cheddar Fritters
  1 cup chopped cured ham $\frac{1}{2}$ cup grated cheddar cheese
(E) Apple Fritters
  1 large Granny Smith apple, peeled, cored, finely chopped
  $\frac{1}{4}$ tsp. each: cinnamon, nutmeg   1 tbsp. brown sugar
(F) Blueberry Fritters
  1 cup blueberries, rinsed, drained   1 tbsp. fresh lemon juice

To the Basic Fritter Batter recipe, stir in ingredients from one of the suggestions above. Heat griddle or skillet to medium; grease pan with canola oil. Pour 4-inch circles of prepared fritter batter onto hot greased griddle (or skillet), 2 at a time. When bubbles are formed in batter, turn over fritters to cook on other side for 1-2 minutes, or until golden. Makes 8-10 (4-inch) fritters.

CORNMEAL PAP A LA CREOLE
(Enid Lopes' traditional Virgin Islands breakfast.)

1 cup milk

1 cup boiling water

1 cinnamon stick

$\frac{1}{4}$ cup granulated sugar

1 cup yellow cornmeal

1 tsp. salt

1 tsp. butter

$\frac{1}{4}$ cup raisins

Bring milk, water and cinnamon to boil in top pot of double boiler. Stir in cornmeal, sugar, salt and butter. Boil, stirring constantly, until mixture thickens. Set cereal pot over bottom pot (with water); stir in raisins. Cover; steam cereal for 15-20 minutes. If desired, add a dollop of butter and more milk for each serving. Serves 1.

SOFT PRETZELS

$1\frac{1}{4}$ cups warm water

1 tbsp. active dry yeast

2 tsp. granulated sugar

$3\frac{1}{2}$-4 cups all-purpose flour

$1\frac{1}{2}$ tsp. salt

2 tbsp. canola oil

1 large egg or $\frac{1}{4}$ cup egg substitute, beaten with 1 tbsp. low-fat milk (for glaze)

butter or Smart Balance spread to grease baking sheets

TOPPINGS: poppy seeds, sesame seeds, caraway seeds; Kosher salt

Have ready: a lightly floured board; 2 heavy 9x12 baking sheets, greased.

Place $\frac{1}{4}$ cup of warm water in a bowl and sprinkle yeast and sugar over it. Stir to dissolve and allow yeast mix to stand until bubbly (about 5 – 10 minutes).

Combine $3\frac{1}{2}$ cups flour with salt. Add remaining cup of warm water, oil and the "proofed" yeast (mixture). Stir to combine.

Pour dough on a lightly floured board; knead dough until smooth and elastic, adding more flour if necessary to prevent sticking.

Preheat oven to 425°.

Lightly grease 2 heavy 9x12-inch baking sheets with butter or Smart Balance spread. Divide dough into 24 pieces and roll each into thin strips, about 10 inches long. Shape them into pretzels by crossing the ends to form a loop; then, by flipping the ends back across the loop.
Or, be creative: form knots or bows.

Place pretzels on prepared baking sheets. For chewy pretzels, cover the dough loosely with a clean linen or cotton towel; allow pretzels to rest in a warm place until puffy, about 15 minutes. You may preheat your oven to 150° for 15 minutes; turn off oven; place trays of pretzels on racks in this oven; close the oven door. (*NOTE: below.)

Then, lightly brush the egg-milk glaze over the pretzels. Sprinkle each pretzel with the desired topping. Bake them in preheated oven at 425° for 15-20 minutes, or until lightly colored.
Makes about 24 pretzels. Yummy – either warm or at room temperature.

*NOTE: If you prefer crunchier pretzels, do not allow them to rest. Bake them immediately after forming them and after glazing/topping them.

"NOW, IF ONLY I COULD COOK"

During a recent newspaper interview, and after he had previously received copies of my published cookbooks, the young journalist paused in his questioning, deeply sighed, and whispered, "Now, if only I could cook".

Everyone can cook. As long as you are willing to provide these three basics:
  1) *The written recipe with instructions.*
  2) *The ingredients suggested in the recipe (or reasonable facsimiles).*
  3) *Pangs of desire or a growling stomach.*

It's a "piece of cake"!

Accordingly, KIRKUS DISCOVERIES reviewers have acknowledged that Marion O. Celenza's cookbooks have displayed "specific, clear and helpful instructions which are easy to follow; the foods are wholesome and healthfully prepared".

Each of my cookbooks has been proof-read by Staff at least a dozen times. The Author-Publisher has match-read the script, as many times. More important, our editorial assistant (who admits to being a "non-cook") reads the text with eyes wide-open. She's a "babe in the woods" and is instructed by every written word and phrase. She must understand every direction and interpret every phrase; she "becomes" the veritable cook.

Cooking is fun! It's the sharing of ourselves with others; it's a mental exercise; and it can be a small challenge. Cooking stirs the creative juices as well as the pancreatic. Cooking gives joys and pleasures to everyone involved __ the Cook and the Participants. It is a therapeutic outlet for those who strive long and hard at their work-a-day tasks. Cooking is a necessity to life. And, if you're good at it, cooking can be a fruitful and rewarding lifetime accomplishment.

A Celebration of the

Midday Meal

Lunch

Sandwiches

Salads

Lunch-In-A-Crust

Soups

Enjoying Lunch Hour at Our Lady of Mercy Academy, Syosset, NY.
With permission: photo by Joan Gordon, Co-Principal

GRILLED ROAST BEEF AND ONIONS PANINI

2 large Italian bread rolls (hoagies)

2 tbsp. olive oil, divided (1 tbsp. for pan; 1 tbsp. for bread spread)

2 large onions, thinly sliced, about 2 cups

salt and freshly ground black pepper, to taste

$\frac{1}{2}$ lb. deli roast beef, thinly sliced

$\frac{1}{4}$ lb. provolone, thinly sliced

2-3 plum tomatoes, thinly sliced, lengthwise

Have ready: a large skillet with a flat lid.

Brush a large skillet with 1 tablespoon olive oil. Cook onions with salt and pepper in skillet over medium-high heat until completely soft and golden brown, about 5 minutes. Remove skillet from heat. Separate tops from bottom of 2 large Italian bread rolls (hoagies). Lightly brush outside of bottom halves of rolls with oil (NOT cut-side).

Layer roast beef, provolone, cooked onions and tomato slices on bottom halves of rolls. Close sandwiches with top halves and gently but firmly, press down on sandwiches with your hands. With remaining oil, brush oil on tops of rolls.

Replace skillet on burner and heat on moderate. Lay the sandwiches top-side down in the skillet. Firmly press the flat lid on top of the sandwiches. (You may wish to place a 2-pound can of tomatoes on the lid to add pressure to the sandwiches.)

Cook until cheese is just melted and pan marks appear on the rolls, about 3-4 minutes. Turn over sandwiches with aid of a spatula and repeat the procedure for another 2 minutes, or until the bottom half of bread is toasted. Serve immediately; cut each panino in half. Depending upon size of rolls, serves 2-4.

Dawn's Baby Shower Luncheon.

CORNED BEEF AND COLESLAW ON RYE
(Start recipe night before or early on day.)

3 cups of cabbage, shredded
1 small red onion, thinly sliced
1 large carrot, pared, grated
6-8 large slices seeded rye (or unseeded)
$\frac{1}{2}$ lb. corned beef, thinly sliced

DRESSING
2 tbsp. white vinegar
$1\frac{1}{2}$ tbsp. Dijon mustard (plus additional mustard to spread on bread)
$1\frac{1}{2}$ tbsp. mild horseradish
$\frac{1}{4}$ cup olive oil
salt and freshly ground black pepper, to taste

Prepare DRESSING. In a large bowl whisk together: vinegar, $1\frac{1}{2}$ tablespoons mustard, horseradish, olive oil, salt and pepper, until dressing is emulsified. Add cabbage, onion and carrots and toss coleslaw to coat thoroughly. Chill the salad, covered, overnight; or at least for 6 hours, before serving.

Spread additional mustard on bottom slices of rye bread. Lay slices of corned beef over bottom halves of bread; spoon and arrange coleslaw over corned beef. Fit top slices of rye bread over the sandwiches, pressing the sandwiches firmly together. If not serving immediately, the sandwiches may be made 5-6 hours in advance, wrapped in waxed sandwich paper and chilled. Serve with Kosher dill pickles. Serves 3-4.

GRILLED CHEESE AND PROSCIUTTO SANDWICH

8 thin slices multi-grain or fiber-enriched light wheat bread
4 thin slices prosciutto, each cut in half, horizontally
8 slices Jarlsberg Swiss cheese, thinly sliced into large squares to fit sandwich bread
1-2 beefsteak tomatoes, sliced into 8 thin slices, 2 slices per sandwich
Dijon mustard

4 large eggs, beaten with 2 tbsp. low-fat milk, or
    1 cup egg substitute and 2 tbsp. low-fat milk, beaten
$\frac{1}{4}$ tsp. freshly ground black pepper
butter or Smart Balance spread to coat the grill pan (or sandwich maker)

Have ready: a grill pan or a sandwich maker, each buttered. Re-butter the pan before each sandwich is cooked.

Beat eggs (or egg substitute) with milk and black pepper in a wide-mouthed bowl. Set aside.

Lay out 4 slices of bread on a glass board. Spread each slice with Dijon mustard.
Place 2 halves of prosciutto on each slice. Follow with 2 slices of cheese and 2 slices tomato.
Cover with top half of sandwich bread.

Butter grill pan (or both sides of sandwich maker). Turn on surface burner to medium-high and allow pan to become hot. With your fingers, dip a sandwich into the beaten egg mix to coat on both sides. Lay the dressed sandwich into the hot pan. Grill sandwich on each side for 3-4 minutes over medium-high. Or, if using a sandwich maker, close the cover of the sandwich maker and cook on burner for 3-4 minutes on each side; repeat procedure for each serving.

Remove prepared sandwiches to a serving platter; cut each on a diagonal. Serves 4.

BAKED EGGPLANT PARMAGIANO AND ASIAGO ON A CIABATTA ROLL

[A Cooking Hint: Follow directions, step by step. It is important to the finished product that certain ingredients combine with other ingredients in a defined "order" of recipe development.]

1-2 round grilled eggplant slices, each $\frac{1}{2}$-inch thick (Select eggplants which measure no
    more than 3-4 inches in diameter.)

salt and black pepper to taste

$\frac{1}{4}$ cup olive oil

For each serving:

2 thin slices, $\frac{1}{4}$-inch thick, beefsteak tomato

2 tbsp. Asiago cheese, grated

2 tbsp. mozzarella, diced

salt, freshly ground black pepper to taste

1 ciabatta roll, split; brush 1 tbsp. olive oil on inside of both halves of roll

    Have ready: a 12-inch grill pan, brushed with olive oil; and a large heat-resistant warming platter.

    First, prepare grilled eggplant slices. Pare eggplant. Cut into slices, $\frac{1}{2}$-inch thick. Rinse slices under cold running water; pat them dry with paper towels.

    You will need $\frac{1}{4}$ cup olive oil, salt and black pepper to brush on each eggplant slice before grilling them.

    Heat a 12-inch grill pan over medium-high; brush pan with olive oil. Lay 2-3 slices of prepared eggplant at a time on the grill. Cook them for 2 minutes on each side; then lower heat to medium and continue to cook eggplant for 2-3 more minutes on each side, until eggplant is lightly browned and tender. Brush grill pan with oil between each cooking session. Transfer eggplant to a heat- resistant platter to keep warm in a 200° oven. Grill all of the eggplant slices in the same way and keep them in the warming oven. (You will re-use grill pan to grill bread.)

    Remove platter of grilled eggplant slices from warming oven. Turn on broiler.

    Over each slice of warm eggplant, lay 1-2 slices of tomato; over the eggplant and tomato, sprinkle 2 tablespoons of each: diced mozzarella and grated Asiago cheese, salt and black pepper to taste. Transfer platter of prepared eggplant to broiler, 5 inches under heating element. Broil eggplant for 1-2 minutes, until cheese melts and starts to brown. Turn off broiler; keep eggplant warm.

    Meanwhile, as the eggplant browns, brush grill pan with olive oil and set to medium-high. Lay both halves of ciabatta, bread-side down on oiled grill and toast them for 1 minute. Then, with a spatula, lay 1 or 2 portions of eggplant parmagiano on toasted bottom half of ciabatta; close with toasted top half, gently pressing down on the sandwich to blend the cheese and tomato. Serve immediately, while quite warm. This recipe: one serving. Suggestions: It will be easier to handle no more then 3-4 servings at a time. Or, you can prepare as directed, a tray of baked or sautéed eggplant parmagiano in advance, and form ciabatta sandwiches with grilled ciabatta halves, cooked eggplant parmagiano, tomato slices and cheeses.

BARBEQUE CHICKEN BREAST SANDWICH
(For cooking on outdoor grill or grill pan on stove burner.)

4 halves thin sliced skinless, boneless chicken breasts, rinsed in cold water, patted dry
    with paper towels

4 green fryer peppers, rinsed, deseeded, cut into strips

2 ripe tomatoes, rinsed, chopped into chunks

1 onion, thinly sliced

4 Kaiser rolls, split in half

(olive oil for grill pan)

Barbeque Sauce (see page 386)

    Have ready: grill pan for vegetables (for outdoor grill) OR
a 12-inch grill pan for stove-top cooking.

    Prepare Barbeque Sauce in advance. Refrigerate if not using within a few hours.
    Assemble the thin chicken breasts and vegetables as directed above. Put vegetables in a bowl
and refrigerate vegetables and chicken, separately, until needed. Then, rinse chicken once more,
in cold water and paper towel- dry. Pour vegetables on an oil-coated outdoor grill pan.
1) Outdoor Grill: fire up grill; set grate about 5 inches above heat. Lay chicken pieces on ½ of
the grate and grill for 2-3 minutes on each side. Baste chicken with Barbeque sauce on both sides
and return them to the grate to cook 4-5 minutes on each side, depending on thickness. Baste
frequently, and regularly turn chicken to cook both sides. Do not overcook. Chicken is ready
when a knife slit runs clear juices.
    Meanwhile, as the chicken cooks, place the oiled pan of vegetables on the empty half of the
grate. Cook vegetables for 4-5 minutes, until onion starts to brown. Use a long-handled spatula to
shuffle the vegetables as they cook.
2A) Stove-top Grill Pan: Preheat oven to 200°. First, grill chicken breasts on a grill pan, 2 at a
time. To start, cook chicken at medium-high for 2 minutes on each side, just enough to implant
grill-pan markings. Then, baste them with Barbeque sauce; lower heat to medium-low, and cook
chicken for 3-4 minutes on each side, basting frequently; or until juices run clear when chicken is
cut with a knife.
    Transfer chicken to a waiting oven pan; baste with Barbeque sauce again; lay a loose foil sheet
over pan and place pan in preheated oven 200° to keep warm, as you cook vegetables.
2B) Brush same grill pan with olive oil; pour vegetables into pan and grill them on medium-high,
tossing them frequently with a spatula, for about 4-5 minutes, or until onion starts to brown.
3) Forming the Sandwich: Cut 4 Kaiser rolls in half, horizontally. On bottom halves of each,
lay 1 portion Barbeque chicken and a serving spoonful (about ½ cup) of grilled vegetables on top
of chicken. Close the rolls; cut each in half, if desired. Serve with a salad from this cookbook.
Serves 4.

PANINO OF ROAST PORK, BROCCOLI RABE, RED PEPPERS & SMOKY MOZZARELLA

(One pound of uncooked broccoli rabe should equal 4 portions,
2 cups, of steamed broccoli rabe for this recipe.)

For each Panino:

3-4 thin slices, $\frac{1}{4}$-inch-thick, roast pork or 3-4 slices prosciutto

$\frac{1}{2}$ roasted bell pepper, deseeded, skin removed (Use packaged jar of roasted peppers in
    water; or roast your own; see page 402)

$\frac{1}{2}$ cup cooked broccoli rabe (steamed with 2 garlic cloves);
    drain broccoli and drizzle with 1 tsp. olive oil

2-3 thin slices smoky mozzarella

1 panino sandwich roll, about 3x6 inches

a sprinkling of fresh ground black pepper

$\frac{1}{2}$ tsp. extra-virgin olive oil

2 tbsp. olive oil for grill pan for every 2 panini you grill in pan

    Have ready: a 12-inch grill pan with a flat lid (or a panino maker); sandwich tongs
or 2 thin spatulas.

    Adjust serving quantities of ingredients. Arrange all ingredients on a board. Cut panini in
half. Assemble as follows: Lay roasted pork slices (or prosciutto) on bottom half of each panino.
On top of pork, place $\frac{1}{2}$ roasted red pepper, broccoli rabe and complete the sandwich with thin
slices of smoky mozzarella. Sprinkle black pepper and drizzle olive oil over ingredients in each
sandwich and close the sandwich with the top half of the panino roll.

    Brush 2 tablespoons olive oil on surface of grill
(or panino maker). Heat pan on medium, for 30 seconds.
Lay 1 or 2 panini on oiled and heated grill pan.
Gently press a flat lid on top of the panini and grill
for 2 minutes. Remove lid and with sandwich tongs
(or 2 spatulas) turn panini over to grill other side.
Return lid to press on panini and grill the other
side of sandwich for another 2 minutes.

    Remove panini to individual serving plates.
Accompany with a salad from this cookbook.
Recipe as written serves 1.

Pancakes: Apple Cheddar, Blueberry Lime, pages 13-16

Turkey Chili Soup, page 304

Zuppa Di Polpeta, page 158

Black Beans and Peppers Soup, page 85

Corn Clam Chowder, page 88

Butternut Squash Crab Soup, page 297

Crunchy Spicy Fish Fillet Sandwich, page 32

Pea Soup, page 103

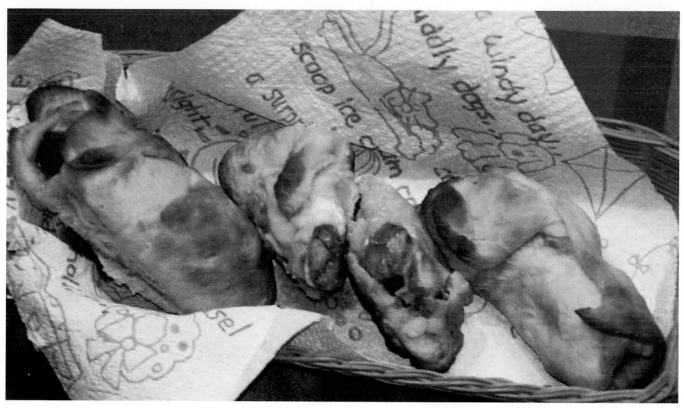

Sausage Provolone Wraps, page 38

Bouillabaisse, page 107

Salmon Fillet Burger, page 36

Tuna Melt, page 34

Shrimp and Scallop Pie, page 75

Creamy Clam Chowder, page 87   **Ham/Apple Open-Faced Sandwich with Brie, page 36**

Salad on a Crust, page 79

Muffuletta, page 41

REUBEN'S REUBEN
(A must have sandwich, bursting with calories. Gotta try it.)

12-16 slices precooked corned beef

4 slices Swiss cheese (low-fat available)

1 cup prepared sauerkraut

$\frac{1}{2}$ cup Thousand Island Dressing (see page 383)

$\frac{1}{2}$ cup butter or Smart Balance spread for skillet

8 slices rye bread (with seeds, optional)

Thousand Island Dressing or "low calorie" Thousand Island Dressing (see page 383)

Have ready: a large skillet.

For both dressing recipes: Combine all ingredients in a large jar with a screw-top lid. Refrigerate until serving.

Prepare the SANDWICHES. Layer several slices of corned beef and 1 slice of cheese on each of the 4 slices of bread. Spoon about 2-3 tablespoons of sauerkraut on each sandwich. Spread dressing on the other 4 slices of bread and place them on top of the sauerkraut.

Melt butter (or Smart Balance spread) in a large skillet over medium-low heat. Lay sandwiches, two at a time, in the skillet and lightly brown on both sides, about 2 minutes for each side. Serves 4.

Dr. Reuben David and Staff enjoy a "Muffuletta" for lunch.

GRILLED VEAL BURGERS PARMAGIANO IN A CIABATTA
(You may substitute ground chicken or ground pork.)

4 large crusty Italian bread rolls

4 slices provolone cheese

4-8 slices beefsteak tomato

BURGERS:

$1\frac{1}{2}$ lbs. ground veal, (or ground chicken, or ground pork)

$\frac{1}{4}$ cup onion, minced

1 tbsp. fresh parsley, minced

$\frac{1}{4}$ tsp. freshly ground black pepper

pinch of salt

$\frac{1}{2}$ cup prepared tomato sauce

2 tbsp. grated Parmesan cheese

COATING FOR BURGERS:

$1\frac{1}{2}$ cups fine Italian bread crumbs

$\frac{1}{4}$ cup grated provolone cheese

salt and freshly ground black pepper, to taste

1 cup prepared tomato sauce

$\frac{1}{4}$ cup olive oil for pan (Brush grill pan with 2 tbsp. olive oil before grilling each pair of burgers.)

Have ready: a 12-inch grill pan, coated with olive oil; a flat lid to fit over the grill pan; a 9x12 baking pan and a sheet of foil.

Preheat oven to 250°.

First, prepare the burgers. In a bowl, thoroughly mix ground veal (or chicken or pork), onion, parsley, $\frac{1}{2}$ cup tomato sauce, grated Parmesan, salt and pepper. Form 4 to 6 thick patties, each about 3x4x$\frac{1}{2}$-inches. Set aside.

Prepare the coating for the burgers by mixing bread crumbs, grated provolone, salt and pepper; spread this mix over a sheet of waxed paper on the work board. Pour 1 cup tomato sauce into a large flat dish with an edge.

Preheat a 12-inch oil-coated grill pan on medium-high. With your hands, dip each formed burger, first into the crumbs mix; then, coat each with tomato sauce; then, coat them again with the crumb mix. Lay prepared burgers, 2 at a time, on the preheated oiled grill pan. Cook them at medium-high for 2-3 minutes on each side. Lower heat to medium; turn burgers over and cover the grill pan with a flat lid. Continue to cook them for 3-4 minutes longer on each side, removing the lid only to turn the burgers over. (You should have formed grill marks on the burgers.)

Transfer burgers to baking pan; lay a sheet of foil over them and place the pan in a preheated oven at 250° to keep warm while you continue to prepare the remaining burgers. After the remaining burgers have been cooked, add them to the pan in the oven; lightly re-cover pan with foil and turn off oven.

Meanwhile, slice open 4 large crusty Italian rolls; be careful not to fully halve the rolls. (You are going to "trap" each burger with trimmings, into its roll.) Into each roll, stuff 1 slice provolone cheese; follow with a warm burger; then, 1 or 2 slices of tomato.
Serve sandwiches while they're still quite warm. Serves 4.

GRILLED VEGETABLES SANDWICH
(Instead, you may roast the vegetables. Directions included.)

1 dozen spears thin asparagus, trimmed, rinsed, drained

2 red bell peppers, rinsed, cored, deseeded, each cut into 4 sections

4-5 baby bella mushrooms, trimmed, rinsed, drained, quartered

1 small onion, thinly sliced

8 garlic cloves

4 (6-inch) pitas (whole wheat available)

2-4 tbsp. olive oil for pan

DRESSING:

2 tbsp. extra-virgin olive oil

1 tbsp. balsamic vinegar

a sprinkling of freshly ground black pepper

   Have ready: a 12-inch grill pan with oven-proof handles, generously coated with olive oil. Or, a well-oiled 9x12 roasting pan.

   Preheat oven to 450°, if roasting the vegetables.

   Arrange prepared vegetables (asparagus, peppers, mushrooms, onion and garlic) on a well-oiled grill pan or roasting pan. Drizzle vegetables with oil and vinegar and sprinkle with freshly ground black pepper.

FOR GRILLING: Turn on stove-top burner to medium-high. Lay the grill pan on the burner and cook vegetables, stirring and shuffling them with a spatula, for 4-5 minutes. Remove from burner; cover pan lightly with foil and keep vegetables warm while you prepare the pitas.

FOR ROASTING: Preheat oven to 450°. Lay vegetables in prepared pan and over them, drizzle with olive oil and balsamic vinegar and sprinkle with freshly ground black pepper. Roast them at 450° for 7-8 minutes. Remove pan from oven and cover lightly with foil to keep vegetables warm while you prepare the pitas.

   Lay pitas on a work board and cut a 3-4-inch slit into each pita. Stuff a portion of cooked mixed vegetables into each pocket. Serve warm. Serves 4.

HAM AND CHEESE ON FRENCH TOAST

4-6 soft whole wheat or potato sandwich buns
4-6 slices low-fat Swiss or Jarlsberg cheese
4-6 slices low-fat boiled ham
2 beefsteak tomatoes (6-8 thin slices)
Dijon mustard spread

BATTER:
3 large eggs, beaten or $\frac{3}{4}$ cup egg substitute
$\frac{1}{2}$ cup low-fat sour cream
$\frac{1}{4}$ tsp. each: salt, freshly ground black pepper

$\frac{1}{4}$ cup butter or Smart Balance spread, for skillet or non-stick 9x12 pan

Have ready: a large skillet; or, a 9x12 non-stick pan; a heat-resistant serving platter; a sheet of foil.

In a large, wide bowl, beat together until foamy: eggs (or egg substitute) and sour cream, salt and pepper. Set aside.

Form the sandwiches. Spread 1 tablespoon mustard on inside of bottom half of bun. Lay 1 slice of cheese and 1 slice of ham over mustard. Place 1-2 slices of tomato over ham/cheese. Cover with top half of bun.

Melt $\frac{1}{4}$ cup butter (or Smart Balance spread) in a large skillet. Dip each sandwich into egg mixture to coat, entirely. Sauté sandwiches over medium heat for 3-4 minutes on each side. Drizzle any remaining egg batter over sandwiches as they cook in skillet. Use a thin-edged metal spatula to turn sandwiches in pan. Cook 2 sandwiches at a time. Remove them to a heat-resistant serving platter; lay a sheet of foil over the sandwiches and keep them warm in a low oven as you complete the project.

Or, you may bake the sandwiches. Preheat oven to 375°. Over low heat on stove burner, melt $\frac{1}{4}$ cup butter (or Smart Balance spread) in 9x12 non-stick pan. Remove pan to work counter. Dip sandwiches into egg mixture and lay them in the melted butter (or Smart Balance spread). Drizzle any remaining egg batter over the sandwiches in pan. Bake them in preheated oven at 375° for 5-6 minutes; then, turn the sandwiches over with a thin spatula and bake the other side for another 5-6 minutes. Remove them to a serving platter. Serve immediately. Serves 4-6.

ROASTED CHICKEN SALAD SANDWICH
(Roasted Turkey may be a substitute for chicken in this recipe.)

2 cups roasted chicken (white/dark meat);
   do not remove all of the skin;
   finely chopped
$\frac{1}{4}$ cup celery, finely chopped
1 small carrot, shredded
$\frac{1}{4}$ cup tart apple with skin, finely chopped
1 tbsp. fresh cilantro, finely chopped
$\frac{1}{2}$ cup low-fat mayonnaise
juice of 1 lime
freshly ground black pepper

8 slices whole grain artisan bread
   (with pistachio nuts and cranberries),
   each slice cut $\frac{1}{2}$-inch-thick

1 cup whole cranberry sauce
   (see page 400 for recipe)

In a large bowl, combine chicken, celery, carrot, apple, lime juice, mayonnaise, cilantro and black pepper. On a board, cut 8 slices bread, $\frac{1}{2}$-inch thick. Spoon and spread about $\frac{1}{2}$ cup chicken salad on each of 4 slices of bread. Cover sandwich with top slice of bread. Serve with $\frac{1}{4}$ cup whole cranberry sauce. Serves 4.

CHINESE SHRIMP OMELET IN A PITA

2 thin chicken breasts, boneless, skinless,
   simmered in $\frac{1}{2}$ cup water until cooked,
   about12-15 minutes (Refrigerate/reserve
   broth up to several days to use
   as soup stock.)
6 jumbo shrimp, peeled, deveined
$\frac{1}{4}$ cup chives, chopped

4 large eggs or 1 cup egg substitute
2 large pitas
1 tbsp. *lite* soy sauce
2-3 splashes Tabasco
2 tbsp. canola oil for skillet
2 cups prepared Slaw Salad
   (see recipes: pages 182, 215, 279)

Have ready: a 9-inch skillet with a cover.

Shred cooked chicken (about 1 cupful) into a large bowl. Beat eggs (or egg substitute) in a bowl. Add to bowl of shredded chicken. Mix prepared shrimp into same bowl. Stir in chives, soy sauce and Tabasco. Warm oil in skillet over moderate heat. Pour the chicken/shrimp/egg mixture into the hot skillet; cover and cook the omelet until just set. Underside should be golden brown. Cut omelet into 2 portions. Slice a wide pocket in the pitas. With help from a spatula, lift each omelet section out of pan and insert into pitas. Serve with a slaw salad from this book. Serves 2.

31

CRUNCHY SPICY FISH FILLET SANDWICH

4 fish fillets (like flounder, grey sole, tilapia); remove bones

4 large soft rolls (about 3x6 inches)

2 tbsp. olive oil, divided

1 cup corn flake crumbs

$\frac{1}{2}$ cup pineapple juice

$\frac{1}{2}$ red bell pepper, deseeded, minced

$\frac{1}{2}$ green bell pepper, deseeded, minced

1 very small (or 1-inch piece) jalapeño pepper, deseeded, minced

    (Wear plastic gloves when handling hot peppers.)

2 garlic cloves, minced

2-inch piece of fresh gingerroot, pared, minced

2 tbsp. fresh parsley, minced

2 tbsp. onion, minced

$\frac{1}{4}$ tsp. freshly ground black pepper

$\frac{1}{8}$ tsp. cayenne pepper

$\frac{1}{2}$ cup coarsely crumbled pretzels

4-8 slices of beefsteak tomato

4 leaves of Boston lettuce, rinsed, patted dry with paper towel

Friends at Lunch.

Preheat oven to 400°.

Have ready: a 9x12 non-stick baking pan, coated with 1 tablespoon olive oil.

Prepare CRUST. On a large sheet of waxed paper combine cornflake crumbs, minced red and green pepper, minced jalapeño, garlic, onion, parsley and gingerroot. Add black pepper, cayenne and ground pretzels. Pour pineapple juice in a wide plate with a rim. Dip each fish fillet into pineapple juice. Lay the slices into prepared crumb mixture to coat on both sides. Then, lay the crusted fillets into the oiled 9x12 non-stick pan. Bake in preheated oven at 400° for 25 minutes.

Cut rolls in half. Lay a baked fillet on bottom of each roll. Cover each with a slice or two of tomato and a leaf of lettuce. Close with top half of roll. Serves 4.

SALMON BURGER ON A CROISSANT

1 tbsp. olive oil for pan

4 large leaves Boston lettuce, rinsed, drained

4 large croissant rolls, split

1 cup all-purpose flour, $\frac{1}{4}$ tsp. freshly ground black pepper

1 can (14.5 oz.) salmon, crumbled (skin and bones discarded)

2 cups unseasoned mashed potatoes (about 3 large all-purpose potatoes)

2 tbsp. onion, finely chopped

1 tbsp. fresh parsley, chopped

$\frac{1}{4}$ tsp. freshly ground black pepper

juice of 1 lemon, strained

2 strips lean, cooked bacon, crumbled

Hungarian paprika for garnish

Preheat oven to 400° (if baking the burgers).

Have ready: a skillet or grill pan, surface rubbed with olive oil; or, if baking, a 9x12 oiled baking pan.

Spread flour with a sprinkling of black pepper over a sheet of waxed paper. Set aside. In a large bowl, combine crumbled salmon into mashed potatoes. Stir in chopped onion, pepper, parsley, lemon juice and crumbled bacon. Form 4 patties with your hands, each about 3x4x1 inches in size. Coat the patties on all sides with flour mixture. Garnish with paprika.

Grill or fry the salmon burgers in a hot oiled skillet or a grill pan at moderate-high, 4-5 minutes on each side. Or: Bake burgers in a preheated oven at 400° for 15 minutes. With a spatula, turn over burgers and continue to bake the other side for an additional 10 minutes. Place burgers inside split croissant rolls and lay a leaf of lettuce on top of burgers before closing the sandwich. Serve immediately. Serves 4.

West Publishing Picnic. Photo: H. Capriglione

TUNA MELT

2 cans (5 oz. each) solid white tuna in water, well-drained, flaked

1 scallion, including some greens, finely chopped

$\frac{1}{4}$ cup fresh Italian parsley, minced

2 tsp. dried tarragon leaves

juice of 1 lemon

grated rind of 1 lemon

1 tsp. Dijon mustard

$\frac{1}{2}$ cup mayonnaise (low-fat available)

$\frac{1}{8}$ tsp. freshly ground black pepper

1 large ripe tomato, thinly sliced (about 8 slices)

$\frac{1}{2}$ cup sharp Cheddar cheese, grated

8 slices Italian bread (sliced $\frac{1}{2}$-inch thick)

2 tbsp. olive oil

Have ready: a 12-inch grill pan, brushed with olive oil and an ovenproof 9x12 metal pan; a sheet of foil for warming.

In a medium-size bowl, combine chopped scallion, parsley, tarragon, lemon juice and zest, mustard, pepper and mayonnaise. Add flaked tuna and mix thoroughly. Lay out 4 slices of bread on a board. Divide the tuna mixture onto the slices. Top each with tomato slices and a sprinkling of cheese. Brush one side of each of the remaining 4 slices of bread, with olive oil. Place these slices of bread, oiled-side up, on top of the cheese.

Preheat oven to 250°.

Heat the oiled grill pan at moderate. Place 2 sandwiches at a time on the grill pan, oiled-side down. Carefully brush top side of sandwich bread with oil. Cook for 2-3 minutes, until nicely browned on bottom side. Turn sandwiches over and cook other side another 2-3 minutes, until browned. Remove sandwiches to metal pan; lightly cover with a sheet of foil and place in a warming oven as you cook the remaining sandwiches. Serve warm. Serves 4.

ROASTED PEPPER AND SARDINES SALAD SANDWICH

1 can sardines in water, drained, chopped

1 tbsp. catsup

1 tbsp. celery, chopped

1 tbsp. pitted spicy green olives, chopped

$\frac{1}{4}$ cup light mayonnaise

1 tbsp. horseradish

1 red bell pepper, cored, deseeded, grilled
   (see page 402, "How to Roast Peppers".)

2 large leaves Boston lettuce, rinsed, drained

4 slices seeded rye, toasted

more spicy olives for garnish

   Grill or roast red pepper as directed on page 402, "How to Roast or Grill Peppers".
Or, you may use ready-prepared roasted peppers from deli department or from a jar.
Slice roasted peppers into narrow strips. Set aside.
   In a small bowl, blend mayonnaise, catsup, celery, olives, horseradish and sardines.
Toast rye bread slices. Divide sardines mix to spread on bottoms of 2 slices toasted rye bread.
Cover each with pepper slices and a leaf of lettuce. Top sandwich with toasted rye bread.
Serve with a bean soup and a potato salad from this book. Serves 2.

STUFFED HAM, TURKEY, CHEESE WRAP
(Processed ham and turkey, and mayonnaise are available in low-fat, low-sodium.
Suggestion: Try thin apple slivers in place of cream cheese spread.)

2 9-inch whole wheat wraps

$\frac{1}{4}$ cup mayonnaise

4-8 leaves Boston lettuce, rinsed, drained

4-8 slices ham

4-8 slices turkey breast

4-8 slices Swiss cheese

STUFFING:

8 oz. cream cheese, softened

2 tbsp. pitted Kalamata olives, chopped

1 tbsp. each: red bell pepper, green bell pepper,
   deseeded, minced

(2 sheets each: waxed paper, aluminum foil; each sheet 12 inches long)

   Lay 2 sheets aluminum foil, each layered with a sheet of waxed paper, on your work table.

   In a small bowl, blend chopped olives and peppers into cream cheese until smooth. Set aside.
Lay 1 whole wheat wrap over each foil/waxed paper; spread mayonnaise over wraps. Lay 2 to 4
leaves Boston lettuce over each wrap; follow with layers of ham, cheese, turkey. Over turkey in
each wrap, spread half of the cream cheese mix in a 4-inch center circle. (Do *not* spead cheese to
the edge of wraps.) With water-dampened hands, tightly bundle and roll the wrap from right to
left. Tightly wrap each formed sandwich wrap in the foil/waxed paper, twisting the edges closed.
Refrigerate until 15 minutes before serving. At serving, diagonally slice each wrap in half to form
2 sandwiches each wrap. Serves 4.

APPLE AND HAM OPEN-FACED SANDWICH WITH BRIE

(Get ready for a delicious, healthy and quick winter's-day lunch.)

<u>For each Open-Faced Sandwich:</u>

1 pre-sliced whole-grain sandwich thin

½ large Red Delicious apple, cored

4 thin slices Brie

1 thin slice low-fat packaged boiled ham
    for each half

sprinkling of cinnamon powder

3 leaves Boston lettuce, rinsed, drained

a small bunch of grapes

Have ready: small flat broiler tray; a thin spatula; a serving plate.
Preheat broiler.
Arrange lettuce on serving plate. Open and lay both halves of thin sandwich bread on a flat broiler tray. Place 1 slice ham on each sandwich bread half. Slice cored apple into 4 thick slices, horizontally. Lay the 2 widest (center) apple rounds, one each, over ham, on top of each sandwich-thin half. Arrange 2 slices of Brie on each half. Sprinkle tops of sandwich halves with cinnamon. Broil 5 inches below broiling element for 2-3 minutes, or until cheese begins to bubble and char. With a thin spatula, transfer both halves of sandwich to lay on top of lettuce leaves on the serving plate. Add a small bunch of seedless red or black grapes. Serve with a small bowl of soup from this cookbook, prepared in advance. Serves 1.

FRESH SALMON FILLET BURGER

1 lb. thin salmon fillet, about ½-inch thick;
    remove skin; cut into 2-3 portions
    (pieces to fit on a bun)

2 tbsp. honey mustard

juice of 1 lemon

1 tsp. finely chopped dill
    (or use dried dill weed)

⅛ tsp. freshly ground black pepper

¼ cup corn flake crumbs

1 tbsp. extra-virgin olive oil

½ cup baby spinach, trimmed, rinsed,
    thoroughly drained

2-3 soft whole wheat potato buns

Have ready: a 12-inch grill pan, brushed with 1 tablespoon olive oil.
In a small bowl, smoothly blend mustard, lemon juice, black pepper and dill. Spread on both sides of salmon portions. Coat salmon on both sides with crumbs. Heat oiled grill pan at medium-high; lay sections of prepared salmon in pan and cook for 2-3 minutes on each side. Remove salmon with a thin spatula to a plate. Lightly grill insides of buns, about 30 seconds. Lay a salmon patty on lower half of each bun. Pack ¼ cup spinach on top of each patty; drizzle olive oil over spinach and close sandwich with top-bun. Serve immediately with a small salad from this cookbook. Serves 2-3.

CRAB CAKES IN A CROISSANT

1 cup fine corn meal
2 cups crab lump meat, finely chopped
2 cups mashed potatoes
1 small onion, diced
1 tbsp. red bell pepper, finely chopped
$\frac{1}{4}$ cup fresh parsley, finely chopped
1 tbsp. lemon juice
1 tbsp. Worcestershire sauce
$\frac{1}{4}$ cup low-fat mayonnaise
2 large eggs or $\frac{1}{2}$ cup egg substitute, beaten
$\frac{1}{4}$ tsp. salt
$\frac{1}{4}$ tsp. freshly ground black pepper
2-3 tbsp. evaporated milk (fat-free available), if needed
1 cup corn flake crumbs
Hungarian paprika
2 tbsp. oil for pan

6-8 large croissant rolls
Boston lettuce leaves, rinsed, drained, patted dry
lemon wedges at serving

Preheat oven to 400° when ready to bake crab cakes.

Have ready: a 9x12-inch baking tin; brush with 2 tablespoons canola oil.

Lay a sheet of waxed paper on a board; coat with 1 cup corn flake crumbs. In a large bowl, thoroughly combine mashed potatoes, corn meal, crab meat, onion, red pepper, parsley, Worcestershire sauce, mayonnaise, beaten eggs (or egg beaters), salt and pepper, lemon juice. Add 2-3 tablespoons evaporated milk if dough is too stiff.

With the aid of a large serving spoon, form 4-inch crab burgers. Coat them with corn flake crumbs. Sprinkle Hungarian paprika over both sides of the crab cakes. At this point, lay the crab cakes on a greased 9x12-inch pan and store in refrigerator for 1 hour.

Then, bake the crab cakes in a preheated oven at 400° for 20 minutes. Cut croissants in half; lay a large lettuce leaf on bottom of each roll. Lay crab cakes on top of lettuce. Squeeze lemon juice over each crab cake and close the sandwich. Serves 6-8 crab cake sandwiches.

BUTTERFLIED SHRIMP CIABATTA

4 ciabatta rolls for sandwiches

8 jumbo shrimp, shelled, deveined,
    butterfly-cut (After removing shrimp
    shells, with a sharp knife, cut fin area
    almost through to the tail to spread-eagle
    the shrimp.)

1 cup all-purpose flour

a pinch of cayenne

$\frac{1}{4}$ tsp. freshly ground black pepper

a sprinkling of salt

2 large eggs, beaten or
    $\frac{1}{2}$ cup egg substitute

$\frac{1}{2}$ cup flat beer (or flat seltzer)

$\frac{1}{4}$ cup canola oil for skillet

2 cups coleslaw (see recipe on page 279)

    Have ready: a large skillet; a flat plate lined with paper towel.

    Prepare coleslaw in advance. Gradually, beat 2 eggs (or egg substitute) in a 2-quart bowl. Whisk in flour mixed with salt, pepper and cayenne until flour mix is incorporated. Slowly, add flat beer or seltzer to form a thick paste. Preheat $\frac{1}{4}$ cup canola oil in a skillet to 320°.
Dip the butterflied shrimp into the batter to completely coat. Fry battered shrimp 3-4 at a time in a preheated skillet, 3 minutes on each side, until golden. Transfer cooked shrimp to a plate lined with a paper towel to absorb excess oil from shrimp.

    After all of the shrimp are fried, cut ciabatta rolls in half and lay 2 shrimp on bottom half of each roll. Mound $\frac{1}{2}$ cup coleslaw on top and place top half of roll lightly upon coleslaw. Serve immediately. If not serving quickly, you may arrange drained shrimp on an oven-proof platter to keep warm in a low oven, at 200° for a few more minutes. Serves 4.

SAUSAGE- PROVOLONE WRAPS

4-6 fully cooked seasoned packaged sausages
    (Suggestion: packaged fully-cooked
    sausages like: Chef Bruce Aidell
    or Hillshire Farms.)

4-6 slices sharp provolone cheese,
    each 4x4 inches, $\frac{1}{4}$-inch thick

1 pkg. dough for crescent rolls

4-6 tsp. honey mustard

    Preheat oven 375°. You will need a 9x15-inch cookie sheet.

    Unroll dough on a cutting board. Evenly divide dough into 4-6 sections. Spread 1 teaspoon honey mustard on each of 4-6 sections of dough. Lay one fully-cooked sausage and 1 slice of provolone on each section of prepared dough. Stretch dough around sausage and cheese to form a package. Lay the sausage wraps, 2 inches apart on an ungreased cookie sheet. Bake in preheated oven, at 375° for 10 minutes, or until golden brown. Serves 4-6.

CUBAN PORK ROAST SANDWICH

10-12 thin slices Cuban Pork Roast
    for 1 12-inch baguette
    (makes 2 sandwiches)
    (see recipe for Cuban Pork Roast,
      page 283)
Aioli (Garlic) Sauce (see page 384);
    use entire recipe for 1 baguette;
    prepare in advance

$\frac{1}{2}$ cup caramelized onions
$\frac{1}{2}$ cup pickled jalapeños
1 tbsp. cilantro, minced
several leaves Romaine lettuce, rinsed, drained,
    patted dry with paper towel
1 12-inch baguette, lightly toasted on inside

NOTE: If serving 4-6 portions (sandwiches), you will need 2-3 (12-inch) baguettes, plus double or triple recipe's ingredients. Each baguette serves 2 portions. Cut baguettes in half, lengthwise; lightly toast insides, just before serving. Then, across each baguette bottom, lay 10-12 thin slices of Cuban Pork Roast. Spread $\frac{1}{2}$ cup Aioli Sauce over pork; follow with $\frac{1}{2}$ cup pickled jalapeños, $\frac{1}{2}$ cup caramelized onions (see recipe below) and a sprinkling of minced cilantro. Cover with leaves of Romaine lettuce and close with top half of baguette. Each recipe serves 2.

CARAMELIZED ONIONS (enough for 6 portions; prepare a day or two in advance; refrigerate; reheat in skillet before serving)

skillet to cook onions
3-4 large white onions, thinly sliced
2 tbsp. olive oil

2 tbsp. butter or Smart Balance spread
1 tbsp. red wine vinegar

Heat oil and butter or Smart Balance spread at medium-high. Add sliced onions and sauté for 10 minutes, frequently shuffling onions in pan. Lower temperature to medium-low and continue to cook onions for 20-30 minutes, shuffling them occasionally as they soften and brown, not allowing onions to burn. Stir in vinegar. Spread $\frac{1}{2}$ cup onions into each baguette as directed above.

POTATO FRITTATA HERO

2 12-inch baguettes, cut in half horizontally; each portion halved, lengthwise
1 recipe for Frittata de Patate e Carciofi (see page 76)
1 large beefsteak tomato, cut into $\frac{1}{2}$-inch slices

Prepare recipe for Fritatta de Patate e Carciofi (see page 76).
Divide the prepared frittata into 4 portions. Lay one warm portion on bottom half of each baguette; top with 1-2 slices tomato; close sandwiches with top halves of baguettes. Wrap each sandwich in foil and lay them on a tray in a warm oven, preheated to 250° for 10 minutes, until heated through. Serve picnic-style with a salad; or package in a thermal carrying case for up to several hours. Serves 4.

SLIDERS

(While my husband attended Georgetown University Dental School, Washington DC, way back in the late 1940's, he had become acquainted with Sliders - those tiny, greasy burgers which sold for 5 cents apiece at White Castle. Arthur Godfrey's comfortable, homespun voice would drawl, "Buy 'em by the bag!" This recipe pretty much follows the format of the original tiny burgers, which dates back to around 1921.)

1 lb. chopped beef chuck

salt

black pepper to taste

2 large yellow onions, shredded, oozing moisture

1 large dill pickle, in 12-16 slivers

12-16 tiny burger buns, split in half; or English muffins

Fire up the outdoor grill; or heat a large oil-greased grill pan on stove burner. Form at least 12-16 tiny balls (1 ounce each) from 1 pound of chopped chuck, about 1 tablespoon per ball. Space 6 balls on the grill (or in the pan); add 1 tablespoon of shredded onion on tops of each beef ball and cook for 2 minutes. Flip the burgers over, onions at bottom. Squash the beef balls with the flat side of a spatula and cook for 2 minutes longer. Place bottom half of a bun (or English muffin) on top; and with a spatula, flip the patty on the bun; then, set the other half of the bun (or muffin) on top; place tiny burgers on a plate. Press down on the Sliders, to allow the juices to stream out of the buns. Insert a sliver of dill pickle into each Slider and serve.

On second thought, until you've become adept at the culinary agility needed to perform this cooking task, start this grilling project, one Slider at a time. Have fun!

Georgetown University Dental School 40th Reunion.

CHIPPED BEEF SANDWICH

(Sometimes referred to as "dried beef", Chipped Beef is a section of meat that has been thinly sliced and cured by smoking or salting. It can be stored for long periods of time without refrigeration. Sold in airtight aluminum tins or in flash-sealed pouches; in delis or specialty food stores. Not highly touted, Chipped Beef has had the reputation for being meat which was produced for people with no cooking ability. My apologies for providing alternate "healthier" ingredients.)

¼ cup butter or Smart Balance spread

½ lb. chipped beef, torn into bite-size pieces

2 tbsp. onion, finely chopped

3 tbsp. all-purpose flour

2½ cups low-fat milk

1 cup low-fat sour cream

salt, pepper, to taste

2 tbsp. fresh parsley, finely chopped

4 English muffins (available whole grain),
    split and toasted

Melt butter (or Smart Balance spread) in a skillet over medium heat. Sauté beef and onion for 5-7 minutes, until onion is soft. Stir in flour for 1 minute; gradually add milk. Cook, stirring until sauce is smooth and thick, about 5-7 minutes. Stir in sour cream, salt, pepper and parsley and continue to cook for 1-2 minutes. Spoon over toasted English muffin halves. Serves 4.

MUFFULETTA

(The Muffuletta is a classic New Orleans sandwich. It's a large, round Italian-style hero with a taste for olives. The oil-soaked olive salad seeps into the thick bread, resulting in an oily, messy, but thoroughly delicious huge sandwich that begs to be shared.)

1 8-inch round loaf of Italian bread

1 cup pitted Kalamata olives, chopped

1 large garlic clove, minced

1 tbsp. onion, minced

1 tbsp. fresh Italian (flat-leaf) parsley, minced

¼ lb. mortadella, sliced

¼ lb. Genoa salami, sliced

¼ lb. capicola, sliced (hot, if you prefer)

¼ lb. mozzarella, sliced

¼ lb. sharp provolone, sliced

freshly ground black pepper to taste

2 tbsp. extra-virgin olive oil, divided

Have ready: lay on a board, a 2-ft. sheet of aluminum foil (bottom layer); and a 2-ft. sheet waxed paper (top layer). To be used as a double wrapper for the Muffuletta.

In a small bowl, combine pitted olives, garlic, onion and parsley. Cut the round loaf of bread in half, horizontally, creating top and bottom halves. With your fingers, press into the soft bread of the halves, to form slight depressions. Place bottom half on foil/paper. Sprinkle 1 tablespoon olive oil and black pepper over inside of bottom half; repeat oil/pepper inside top half. Over bottom half, layer mortadella, salami, capicola, mozzarella and provolone. Spoon olives mix over meat/cheese. Fit top half of loaf over filled bottom half. Press down gently on Muffuletta. Tightly wrap sandwich in paper/foil. Allow Muffuletta to sit for at least 30 minutes. Then, remove wrapper and cut sandwich into quarters (or more). Serves 4-6.

BAKED PORK CUTLET BAGUETTE
(Thin metal skewers/sandwich picks are preferable to wooden picks which
may easily break off inside the sandwich.)

HERO SANDWICH:

1 long baguette, about 15-18 inches, halved horizontally; whole grain bread available

6-8 slices prosciutto

2 cups arugula (rocket), rinsed, drained, patted dry with paper towel

6 prepared pork cutlets, cooked as directed in recipe, below

MARINADE FOR PORK CUTLETS:

2 tbsp. olive oil

$\frac{1}{4}$ cup Asian plum sauce

$\frac{1}{4}$ cup *lite* ginger soy sauce

$\frac{1}{4}$ cup pineapple juice

3 round slices canned pineapple, halved

1 cup corn flake crumbs

TIna's Round-up Barbeque.
Photo: T. Miller

Preheat oven to 375°.

Have ready: a 9x12x1$\frac{1}{2}$-inch non-stick pan and a large serving platter.

Spread corn flake crumbs on a sheet of waxed paper. In a small bowl, blend plum sauce, ginger soy sauce and pineapple juice. Brush bottom of a 9x12x1$\frac{1}{2}$-inch pan with olive oil. Working one cutlet at a time, dip each cutlet into marinade to coat on both sides. Press one side of coated cutlet into cornflake crumbs; lay a slice of prosciutto on top-side of sauce-coated cutlet. Turn over prosciutto side onto corn flake crumbs, to coat with crumbs. Place each prepared pork cutlet in the pan, prosciutto-side down.

Bake cutlets in preheated oven at 375° for 15-17 minutes, turning cutlets over, prosciutto side, up, at the seven-minute mark and continue to bake them.

As cutlets are baking, rinse and drain arugula; cut baguettes in half, horizontally, and lay them on the serving platter. With the aid of a spatula, lay each prepared pork cutlet on bottom half of baguette. Add a half-slice of pineapple and a portion of arugula and close the baguette with its top half. Use metal picks to close the sandwich. Serves up to 6.

ARLINE'S CROQUE MONSIEUR
(Years ago, my best friend, Arline Scaglione, introduced us to
"Croque Monsieur", the French version of the ham and cheese sandwich.
At our Saturday evening supper parties, Arline would arrive with all of the
ingredients, plus her electric sandwich maker. No wonder, my parties were so successful!)

8 slices, $\frac{1}{2}$-inch thick, French or Italian loaf bread

8 thin slices cured ham (about 12 oz.)

Dijon mustard

(4 fried eggs, if you want to serve "Croque Madame")

BÉCHAMEL SAUCE:

2 tbsp. butter or Smart Balance spread

2 tbsp. all-purpose flour

$1\frac{1}{2}$ cups evaporated milk (fat-free available)

$\frac{1}{8}$ tsp. freshly ground black pepper

$\frac{1}{8}$ tsp. ground nutmeg

pinch of salt

$\frac{1}{2}$ lb. (about $1\frac{1}{2}$ cups) Gruyere cheese, grated

$\frac{1}{4}$ cup Parmesan cheese, grated

"Best Friends" at a Wedding Rehearsal Dinner.

Have ready: a buttered 9x12-inch baking sheet.
Preheat oven to 400°.

Prepare Béchamel SAUCE. Melt butter (or Smart Balance spread) in a small saucepan on medium-low heat until it starts to bubble. Whisk in flour and cook, stirring until smooth, about 2 minutes. Slowly add milk, whisking continuously, cooking until thick. Remove from heat. Stir in salt, pepper and nutmeg, Parmesan cheese and $\frac{1}{4}$ cup of grated Gruyere. Set aside.

Prepare the SANDWICHES. Lay out slices of bread on a buttered baking sheet and toast them in preheated oven at 400°, a couple of minutes on each side, until lightly toasted. (Do not turn off oven.) Lightly spread mustard on 4 slices of bread. Add 2 slices of ham on each of 4 slices of bread; spread remaining Gruyere cheese on top of ham. Top with remaining 4 slices of toasted bread slices.

Spoon Béchamel Sauce over tops of sandwiches. Sprinkle with remaining Gruyere cheese. Place the tray in a preheated oven at 400° and bake sandwiches for 5 minutes. Then, turn on broiler and broil for an additional 3 minutes, until cheese topping is bubbly and lightly browned.

If you top this sandwich with a fried egg it becomes a "Croque Madame".
Makes 4 sandwiches.

ROASTED CHICKEN SANDWICH AND TOMATO-AVOCADO SALAD

1) The SANDWICH:
   2 slices of artisan whole grain bread for each sandwich, each slice $\frac{1}{2}$-inch thick
   Carved slices of roasted chicken (with crisp skin) from breast, legs, thighs; set aside
   4 large leaves Boston lettuce, rinsed, drained

2) Sandwich FILLING: In a 1 qt. bowl make a mix with:
   1 celery stalk with greens, finely chopped
   $\frac{1}{4}$ cup finely chopped red onion
   $\frac{1}{4}$ cup finely deseeded, chopped sweet red pepper
   $\frac{1}{4}$ cup finely deseeded, chopped green bell pepper
   1 hard boiled egg, mashed
   1 tbsp. honey mustard spread
   1 tbsp. low-fat mayonnaise
   1 tbsp. prepared horseradish
   $\frac{1}{4}$ tsp. black pepper
   $\frac{1}{4}$ tsp. Hungarian paprika
   juice from 1 lemon (remove seeds)

3) Form the SANDWICH: Spread about $\frac{1}{2}$ cup sandwich filling (see above) on each of 4 thick slices whole grain artisan bread. Lay a couple of slices of roasted chicken over Filling and top with a large leaf of Boston lettuce. Hold each sandwich together with 2-3 metal sandwich picks.

4) A Salad ACCOMPANIMENT: (Prepare just before serving.)
   2 Hass avocados, peeled, cut into small cubes (sprinkle lemon juice over avocado)
   2-3 ripe plum tomatoes, chopped
   $\frac{1}{4}$ cup pitted, chopped Kalamata olives
   $\frac{1}{2}$ cup Feta cheese, crumbled
   freshly ground black pepper, olive oil, red wine vinegar, to taste

   On each of 4 dinner plates (or 10-inch glass plates), lay one large leaf of Boston lettuce. Over the lettuce on each plate, spoon one portion of prepared avocado cubes, 1 tablespoon chopped tomato, a sprinkling of chopped olives and a scattering of crumbled feta cheese. Drizzle olive oil and red wine vinegar over each plate, to taste. Sprinkle with black pepper. Cut each roasted chicken sandwich in half and with aid of a thin spatula, place 2 halves of sandwich next to salad on each plate. Serves 4.

GRILLED PORK CUTLETS AND PEPPER HERO
(You may prepare this sandwich with veal cutlets. Do not pound cutlets.)

4 pork (or veal) cutlets, about 3x6 inches; do not pound cutlets

$\frac{1}{2}$ cup Italian seasoned bread crumbs

$\frac{1}{4}$ cup Parmesan cheese, grated

2 red bell peppers, cored, deseeded, each cut into 4 sections

2 green bell peppers, cored, deseeded, each cut into 4 sections

4-5 whole garlic cloves

2 tbsp. olive oil (or more)

$\frac{1}{4}$ cup pitted Kalmata olives, sliced

2 12-inch baguettes, halved horizontally; cut each half-section into 2 pieces, vertically

   (You are preparing 4 baguette sandwiches, 2 sandwiches per baguette.)

Preheat oven to warm at 200°.
Have ready: a 12-inch grill pan with ovenproof handle; and a 9x12-inch baking pan.

Rub grill pan with olive oil. Set aside. Coat pork (or veal) cutlets on both sides in a mixture of crumbs and Parmesan cheese. Heat oiled grill pan on medium-high for several minutes. Lay prepared breaded cutlets in a oiled grill pan and cook them, 2 at a time, on medium-high for 2-3 minutes. Lower heat to medium and continue to cook them for another 2 minutes. Turn cutlets over and repeat cooking directions. Transfer grilled cutlets to a baking pan to warm in a low oven at 200°.

Oil bottom of grill pan, if needed, and turn up heat to medium-high. Pour sectioned peppers and garlic into grill pan for 5-6 minutes, frequently using a large Teflon spatula to move peppers in grill pan to prevent burning and sticking. Lower heat under pan and cook peppers for a couple of minutes longer, until they are softened. Remove pan from heat.

Set halved baguettes (4 sections) on a work board. Lay one warm cooked cutlet on each bottom half. Top with a spoonful of sliced olives and lay 4 slices of peppers (2 red, 2 green) on top of olives. Include a garlic clove, as desired. Top with upper half of baguette. With your hand, press down on sandwich to assist in blending the tastes. Cut each portion in half just before serving. Serves 4.

HINT: You may wish to "lightly" grill inside bottom and top halves of baguettes before building the sandwich.

GRILLED BREADED CHICKEN CUTLET ON WHOLE WHEAT SOFT ROLL
(You may substitute turkey cutlets in this recipe. Or, try this sandwich with Breaded Fillet of
Flounder. *NOTE below: for Preparation of Grilled Breaded Fillet of Flounder Sandwich.)

4 grilled breaded chicken (or turkey) cutlets (see recipe below)

4 whole wheat soft sandwich rolls, each split in half

4 slices ($\frac{1}{4}$-inch thick) Virginia ham

4 thin slices ($\frac{1}{2}$-inch thick) canned pineapple in rings, lightly grilled on each side

4 large leaves Boston lettuce, rinsed, drained, air-dried

1) Prepare CUTLETS. Cutlets may be prepared in advance. Refrigerate covered. Re-warm in
low oven when needed.

GRILLED BREADED CHICKEN (or TURKEY) CUTLETS
2 chicken cutlets, halved (4 pieces), rinsed in cold water, patted dry with paper towels
$\frac{1}{2}$ cup Italian seasoned bread crumbs
$\frac{1}{4}$ cup Parmesan cheese, grated
1 tbsp. olive oil for grill pan

Preheat oil-coated 12-inch grill pan with ovenproof handle, just before cooking
chicken cutlets.

Spread crumbs mixed with cheese on a sheet of waxed paper. Coat both sides of chicken with
crumbs mix. Increase burner to medium-high and lay 2 cutlets at a time in grill pan to cook for
3 minutes on each side. Lower heat to medium and cook each side for an additional 4-5 minutes.
Transfer cooked cutlets to an oven-proof platter to keep warm in a low oven at 200°.
Cook remaining cutlets in a similar way.

2) Prepare SANDWICHES. Lay opened whole wheat soft rolls on a work board. Lay one grilled
cutlet on each bottom half of roll. Lightly grill pineapple slices on one side. Lay one slice
Virginia ham on top of chicken followed by a slice of grilled pineapple. Cover with a leaf of
lettuce and top half of roll. Cut each sandwich in half when serving. Serves 4.

*NOTE: Preparation of GRILLED BREADED FILLET OF FLOUNDER SANDWICH may
follow same recipe (see above); omit Parmesan cheese from crumb coating. Depending upon
thickness of fish, flounder fillet may be grill pan-ready in 10-12 minutes, about 5-6 minutes on
each side. Adjust cooking accordingly.

BAKED BREADED CHICKEN CUTLET, ROASTED PEPPER
AND PROVOLONE HERO
(You may substitute turkey cutlets in this recipe.)

2 tbsp. olive oil

4-6 cooked breaded chicken cutlets (see recipe below)

1 loaf Italian hero bread or French bread (about 12-16 inches long);
    (whole wheat Italian hero bread available)

2-3 red bell peppers, roasted, peeled, deseeded, each sliced into 4 vertical sections
    (see page 402 "How to Roast Peppers" or use prepared roasted peppers in a jar.)

4-8 thin slices provolone cheese

$\frac{1}{2}$ cup pitted Kalamata olives, sliced

(6 metal sandwich picks for each hero)

(2 feet of freezer wrap)

1) <u>Prepare CUTLETS</u>. Cutlets may be prepared in advance. Wrap and refrigerate or freeze until needed. Warm cutlets thoroughly before using in hero.

BAKED ITALIAN-STYLE CHICKEN CUTLETS

4-6 thin sliced chicken cutlets, skin removed,
    rinsed in cold water, patted dry with
    paper towel

$\frac{1}{4}$ cup honey mustard spread

juice of 1 lemon

1 tbsp. olive oil

1-1$\frac{1}{2}$ cups Italian seasoned bread crumbs

2 tbsp. Parmesan cheese, grated

1 tbsp. olive oil for baking pan

Preheat oven to 375°.
Have ready: 7x9-inch baking pan, bottom greased with olive oil.

Combine mustard, lemon juice and olive oil in a small bowl. Brush both sides of cutlets with this mixture. Spread crumbs, mixed with Parmesan cheese on a sheet of waxed paper. Coat both sides of chicken with crumbs mix; lay the cutlets in prepared 7x9-inch pan and bake them in a preheated oven at 375° for 15-20 minutes. After 8 minutes, turn them over to bake the other side. Do not overcook chicken. A small slit in cooked cutlet should show clear juices.

2) <u>Prepare the HERO</u>. Lay 2 feet of freezer wrap on cutting board. Lay hero on freezer wrap on the cutting board. Slice hero in half lengthwise. Lay 4-6 cooked breaded cutlets on bottom half of loaf. Place 4-8 slices provolone cheese on top of cooked cutlets. Sprinkle surface with sliced olives and top with sections of roasted peppers. Brush inside of top half of hero bread with 2 tablespoons olive oil. Close the hero, firmly pressing the loaf with your fingers to help to seal in flavors. Insert 6-8 metal picks into hero, every few inches. Wrap the hero in the freezer wrap. Keep hero warm. Serve within a couple of hours. Makes 8-10 portions if using 12 to 16-inch loaf.

PORK DIM SUM

1 lb. finely ground lean pork
3-4 scallions with some greens, finely chopped
1 can (2½ oz.) bamboo shoots, drained, rinsed, (drained again), chopped
1 tbsp. *lite* ginger soy sauce
1 tbsp. dry sherry
2 tsp. sesame oil

2 tsp. fine granulated sugar
1 egg white from large egg, lightly beaten
2 tbsp. cornstarch
2 dozen wonton wrappers (May be purchased in dairy section of Asian specialty stores and many supermarkets.)

Have ready: a large bamboo steamer or a large, round, sloping steamer with basket.

In a bowl, combine thoroughly: finely ground pork, scallions, bamboo shoots, soy sauce, sherry, sesame oil, sugar and beaten egg white. Stir in cornstarch, mixing well.

On surface of a large board, spread out wonton wrappers. Place 1 spoonful of pork mixture in center of each wonton wrapper. Brush the inside edges of each wrapper with water; bring sides of wrappers together towards the center of the filling, pinching firmly together.

Line a steamer basket with a clean, damp linen or cotton tea towel and arrange the wontons within the towel. Cover the steamer and cook for 5-7 minutes until wontons are cooked through. Transfer to a serving plate. Serves 5-6.

STELLA WU'S SHRIMP TOAST

1 lb. small shrimp
1 cup water
3 scallions with some greens, finely chopped
6 water chestnuts, minced
1 tbsp. *lite* soy sauce
1 tbsp. sherry
¼ tsp. salt, or to taste

¼ tsp. freshly ground black pepper
2 egg whites, beaten
4 tbsp. sesame seeds
8 slices white or whole grain bread
peanut oil for frying
fresh parsley, finely chopped for garnish

Have ready: a large skillet; a food processor.

Wash shrimp in shells; drain. Put shrimp in a medium-size sauce pan with 1 cup water. Cover pot, bring to a boil and steam shrimp for 1 minute. Remove pot from heat and drain shrimp in colander. Run cold water through shrimp in colander for 15 seconds (to stop cooking); drain again. Peel shrimp. Process peeled shrimp, water chestnuts and scallions in a food processor until finely ground. Transfer to a large bowl and stir in soy sauce, sherry, salt, black pepper and beaten egg whites. Spread the shrimp mixture on one side of each of the 8 slices of bread. Spread sesame seeds on top of shrimp mixture, patting down seeds securely with round side of a large spoon. Cut each slice of prepared bread in half. Heat enough oil in bottom of skillet (about ¼ cup) to moderate and fry shrimp bread slices until golden. Drain them on paper towels; then transfer to warm serving platter. Sprinkle with chopped parsley. Serves 5-6.

CHINESE SHRIMP EGG ROLLS
Reprinted from: MENU LOG: A Collection of Recipes as Coordinated Menus
by Marion O. Celenza, page 67.
(May be prepared in advance and frozen. *NOTE below: Egg Rolls with Pork.)

1 lb. small shrimp, peeled, washed and drained
1 pkg. fresh Chinese vegetables: 8 oz. bok choy, bean sprouts, bamboo shoots (chopped)
1 large celery stalk, chopped fine
2 garlic cloves, minced
1 small onion, chopped fine
1 small Chile (or Thai) pepper, deseeded and chopped fine
1 pkg. dry Chinese stir-fry mix (i.e., Durkee, Taste of Thai, Sun Bird)
2 tbsp. cornstarch
3 tbsp. water
1 lb. soft tofu, mashed
2 tbsp. sesame oil
$\frac{1}{4}$ cup spicy Szechwan sauce
2 tbsp. ginger soy sauce
12 egg roll wraps (purchased in produce section of food stores)
Peanut oil for frying
Accompaniments: Chinese hot mustard, peach nectar

Have ready: a small skillet, an electric fry pan.

In a large bowl, mix shrimp, Chinese vegetables (rinsed once), celery, garlic, onion and pepper. Stir in package of dry stir-fry mix and cornstarch. Sprinkle 3 tablespoons water over mix and toss ingredients until combined. Pour into small skillet and simmer uncovered for 2 minutes. Pour back into large bowl and add mashed tofu. Add sesame oil, Szechwan and ginger soy sauce. Mix thoroughly.
On board, lay out the egg roll wraps. With a large spoon, scoop a compact bundle of filling and arrange vertically across center of wrap. Prepare one at a time. Roll up, wrap tightly and tuck in ends. Set seam-side down on a large plate or board. Prepare rest of rolls in same way.
Pour $\frac{1}{2}$-inch-high peanut oil into electric frying pan and preheat oil to 340°. Fry 4 rolls at a time, turning every 2 minutes until golden in color. Remove rolls with slotted spoon to paper towels and drain. If not serving immediately, keep them warm in low oven. Accompany rolls with Chinese hot mustard/peach sauce. (If freezing, after the rolls have cooled, wrap in a sheet of foil lined with plastic wrap.)

*NOTE: CHINESE PORK EGG ROLLS may be prepared with shredded pork instead of shrimp. Use 3 pork cutlets (about 1 lb.). Pound the cutlets to thin. Pile them on each other and with a sharp knife, cut them into julienne strips. Substitute shredded pork for small cleaned shrimp and proceed as directed in recipe.

SANDWICH SPREADS AND DIPS

1) CREAM CHEESE, PEPPERS & OLIVES

    12 oz. low-fat cream cheese, at room temperature
    1 tbsp. red bell pepper, finely chopped
    1 tbsp. green bell pepper, finely chopped
    2 tbsp. pitted Kalamata olives, finely chopped

Mash cream cheese with a fork and blend smoothly. Combine rest of ingredients to blend into cream cheese paste. Spread on triangles of firm bread, or crackers; or on firm raw vegetables or fruit: carrots, celery, apples.

2) CREAM CHEESE, WALNUTS & CRANBERRY RAISINS

    12 oz. low-fat cream cheese, at room temperature
    2 tbsp. walnuts, finely chopped
    2 tbsp. cranberry raisins, finely chopped

Mash cream cheese with a fork and blend smoothly. Combine rest of ingredients to blend into cream cheese paste. Spread on triangles of firm bread, or crackers; or on firm raw vegetables or fruit: carrots, celery, apples.

3) CREAM CHEESE & SCALLION SPREAD

    $\frac{1}{2}$ lb. cream cheese
    $\frac{1}{4}$ cup sour cream
    $\frac{1}{4}$ cup scallions, with some greens, chopped
    pinch of salt
    $\frac{1}{4}$ tsp. garlic powder

Mash cream cheese with a fork and blend smoothly. Combine rest of ingredients to blend into cream cheese paste. Spread on triangles of firm bread, or crackers; or on firm raw vegetables or fruit: carrots, celery, apples.

GUACAMOLE (AVOCADO DIP)

[A Cooking Hint: Dip peeled avocado, banana or apple into lemon juice (or other citrus juice) to prevent its discoloration.]

2 ripe Hass avocados
2 tbsp. lemon juice
3 cherry tomatoes, chopped
1 tsp. garlic powder

1 tbsp. onion, minced
1 tbsp. fresh cilantro, minced
$\frac{1}{2}$ tsp. Hungarian paprika
2 tbsp. pignola for garnish

Have ready: a small bowl for dip, sitting on a 12-inch platter.

Peel avocados. Mash them in a medium-size bowl (discard stones). Add lemon juice, garlic powder, chopped tomatoes, minced onion and cilantro. Pack and mound dip into a small serving bowl. Sprinkle with paprika; insert pignola over avocado ball (like a porcupine). Place bowl in center of a platter; scatter corn chips around dip bowl. Serves 4-6.

Additional *SALAD RECIPES*

from **ALL ARE WELCOME TO THIS TABLE**
(Dinner Menus)

[A Cooking Hint: Remove prepared salad dressing made with oil, from refrigerator 1 hour prior to serving. Bring to room temperature; shake or stir ingredients thoroughly prior to using. Suggestion: Chill salad plates/ bowls in refrigerator for 5 hours before serving.]

SMOKED SALMON AND LENTIL SALAD ON A BED OF ARUGULA

2 cups lentils, rinsed in cold water, drained

4 cups water

1 celery stalk, trimmed, finely chopped

1 onion, chopped

1 carrot, pared, finely chopped

1 tsp. dried thyme

$\frac{1}{4}$ tsp. allspice

$\frac{1}{4}$ cup fresh parsley, minced

$\frac{1}{4}$ cup white wine vinegar

freshly ground black pepper and salt to taste

1 tbsp. Dijon mustard

$\frac{1}{4}$ cup olive oil, divided

8 oz. smoked salmon, thinly sliced, cut into strips

3 cups arugula, trimmed, rinsed, drained thoroughly

2 tbsp. balsamic vinegar

2 tbsp. extra-virgin olive oil

Lunch at the Pool.

Have ready: a large round glass serving platter.

Simmer lentils in 4 cups water for 1 hour or until lentils are tender. While lentils are cooking, in a small skillet over moderate heat, cook celery, onion and carrot in 2 tablespoons olive oil for 4-5 minutes until softened and lightly browned. Drain lentils and pour them into a mixing bowl. Add cooked celery, onion and carrot mix. Stir in parsley, thyme, allspice, pepper and salt, mustard, vinegar and the remaining 2 tablespoons olive oil. Fluff up the lentil salad and allow to come to room temperature.

Before serving, in a large bowl, toss prepared arugula with 2 tablespoons balsamic vinegar and 2 tablespoons olive oil. Arrange greens on bottom of a large round glass serving platter. Lay strips of smoked salmon over the bed of arugula, around the edge of the platter. Pour cooked lentil mixture into center of arugula bed. Serve at room temperature or chill for 1 hour. Serves 4.

TOMATO BASKETS OF EGGS AND SHRIMP

[A Cooking Hint: Never cook eggs in boiling water; simply simmer them for desired consistency. For example: soft-cooked – 3 minutes, hard cooked – 5-7 minutes. A pinch of salt added to water will prevent the yolk from escaping through a crack you may have inadvertently made in the egg shell.]

4 large ripe tomatoes, halved

2 tbsp. fresh lemon juice

¼ cup mayonnaise (low-fat available)

bed of lettuce, rinsed, drained thoroughly

8 large cooked, peeled shrimp

4 large hard cooked eggs, shelled

1 tbsp. extra-virgin olive oil

salt and freshly ground black pepper, to taste

Lay a bed of lettuce on a large glass platter. Halve the tomatoes; remove seeds but not the pulp and drain extra juices. Arrange prepared tomato halves on the bed of lettuce around the platter. Sprinkle insides of tomato with lemon juice, olive oil, salt and pepper.

Shell the hard cooked eggs. Cut the whites of the eggs in half, in such a way as to remove the whites from the yolk, leaving yolks intact. Dice the whites and place in a small bowl. In the same bowl, blend mayonnaise with diced egg whites. Carefully, cut yolks in half; place each yolk half into hollow of each tomato half. Evenly spoon mayonnaise-egg white mixture over each tomato/egg half. Garnish each half with a cooked shrimp. Serves 6-8.

SPICY COLE SLAW

Reprinted from: MENU LOG: A Collection of Recipes as Coordinated Menus
by Marion O. Celenza, page 209.

1 small head white cabbage, remove outer
   leaves and core; finely shredded

1 carrot, pared, shredded

½ cup finely shredded red cabbage

½ cup Miracle Whip dressing

¼ tsp. salt

¼ cup cider vinegar

1 tbsp. prepared horseradish

1 small onion, minced

1 tsp. sugar

¼ tsp. black pepper

juice of 1 lemon

1 tsp. celery seed

In a small bowl, blend Miracle Whip, cider vinegar, lemon juice, salt, sugar, black pepper, horseradish, celery seed. Finely shave cabbage (do not use outer leaves or center stalk). In a large salad bowl, place shredded cabbages, and add shredded carrot, minced onion. Pour dressing over salad. Toss and mix thoroughly. Refrigerate. Toss again before serving. Serves 6.

Salads

BLACK AND GREEN BEANS WITH CHOPPED EGG SALAD

1 can (1 lb.) black beans, rinsed in cold water,
    drained
$\frac{1}{2}$ lb. green beans, trimmed, rinsed,
    cut into $\frac{1}{2}$-inch pieces
$\frac{1}{4}$ cup fresh lemon juice
$\frac{1}{4}$ cup extra-virgin olive oil
2-3 scallions with some greens, rinsed, chopped
1 large celery stalk, trimmed, rinsed, chopped

3 cups romaine lettuce, rinsed,
    spun dry, shredded
2 hard cooked large eggs, chopped
a sprinkling of hot red pepper flakes
salt and freshly ground black pepper, to taste

Have ready: 4 chilled salad plates, lined with lettuce.

Blanch green beans in boiling water for 3-5 minutes, until just tender; drain in colander. Refresh them under cold running water. Drain. Blanch canned and rinsed black beans in boiling water for 5-6 seconds; drain.

In a bowl, whisk lemon juice, red pepper flakes and salt and black pepper to taste. Gradually add oil in a stream, whisking the dressing until it is emulsified. Add green and black beans, scallions, celery and toss to mix thoroughly. Divide chopped romaine among 4 salad plates; spoon portions of bean mixture over each bed of lettuce and sprinkle each with chopped eggs. Serves 4.

BROWN RICE AND PIGNOLA SALAD

2 tbsp. butter or Smart Balance spread
$\frac{1}{2}$ tsp. salt
1 cup brown rice
$2\frac{1}{2}$ cups water
$\frac{1}{4}$ cup fresh Italian parsley leaves, minced
1 small red bell pepper, deseeded, sliced
$\frac{1}{4}$ cup pignola (pine nuts), lightly toasted

$\frac{1}{4}$ cup fresh lime juice
 salt and freshly ground black pepper, to taste
2 tbsp. olive oil
Boston lettuce leaves

Have ready: a large platter lined with lettuce leaves.

In a 2-quart pot with a lid, combine water, salt, butter (or Smart Balance) and bring to a boil. Stir in brown rice. Cover pot and cook rice for 30-35 minutes or until tender and liquid is absorbed. Transfer to a bowl and allow rice to cool, tossing it occasionally. Stir in parsley, red pepper and pignola.

In a small bowl, combine lime juice with salt and pepper to taste; add olive oil in a stream, whisking the dressing until it is emulsified. Toss the rice mixture with the dressing and transfer the salad to a platter lined with lettuce leaves. Serves 4.

LIGHT AND EASY DOES IT (With Variations)

[A Cooking Hint: Rinse all vegetables and fruits prior to eating; this means berries, oranges, apples and melons as well. Drain greens and berries thoroughly. Gently pat dry berries with paper towels.]
(A simple healthy "Lunch for One". Prepare early on the day of serving.)

1 cup low-fat cottage cheese, or low-fat ricotta cheese
2 large Boston lettuce leaves, or 4-5 tender leaves escarole, rinsed in cold water, drained
2 slices ripe beefsteak tomatoes, or 2 plum tomatoes, quartered, or
    4-6 cherry or grape tomatoes (Rinse tomatoes under cold water before preparing.)
½ ripe avocado, peeled, sliced, sprinkled lightly with lemon juice to retard discoloration

Selections to add to/combine with cottage cheese or ricotta (if desired):
1 large celery stalk, trimmed, rinsed, chopped
1 carrot, pared, chopped
½ red bell pepper, rinsed, deseeded, chopped
1 small onion, chopped
½ cup chopped apple or pear, with skin
    (Rinse apple/pear under cold water before preparing.)
½ cup red grapes or strawberries; or blueberries; or blackberries; or raspberries
    (Rinse gently and drain berries before preparing.)
1 small banana, sliced into rounds
1 navel orange, peeled, cut into small chunks
    (or other seasonal fruits such as: peaches, apricots, plums)

    Lay lettuce leaves (or escarole) on a chilled luncheon plate. On top of greens, place selected tomatoes and avocado. Stir selected fruit or vegetables into cottage cheese (or ricotta). Spoon cheese mix over salad base, in center of plate. If desired, sprinkle a little black pepper over cheese mixture. Chill salad in refrigerator until serving.

Homemakers Council of Nassau County
(Rockville Centre), Guest Speaker.

SALMON SALAD ON A BED OF SPINACH
(A 30 minute lunch for 2.)

1 can (8 oz.) wild Alaska pink salmon or $\frac{1}{2}$ lb. fresh fillet of wild Alaska salmon, grilled

1 celery stalk, with greens, chopped

1 tbsp. hot cream-style horseradish

2 tbsp. mayonnaise (low-fat available)

2 plum tomatoes, each quartered

2 cups baby spinach, rinsed, drained

1 ripe Hass avocado, peeled, sliced (sprinkle with lemon juice to avoid discoloration)

1 medium- size carrot, pared, shredded

2 celery stalks, trimmed, stuffed with prepared Hummus with Garlic; or (*NOTE: below)

2 1-inch thick slices Italian bread

$\frac{1}{4}$ cup Cheddar cheese or Jarlsberg, shredded

*NOTE: Instead of using prepared Hummus with Garlic, you may prepare the hummus with garlic by mashing ceci (1 lb. can) with 4-5 garlic cloves (minced, or roasted and mashed).

Have ready: 2 8-inch salad plates, chilled.

1) If using fresh salmon, grill salmon fillet for 2 minutes on both sides on medium-high. Place salmon in a small bowl and break the fillet into flaky pieces with a fork. Stir in chopped celery, mayonnaise and horseradish.

2) If using canned salmon, discard pieces of salmon skin and bones. Place canned salmon in a small bowl; stir in chopped celery, mayonnaise and horseradish.

Lay a bed of spinach on each salad plate. Line a layer of avocado slices on top of spinach. Spoon half of salmon mixture on top of each bed of spinach/avocado. Garnish each plate with shredded carrot and plum tomato quarters.

Stuff 2 celery stalks (with greens) with prepared hummus with garlic. Lay one stuffed celery stalk on each salad plate. Pack 2 tablespoons shredded Cheddar (or Jarlsberg) on each slice of Italian bread. Broil slices of bread with cheese for 1 minute under broiler. Remove grilled cheese toasts, one to each salad plate. Serve immediately. Serves 2.

CECI WITH TUNA SALAD

[A Cooking Hint: Remove prepared salad dressings made with olive oil from refrigerator 1 hour prior to serving. Bring to room temperature. Shake to stir ingredients thoroughly prior to using. Chill salad plates and bowls.]

1 lg. can (20 oz.) ceci (garbanzo beans), rinsed, drained

black pepper and salt to taste

3 cups red leaf lettuce, washed, drained

1 small yellow onion, chopped

1 tbsp. pimiento pepper, finely chopped (Wear plastic gloves when handling hot pepper.)

1 tbsp. olive oil

6 plum tomatoes, halved

2 cans (8 oz. each), Italian tuna fish in olive oil

$\frac{1}{2}$ pitted chopped Kalamata olives

Lemon-Oil Dressing (see page 379) Refrigerate dressing until serving.

On a large glass platter with an edge, lay a bed of red leaf lettuce. Brown onion in olive oil in a small saucepot. Add ceci, pimientos, pepper and salt and stir to blend. Simmer the mix for 1-2 minutes.

Pour warm bean mix over the bed of red leaf lettuce. With a fork, flake the tuna in a bowl. Spoon equal portions of tuna over bean mix. Garnish with tomato wedges and olives. Shake jar of dressing to thoroughly blend. Drizzle Lemon-Oil Dressing over salad. Serve warm. Serves 6.

· ·

TUNA STUFFED CELERY

a few large lettuce leaves to garnish an 8-inch plate

1 can (7 oz.) tuna, mashed

1 pkg. (8 oz.) low-fat cream cheese

2 tbsp. Kalamata olives, pitted, chopped

6 celery stalks, with greens, trimmed, rinsed, patted dry with paper towels

2 large beefsteak tomatoes, sliced into rounds

Have ready: 2-3 chilled glass salad plates, lined with lettuce leaves.

In a 1-quart bowl, blend until spreadable: cream cheese, mashed tuna and chopped olives. Stuff this mixture into cavities of celery stalks.

Lay tomato slices over a bed of lettuce on each 8-inch plate. Place stuffed celery stalks over tomatoes. Serves 2-3.

SHRIMP IN GINGER SALAD

1 lb. (about $2\frac{1}{2}$ cups) snow peas, trimmed, discard strings

1 red bell pepper, deseeded, cut into thin strips (julienne)

$\frac{3}{4}$ lb. small shrimp (about 28-30), rinsed in cold water, drained

$\frac{1}{2}$ cup plain yogurt

$\frac{1}{4}$ cup mayonnaise (low-fat available)

1 tsp. curry powder

1 tbsp. fresh gingerroot, peeled, minced

1 tbsp. Dijon mustard

1 tbsp. fresh lemon juice

$\frac{1}{2}$ tsp. granulated sugar

salt and freshly ground black pepper to taste

3-4 beds of Boston lettuce leaves, rinsed, drained,
    to be used as edible bowls

3-4 flour tortillas, $7\frac{1}{2}$ inches

Have ready: 3-4 chilled salad plates, lined with Boston lettuce.

First, prepare the tortillas by preheating oven to 375°. Press tortillas, one at a time, to fit inside a small pie pan ($5\frac{1}{2}$-inch bottom). Prick surface with a fork in several places; bake at 375° for 1-2 minutes. Remove baked tortilla and set aside to act as a "bowl" for the salad.

In a pot of boiling water, blanch snow peas and red pepper strips for 15 seconds; transfer with a slotted spoon to a bowl of cold water with ice to stop the cooking process. Drain the vegetables; pat dry; cut snow peas lengthwise into thin strips.

To the same pan of boiling water, add shrimp. Remove pan from heat and allow shrimp to rest, covered, for 5 minutes. Then, drain shrimp in a colander and rinse them in the colander, under cold running water until cooled. Shell the shrimp.

In a bowl whisk together: yogurt, mayonnaise, gingerroot, mustard, lemon juice, curry powder, sugar, salt and pepper to taste. Stir in shrimp and vegetables. Line chilled plates with leaves of Boston lettuce. Place baked tortilla "bowl" on lettuce. Divide salad among 3-4 baked tortilla flour bowls. Serves 3-4.

PASTA SALAD WITH PEPPERS AND GOAT CHEESE

1 lb. rotelle pasta

2 tbsp. olive oil

2 garlic cloves, minced

1 small onion, finely chopped

1 red bell pepper, deseeded, cut into thin
   strips (julienne)

1 yellow bell pepper, deseeded, cut into thin
   strips (julienne)

$\frac{1}{2}$ cup dry vermouth

$\frac{1}{4}$ cup pitted Kalamata olives, sliced

 salt and freshly ground black pepper, to taste

$\frac{1}{4}$ cup fresh basil leaves, rinsed, dried,
   shredded

1 cup goat cheese (about 4 oz.), crumbled

In a skillet, cook garlic and onion in olive oil over moderate heat for 1 minute; add peppers and cook the mixture, stirring, for 5 minutes, or until peppers are just tender. Add wine and olives. Bring wine mix to a boil until it is reduced by half. Season with salt and pepper to taste and stir in basil.

Meanwhile, boil a large pot of water to cook the rotelle, al dente, for 8-10 minutes (or as directed on the package). Drain pasta, reserving $\frac{1}{2}$ cup cooking water. In a small bowl, whisk two-thirds of the goat cheese with the reserved pasta water until cheese is melted and mixture is smooth. Add cheese mixture to pasta and pepper mixture in a large serving bowl; gently toss to mix thoroughly. Sprinkle pasta with remaining goat cheese. Serves 4.

POTATOES, CORN, CHERRY TOMATOES SALAD

2 lbs. small red potatoes, scrubbed,
   cut into 1-inch wedges

1 can (1 lb.) corn kernels

1 small red onion, finely sliced

1 dozen cherry or grape tomatoes, halved

$\frac{1}{4}$ cup fresh basil leaves, rinsed, drained

 salt and freshly ground black pepper to taste

$\frac{1}{2}$ cup pitted olives, sliced, for garnish

Olive Oil and Red Wine Vinegar Dressing (see page 376)

Prepare Olive Oil and Red Wine Vinegar Dressing in advance and refrigerate until 1 hour prior to serving. Shake dressing thoroughly before using. In a large saucepan, cook potatoes in enough boiling water to cover, for 10-12 minutes or until tender, yet firm. Drain; gently run cool water in pot with potatoes to allow them to cool. Drain again.

In a large serving bowl, combine potatoes, corn, onion, tomatoes, basil leaves, salt and black pepper to taste and $\frac{1}{2}$ cup of the dressing. Gently toss salad. Garnish with olive slices. Serves 6.

A SATURDAY NIGHT IN THE SUMMER PASTA SALAD
(Mama made some delicious Pasta Salads. This recipe happens to be my favorite.
Name the beans: chick peas, ceci or garbanzo beans- they're delicious and good for you.
Mama would serve this salad to accompany sirloin steak or hot dogs, her favorite "fun food".)

1 lb. penne rigati, or 1 lb. rotini pasta, for salads (may be purchased tri-colore)

½ cup Parmesan cheese, grated

1 small carrot, pared, shredded, for garnish

DRESSING:

2-3 large garlic cloves, sliccd or minced (if you prefer not to "notice" that garlic
    is in the recipe)

1 cup mayonnaise (low-fat available)

1 tbsp. mustard

2 tbsp. extra-virgin olive oil

⅓ cup white wine vinegar

2 tbsp. balsamic vinegar

1 celery stalk with greens, trimmed, chopped

¼ cup sun dried tomatoes, soaked in hot water for 5 minutes, drained and slivered

1 small red onion, chopped

¼ tsp. salt, ¼ tsp. freshly ground black pepper

½ lb. sharp provolone, cut in ½-inch cubes

1 can (1 lb.) ceci (chick peas), rinsed in cold water, drained

6 slices Genoa salami, slivered (cut in julienne strips)

6-8 small peperoncini (tiny pickled peppers)

¼ cup fresh Italian (flat-leaf) parsley, finely chopped

a sprinkling of hot red pepper flakes

   Prepare dressing before cooking pasta. In a glass or ceramic bowl, blend thoroughly: the vinegars, mayonnaise, olive oil, mustard, garlic, salt and pepper, parsley and hot pepper flakes.
   Cook rotini (or penne rigati) in a large pot of boiling water, al dente (according to directions on package). Drain pasta; rinse in cool water and drain again, thoroughly.
   Pour pasta in a very large serving bowl. Stir in chopped celery, onion, ceci, tomato strips, salami, provolone and peperoncini. Spoon dressing over the pasta mixture and toss to mix thoroughly. Garnish top of salad with Parmesan cheese and shredded carrot. Cover and chill the salad for 1 hour. You may prepare this salad 2 days in advance; cover and refrigerate. Serves 6.

VEGETABLE PASTA SALAD

1 lb. mini-mostacciolli rigati (for salads)
½ cup frozen peas
1 cup fresh green beans, cut into 1-inch segments
1 carrot, pared, finely chopped
¼ cup red onion, finely chopped
¼ cup each: red bell pepper, green bell pepper, deseeded, finely chopped
¼ cup pitted Sicilian and Kalamata olives, sliced
½ cup Genoa salami, slivered (about 3-4 slices), optional
    (For variety, instead of salami, use: 1 cup tiny shrimp, shelled or
    1 cup chopped grilled chicken.)

a bed of mixed greens: red leaf and green leaf lettuces, arugula, rinsed, drained

CREAMY LIME DRESSING:
1 cup mayonnaise, low-fat available
¼ cup fresh lime juice
2 tbsp. cider vinegar
2 tbsp. low-fat milk
2 tbsp. fresh parsley, chopped
¼ tsp. freshly ground black pepper
½ tsp. salt, or to taste

   In a small bowl, thoroughly blend all of the dressing ingredients. Refrigerate until needed.
   Cook pasta in enough boiling water as directed on package. At the 5 minute mark, as the pasta boils stir in green beans and peas. Cook pasta, green beans and peas for an additional 5-7 minutes, until pasta is al dente. Drain and place the pasta mix into a large mixing bowl. Mix olives, carrot, onion, red and green peppers and salami (or shrimp, or chicken) into the cooked pasta mixture. Empty the bowl of prepared dressing into the pasta salad mixture; toss salad to cover thoroughly.
   Line a 12-inch platter with a rim, with salad greens; pour prepared pasta salad into the platter, over the greens. Serve immediately, at room temperature or refrigerate briefly until needed. Bring to room temperature before serving. Serves 6.

AVOCADO SALAD

[A Cooking Hint: Dip peeled avocado, banana or apple into lemon juice or other citrus juice to prevent its discoloration.]

4-6 cups combined: baby spinach, red leaf and green leaf lettuces and arugula
   (about 1½ cups of each vegetable)

2 ripe but firm Hass avocados pared, cut into ½-inch slices; sprinkle with lemon juice
   to prevent discoloration

2 beef steak tomatoes, cut into ½-inch slices; sprinkle slices with ½ cup Pepper Jack
   cheese, finely chopped

1 carrot, pared, shredded

4-6 celery stalks, each cut into 2 sections and stuffed with Cream Cheese, Peppers and
   Olive Spread (see page 50)

1 can (3.75 oz.) sardines in water, drained, chopped into chunks

4 slices, ½-inch thick, pumpernickel with raisins bread

Lemon-Oil Dressing (see page 379)

Preheat Broiler.

Have ready: a 15-inch glass platter and an oiled broiler pan.

Prepare Lemon-Oil Dressing in advance. Refrigerate until 1 hour before serving.

Lay a blend of prepared salad greens over the glass platter. Arrange avocado slices over the greens. Lay slices of tomato and cheese on an oiled broiler pan. Broil them 5 inches below broiler element for 2-3 minutes. With aid of a thin metal spatula, lay broiled tomato/cheese slices around the platter. Strew sardines chunks over surface of filled platter. Garnish with shredded carrot. Cut slices of pumpernickel raisin bread in half, diagonally. Insert cheese-spread filled celery segments around edge of platter; insert diagonal half-slices of bread around edge of platter. Drizzle entire salad platter with Lemon-Oil Dressing. Serve portions with aid of a wide spatula or a large serving spoon onto individual salad plates, making sure every portion includes stuffed celery and bread slices. Serves 4.

LEFTOVER THANKSGIVING TURKEY SALAD

3-4 cups leftover roasted turkey meat from carcass, legs, breast, chopped

1 red onion, chopped

1 red apple, like Fuji or Paula Red, chopped, with skin

1 large celery stalk, trimmed, chopped with greens

1 carrot, pared, shredded

$\frac{1}{2}$ cup candied walnuts (Toss walnut halves with 2 tbsp. honey and 1 tsp. cinnamon; lay them on a sheet of foil and roast nuts in oven at 300° for 8-10 minutes; OR use packaged glazed walnuts.)

Bed of Boston lettuce for each serving

1 large beefsteak tomato, sliced into large rounds, $\frac{1}{4}$-inch thick

2 hard-cooked eggs, shelled

Creamy Honey Mustard Dressing (see page 377)

Dill weed for garnish

Prepare dressing in advance and refrigerate until needed. Stir well before serving.

Place chopped leftover turkey meat in a bowl. Add red onion, apple, celery, walnuts and shredded carrot. When ready to serve, spoon dressing over chopped turkey salad; toss to mix thoroughly.

Prepare a salad plate for each serving: lay a bed of Boston lettuce on bottom of plate. Add 1 or 2 slices of tomato. Then, pack about 1 cup of turkey salad over the bed of lettuce. Finely chop hard-cooked eggs and sprinkle them over the salad plate. Garnish with chopped dill weed. Serves 3-4.

Louise and Don have been blessed with 60 years of marriage.

PASTA AND SOY BEAN SALAD

1 lb. (about 2 cups) cooked soy beans-edible variety (*NOTE: below)

1 can (1 lb.) black beans, rinsed in cold water, drained

1 can (1 lb.) corn kernels (less-salt variety) rinsed in cold water, drained

1 small red pepper, deseeded, chopped

1 small poblano, deseeded, finely chopped

    (Wear plastic gloves when handling hot peppers.)

2-3 garlic cloves, minced

2 tbsp. finely chopped red onion

$\frac{1}{4}$ cup sun dried tomatoes, slivered

1 carrot, pared, shredded

$\frac{1}{4}$ cup pitted, black olives, chopped

$\frac{1}{4}$ cup red grapes, rinsed, halved

$\frac{1}{2}$ cup packaged seasoned croutons (optional)

2 cups tiny maruzzelle pasta (seashells), cooked according to directions on package

$\frac{1}{4}$ cup fresh cilantro, chopped

2 tbsp. extra-virgin olive oil

2 tbsp. red wine vinegar

$\frac{1}{4}$ tsp. freshly ground black pepper, dash of cayenne

$\frac{1}{4}$ tsp. salt

$\frac{1}{4}$ cup ricotta salata, diced

$\frac{1}{4}$ cup freshly grated Asiago cheese for garnish

    *NOTE: You will need a couple pounds of soybeans in shells to fill 2 cups. Cook edible soybeans as follows: Slit open pods; pop out beans into a bowl. Rinse beans in cold water. Drain. Pour them into a pot with a lid. Add $\frac{1}{2}$ cup water. Bring beans to a boil; simmer them for 10-15 minutes until tender. Do not add salt to water; at cooking stage, salt will toughen the beans. Drain beans into a bowl and chill bowl in refrigerator. (Or, you may purchase "cooked" soybeans, sold in packages, available in produce department.)

    In a 2-quart bowl, mix cooked soybeans, black beans and corn kernels. Add poblano, red pepper, garlic, onion, sun dried tomatoes, grapes, olives, cooked pasta, diced ricotta salata, croutons, and all but 2 tablespoons of cilantro. Garnish salad with 2 tablespoons cilantro and Asiago Cheese.

    In a small bowl or jar, blend oil, vinegar, salt, pepper and cayenne. Shake dressing thoroughly and drizzle it over the bean salad. Mix thoroughly. Lay a sheet of waxed paper over salad and allow to sit for one hour at room temperature.

    Refrigerate salad for at least one-half hour before serving. May be prepared a day or two in advance and refrigerated. Store leftovers in refrigerator. Serves 6-8.

POTATO SALAD WITH BEANS

8 small Red Bliss potatoes, scrubbed, halved (or if large enough, quartered)

1 can (1 lb.) red kidney beans, rinsed in cold water, drained

1 lb. (about 2 cups) cooked soybeans, edible variety (*NOTE: below)

$\frac{1}{4}$ cup red bell pepper, deseeded, chopped

$\frac{1}{4}$ cup green pepper, deseeded, chopped

1 tbsp. Chile pepper, deseeded, minced – (optional);

    (Wear plastic gloves when handling hot peppers.)

$\frac{1}{4}$ cup red onion, chopped

1 dozen cherry or grape tomatoes, rinsed, drained

$\frac{1}{2}$ cup firm cheese, like Gouda,

    Emmentaler or provolone, cut into $\frac{1}{2}$-inch cubes

2 tbsp. Italian parsley, chopped

$\frac{1}{2}$ tsp. salt

$\frac{1}{4}$ tsp. freshly ground black pepper

$\frac{1}{2}$ cup oil-cured olives, pitted

2 tbsp. extra-virgin olive oil

2 tbsp. white wine vinegar

more chopped Italian parsley, for garnish

leaves of Boston lettuce to line individual salad bowls

    *NOTE: You will need a couple pounds of soybeans in shells to fill 2 cups. Cook edible soybeans as follows: Slit open pods; pop out beans into a bowl. Rinse beans in cold water. Drain. Pour them into a pot with a lid. Add $\frac{1}{2}$ cup water. Bring beans to a boil; simmer them for 10-15 minutes until tender. Do not add salt to water; at cooking stage, salt will toughen the beans. Drain beans into a bowl and chill bowl in refrigerator. (Or, you may purchase "cooked" soybeans, sold in packages, available in produce department.)

    Simmer potatoes in a couple inches of water for 10 minutes, until tender. Do not overcook. Drain and set aside to cool.

    In a 2-quart bowl, mix cooked soybeans, kidney beans, potatoes, chopped peppers, onions, tomatoes, cheese cubes, parsley, salt, pepper, olive oil and white wine vinegar. Toss gently to blend the tastes. Sprinkle pitted olives over surface of salad; garnish with minced parsley. Cover with waxed paper and allow to sit in refrigerator for at least one-half hour to blend the tastes.

    Serve in individual salad bowls lined with Boston lettuce. Serves 6-8.

GRILLED CALAMARI, SHRIMP, SCALLOPS SALAD

3 cups calamari (squid) rings and tentacles, rinsed in cold water, drained

1 dozen or more jumbo shrimp, shelled, cleaned, rinsed in cold water and drained

1 dozen or more sea scallops, rinsed in cold water, drained

1 lg. can ceci (chick peas) about 1 lb. rinsed in cool water, drained

2 Portobello mushrooms, rinsed, cut into $\frac{1}{4}$-inch slices

1 red onion, thinly sliced

2-3 garlic cloves, minced

2 tbsp. olive oil   oil for grill pan

juice of 1 lemon   1 lemon thinly sliced

$\frac{1}{4}$ cup balsamic vinegar

1 tbsp. dried oregano

$\frac{1}{4}$ tsp. salt

$\frac{1}{4}$ tsp. coarsely ground black pepper

a pinch of hot red pepper flakes

10 oz. baby arugula, rinsed in cool water, drained

You will need a large 15-inch grill pan, brushed with olive oil; and a large heat-proof salad bowl. Line the sides of the salad bowl with prepared arugula.

Prepare seafood as directed above. In a small bowl blend oil, lemon juice, vinegar, garlic, oregano, salt and peppers. Combine calamari, shrimp, scallops, ceci, mushrooms and onion in a large bowl and pour dressing mix over the seafood mix. Toss with two spoons to coat seafood thoroughly.

Preheat oiled grill pan on stove burner, set at medium-high. Pour half of the amount of the coated seafood/vegetables onto the grill pan. Grill on medium-high heat for 3-4 minutes, using a heat-proof spatula to toss and cook the mix. Transfer grilled mix to a salad bowl; then, pour remaining uncooked seafood mix to grill pan to complete the job. Grill and toss for another 3-4 minutes and add mix to prepared salad bowl. Garnish with thin slices of lemon. Serve warm. Serves 4-6.

TUNA AND AVOCADO-PINEAPPLE SALAD
(Double the recipe for 4-6 portions.)

2-3 cups arugula, trimmed, rinsed, drained

1 can (5 oz.) solid tuna fish in water
4 pearl onions, remove skin, finely chopped
6 cherry or grape tomatoes, chopped
1 tbsp. prepared horseradish

1 ripe, but firm Hass avocado, for slicing
2-3 slices, 1-inch thick, fresh pineapple, cut into circles
6 cherry or grape tomatoes, each halved
2 hard-cooked eggs, shelled (hard-cook eggs a couple of hours in advance of serving)
2-3 tbsp. lemon juice

1 cup Honey Mustard Dressing (see page 377)

Prepare Honey Mustard Dressing in advance and refrigerate until 1 hour prior to serving.
Spread a layer of prepared arugula on 2 to 3 flat 8-9-inch salad plates. Set aside. In a 1-quart bowl, fork-mash canned solid tuna. Stir until mixed: chopped pearl onions, chopped tomatoes, horseradish and $\frac{1}{2}$ cup Honey Mustard Dressing. Just before serving, lay a ring-slice of pineapple in center of each bed of arugula. Spoon a portion of the tuna mix into each pineapple ring. Cut and peel off skin from avocado; cut 9-10 avocado slices off the stone and discard stone. Arrange 3-4 slices of avocado around the tuna-filled pineapple ring. Thinly slice the eggs into rounds and garnish the salad plate with sliced eggs and cherry tomato halves; sprinkle avocado with lemon juice. Drizzle remaining $\frac{1}{2}$ cup Honey Mustard Dressing over entire salad. Serves 2-3.

Telecare TV taping for "Good News with Msgr. Jim Vlaun".

ANTIPASTO SALAD OF TOMATO, ARTICHOKES, SMOKY MOZZARELLA AND OLIVES

4 large leaves Boston lettuce, rinsed, drained, patted dry with paper towels

8 ripe, firm plum tomatoes, rinsed, quartered

1 lb. ball smoky mozzarella, sliced

1 can (about 1 lb.) unseasoned artichoke hearts, in water; or 1 pkg. frozen unseasoned artichokes, cooked according to directions on package, drained and cooled to room temperature. Halve or quarter the artichokes.

about 2 dozen Kalamata olives, pitted

2 garlic cloves, minced

2 tbsp. extra-virgin olive oil

a sprinkling of freshly ground black pepper, to taste

2 tbsp. grated Asiago cheese

8 basil leaves

Have ready: a 15-inch flat platter.

Line a large flat platter with prepared lettuce leaves. Arrange quartered plum tomatoes over the lettuce. Follow with quartered artichokes and sliced smoky mozzarella. Strew pitted olives over surface of salad plate and sprinkle with minced garlic, grated Asiago cheese, black pepper and olive oil. Tuck in basil leaves. Refrigerate for $\frac{1}{2}$ hour. Serves 4. Seasoned bread crisps make a tasty accompaniment.

SALAD OF RED PEPPER, AVOCADO AND PAPAYA

10 oz. salad greens (Combine from: green leaf, red leaf, romaine, arugula), rinsed, drained, chopped

3 scallions with some greens, finely chopped

1 large red bell pepper, cored, deseeded, thinly sliced

1 small ripe papaya, halved; scoop out seeds, cut into quarters and peel off skin

1 ripe, not soft, avocado, peeled, stone removed, sliced (sprinkle with lime juice to prevent discoloration)

$\frac{1}{4}$ cup toasted pumpkin seeds

Islands Spicy Dressing (see page 381)

Blend all dressing ingredients for Islands Spicy Dressing in a small bowl. Refrigerate until needed. Shake thoroughly before using.

On a large platter with a rim, lay a bed of mixed chopped greens. Arrange thin slices of red pepper, papaya slices and slivers of avocado all over surface of greens. Drizzle dressing over salad and gently toss to combine. Sprinkle salad with toasted pumpkin seeds. Serves 6.

SARDINES AND EGG SALAD

green leaf lettuce, red leaf lettuce

1 can ($\frac{3}{8}$ oz.) sardines in water

4 thin slices cucumber rounds

2 thick slices beefsteak tomato

1-2 celery stalks, cut into sticks

1-2 carrots, pared cut into sticks

$\frac{1}{4}$ cup chopped red onion

a few Greek black olives

2-3 radishes trimmed, cut like a flower

1 small sweet red pepper, deseeded,
   thinly sliced in rings

1 hard cooked egg, quartered

2-3 scallions with greens

Bleu Cheese Dressing (see page 379)

Prepare Bleu Cheese Dressing and refrigerate until needed.

Arrange lettuce to cover a large flat plate. Lay sardines in a circle in center of plate. Layer cucumber and tomato slices around them and then arrange carrot and celery around tomatoes. Scatter chopped onion and olives on top of sardines. Garnish plate with flowered radishes, egg quarters and pepper rings. Lay the scallions on top of salad. Spoon 2-3 tablespoons Bleu Cheese Dressing over salad. Store remainder of dressing in refrigerator and use within 2 weeks. Serve salad with crisp whole grain crackers. Serves 1 generous portion.

PINEAPPLE SALSA

[A Cooking Hint: Rinse all vegetables and fruits prior to eating; this means berries, oranges, apples, pineapples and melons as well. Drain greens and berries thoroughly. Gently pat-dry berries with paper towels.]

1 pineapple (With sharp knife cut off shrub at top of pineapple, and slice off bottom.
   Slice pineapple into 1-inch rounds; then cut off rind from each round; chop
   the fruit in chunks and place in a large bowl. Reserve juice.)

juice of 1 lime

1 small red bell pepper, cored, deseeded, finely chopped

1 small fresh Chile pepper, deseeded, minced
   (Wear plastic gloves when handling hot peppers.)

1 large garlic clove, minced

1 scallion, including some greens, chopped finely

$\frac{1}{4}$ cup fresh mint, finely chopped

$\frac{1}{4}$ cup fresh cilantro, finely chopped

dash of salt

Place all prepared ingredients into a large decorative serving bowl. Add juices, herbs and a dash of salt. Toss to fully combine. Refrigerate salsa until ready to serve. Serves 8.

INSALATA ALLA CAMPAGNA

*[A Cooking Hint: Always chill salad vegetables before assembling salad;
chill salad plates.]*

10 oz. pkg. mixed salad greens (a blend of arugula, spinach, chicory, romaine, red leaf),
   rinsed, drained
2-3 fresh ripe peaches, rinsed, patted dry with paper towels
6 fresh ripe figs, like Calimyrna, Kadota, Brown Turkey, rinsed
1 cup gorgonzola cheese, coarsely crumbled

Balsamic Vinegar and Olive Oil Dressing (see page 376)

Prepare Balsamic Vinegar and Olive Oil Dressing in advance. Refrigerate until 1 hour before using.
Shake well before using.
   Set out 4 chilled salad plates.
   In a large salad bowl combine prepared salad greens (sometimes packaged in a combination of greens). Divide mixed greens on each of 4 salad plates.
   Slice each peach in 6-8 wedges and arrange around edge of salad plates. Discard pits.
Trim stems off figs; quarter each fig lengthwise and arrange 6 sections over each salad plate.
   Sprinkle $\frac{1}{4}$ cup crumbled gorgonzola over each salad. Refrigerate salads if not serving immediately. At serving, thoroughly shake dressing and drizzle over each plate. Serves 4.

SPINACH PARMESAN SALAD

10 oz. pkg. baby spinach, rinsed, drained
1 medium-size carrot, pared, shredded
1 small red onion, finely sliced
$\frac{1}{2}$ cup red grapes, halved
$\frac{1}{2}$ cup Parmesan cheese, shredded

Lemon-Oil Dressing (see page 379)

Prepare Lemon-Oil Dressing in advance. Refrigerate dressing until 1 hour prior to serving.
Shake dressing thoroughly before serving.
   In a large salad bowl, combine spinach, carrot, onion and grapes. Sprinkle Parmesan cheese over salad. Refrigerate salad until ready to serve, up to 4-5 hours. Sprinkle dressing over salad.
Toss to coat thoroughly. Serves 4-6.

ANTIPASTO DI POMIDORI E FUNGHI

4 large ripe tomatoes, rinsed, sliced $\frac{1}{4}$-inch thick

6-8 large fresh white mushrooms, trimmed, rinsed thoroughly, thinly sliced

$\frac{1}{4}$ cup fresh marjoram or 2 tbsp. dried marjoram

2 tbsp. balsamic vinegar

2 tbsp. extra-virgin olive oil

salt and freshly ground black pepper, to taste

   Slice tomatoes and arrange them in overlapping rows around a large round serving platter. Sprinkle them with half of the marjoram and 1 tablespoon each, vinegar and oil Arrange thin slices of mushrooms around the platter, on top of the tomatoes; sprinkle with marjoram and vinegar and oil. Serve with thin slices of crusty artisan bread. Serves 6.

ANTIPASTO DI MELONE E PROSCIUTTO
[A Cooking Hint: Chill melons in paper bags in the refrigerator to prevent the spread of their odors.]

1 cantaloupe melon, rinsed thoroughly, patted dry

$1\frac{1}{2}$ dozen very thin slices prosciutto

1 cup pitted oil-cured olives

2 lemons, rinsed, each cut into 6 wedges

   Halve the washed and dried melon. Spoon out seeds and discard. Cut each half into 4-6 thin crescent wedges; cut off rind from pulp and discard. Arrange melon slices on a round serving platter, radiating from center (like a sun-burst). Between each melon slice lay a curly twist of prosciutto. Sprinkle olives over the platter. Serve with a small bowl of lemon wedges.
Serves 6-8.

3-CHEESE CROSTATA WITH BROCCOLI AND RED PEPPERS

[A Cooking Hint: Many recipes may be partially or entirely prepared in advance; pre-planning recipes saves time.]

(For a thick, crunchy crust, try a loaf of *Italian Bastone with sesame seeds*. Cut the loaf in half, vertically; lay open halves, side by side; with your fingers, depress soft insides of the bread; spread TOPPING over the bread; continue with baking instructions, below.)

olive oil for coating 12-inch round pizza pan

1 lb. portion ready-to-use pizza dough (Sold in supermarkets and bakeries;
    whole wheat available.)

$\frac{1}{2}$ cup Parmesan cheese, finely grated

TOPPING:

1 cup sharp provolone cheese, shredded

1 cup low-fat ricotta

1 cup Asiago cheese, grated, in 2 portions

2 cups broccoli florets, rinsed, drained

1 large red bell pepper, deseeded, sliced into thin strips

$\frac{1}{2}$ cup pitted Kalamata olives

salt and freshly ground black pepper, to taste

2-3 tbsp. extra-virgin olive oil

1 tsp. hot pepper flakes, or to taste (Wear plastic gloves when handling hot pepper.)

Preheat oven to 375°.

Coat a 12-inch round pizza pan with olive oil.

Prepare CRUST. If dough has been frozen, soften to room temperature. Place frozen ball of dough (or dough section) in a bowl coated with olive oil for 2 hours. During that time, turn dough once. Then, stretch dough over a lightly oiled 12-inch pizza pan. Form a slightly raised dough rim around edge of pan. Dough should be about $\frac{1}{2}$-inch thick. Sprinkle finely grated Parmesan over the dough in the pan. Partially bake crust in preheated oven at 375° for 5 minutes. Remove crust in pan from oven.

Prepare TOPPING. In a bowl, combine provolone, ricotta and $\frac{1}{2}$ cup grated Asiago; sprinkle and blend in salt and pepper. Spread over prepared pizza crust. Arrange broccoli florets and red bell pepper over mixed cheese topping. Scatter pitted olives over top and sprinkle remainder of Asiago cheese ($\frac{1}{2}$ cup) and hot pepper flakes over surface of crostata. Drizzle crostata with 2-3 tablespoons extra-virgin olive oil.

Bake crostata in preheated oven at 375° for 15-20 minutes. Do not overcook. Allow to rest for a few minutes. Slice into 4-6 wedges and serve very warm. Add a salad from this book. Serves 2-3.

APPLE, HAM AND CHEDDAR WHOLE WHEAT CROSTATA
[A Cooking Hint: Many recipes may be partially or entirely prepared in advance;
pre-planning recipes saves time.]
(For a thick, crunchy crust, try a loaf of *Italian Bastone with sesame seeds*. Cut the loaf in half,
vertically; lay open halves, side by side; with your fingers, depress soft insides of the bread;
spread TOPPING over the bread; continue with baking instructions, below.)

olive oil for coating 12-inch round pizza pan

1 lb. whole wheat packaged dough (found in supermarket deli department)

$\frac{1}{2}$ cup sharp Cheddar cheese, shredded, plus $\frac{1}{4}$ cup to sprinkle over dough (crust)

TOPPING:

1 large or 2 small Granny Smith apples, cored; leave skin; thinly sliced

$\frac{1}{4}$ cup fresh lemon juice

2 tbsp. brown sugar

1 tsp. ground cinnamon

$\frac{1}{2}$ cup cranberry raisins

$\frac{1}{2}$ cup chopped pecans

$\frac{1}{2}$ cup sharp Cheddar cheese, in tiny chunks

2 tbsp. butter or Smart Balance spread, diced

$\frac{1}{2}$ lb. low-fat Virginia ham, shredded

Preheat oven to 375°.

Have ready: a greased 12-inch pizza pan.

Prepare CRUST. If dough has been frozen, soften to room temperature. Place ball
of dough (or dough section) in a bowl coated with olive oil for 2 hours. Turn dough once during
that time. Then, stretch dough over a lightly oiled 12-inch round pizza pan. Form a slightly
raised dough rim around the edge of the pan. Dough should be about $\frac{1}{2}$-inch thick.
Sprinkle $\frac{1}{4}$ cup shredded Cheddar cheese over the dough in the pan. Partially bake crust in
preheated oven, at 375° for 5 minutes. Remove pan from oven.
Prepare TOPPING. Blend brown sugar and cinnamon in a bowl; pour lemon juice into a
small bowl. Dip apple slices into lemon juice; then, into sugar mix. Arrange sliced apples over
the surface of the crust. (Suggestion: Starting around outer rim, arrange apples to create a spiral
affect, ending in center of crostata.) Combine pecans with remainder of brown sugar mix; toss
nuts to coat with sugar. Spread sugared nuts over coated apples in pan. Scatter cranberry raisins
over apples and nuts. Spread shredded ham over the crostata. Top with chopped Cheddar and dot
with butter (or Smart Balance).
Just before serving, bake crostata in preheated oven at 375° for 15-20 minutes. Do not
overcook. Serves 4-6 wedges.

SPINACH QUICHE

1 ready-bake 9-inch pie crust
1 lb. baby spinach, rinsed, drained
1 cup water (for steamer)
1 lb. low-fat ricotta cheese
2 eggs or $\frac{1}{2}$ cup egg substitute
$\frac{1}{4}$ cup sour cream (fat-free available)

$\frac{1}{4}$ cup onion, minced
$\frac{1}{2}$ tsp. salt
$\frac{1}{2}$ tsp. freshly ground black pepper
1 tbsp. dried basil
1 cup Asiago cheese, grated
   (bring to room temperature)
$\frac{1}{4}$ cup butter or Smart Balance spread

Preheat oven to 350°.
Have ready: one 9-inch pie pan with inserted ready-bake pie crust.
Over 1 cup water, steam spinach in upper portion of steamer pot for 1 minute. Remove and drain spinach from pot to a bowl and allow to cool.
In a large bowl, combine ricotta, eggs, sour cream, onion, salt, pepper, basil and Asiago cheese. Stir in spinach.
Pour this filling into the pie crust. Dot with butter (or Smart Balance spread). Bake pie in preheated oven at 350° for 45 minutes or until a knife, inserted at center of pie, returns clean. Cool quiche to room temperature and serve. Serves 6.

SHRIMP-APPLE CHEDDAR CROSTATA

2 tbsp. olive oil, divided
1 portion (1 lb.) whole wheat pizza dough
   (sold in supermarket Dairy Dept.)
2 cups extra-sharp Cheddar cheese, divided
1 large red delicious apple, cored,
   sliced into $\frac{1}{2}$-inch rounds

6-8 jumbo shrimp, shelled, deveined,
   butterflied
3-4 sun dried tomato halves, sliced into strips
1 tbsp. Spanish paprika (smoky)
6 strips bacon

Preheat oven to 450°.

Have ready: a pizza pan to fit a 12-inch pizza; rub pan with 1 tablespoon olive oil.
Stretch dough to make a 12-inch round pizza. Sprinkle top of dough with 1 cup Cheddar. Arrange apple rounds over pizza; set butterflied shrimp over apples; scatter tomato strips. Sprinkle with remainder of Cheddar and 1 tablespoon of paprika. Drizzle pie with remainder of olive oil and lay 6 strips of bacon across top of pie. Bake in preheated oven at 450° for 15-20 minutes. Bacon will crisp; cheese will melt. Remove from oven to rest for several minutes. Serve hot. Serves 3-4.

SHRIMP AND SCALLOP PIE

oil to coat a deep 8-inch pie plate

1 lb. all-purpose potatoes, pared, cut into chunks

3 garlic cloves, minced

$\frac{1}{4}$ cup canola oil, divided

$\frac{1}{2}$ cup scallions with some greens, minced, trimmed

1 lb. small white mushrooms, rinsed, drained, chopped

1 small red bell pepper, deseeded, chopped

2 tbsp. all-purpose flour

1 cup evaporated milk (fat-free available)

$\frac{1}{4}$ cup sherry

1 lb. small shrimp, shelled, rinsed, thoroughly drained and patted dry with paper towel

1 lb. bay scallops, rinsed, thoroughly drained and patted dry with paper towel

3 tbsp. evaporated milk for mashed potatoes

2 tbsp. fresh parsley, chopped, for garnish

Preheat oven to 350°.

Have ready: an oiled deep 8-inch pie plate.

Place potatoes in a pan of cold water to cover. Bring to a boil over high heat. Reduce to simmer and cook until tender, about 30 minutes.

Meanwhile, heat 2 tablespoons canola oil in a heavy saucepan and cook minced garlic and scallions for 2 minutes; add mushrooms and red pepper and sauté 2 minutes longer. Sprinkle flour over this mixture and stir thoroughly to blend. Slowly add and stir in evaporated milk; bring to a boil. Add and stir in sherry and shrimp/scallops and immediately remove from heat.

Remove potatoes from heat and drain. Add 1 tablespoon canola oil. Mash potatoes until fluffy, adding remaining tablespoon of canola oil (and a few tablespoons of evaporated milk, if potatoes are too dry).

Pour shrimp/scallop mixture into an 8-inch deep-dish pie plate. Spoon potatoes on top of seafood mix and spread evenly with a fork. Make furrows with the tines of the fork across the top of potatoes. Bake pie in preheated oven at 350° for 25 minutes, or until tips of potato furrows are golden brown. Garnish with parsley and serve. Serves 6.

FRITTATA DE PATATE E CARCIOFI

2 tbsp. olive oil for skillet; 2 tbsp. olive oil for 9x12x3-inch pan

3 large all-purpose potatoes, pared, halved, cut into narrow slices, $\frac{1}{4}$-inch thick;
 after slicing, place potatoes in a bowl of cold water to prevent discoloration.
 Drain potatoes just before cooking.

1 large onion, finely sliced

2 garlic cloves, chopped

6 sun dried tomato halves, cut into strips

1 can (1 lb.) unseasoned artichoke hearts in water, drained, each quartered

$\frac{1}{2}$ cup pitted black olives, sliced

1 lb. ricotta

6 large eggs, beaten or $1\frac{1}{2}$ cups egg substitute

$\frac{1}{4}$ cup milk

$\frac{1}{2}$ cup Asiago cheese, grated

1 tsp. dried oregano

$\frac{1}{2}$ tsp. salt

$\frac{1}{2}$ tsp. freshly ground black pepper

Preheat oven to 375°.

Have ready: a large skillet with a cover and a 9x12x3-inch baking pan coated with olive oil.

At medium heat in a large skillet, warm olive oil and cook onion, sun dried tomatoes and garlic for 1-2 minutes, scraping bottom of skillet to prevent sticking. Drain potatoes and pour and spread them into skillet. Cook potatoes for 5-6 minutes, using a wide metal spatula to occasionally scrape bottom of skillet and to toss potatoes to cook until tender.

Spread half of the potato mix over the bottom of a well-oiled 9x12 baking pan. In a bowl combine ricotta, olives and artichokes. Spoon this mixture into the 9x12 pan and spread over the potatoes. Cover the ricotta mix with remainder of potatoes, pressing surface of potato casserole with the back of a large spoon or flat part of the spatula.

Beat together: eggs, milk, half of Asiago cheese, oregano, salt and pepper. Carefully, pour the egg mixture over the potato casserole. Sprinkle surface of frittata with remainder of Asiago and bake frittata in a preheated oven at 375° for 20-25 minutes or until golden brown. Cut into sections and serve with a spatula. Serves 6.

SALMON-STUFFED POTATOES

4-6 large Idaho baking potatoes
1 can (about 8 oz.) pink salmon; remove skin and bones
$\frac{1}{4}$ cup finely chopped sweet red pepper
3 scallions with greens, finely chopped (Reserve 2-3 tbsp. for garnish.)
$\frac{1}{4}$ tsp. salt
$\frac{1}{4}$ tsp. finely ground black pepper
1 tbsp. finely chopped parsley
1 tbsp. olive oil
Hungarian paprika for additional garnish

Preheat oven to 400°.

Bake large potatoes in a preheated oven at 400° for about 1 hour and 10 minutes. Remove potatoes from oven and lower oven temperature to 350°. Cut off a large triangle of potato skin from the flat part of each potato and discard pieces of potato skin.

With a tablespoon, scoop out most of the cooked potato into a medium-size bowl. Set potato shells aside.

Add can of salmon (skin and bone fragments removed) to the potatoes in the mixing bowl. Mash with hand masher. Add and thoroughly mix finely chopped red pepper, chopped scallions, parsley, salt, pepper and olive oil. (Reserve some chopped scallions for garnish.)

Stuff each of the potato shells with equal portions of this mix. Sprinkle tops of stuffed potatoes with finely chopped scallions and paprika. Return prepared stuffed potatoes to oven at 350° for an additional 10 minutes. Serves 4-6.

COD PUFFS

1 lb. salted cod, boned and skinned

$\frac{1}{4}$ cup fresh parsley, minced

$\frac{1}{4}$ cup scallions with some greens, minced

$\frac{1}{4}$ cup onion, minced

1 tsp. baking soda

1 large egg or $\frac{1}{4}$ cup egg substitute

1 tsp. finely ground black pepper

$1\frac{1}{2}$ tsp. garlic powder

$\frac{1}{2}$ tsp. Tabasco, or to taste

$\frac{1}{2}$ cup evaporated milk (fat-free available)

$\frac{3}{4}$ cup water

$1\frac{1}{2}$ cups all-purpose flour

canola oil, for frying

Tartare Sauce at serving (see page 385)

Have ready: a large heavy skillet.

Soak salted cod in cold water to cover for 2 hours. Drain and rinse thoroughly. Blanch the fish in boiling water to cover for 5 minutes. Drain thoroughly and allow to cool.

Use a fork to finely shred the salted cod in a large bowl. Add parsley, scallions, onion and baking soda and stir to combine well. In a separate bowl whisk egg until frothy; add it to salted cod mixture along with pepper, garlic powder and Tabasco. Stir in evaporated milk and $\frac{3}{4}$ cup of water. Sprinkle flour over the salted cod mixture and stir to combine well. Add more Tabasco, if desired.

Place a large skillet, filled halfway with canola oil over medium heat. Heat oil until a speck of flour dropped into it sizzles and turns brown. Use a tablespoon to shape codfish mixture into balls the size of golf balls. Carefully lay them, a few at a time, into the oil and fry them until golden, about 5 minutes.

Turn and fry the other side until golden, another 5 minutes. Use a slotted spoon to remove codfish puffs and drain them on paper towels. Continue forming and frying the remaining puffs. Keep cooked codfish puffs in a warming oven at 200° up to an hour before serving.

Serve on toothpicks, accompanied by Tartare Sauce. Makes about 24-26 puffs.

SALAD ON A CRUST

1 lb. portion ready-to-use pizza dough (sold in supermarkets and bakeries)
$\frac{1}{2}$ cup Asiago cheese, grated
TOPPING:
$\frac{1}{4}$ cup red bell pepper, deseeded, finely chopped
$\frac{1}{4}$ cup green pepper, deseeded, finely chopped
3 medium-size white mushrooms, trimmed, rinsed, drained, thinly sliced
1 small tin ($2\frac{1}{2}$ oz.) flat anchovies, chopped
2 tbsp. olive oil

SALAD TOPPING:
2 cups green leaf lettuce, trimmed, rinsed, drained
2 cups red leaf lettuce, trimmed, rinsed, drained
1 cup baby arugula, trimmed, rinsed, drained
4-5 plum tomatoes, rinsed, chopped with juice
1 cup pitted Kalamata olives
$\frac{1}{2}$ cup sharp provolone cheese, diced
$\frac{1}{4}$ cup Parmesan Cheese Dressing (see page 381)

Prepare dressing in advance and refrigerate until 1 hour prior to using;
shake well to blend.

Preheat oven to 375° just before preparing crust.

Have ready: 12-inch pizza pan, coated with olive oil; or
9x12 baking pan, olive-oil coated.
Prepare the CRUST. If dough has been frozen, soften to room temperature. Place ball
or section of dough in an oil-coated bowl for 2 hours. Turn dough once during this time.
Then stretch dough over a lightly oiled pan. Dough should be about $\frac{1}{2}$-inch thick. Sprinkle
Asagio cheese over the dough.
Prepare the TOPPING. In a small bowl, combine finely chopped red and green peppers,
mushrooms and anchovies with 2 tablespoons olive oil. Spread this mixture over the dough in the
pan and pat it down on the dough with a spatula or your hands.
Bake the crust in a preheated oven at 375° for 10-12 minutes. Do not overcook.
While the crust is baking, Prepare SALAD TOPPING. Combine the lettuces, arugula,
chopped tomatoes, olives and provolone in a bowl. Toss with $\frac{1}{4}$ cup of Parmesan Cheese
Dressing. Remove pizza from oven and pour and spread salad over the crust. Slice pizza into
sections (or wedges) and serve. Serves 3-4.

Variations on this recipe: For anchovies, substitute 6 slices Genoa salami, cut into strips. Spread
salami strips over crust. Continue as directed.

Additional *SOUP RECIPES*

from ALL ARE WELCOME TO THIS TABLE
(Dinner Menus)

*[A Cooking Hint: Most soups may be prepared in advance and frozen in containers.
Thaw in refrigerator. Heat soup thoroughly on lo-medium burner.
Suggestion: The hostess may wish to add a special touch by warming hot soup/ hot pasta plates
before serving the dish. You may warm plates in a low oven, microwave, dishwasher, or by simply
running hot water over them.]*

HOMEMADE CHICKEN STOCK

2 chicken legs, 2 chicken wings, rinsed in cold water
6 cups water
1 celery stalk, chopped
1 carrot, pared, chopped
1 small onion, chopped
1 garlic clove, chopped
1 bay leaf
salt and freshly ground black pepper to taste

    In a 4-quart soup pot with lid, simmer all ingredients in 6 cups water for 35-40 minutes. Remove chicken meat from legs and wings and add to stock. (Discard skin and bay leaf.) Or, add chopped celery and mayo to chicken meat and enjoy a delicious chicken salad sandwich. Makes 6 cups chicken stock.

SCOTCH BROTH
("DOUBLE-SCOTCH")

2 lbs. boneless breast of lamb, cubed for stew
8 cups water
$\frac{1}{2}$ cup barley
2 tbsp. olive oil
2 carrots, pared, chopped
1 white turnip, peeled, diced
2 celery stalks, trimmed, chopped
1 onion, finely chopped

$\frac{1}{2}$ tsp. salt
$\frac{1}{2}$ tsp. freshly ground black pepper, or to taste
2 bay leaves
1 tsp. dried thyme
$\frac{1}{2}$ cup Scotch whiskey

    Over moderate high, heat olive oil in a large soup pot and cook lamb cubes and chopped onion for 5 minutes, until lightly browned. Pour in water and barley and simmer for 1 hour, until barley is tender. Stir in carrots, turnip, celery, salt, pepper, bay leaves and thyme; cover pot and simmer soup for 15-20 minutes. Stir in Scotch whiskey during last 2 minutes. Remove and discard bay leaves. Serves 6.

CREAM OF ASPARAGUS SOUP

6-8 cups water

2 lbs. asparagus, trimmed, rinsed

2 large all-purpose potatoes, pared, chopped

1 large leek, trimmed, chopped

$\frac{1}{2}$ tsp. salt, or to taste

$\frac{1}{2}$ tsp. freshly ground black pepper

$\frac{1}{4}$ tsp. cayenne pepper

2 tbsp. olive oil

1 egg yolk or $\frac{1}{4}$ cup egg substitute

$\frac{1}{2}$ cup low-fat evaporated milk

1 cup white Cheddar cheese, finely chopped

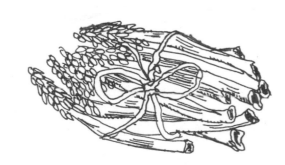

cook's string

Have ready: a food processor.

Cut off 2-inch tips from asparagus and tie the tips in a few bunches with cook's string. Cut up the rest of the asparagus spears into small pieces. Put cut asparagus, chopped pared potatoes and leek, plus bundles of asparagus tips in a large soup pot with cover. Fill pot with 6-8 cups of water, enough to completely cover the vegetables.

Cover pot and bring to a simmer for 15 minutes. Remove bunches of asparagus and set them aside. Continue to cook rest of vegetables until quite soft. Remove only the cooked vegetables, a couple of cupfuls at a time to a food processor; purée the cooked vegetables. Then, return the purée to the soup pot. Season with salt, black pepper, cayenne and olive oil. In a small bowl beat evaporated milk together with egg yolk (or egg substitute) and stir this mixture into asparagus soup. Remove string from asparagus tips and add tips to the soup pot. Bring soup to simmer and allow to thicken slightly. (Do not boil soup.) Stir soup continuously over a low simmer for a few minutes. Serve with croutons. Serves 6-8.

ZUPPA DI PESCE
(Easy to prepare; deliciously elegant to serve.)

about 2 pounds fleshy fish, including skin and a head or two, from:
    cod, whiting, bluefish (one, two or all three); cut fish into strips and remove bones
1 cup squid, cleaned, chopped
$\frac{1}{2}$ lb. sea scallops, cut into chunks
6-8 mussels, scrubbed
$\frac{1}{4}$ cup olive oil
4 cups water
1 cup dry white wine, like Soave or Chardonnay
2 cups (1 large can) plum tomatoes, mashed with juice
1 celery stalk, chopped
4 garlic cloves, minced
1 large onion, chopped
$\frac{1}{4}$ cup fresh Italian parsley, chopped
2 bay leaves
salt and freshly ground black pepper, to taste
$\frac{1}{4}$ tsp. hot pepper flakes

6 chunks (2-inch squares) crusty Italian bread, toasted in oven for a few minutes just
    before serving

Prepare fish stock by simmering chunks of boneless fish (and heads) in 4 cups water. Add onion, celery, garlic, bay leaves and parsley and continue to simmer for 30 minutes. Strain the stock. Set aside. Discard fish skin, bones and heads; return chunks of fish and vegetables to the bowl of strained stock.

To a clean soup pot, heat $\frac{1}{4}$ cup olive oil and cook scallops, squid and mussels for a few minutes. Stir in tomatoes and cook for 10 minutes; stir in fish stock and chunks of fish/vegetables. Add salt, pepper, hot pepper flakes and wine and continue to simmer for another 5-7 minutes. Discard bay leaves.

Meanwhile, toast chunks of Italian bread in oven for a few minutes until crisp. Place a chunk of toast into each serving bowl and ladle soup directly from the soup pot into serving bowls over the toasts. Serves 6-8

PASTA E FAGIOLI
("Pasta Fazool")

2 tbsp. olive oil

6 cups water

2 cans (1 lb. each) cannellini beans, rinsed in cold water, drained

1 medium onion, chopped

4 garlic cloves, minced

2 celery stalks, trimmed, finely chopped

4 ripe plum tomatoes, chopped

1 large carrot, trimmed, finely sliced into rounds

salt, freshly ground black pepper to taste

$\frac{1}{4}$ cup fresh parsley, chopped

1 tbsp. dried oregano

2 cups pork sausage meat, crumbled; discard casing

1 cup tiny shells pasta

$\frac{1}{2}$ cup Parmesan cheese, grated

Have ready: a food processor.

Heat 2 tablespoons olive oil in a large soup pot at medium-high. Crumble sausage meat into hot oil; add chopped onion and garlic, stirring frequently, breaking up sausage meat into small chunks. Simmer until sausage is cooked and onion is lightly browned, about 4-5 minutes. Scrape bottom of pot to prevent meat from sticking. Pour 6 cups water into pot; add and stir in chopped tomato, chopped celery, carrot rounds, parsley, oregano, salt and pepper. Bring pot to boil; then cover and simmer soup for 15 minutes. Stir in 1 can of rinsed and drained beans. Purée remainder of beans (1 lb. can) in food processor and stir the bean purée into the soup pot. Stir in tiny shells pasta and simmer soup 10 minutes longer, stirring continuously. Sprinkle with cheese. Serves 4-6.

Tailgating at Giants.

SPICY BLACK BEANS AND PEPPERS SOUP
[A Cooking Hint: Dried beans have a pantry life up to 2 years.
However, the older they are, the longer they must be soaked before using.]

8 cups water

1 lb. dried black beans, rinsed, drained; soak beans in hot water overnight;
   drain and rinse again

3 strips prosciutto, cut into small pieces

1 onion, finely chopped

1 celery stalk, trimmed, chopped

1 carrot, pared, shredded

1 all-purpose potato, pared, diced

1 small red bell pepper, deseeded, chopped

1 small green bell pepper, deseeded, chopped

1 small jalapeño pepper, deseeded, chopped
   (Wear plastic gloves when handling hot pepper.)

3 fresh ripe plum tomatoes, peeled, chopped in juice (*NOTE: below)

1 tsp. dried thyme

1 tbsp. dried oregano

$\frac{1}{2}$ tsp. salt

$\frac{1}{2}$ tsp. freshly ground black pepper

$\frac{1}{2}$ cup sour cream (fat-free available)

*NOTE: Remove skins from tomatoes by immersing them in boiling water for 1 minute.
Remove tomatoes from boiling water and plunge them into cold water; peel off skin with fingers.

Have ready: a food processor to purée beans.

In a large soup pot with a cover, brown onion in olive oil; at same time sauté prosciutto until crisp. Scrape bottom of pot to loosen leavings. Add soaked beans and pour in 8 cups water. Stir in celery, carrot, potato, green, red and jalapeño peppers, tomatoes, herbs and spices. Cover pot and bring to simmer for 2 hours, until beans are tender. Stir soup occasionally. Remove 3 cups cooked beans from soup pot and purée in food processor. Return purée to soup pot; add purée to soup and continue to simmer for 10 minutes longer. Add a dollop of sour cream to each serving bowl. Serves 6-8.

MANHATTAN CLAM CHOWDER

2 doz. cherrystone clams; have fishery shuck clams and store them in containers with
their liquid. Store containers in refrigerator, up to 1 day. Just before using, drain liquid
from containers into a large bowl, through a fine sieve. Reserve liquid. More liquid
may be needed to total 4 cups, including clam juices.
Lay clams on a glass board; remove any unwanted excrement from their stomach ;
chop clams to use in this recipe. Refrigerate clams in a bowl until needed.

1 tbsp. olive oil

3 strips lean prosciutto

1 lg. yellow onion, finely chopped

2 large all-purpose potatoes, pared, cut into $\frac{1}{2}$-inch cubes

6 fresh ripe tomatoes, rinsed, peeled, chopped (with juices) (*NOTE: below)

5 cups water

1 cup dry white wine, like Pinot Blanc

1 tsp. dried thyme

1 tbsp. dried oregano

$\frac{1}{4}$ cup fresh parsley, minced

salt, to taste

$\frac{1}{2}$ tsp. freshly ground black pepper

1 cup saltine crackers, crumbled

*NOTE: Remove skins from tomatoes by immersing them in boiling water for 1 minute;
remove tomatoes from boiling water and plunge them into cold water; peel off skin with fingers.

In a large soup pot, sauté prosciutto and onion in hot oil over medium heat for 5 minutes until
onion is tender. Add 5 cups water, cubed potatoes, chopped tomatoes and juice, wine, herbs and
spices. Simmer soup for 15 minutes. Add chopped clams and simmer soup for 3 minutes longer.
Serve hot in bowls. Sprinkle each bowl with crumbled saltine crackers at serving. Serves 6.

. . . .

CREAMY MANHATTAN CLAM CHOWDER

Follow recipe for MANHATTAN CLAM CHOWDER. Decrease amount of water
to $3\frac{1}{2}$ cups. Add $1\frac{1}{2}$ cups (1 can) low-fat evaporated milk at the same time when adding water,
wine, tomatoes etc.

CREAMY CLAM CHOWDER

[A Cooking Hint: 1) Store freshly harvested or fishery - bought shellfish ON ICE, in refrigerator, for no longer than the next day. 2) Or, freeze for a couple of weeks.
Notes on Freezing Clams/Mussels: remove clams or mussels from shells and place in a container to freeze; discard shells. However, freshly prepared stuffed clams or mussels (for baking) can be prepared, using their own pre-scrubbed shells. After stuffing the clam or mussel shells, arrange them on trays and freezer wrap. Store in freezer for up to a couple of weeks. Bake or broil as directed in your recipe, just before serving.]

3 doz. cherrystone clams, shucked, discard shells; have fishery shuck the clams and store them in containers with their liquids. (Store the containers in refrigerator, up to 1 day. Just before using, drain liquid from container into a large bowl, through a fine sieve. Reserve liquid. More water may be needed to total 4 cups liquid, including clam juices. Lay clams on a glass board; remove any unwanted contents from their stomachs; chop clams into small chunks. Place in a bowl. Set aside.)

1 tbsp. olive oil

3 strips bacon

1 lg. yellow onion, finely chopped

2 cups low-fat milk

2 cups low-fat evaporated milk or half-and-half

3 cups pared all-purpose potatoes, diced

1 small carrot, pared, minced

1 celery stalk (with greens) trimmed, finely chopped

$\frac{1}{2}$ tsp. salt

$\frac{1}{2}$ tsp. freshly ground black pepper, dash of cayenne

$\frac{1}{2}$ cup finely chopped Italian parsley

Have ready: a 4-quart pot with lid.

Heat oil in pot. Cook bacon just until crisp. Drain on paper towels. Remove all but 1 tablespoon fat from pot. Add onion and cook over moderate heat until softened, about 3-4 minutes. Add 4 cups water/clam liquid, 2 cups milk, 2 cups evaporated milk, potato, carrot and celery. Stir to blend thoroughly. Cover pot. Bring to boil and simmer chowder for 10-12 minutes until vegetables are tender.

Add bowl of chopped clams, salt, black pepper and cayenne. Cook just until clams are heated through. *Do not allow to boil, or clams will become tough.* Stir in chopped parsley. Check and taste; adjust seasoning, if needed. Serve immediately. Serves 6.

CORN-CLAM CHOWDER

2 doz. Little Neck clams in shell, scrubbed under cold running water; discard any closed
  clams which do not open when lightly tapped; keep clams cold, on ice and
  in refrigerator

$\frac{1}{2}$ cup dry white wine, like Pinot Grigio

2 tbsp. olive oil

1 small onion, minced

1 small jalapeño pepper, deseeded, finely chopped

  (Wear plastic gloves when handling hot peppers.)

1 small carrot, pared, finely chopped

1 small all-purpose potato, pared, finely chopped

$\frac{1}{4}$ cup flour

4 cups water

1 can (12 oz.) evaporated milk, fat-free available

$\frac{1}{4}$ cup parsley, finely chopped

1 tsp. ground nutmeg

1 tsp. salt

$\frac{1}{2}$ tsp. freshly ground black pepper

1 cup canned or frozen corn kernels

   In a large soup pot, at medium-heat, lightly brown onion in oil for 2-3 minutes. Stir in carrot, potato and pepper and cook for 2-3 minutes longer. Pour in $\frac{1}{2}$ cup wine, 4 cups water and 1 can evaporated milk. Cover and bring to simmer for 15 minutes. Remove 1 cup only liquid from soup pot and stir in $\frac{1}{4}$ cup flour to make a smooth paste. Return the thickened stock to soup pot, stirring as soup simmers. Add and blend in salt, pepper, nutmeg and parsley. Stir in corn kernels and float the clams on top the soup; simmer for several minutes longer until clams open. Discard any clams which do not open. Accompany servings with small bowls to discard shells. Serve immediately. Serves 5-6.

TOMATO AND FENNEL SOUP WITH SHRIMP

2 tbsp. olive oil

1 large onion, finely sliced

1 large fennel bulb, trimmed, halved, finely sliced; reserve fennel fronds for garnish

1 small all-purpose potato, pared, diced

4 cups water

2 cups chopped, skinned tomatoes (*NOTE: below);
    discard seeds, reserve tomato juices

2 cups canned tomato juice

1 bay leaf

$\frac{1}{2}$ lb small shrimp, shelled, rinsed in cold water

$\frac{1}{2}$ tsp. salt

$\frac{1}{2}$ tsp. freshly ground black pepper

$\frac{1}{4}$ cup chopped fennel fronds, for garnish

    *NOTE: Remove skins from tomatoes by immersing them in boiling water for 1 minute; remove tomatoes from boiling water and plunge them into cold water; peel off skin with fingers.

    Clean shrimp and refrigerate over ice as you prepare the soup recipe. In a large soup pot over medium heat, cook onion and fennel in olive oil for 5 minutes until tender. Pour 4 cups water, tomato juice, chopped tomato and diced potato into the pot. Cover pot and bring to a boil; then lower heat to simmer for 20 minutes. Stir in bay leaf, salt, pepper and cleaned shrimp and simmer for 5 minutes longer. Remove bay leaf and discard. Garnish each bowl with chopped fennel fronds at serving. Serves 6.

Feeding the Dolphins. Photo: R. Bastien

VEGETABLE BEEF SOUP
(Most canned vegetables are offered less-salt variety.)

2 tbsp. olive oil

1 lb. lean beef for stew, cut into small cubes

1 can (1 lb.) chopped tomatoes in juice

1 large onion, finely chopped

3 garlic cloves, minced

2 large carrots, pared, sliced into narrow rounds

2 celery stalks, trimmed, chopped

$\frac{1}{4}$ wedge of a large cabbage, shredded

1 all-purpose potato, pared, cubed

1 small green bell pepper, deseeded, chopped

2 cups fresh green beans, trimmed, cut into pieces

$\frac{1}{2}$ cup frozen peas

1 small can (8 oz.) corn kernels

$\frac{1}{2}$ tsp. salt

$\frac{1}{2}$ tsp. freshly ground black pepper

1 bay leaf

1 tbsp. oregano

8 cups water

1 beef shin bone

Have ready: a large soup pot; a large skillet.

In a large soup pot, pour 8 cups of water; add shin bone. Cover pot and bring to a boil; lower heat and simmer for 30 minutes.

Meanwhile in a large skillet at medium heat, cook beef cubes, onion and garlic in 2 tablespoons olive oil for 3-4 minutes until lightly browned. Stir in chopped tomatoes and juice, and simmer for 15 minutes.

Remove shin bone from soup pot and discard. Spoon tomato mixture into soup pot; add celery, carrots, cabbage, green pepper, green beans, cubed potato, peas and corn. Stir in bay leaf, salt, pepper and oregano. Cover pot and bring to a boil; then lower heat to simmer soup for 30 minutes or until vegetables are tender. Taste soup; adjust spices, if needed. Discard bay leaf before serving. Serve with crisp toasts of Italian bread. Serves 6-8.

BEEF BOLOGNESE SOUP

2 tbsp. olive oil

1 lb. lean ground beef

1 large onion, finely chopped

2 garlic cloves, minced

1 small can (6 oz.) tomato paste

1 can (1 lb.) chopped tomatoes in juice

6 cups water

1 carrot, finely chopped

1 small red bell pepper, deseeded, chopped

1 tsp. dried oregano

1 tsp. dried basil

pinch of hot red pepper flakes

$\frac{1}{2}$ tsp. salt

$\frac{1}{2}$ tsp. freshly ground black pepper

$\frac{1}{2}$ cup Parmesan cheese, grated

$\frac{1}{4}$ lb. tagliatelle pasta, broken into small pieces

more grated Parmesan cheese for garnish

In a large soup pot, over medium heat, lightly brown onion, garlic and ground beef in olive oil, about 5 minutes. In a small bowl, stir small can of tomato paste into 1 cup warm water; set aside. Add chopped tomatoes in juice to soup pot, scraping bottom of pot to remove leavings. Pour remaining 5 cups water into soup pot; add chopped carrot, red pepper, oregano, basil, salt, pepper and hot pepper flakes. Cover pot and bring to simmer for 20 minutes. Stir in and blend liquefied tomato paste. Continue to simmer for another 15 minutes. Maintain a low simmer and stir in cut tagliatelle to simmer for 12-14 minutes until pasta is just tender. Stir in $\frac{1}{2}$ cup Parmesan cheese. Serve in warm bowls with Italian artisan bread. Garnish with more Parmesan cheese at serving. Serves 6.

VEAL IN LEMON SOUP

[A Cooking Hint: "Deglazing" is a term used when meat is fried or cooked in a skillet or in a pan in the oven. The pan is "deglazed". Liquid is added to the pan to loosen and dissolve the remaining bits of sautéed/ roasted food (as when making gravy). Deglazing dissolves the caramelized juices stuck to bottom of pan.]

2 tbsp. olive oil

1 lb. boneless veal in 1-inch cubes

2 cups low-sodium beef stock

3 cups water

1 large onion, minced

1 large carrot, shaved into curls

1 large celery stalk, finely chopped

2 large garlic cloves, minced

$\frac{1}{4}$ cup fresh lemon juice

grated rind from 1 lemon

1 cup small white mushrooms, chopped

$1\frac{1}{2}$ cups fat-free evaporated milk

$\frac{1}{4}$ cup fresh parsley

1 tsp. salt

$\frac{1}{2}$ tsp. freshly ground black pepper

1 tsp. nutmeg

$\frac{1}{2}$ cup orzo

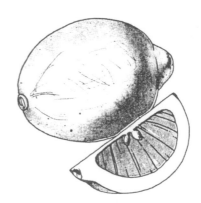

In a large soup pot at medium heat, cook onion, garlic, mushrooms and veal cubes in olive oil until onion is lightly browned, stirring frequently to cook veal about 5-7 minutes. Scrape bottom of pot to loosen leavings. Pour beef stock and water into the soup pot; add carrots, celery, lemon juice and lemon rind, herbs and spices. Cover and bring to a boil; then lower heat to simmer for 15 minutes. Remove 2 cups of only liquid to a bowl; blend evaporated milk and nutmeg into the liquid and return bowl of creamy liquid to the soup pot. Mix thoroughly; bring soup to simmer. Stir in $\frac{1}{2}$ cup orzo and continue to simmer soup for 10 minutes, stirring frequently. Serves 6.

CHILLED TOMATO, CARROT AND ORANGE SOUP

6 ripe tomatoes, skin removed (*NOTE: below), each cut in half, seeds removed,
    chopped with juice
3 large navel oranges, peeled, sectioned, membrane/pith removed
2 celery stalks, trimmed, chopped
3 carrots, trimmed, pared, grated
2 cups tomato juice
$\frac{1}{4}$ tsp. Tabasco sauce
salt to taste
fresh mint sprigs for garnish

*NOTE: Remove skins from tomatoes by immersing them in boiling water for 1 minute; remove tomatoes from boiling water and plunge them into cold water; peel off skin with fingers.

Have ready: a blender; a large glass pitcher to store soup.

Prepare tomatoes, oranges, celery and carrots as directed. Place them in a large bowl. Have a large glass pitcher ready to store soup after the vegetables and fruits are blended.

Purée fruits and vegetables until smooth, a ladleful at a time, in a sturdy blender. (For this recipe, a blender is preferred to a food processor because a blender will create a smoother soup.) Pour soup into a large glass pitcher. Stir in 2 cups tomato juice, Tabasco and salt to taste. Cover pitcher and chill soup in refrigerator for a couple of hours, until soup is cold. Serve in cold bowls; garnish each bowl with a sprig of mint. Serves 6.

Good Friends.

93

GAZPACHO

1 large cucumber, peeled, quartered, diced

2 green bell peppers, cored, deseeded, chopped fine

$\frac{1}{2}$-inch piece fresh hot Chile pepper, deseeded, chopped
    (Wear plastic gloves when handling hot peppers.)

6 ripe tomatoes, skin removed (*NOTE: below); halved,
    deseeded, chopped

1 onion, finely chopped

4 garlic cloves, chopped

2 tbsp. olive oil

2 tsp. balsamic vinegar

$\frac{1}{2}$ tsp. ground cumin

$\frac{1}{4}$ tsp. (or more) freshly ground black pepper

salt to taste

$\frac{1}{4}$ cup fresh cilantro, finely chopped

2 tbsp. fresh parsley, finely chopped

2 cups tomato juice

A Bird at the Feeder.

*NOTE: Remove skins from tomatoes by immersing them in boiling water for 1 minute; remove tomatoes from boiling water and plunge them into cold water; peel off skin with fingers.

Have ready: a food processor or a blender.

Combine diced cucumber, chopped tomatoes, Chile and green peppers, onion, garlic, olive oil, vinegar, herbs and spices in a large bowl. Purée *half of this mixture* with enough tomato juice to make a smooth blend. Transfer puréed soup to a large container as you work. Stir to blend remaining vegetable mixture and tomato juice into the container of puréed soup. Taste and adjust spices, if needed. Cover the container and refrigerate to chill for several hours. Serves 4.

COOL CUCUMBER AND SMOKED SALMON SOUP
(Start preparation early on the serving day; or on day before.)

2 tbsp. olive oil

1 large onion, finely chopped

1 large (or 2 small) cucumbers, pared, deseeded and thinly sliced

1 small all-purpose potato, pared, diced

1 large celery stalk with greens, trimmed, finely chopped

5 cups packaged low-sodium vegetable stock;

    or, Homemade Vegetable Stock (*NOTE: below)

$1\frac{1}{2}$ cups light cream; or, 1 can (12 oz.) low-fat evaporated milk

$\frac{1}{2}$ lb. smoked salmon, finely sliced, chopped

$\frac{1}{4}$ cup fresh chives, minced

salt to taste

$\frac{1}{2}$ tsp. freshly ground black pepper

fresh dill sprigs for garnish

*NOTE: Prepare homemade VEGETABLE STOCK: Pour 5 cups of lightly salted water into a 2-quart pot and bring to a boil. Combine: 1 celery stalk with greens, chopped, 1 small onion, chopped, 1 small carrot, pared and chopped. Stir vegetables into boiling water and simmer stock for 30 minutes. Drain stock water from pot and pour into a bowl; purée vegetables and return purée to liquid. Or, allow cooked solid vegetables to remain in stock liquid.

Have ready: a blender; a large glass or plastic container to store soup in refrigerator. *Store cream (or evaporated milk), smoked salmon and chives in refrigerator until needed.*

Heat oil in a large soup pot over medium heat and cook onion for 2-3 minutes to soften. Add prepared cucumbers, potato, celery and stock. Bring pot to boil; then, lower heat, cover pot and simmer soup for 20 minutes until vegetables are tender.
Allow soup to cool slightly; then transfer a ladleful at a time, to a blender. Purée soup solids and return them to the soup pot to combine with remaining soup liquid. Transfer the puréed soup into a large container with a cover. Refrigerate soup for several hours or overnight.
(*Reminder:* Store cream, smoked salmon and chives in refrigerator until needed in recipe.)
Several hours before serving, remove soup from refrigerator. Stir in cream (or evaporated milk), chopped smoked salmon and chives until well-blended. Return the container of soup to refrigerator and chill for 1 hour to allow flavors to blend. Taste and adjust seasonings, if desired. Ladle soup into chilled bowls and garnish with sprigs of dill. Serves 6.

SPICY BLACK BEAN AND CHILI SOUP

1 lb. black beans; soak rinsed beans in enough water to cover, overnight

2 tbsp. olive oil

1 onion, finely chopped

1 small red bell pepper, cored, deseeded, chopped

1 cup canned chopped tomatoes with juice

1 tsp. ground cumin

$\frac{1}{2}$ tsp. freshly ground black pepper

8 cups water

$\frac{1}{4}$ cup fresh cilantro, finely chopped

2 strips lean bacon

3-4 large garlic cloves, minced

1 carrot pared, shaved

1 tsp. chili powder, or to taste

$\frac{1}{2}$ tsp. salt, or to taste

$\frac{1}{2}$ cup brown rice

Rinse beans again, in cold water. In a large soup pot over moderate heat, brown onion and garlic and cook bacon in olive oil for a few minutes until bacon is crisp. Stir in red pepper, carrot, tomatoes and juice, herbs and spices. Simmer for 5 minutes. Pour 8 cups water into the pot and stir in presoaked beans. Cover pot and bring to a boil; then lower heat to simmer for 1 hour. After 15 minutes, stir brown rice into simmering soup and continue to cook for 45 minutes, or until beans are tender. Serves 8-10.

DICK'S ONION SOUP
[A Cooking Hint: To prepare onions without crying or have your nose runny, work with onions under running water.]

6 tbsp. butter or Smart Balance spread

2 lbs. yellow onions, thinly sliced

1 tsp. salt

2 quarts water

$\frac{1}{2}$ cup dry vermouth

$\frac{1}{2}$ lb. mozzarella, cubed

2 tbsp. olive oil

3 tbsp. all-purpose flour

$\frac{1}{4}$ tsp. freshly ground black pepper

6 beef Bovril, bouillon cubes

3 tbsp. brandy

$\frac{1}{2}$ cup Parmesan cheese, grated

Another $\frac{1}{2}$ cup grated Parmesan and hard Italian biscuits (frizelle, rusks) at serving

Have ready: 2 soup pots. At serving: Preheat broiler to 450°.

In a large, heavy soup pot with a cover, cook onions in oil and butter (or Smart Balance spread) over medium heat for 10-15 minutes, until soft. Add and stir in flour, salt, pepper. In another pot, bring 2 quarts water to a boil; remove from heat and dissolve beef bouillon cubes. Add this liquid mixture to the soup pot; stir in wine and brandy. Cover pot and bring to a boil; then, lower to simmer gently for 30 minutes. When ready to serve, ladle soup into ovenproof crock bowls. Float a biscuit on top of each bowl. Combine grated Parmesan and cubed mozzarella and distribute over each biscuit in bowls. Brown cheese in bowls in preheated broiler, 5-6 inches below broiling element for 2-3 minutes or until cheese is golden. Sprinkle with more Parmesan. Serves 6. *CAUTION:* Serve hot; be careful not to burn your mouth.

CREAM CHEESE AND BROCCOLI SOUP

2 tbsp. olive oil

2-3 cups broccoli florets and stems; divide broccoli stalks into small florets; chop stems
　　into small pieces and keep separate from florets

1 large leek, trimmed, thinly sliced

1 small onion, chopped

1 medium-size carrot, finely chopped

$\frac{1}{4}$ cup white rice

6 cups water

1 tsp. salt

$\frac{1}{2}$ tsp. freshly ground black pepper

1 tsp. ground nutmeg

1 bay leaf

$\frac{1}{4}$ cup light cream, or low-fat evaporated milk

8 oz. low-fat cream cheese, cut into small chunks, softened

packaged croutons for garnish at serving

In a large soup pot, cook onion, leek and carrot in oil for 4 minutes, stirring frequently, until onion is softened. Add broccoli stems, rice, water, salt, pepper, nutmeg and bay leaf. Bring just to a boil; cover pot; then, reduce heat to simmer for 15 minutes. Stir in broccoli florets and continue to cook, covered, for 15-20 minutes, until rice and vegetables are tender. Remove bay leaf and discard.

Stir in cream (or evaporated milk) and softened cream cheese. Simmer soup over low heat for 3-4 minutes, stirring occasionally, until thoroughly heated. Serve in warm bowls, garnished with croutons. Serves 6.

Dogs at Suppertime.

FRESH TOMATO SOUP

2 tbsp. olive oil

3 lbs. ripe plum tomatoes, skin removed (*NOTE: below)

1 large onion, finely chopped

1 large carrot, finely chopped

2 garlic cloves, finely chopped

1 celery stalk with greens, finely chopped

6 cups water

1 tsp. dried marjoram

$\frac{1}{2}$ cup low-fat evaporated milk

$\frac{1}{4}$ cup fresh basil leaves, chopped

1 tsp. salt

$\frac{1}{2}$ tsp. freshly ground black pepper

*NOTE: To remove skins from tomatoes, immerse them in boiling water for 1 minute; remove and plunge them into cold water; peel off skin with fingers.

Have ready: a food processor or blender.

It is important that ripe tomatoes are used in this recipe. After you've skinned the tomatoes, cut them in half and scoop out seeds into a sieve, catching the juices into a small bowl. Reserve juices; discard seeds in sieve. Chop tomatoes.

Heat olive oil in a large soup pot. Cook onion, garlic, carrot, celery in oil over low-medium heat for 3-4 minutes, stirring occasionally. Add tomatoes and juice; stir in water and marjoram. Cover pot and reduce heat to simmer for 45 minutes, stirring occasionally, until vegetables are soft. Allow soup to cool slightly. Then, transfer soup solids with enough liquid to moisten, in small batches to a food processor or blender. Return puréed vegetables to remaining liquid in soup pot. Cook soup on low-medium heat. Stir in evaporated milk, basil, salt and pepper and heat soup thoroughly. Do not boil.

Ladle soup into warmed bowls and serve immediately. Serves 6.

CREAM OF MUSHROOM SOUP

[A Cooking Hint: Add and dissolve bouillon cubes to soup for extra body if soup seems too thin. Also, try dissolved bouillon in rice for added flavor.]

2 lbs. white mushrooms, rinsed, trimmed, finely sliced

2 tbsp. butter or Smart Balance spread

1 small onion, finely chopped

1 shallot, finely chopped

2 tbsp. olive oil

4 tbsp. flour

$\frac{1}{4}$ cup sherry wine

8 cups packaged low-sodium chicken broth;
    (or: Homemade Chicken Stock, page 81)

1 cup light cream or low-fat evaporated milk

2 tbsp. fresh parsley, chopped

2 tbsp. fresh lemon juice

$\frac{1}{2}$ tsp. freshly ground black pepper

1 tsp. salt

$\frac{1}{2}$ cup low-fat sour cream, to garnish

Have ready: a food processor or blender; a large skillet; a large soup pot.

In a large skillet, melt butter (or Smart Balance spread) and sauté mushrooms. Season with salt and pepper. Cook, stirring frequently, for 7-8 minutes on medium heat until mushrooms are golden brown. Remove from heat and set aside.

In a large soup pot, over medium heat, cook chopped shallot and onion in olive oil for 2-3 minutes, until softened. Stir in flour and continue to cook for 2 more minutes. Add stock and sherry and thoroughly blend. Remove about one-quarter cooked mushrooms to a small bowl. Add the remainder to the soup pot. Reduce heat under soup pot and simmer gently for 20 minutes, stirring soup occasionally. Remove from heat and allow soup to cool slightly. Then, transfer soup in batches, to a food processor, or blender. (If using a food processor, drain the liquid from the mushrooms mixture and food process solids, only.)

Purée mushrooms mixture with just enough soup liquid to moisten; then, return the puréed mushrooms to the soup pot with remaining liquid. Stir the small bowl of cooked mushroom slices into the soup pot; add evaporated milk, parsley and lemon juice. Cook assembled soup for about 5 minutes. Ladle soup into warmed soup bowls and garnish each bowl with a dollop of sour cream. Serves 6-8.

VEGETARIAN MINESTRONE

[A Cooking Hint: Dried beans have a pantry life of up to 2 years. However, the older they are, the longer they must be soaked before using.]

1 pkg. (1 lb.) dried beans mix (Follow directions on package and soak rinsed beans, overnight, in water, to cover.)

$\frac{1}{2}$ cup barley

2 large carrots, pared, thinly sliced into rounds

1 large celery stalk with greens, trimmed, finely chopped

1 large all-purpose potato, parcd, diced

1 large onion, finely chopped

2 medium-size ripe tomatoes, skin removed, chopped with juice (*NOTE: below)

1 cup prepared tomato purée

10 cups water

$\frac{1}{2}$ cup frozen peas

$\frac{1}{2}$ cup fresh green beans, trimmed, cut into 1-inch segments

1 zucchini, rinsed, chopped into $\frac{1}{2}$-inch cubes (about 1 cup)

1 lb. can ceci (chick peas), rinsed in cold water, drained

1 tsp. salt

$\frac{1}{2}$ tsp. freshly ground black pepper

1 tbsp. dried oregano

1 cup orecchiette (little ears) pasta

$\frac{1}{2}$ cup Asiago cheese, grated

2 tbsp. olive oil

*NOTE: To remove skin from tomatoes, immerse tomatoes in boiling water for 1 minute; remove them from boiling water and plunge them into cold water. Peel off skin with fingers.

Soak beans overnight, in enough water to cover (or, as directed on package).

In a large soup pot with a lid, lightly brown onion in olive oil for 2-3 minutes, until tender, scraping bottom of pot to prevent sticking. Pour 4 cups water into the pot; add beans and barley. Cover pot and bring to boil. Then, lower heat to simmer for 1 hour.

Add tomato purée, chopped tomatoes and juice, carrots, celery and potato. Stir in remaining 6 cups of water. Replace cover and bring to boil. Then, lower heat to simmer; cook soup for 30 minutes. Stir in green beans, peas, zucchini, ceci, oregano, salt/pepper and pasta. Continue to simmer for 15 minutes. Remove pot from burner and stir in cheese. Serve soup with seasoned bread toasts. Serves 6-8.

CHEDDAR CHEESE-VEGETABLE CHOWDER

[A Cooking Hint: To remove excess salt from food, add 1 teaspoon each: granulated sugar and white vinegar to the pot; or, add a few slices raw potato to the soup.]

2 tbsp. olive oil

1 large onion, finely chopped

1 large leek, halved lengthwise, thinly sliced

2 large garlic cloves, minced

6 tbsp. flour

6 cups packaged low-sodium vegetable stock; or (*NOTE: below)

2-3 large carrots, pared, diced

2 celery stalks with greens, chopped

1 large all-purpose potato, pared, diced

1 parsnip, pared, diced

$\frac{1}{2}$ tsp. dried thyme

1 bay leaf

1 tsp. salt

$\frac{1}{2}$ tsp. freshly ground black pepper

2 cups light cream or low-fat evaporated milk

1 lb. sharp Cheddar cheese, grated

$\frac{1}{4}$ cup fresh parsley, chopped, for garnish

*NOTE: recipe for HOMEMADE VEGETABLE STOCK

1 celery stalk, chopped, 1 small onion, chopped, 1 carrot, pared, chopped

Add celery, onion, carrot to 6 cups salted boiling water; simmer for 30 minutes; drain stock and pour liquid into a bowl. Purée vegetables and return the purée to the liquid. Stir vegetable stock into recipe. Or allow cooked solid vegetables to remain in liquid.

In a large soup pot, over medium heat, cook onion, leek and garlic in olive oil for 5 minutes, until vegetables begin to soften. Stir in flour and cook 2 minutes. Add 1 cup of stock; stir and scrape bottom of pot. Bring to a boil, stirring frequently and slowly stir in rest of stock.

Add carrots, celery, parsnip, potato, herbs and spices. Reduce heat; cover pot and cook gently for 35 minutes, stirring occasionally, until vegetables are tender. Remove and discard bay leaf. Stir in cream (or evaporated milk) and continue to simmer over low heat for 4-5 minutes. Add cheese, a handful at a time, stirring continuously for 1 minute after each addition, until cheese is melted.

Ladle soup into warmed bowls; garnish with parsley. Serves 6.

AVGOLEMONO WITH TURKEY

10 cups water

1 turkey leg, 1 turkey wing with skin, rinsed in cold water

1 large yellow onion, chopped

2 large celery stalks with greens, chopped

1 large carrot, pared, sliced in rounds

6 large garlic cloves, chopped

$\frac{1}{2}$ cup fresh parsley, chopped

1 tsp. salt, to taste

1 cup long-grain rice

2 bay leaves

$\frac{1}{2}$ tsp. crushed black peppercorns

4 egg yolks, beaten, or 1 cup egg substitute

1 tbsp. dried oregano

$\frac{1}{2}$ cup fresh lemon juice

more salt/pepper, if needed

Have ready: a large soup pot with a cover.

Bring 10 cups of water to boil in a large soup with a cover. Add turkey leg and wing to the boiling water. Cover pot; lower heat to simmer for 1 hour. Skim foam off top of pot as needed.

As the turkey stock is cooking, prepare the raw vegetables, placing chopped onion, garlic, celery and carrot in a bowl. After 1 hour, transfer soup pot from burner to work table and remove turkey leg/wing to a bowl; set aside.

Add the bowl of vegetables to the stock pot. Stir in parsley, bay leaves, salt and peppercorns. Cover pot and bring pot to boil. Stir in rice; replace cover and simmer soup for 30 minutes. As soup cooks, remove skin from turkey leg/wing and discard. Remove meat from leg/wing to a glass board and chop the turkey meat into bite-size pieces. Stir turkey meat into soup pot as soup continues to cook.

Meanwhile, in a quart-size mixing bowl, whisk eggs, oregano and additional salt/pepper, if needed. Whisk lemon juice into egg mixture, a little at a time. Just before serving the soup, carefully whisk the egg/lemon mixture to blend into the soup pot as it simmers. Remove and discard bay leaves. Serve immediately. Serves 6-8.

HEARTY PEA SOUP
Reprinted from: MENU LOG: A Collection of Recipes as Coordinated Menus
by Marion O. Celenza, page 231.

10 cups water

1 tsp. dried thyme leaves

1 ham bone; or 4 strips cooked bacon,

    crumbled; or 3 links cooked sausage,

    cut in rounds

1 carrot, finely chopped

1 onion, finely chopped

1 lb. dry green split peas, rinsed in cold water

1 bay leaf

1 potato, peeled and diced

1 large celery stalk with greens, chopped

1 tsp. salt

$\frac{1}{4}$ tsp. black pepper

dash of cayenne

    Rinse and pick over peas in a colander. In a 6-quart soup pot with cover, pour 10 cups water. Add split peas, ham bone (or crumbled cooked bacon or cooked sausage rounds), onion, potato, celery, carrot, spices and herbs. Cover pot; bring to a boil; then, simmer gently for 2 hours, stirring the soup occasionally. Add a little more water if soup is too thick. Do not strain. Remove ham bone from pot and cut off meat from the bone. Return meat to the soup pot; discard the bone and bay leaf. Continue to simmer 10 minutes longer. Serve with plain croutons or pepper frizelle. Serves 6-8.

LENTIL SOUP
Reprinted from: MENU LOG: A Collection of Recipes as Coordinated Menus
by Marion O. Celenza, page 95.

1 lb. pkg. lentils, rinsed in colander, drained

10 cups water

2 tbsp. olive oil

3 strips cooked bacon, crumbled;

    or 3 cooked sausages, chopped;

    or 1 ham bone with scraps

1 large celery stalk with greens, chopped

1 all-purpose potato, pared, chopped

1 large carrot, pared, chopped

1 onion, chopped

$\frac{1}{2}$ tsp. dried thyme

$\frac{1}{2}$ tsp. dried oregano

1 bay leaf

1 tsp salt, or to taste

$\frac{1}{2}$ tsp. black pepper

1 tsp. chili powder

$\frac{1}{2}$ cup uncooked rice; or

    1 cup uncooked ditalini pasta

    In a 6-quart soup pot with a cover, cook bacon to crisp; or, brown chopped sausages in olive oil. Scrape bottom of pot to dislodge any leavings, before adding water to pot. If selecting a ham bone, add ham bone to 10 cups water and simmer for 30 minutes. Then, remove any meat from bone and set aside; discard bone.

    In 10 cups of water, add and combine: lentils, all vegetables, herbs and spices. Cover pot; bring to a boil. Then, lower heat and simmer soup for an additional 2 hours. During last 25 minutes, stir in rice; or, during last 10 minutes, stir in ditalini. (During last 5 minutes, stir in cooked meat selection.) Discard bay leaf before serving. Serve with crusty Italian bread. Serves 6-8.

MUSSELS WITH SAFFRON SOUP
*[A Cooking Hint: Store mussels in shells on ice, in refrigerator, for
no longer than the next day.]*

5 lbs. mussels, scrubbed with a stiff brush under cold running water; discard any
   broken mussels and those with open shells that do not close when tapped.
   Pull off "beards" and scrape off barnacles. (*NOTE: below)

1 cup dry white wine, like Pinot Blanc

2 tbsp. olive oil

2 large shallots, finely chopped

1 leek, halved lengthwise, thinly sliced

a couple pinches of saffron threads

$1\frac{1}{2}$ cups light cream or low-fat evaporated milk

up to 5 cups additional water

1 tbsp. cornstarch dissolved in $\frac{1}{4}$ cup water

1 tsp. salt, or to taste

$\frac{1}{2}$ tsp. freshly ground black pepper

2 tbsp. fresh cilantro, chopped

   *NOTE: Serve this soup, or any soup with seafood, when made. Do not store leftover soup
with mussels or clam shells in refrigerator. You may freeze leftover seafood soup for 1-2 weeks;
remove mussels or clams from their shells before freezing soup.

   Have ready: a large, heavy pan; a large soup pot.

   Put mussels and wine in a large, heavy pan with a cover over high heat. Cover pan tightly and
cook for 4-5 minutes, or until mussels open; shake pot occasionally. Discard any mussels which
do not open after cooking. Allow mussels to cool a little.
   Remove mussels from shells, adding any additional juices from the mussels to the cooking
liquid. Strain cooking liquid through a fine sieve. Add enough water to the liquid to make 6 cups.
   Heat oil in a large soup pot with a cover; cook shallots and leek until softened. Stir in the
mussels cooking liquid and saffron. Cover pot and bring to a boil; then, reduce heat to
simmer 15-20 minutes until vegetables are tender and the flavors blend. Add cream; stir and
bring to a boil. Stir in cornstarch/water mixture and gently boil for 2-3 minutes until slightly
thickened. Stir frequently. Add mussels and cook for 1-2 minutes to heat thoroughly. Stir in
cilantro, salt and pepper. Ladle soup into warmed bowls and serve. Serves 6.

SHRIMP BISQUE

1 lb. small shrimp, shelled, cleaned, rinsed in cold water, drained;
    store shrimp in refrigerator over ice while you prepare soup (*NOTE: below)
2 tbsp. olive oil
1 onion, finely chopped
2 garlic cloves, minced
1 celery stalk with greens, minced
6 cups water
$\frac{1}{2}$ cup sherry
12 oz. light cream or low-fat evaporated milk
$\frac{1}{4}$ cup long-grained rice
2 tbsp. tomato paste stirred into $\frac{1}{2}$ cup hot water
juice of 1 lemon
1 tbsp. grated lemon zest
$\frac{1}{2}$ tsp. salt, or to taste
$\frac{1}{2}$ tsp. freshly ground black pepper
1 bay leaf
$\frac{1}{4}$ cup parsley finely chopped, for garnish

    *NOTE: A delicious CRAB BISQUE may be prepared from this recipe. Make the following additions/substitutions:
    1) Substitute 2 cups crab meat, finely chopped, for shrimp
    2) Substitute $\frac{1}{2}$ cup brandy for sherry
    3) Add 1 tsp. ground nutmeg

Have ready: a large soup pot with a cover.

    In a large soup pot over medium heat, cook onion, garlic and celery in olive oil. Pour water and light cream (or evaporated milk) into the pot and blend thoroughly. Stir tomato paste into hot water; add bay leaf, lemon juice and zest, salt, pepper and rice. Cover pot and simmer for 20 minutes, until rice is tender. Stir in prepared shrimp and sherry; continue to simmer 5 minutes longer. Remove bay leaf and discard.
    Serve soup in warmed bowls; garnish with parsley. Serves 4-6.

SALMON-A-LEEKIE

1 lb. salmon fillet, rinsed, patted dry with paper towels; remove skin;
    cut into $\frac{1}{2}$-inch cubes

2 tbsp. olive oil

1 large onion, finely sliced

2-3 large leeks, including some greens, trimmed, rinsed, finely sliced into rounds

2 large carrots, pared, cut into 2-inch chunks

4 large all-purpose potatoes, pared; dice 2 potatoes; halve 2 potatoes

1 cup low-fat evaporated milk

8 cups water, divided (2 cups, 6 cups)

1 bay leaf

1 tsp. salt, or to taste

$\frac{1}{2}$ tsp. freshly ground black pepper

1 head of escarole (about $1\frac{1}{2}$ lbs.), trimmed; rinsed several times in cold water, drained

Have ready: a large soup pot with a cover; a 2-quart pot.

In a large soup pot, cook onion and leeks in olive oil over medium heat for 5 minutes, until vegetables are tender. Set aside.

In a 2-quart pot, bring 2 cups water to boil and cook 2 pared halved potatoes for 20 minutes until just tender. Remove potatoes to a bowl and mash them with 1 cup evaporated milk. Set aside. Save the potato water for later.

Return heat under the soup pot. Pour 6 cups water, including the potato water, into the soup pot, scraping bottom of the pot, to loosen leavings from onion/leeks. Add cleaned escarole and carrot chunks; cover pot and cook for 10 minutes. As pot continues to lightly boil, add diced potatoes, bay leaf, salt, pepper and salmon cubes. Re-cover pot and bring to a quick boil; then, simmer soup for another 5 minutes. Stir in mashed potatoes and simmer soup for 5 minutes longer to thicken soup.

Taste soup and adjust seasonings, if necessary. Remove bay leaf and discard. Serves 6.

Tomatoes, Artichokes, Smoky Mozzarella, Olives Salad, page 68

Shrimp in Ginger Salad, page 58

Arugula, Heirloom Tomatoes, Walnuts Salad, page 207

Insalata Di Toscana, page 184

Pasta, Prosciutto, Broccoli, Smoky Mozzarella Salad, page 137

Salmon Burger on a Croissant, page 33

Potatoes, Corn, Tomato Salad, page 59

Wraps, page 35

Insalata Alla Campagna, page 70

Potatoes and Beans Salad, page 65

Grilled Cheese, Prosciutto, Tomato Sandwich, page 23

A Saturday Night in the Summer Pasta Salad, page 60

Mushrooms Stuffed with Sundried Tomatoes, Prosciutto and Olives, page 299

Crab Cake on a Croissant, page 37

Chicken Cutlets, Roasted Peppers, Provolone Hero, page 47

Avocado Dip, page 400

BOUILLABAISSE

Reprinted from: MENU LOG: A Collection of Recipes as Coordinated Menus
by Marion O. Celenza, page 254.

1 lb. fleshy fish (cod, haddock, scrod, halibut, whiting, etc.), skinned and boned

1 lb. scallops, halved, if they are large

1 lobster, cut into sections; or 2-3 crabs or crab claws

1 lb. large shrimp, shelled, cleaned

$\frac{1}{2}$ lb. squid, cleaned, sliced into rings (include tentacles)

2 dozen cherrystone clams, shucked; strain liquid through a fine strainer
    and add to the stew

1 can (1 lb.) plum tomatoes, mashed in juice

10 cups water

2 tbsp. olive oil

4-6 white mushrooms, rinsed, sliced

3 scallions with some greens, chopped

3 garlic cloves, minced

1 bay leaf

1 tbsp. parsley, chopped

$\frac{1}{2}$ tsp. thyme

1 tsp. salt

$\frac{1}{2}$ tsp. black pepper

1 piece orange peel, 3-4 inches

3-4 whole cloves

$\frac{1}{4}$ cup dry sherry

1 cup dry white wine

$\frac{1}{4}$ cup brandy

a couple pinches saffron

a dash of hot red pepper flakes

Have ready: a 6-quart soup pot with a cover.

In a large soup pot, simmer garlic, onion, mushrooms and scallions in olive oil until tender. Scrape bottom of pot to loosen leavings. Add tomatoes, water, herbs, peel, spices, wines (all ingredients except seafood). Combine thoroughly. Cover pot and simmer for 30 minutes. Add fish and shellfish with liquid. Simmer the stew for 15 minutes longer. Remove bay leaf and discard. Serve in warmed bowls, over toasted chunks of French bread. Bon appétit! Serves 6-8.

We Remember and Honor Our Family Who Served in the Military

Uncle Raphael Orlando
Chaplain Italian Army WWI

Zachary Sansone
Cpl. US Army Infantry WWII

John Sansone
Tech. Sgt. US Army WWII

Frank Sansone
PFC US Army MP

Cosimo Orlando
US Army WWII

Joseph F. Colantuono
PFC US Army WWII (Decorated War Hero)

Michael R. Colantuono
Staff Sgt. US Army WWII

Armand V. Colantuono
Cpl. US Army Korean War

Arthur E. Colantuono
Cpl. US Army Vietnam War

James N. Orlando
Cpl. US Army Signal Corps

John L. Celenza
Lieut. jg US Marines, DDS

Albert P. Shea
Staff Sgt. US Army WWII

Casseroles
and
One-Pot Suppers

....and the SERVICEMEN and WOMAN who shared their lives with our family members...

Francis Colantuono	Pvt. US Army WWI, m. (aunt) Susie Orlando
James De Pascale	US Army, m. (cousin) Rita Colantuono
Herbert L. Lewis	Pfc. US Army Air Corps, m. (cousin) Gloria Colantuono
Joseph Lamendola	Sgt. US Army, m. (cousin) Rose Sansone
Dorothy M. Ricker	Seaman 1st Class US Navy, WWII, m. (cousin) John Sansone
Donald G. Kloenne	Radioman 3rd Class USN Armed Guard, m. (cousin) Louise Orlando
Joseph Viera	Pfc US Army (303 Signal Operation Battalion), m. (cousin) Theresa Viera
Richard Erdmann	ES US Navy Weather Service, m. (cousin) Doris Orlando
Cliff Miller	Machinists' Mate L 2nd Class V6 US Navy, m. (cousin) Tina Mazza

Louis Capriglione
Lieut. jg US Navy WWI, WWII

Ralph Mazza
Captain US Army Signal Corps

Vincent Mazza
Pvt. US Army WWII

Albert Capriglione
2nd Class Petty Officer US Coast Guard

NEAPOLITAN STEW

(This stew, without the pasta, may be prepared a day or two in advance. Cover pot and refrigerate. Before serving, heat stew thoroughly as you prepare the pasta.)

2 tbsp. olive oil

1 small yellow onion, chopped

4 large garlic cloves, sliced

1 Italian sweet red pepper, rinsed, deseeded, sliced into rings

2 Italian mildly hot green peppers, rinsed, deseeded, sliced into rings

1 zucchini, about 6-8 inches long, unpared, rinsed, trimmed, cut into $\frac{1}{2}$-inch rounds

6-8 small or 5 medium-size white mushrooms, rinsed, trimmed, quartered

6-8 small broccoli florets, rinsed

3 plum tomatoes, rinsed, chopped with juice

2 cups prepared tomato sauce

1 tbsp. oregano

$\frac{1}{4}$ cup Gaeta olives, pitted

4 leaves fresh basil, torn

1 tsp. salt

$\frac{1}{4}$ tsp. freshly ground black pepper

2 bay leaves

$\frac{1}{2}$ cup red table wine, like Burgundy

$\frac{1}{2}$ cup Parmagiano Reggiano cheese, grated; more for garnish

3 links Italian sweet fennel sausage, sliced in rounds (Sausage will easily slice if frozen.)

1 doz.-14 meatballs (*NOTE: recipe below)

1 lb. tagliatelle, cooked in enough water, al dente, according to directions on package

MEATBALLS:

1 lb. mixed: ground beef, ground pork

$\frac{1}{2}$ cup finely ground unseasoned Italian bread crumbs

1 tbsp. fresh parsley, finely chopped

1 egg, beaten, or $\frac{1}{4}$ cup egg substitute

$\frac{1}{4}$ tsp. ground nutmeg

pepper and salt to taste

Combine all meatball ingredients in a bowl; mix thoroughly. Form 12-14 meatballs, about 1 tablespoon each. Set aside.

Slice sausage into $\frac{1}{2}$-inch rounds. (Sausages will slice easily if frozen.) Set aside with meatballs.

In a large stew pot, with a lid, over medium heat, brown meatballs, sausages, onion and garlic in olive oil, making certain to lightly brown all sides of meatballs and sausages. Scrape bottom of pot to prevent sticking and burning. Do not overcook. Pour in tomato sauce and chopped tomatoes with juices, herbs and spices. Cover pot with lid and adjust heat to simmer for 15 minutes. Add red and green peppers, zucchini, broccoli florets and mushrooms; continue to simmer the stew, gently for 10-12 minutes. Stir in wine and cheese. Remove from heat. Remove bay leaves and discard.

During last 15-20 minutes, set pasta pot with enough salted water to boil the tagliatelle. Prepare pasta only when ready to serve. Drain cooked pasta and pour into a serving bowl. Serve Neapolitan Stew over a portion of tagliatelle in individual serving bowls. Garnish each portion with cheese. Toasty frizelles and a glass of Burgundy make a tasty accompaniment. Serves 6.

VENETIAN VEAL STEW WITH RISI E BISI

[A Cooking Hint: Stew- type dishes taste even better when leftovers are reheated.
Hint: cook double stew quantity and freeze half for another meal.]

2 tbsp. olive oil

1 onion, finely chopped

1 strip lean bacon, diced, cut with scissors

1 lb. boneless veal, cubed

1 cup Arborio rice

2 cups freshly shelled peas

   (You may use frozen peas.)

2 cups low-salt chicken stock

$\frac{1}{2}$ cup brandy

$\frac{1}{4}$ tsp. freshly ground black pepper

salt to taste

1 tbsp. fresh thyme, minced or

   1 tsp. dried thyme

$\frac{1}{4}$ cup Pecorino Romano cheese,

   grated for garnish

Heat oil over medium-high in a large stock pot and cook onion, chopped bacon and veal cubes on all sides for 5-7 minutes, until onion is golden and veal is lightly browned. Pour chicken stock into pot; stir in rice. Cover pot and cook on simmer for 15 minutes, stirring often. Stir in peas, brandy, salt, pepper and thyme and continue to simmer the stew for another 10 minutes, until rice and peas are tender. Spoon into individual bowls. Garnish with Pecorino Romano cheese and serve with crusty Italian bread. Serves 4.

SHRIMP IN CREAMY TOMATO SAUCE

1 lb. large shrimp, shelled, cleaned,

   rinsed, drained

2-3 tbsp. olive oil

1 lb. linguine pasta

$\frac{1}{4}$ cup Parmesan cheese, grated, at serving

SAUCE:

2 cups ricotta

$\frac{1}{2}$ cup pitted oil-cured olives, chopped

4 scallions, trimmed, chopped

$\frac{1}{4}$ cup fresh basil leaves, slivered

4 ripe plum tomatoes, chopped with juice

2 tbsp. olive oil

$\frac{1}{4}$ tsp. salt

$\frac{1}{4}$ tsp. freshly ground black pepper

Sauté cleaned shrimp in 2-3 tablespoons olive oil at medium-high for 3-4 minutes, moving them as they cook in the skillet with a spatula. Remove from heat; set aside and keep them warm.

In a large bowl, beat ricotta with a fork until smooth Stir in olives, scallions, basil, tomatoes, 2 tablespoons olive oil , salt and pepper. Set aside.

Meanwhile, cook pasta al dente, according to directions on package; drain.

In a large serving bowl, pour drained pasta; add sauce and warm shrimp to the pasta and toss to mix. Serve immediately with grated Parmesan. Serves 4.

SPICY BLACK BEAN CHILI

1 lb. dried black beans

2 tbsp. olive oil

1 large onion, chopped

6 garlic cloves, minced

1 large celery stalk, trimmed, chopped

8 cups water

2 cups low-salt chicken broth (or Homemade Chicken Broth; see recipe on page 81.)

1-2 Chile peppers, deseeded, chopped (Wear plastic gloves when handling hot peppers.)

1 can (1 lb.) plum tomatoes with juice, chopped

1 red bell pepper, deseeded, chopped

1 tbsp. dried oregano

1 tbsp. ground cumin

$\frac{1}{4}$ cup fresh cilantro, chopped

2 tbsp. fresh lime juice

salt and freshly ground pepper, to taste

Have ready: a blender.

In a large bowl, soak beans in enough water to cover for 1 hour; drain. In a large soup pot, heat oil and cook onion, garlic and celery until tender, about 2-3 minutes. Add beans, 8 cups water, 2 cups chicken stock, Chile/red bell peppers, plum tomatoes, juice, oregano, cumin, salt and pepper to taste. Cover pot to cook at simmer for 1 hour, or until beans are tender.

Remove 2 cups of black beans and set aside. In a blender, purée the pot of soup a cupful or two at a time. Return puréed chili to pot; stir in the 2 cups cooked beans (not puréed). Stir in cilantro and lime juice and simmer chili for 30 minutes, stirring occasionally. This chili may be frozen or cooked several days in advance and refrigerated. Heat thoroughly before serving. Serve with tortilla chips and Guacamole Dip (see page 50). Serves 4-6.

SAUSAGE CHILI

[A Cooking Hint: Many recipes may be partially or entirely prepared well in advance to serving. Accordingly, you will be able to allow time for food preparation.]
(Prepare brown rice in advance. Add saffron to rice.)

2 tbsp. olive oil

6 links of Italian sweet pork sausage

    (For a spicier taste, include 2 or 3 hot sausage links)

$\frac{1}{2}$ lb. lean chopped beef, crumbled

1 can (1 lb.) red kidney beans, rinsed in cold water, drained

$1\frac{1}{2}$ cups prepared tomato sauce ($\frac{1}{4}$ cup water, if needed)

1 small green bell pepper, deseeded, chopped

1 small red bell pepper, deseeded, chopped

1 small chili pepper, deseeded, chopped (Wear plastic gloves when handling hot pepper.)

2 garlic cloves, minced

1 onion, chopped

3-4 white mushrooms (about 1 cup), chopped

2 ears corn, each cut into 4 pieces

1 cup cooked brown rice

$\frac{1}{2}$ tsp. salt

$\frac{1}{4}$ tsp. black pepper

1 tbsp. chili powder

a pinch of saffron to cook with brown rice

1 cup sharp Cheddar cheese in small cubes

$\frac{1}{4}$ cup Tequila

    Have ready: a large skillet with cover.

    Warm olive oil over moderate heat; brown sausage links on all sides. Remove sausages to a plate and set aside. Add crumbled chopped beef and all peppers and onion to pan and cook, stirring frequently, for 4-5 minutes, scraping bottom of pan to prevent leavings from sticking. Stir in tomato sauce, garlic, mushrooms, corn pieces, salt, black pepper and chili powder and simmer for 5 minutes. Cut sausages into 1-inch chunks and return to chili mixture. Stir in kidney beans and cooked saffron- seasoned brown rice. Stir in $\frac{1}{4}$ cup water if needed. Dot surface with Cheddar cheese and cover pan; continue to simmer 2-3 minutes longer. Stir in Tequila. Serve hot with tortilla chips. Serves 4.

MULLIGAN STEW

[A Cooking Hint: Stew-type dishes taste even better when leftovers are reheated.
Hint: cook double stew quantity and freeze half for another meal.]
(A version of an Irish Stew, served as a St. Patrick's Day dinner.)

3 lbs. lean beef for stew, cut into 1-inch cubes

1 tsp. salt

$\frac{1}{2}$ tsp. freshly ground black pepper

$\frac{3}{4}$ cup all-purpose flour, divided

2 tbsp. olive oil, divided

3 large carrots, pared, sliced into narrow rounds

2 cups turnips (1 medium-size), pared, cut into 1-inch chunks

1 large white onion, finely sliced

1 cup fresh or frozen peas

3 all-purpose potatoes, pared, each halved, then cut into $\frac{1}{2}$-inch slices

1 can (6 oz.) tomato paste, stirred into 1 cup hot water

$1\frac{1}{2}$-2 cups water, divided

1 cup stout

2 bay leaves

Have ready: a 6-quart ovenproof casserole pan.

Sprinkle beef cubes with salt and pepper. Dredge seasoned beef cubes in $\frac{1}{2}$ cup flour, coating thoroughly. Heat 1 tablespoon olive oil in a 6-quart ovenproof casserole pan. Brown meat on all sides over medium-high heat. Use more oil as needed. Set aside.

Pour $\frac{1}{2}$ cup water into the casserole pan and scrape bottom of pan to loosen any leavings. Return beef to casserole. Add enough water to cover meat by 1 inch. Bring to a boil and cook for 5 minutes. Reduce heat and simmer for 2 hours. Skim the stew with a paper towel (discard).

Add carrots, turnips, onion, potatoes and tomato paste stirred into 1 cup hot water; season with additional salt, pepper as desired. Lay 2 bay leaves across surface of stew. Simmer stew until vegetables are tender, about 45 minutes, adding water as necessary to just cover the stew. In last 15 minutes, stir in peas.

In a small bowl, combine remaining $\frac{1}{4}$ cup flour with $\frac{1}{2}$ cup of the cooking liquid and whisk into a smooth paste. Stir this mixture into the stew. Stir in stout and simmer for an additional 10 minutes. Remove and discard bay leaves. Serves 6.

TURKEY STEW

[A Cooking Hint: Stew-type dishes taste even better when leftovers are reheated.
Hint: cook double stew quantity and freeze half for another meal.]

4 links sweet Italian sausage, with fennel seed

3-4 tbsp. olive oil, divided

2 cups water

2 turkey legs

1 red onion, chopped

1 large celery stalk, chopped

3-4 garlic cloves, minced

1 tbsp. dried thyme leaves

1 tsp. sage leaves

2 bay leaves

$\frac{1}{2}$ tsp. salt, or to taste

$\frac{1}{2}$ tsp. freshly ground black pepper

1 can (28 oz.) peeled tomatoes with juice

1 dozen-15 Brussels sprouts, each cut in half

1 cup white wine, like Pinot Blanc

4-5 medium-to-large sweet potatoes, pared,
    cut into chunks

$\frac{1}{2}$ tsp. ground cinnamon

$\frac{1}{4}$ tsp. ground cloves

1 tsp. brown sugar

2 tbsp. butter or Smart Balance

1 tbsp. fresh cilantro, minced

Have ready: a large skillet with a cover; a large buttered 9x12 casserole dish; a sheet of foil.

First prepare whipped sweet potatoes. Simmer pared sweet potato chunks in a saucepan with just enough water to cover, for 10-15 minutes until tender. Drain. Pour them into a large bowl. Add cinnamon, cloves, brown sugar, butter (or Smart Balance). Put them through a ricer; then, whisk to make smooth. Spoon whipped sweet potatoes around a buttered 9x12 casserole dish, leaving a wide space at center. Set aside.

Heat 2 tablespoons olive oil in a large skillet and cook sausages over moderate heat, on all sides, about 8-10 minutes. Transfer to a plate and refrigerate sausages while you continue the preparation.

In same skillet, over moderate heat, cook onion, celery and garlic, scraping bottom of pan to remove leavings. Add 1-2 tablespoons more oil; add turkey legs and cook them on both sides, 10 minutes on each side, until turkey is lightly browned.

Scrape bottom of skillet; stir in tomatoes with juice, 1 cup white wine, thyme, sage, salt, pepper and bay leaves. Place lid on top of turkey in skillet and continue to cook at moderate-low for another 20 minutes, turning over turkey legs. Add a little more wine if sauce begins to dry. Stir halved Brussels sprouts into sauce; replace lid and cook the turkey and vegetables for an additional 7-8 minutes, until sprouts are just tender. (Do not overcook.) Remove skillet from burner. Remove turkey legs and slice meat from legs, returning meat to vegetable/sauce skillet.

Preheat oven to 325°.

Remove sausages from refrigerator and quarter each sausage into lengthwise strips. Add sausages to vegetable/sauce/turkey skillet. With the aid of a large spatula and a serving spoon, carefully transfer the contents in the skillet to the center of the 9x12 casserole dish with a border of whipped sweet potatoes.

Loosely lay a sheet of foil over casserole dish and bake in preheated oven at 325° for 15-18 minutes. Remove and discard bay leaves. Sprinkle sweet potatoes with minced cilantro. Serves 4.

"CAPTAINS COURAGEOUS" CHICKEN STEW

[A Cooking Hint: In the actual preparation of a recipe, place all of the ingredients and utensils atop your work counter.]

$\frac{1}{2}$ cup all-purpose flour

$\frac{1}{2}$ tsp. salt

$\frac{1}{2}$ tsp. freshly ground black pepper

1 large broiler chicken, rinsed in cold water, patted dry and cut into 12 pieces;
    or 12 assorted pieces: thighs, breast halves, legs

$\frac{1}{4}$ cup canola oil

1 large onion, thinly sliced

1 green bell pepper, deseeded, thinly sliced

1 red bell pepper, deseeded, thinly sliced

2-3 garlic cloves, minced

2 Portobello mushrooms, rinsed, patted dry, each sliced into $\frac{1}{2}$-inch pieces

3 large sweet potatoes or yams, pared, each cut lengthwise, into 4 pieces

1 can (1 lb.) stewing tomatoes

$\frac{1}{2}$ cup sweet vermouth

$1\frac{1}{2}$ tsp. curry powder

$\frac{1}{2}$ tsp. dried thyme leaves

$\frac{1}{4}$ cup currants

$\frac{1}{4}$ cup chopped almonds with skin

Preheat oven to 350°.

Have ready: a large skillet and a large 10x15x4-inch oiled roasting pan.

Combine flour, salt and pepper in a large flat dish. Coat chicken pieces in the flour mixture. Heat oil in a large skillet over medium heat. Cook chicken on all sides, about 2-3 minutes a turn, until evenly browned. Remove from skillet to an oiled 10x15x4-inch roasting pan. Set aside.

Reduce heat in skillet to low and add onion, peppers, garlic, curry powder and thyme. Stir in tomatoes, currants and sweet vermouth; cook sauce for 5 minutes, scraping bottom of skillet to remove any leavings.

Add sliced sweet potatoes and Portobellos to roasting pan with chicken. Spoon sauce all over chicken and vegetables. Sprinkle almonds over top. Bake casserole in preheated oven, uncovered, for 25-30 minutes, or until potatoes are tender. Add a little more vermouth if sauce becomes too thick. Serves 6.

VENISON STEW
("I'm Game!")

$\frac{1}{4}$ cup all-purpose flour

$\frac{1}{2}$ tsp. salt

$\frac{1}{2}$ tsp. freshly ground black pepper

1 tbsp. dried oregano

3 lbs. venison (or beef chuck), cut into 1-inch cubes

$\frac{1}{4}$ cup olive oil

1 cup hearty Burgundy wine; water as needed

2 cups canned crushed tomatoes

1 large onion, thinly sliced

2 large carrots, pared, sliced in thin rounds

2 celery stalks, cut into small chunks

6 baby bella mushrooms, rinsed, trimmed, halved or quartered

3-4 large potatoes, pared, cut into small chunks

1 cup fresh or frozen peas

1 tbsp. fresh parsley, chopped

2 bay leaves

Have ready: a large stew pot with a cover.

Season flour with salt, pepper and oregano. Dredge venison (or beef) in the seasoned flour.

Heat oil in a large stew pot over medium-high. Add meat and brown on all sides.
Add tomatoes, onion, carrots, celery and mushrooms. Pour wine over meat mixture in pot and add
enough water to cover ingredients by 1 inch. Lay 2 bay leaves across top. Bring stew to a boil.
Cover and reduce heat to simmer; cook for 45 minutes, adding more Burgundy (or water)
as necessary, to keep meat well covered.

Stir in potato chunks and continue to simmer for 35 minutes. Add peas and simmer an
additional 10 minutes. Taste and adjust seasonings, if needed. Remove bay leaves and discard.
Ladle stew into bowls and sprinkle with chopped parsley. Serve with hearty artisan bread and
Burgundy wine. Serves 6.

SAUSAGE AND CAULIFLOWER STEW

*[A Cooking Hint: A little lemon juice added to cauliflower cooking water will keep the
florets white. Adding a piece of bread to the water will reduce the cooking odor.
Over-cooking cauliflower will discolor it.]*

2 tbsp. olive oil

4-6 links sweet Italian pork sausages

1 head cauliflower, rinsed, drained, cut into florets (You may use orange cauliflower,
    in season.)

2 cups Homemade Chicken Broth (see page 81); or packaged low-salt chicken broth

1 large ripe tomato, finely chopped, with juice

1½ tsp. dried oregano

½ tsp. salt, to taste

½ tsp. freshly ground black pepper

1 cup feta cheese, crumbled

2 cups fine unseasoned bread crumbs

2 tbsp. olive oil

Preheat oven to 350°.

Have ready: a 9x12-inch oil-greased baking pan; a sheet of aluminum foil.

Brown sausages on all sides in hot oil in a skillet at medium-high
for 5-7 minutes. Cut each cooked sausage into 2-3 chunks. Place cauliflower
florets in a 9x12 oil-greased pan. Pour broth over cauliflower.
Sprinkle with chopped tomato, oregano, salt and pepper and toss well.
Arrange sausage chunks in the pan with cauliflower. Sprinkle feta
cheese and toss well. Cover pan with a sheet of foil and bake in
preheated oven at 350° for 45 minutes. Remove foil and continue
to bake until cauliflower is tender, about 30 minutes longer.

In a small bowl, toss bread crumbs with 2 tablespoons olive oil.
Sprinkle crumbs over the sausage/cauliflower. Bake until crumbs are
golden brown, an additional 15-20 minutes. Serves 4.

BEEF STEW WITH DUMPLINGS

[A Cooking Hint: Stew-type dishes taste even better when leftovers are reheated.
Cook double the stew quantity and freeze half for another meal.]

STEW:

3 lbs. lean boneless beef for stew,
    in 1-inch cubes
6 tbsp. flour
1 tsp. salt
½ tsp. black pepper
1-2 onions, coarsely chopped
1 green bell pepper, deseeded, cut into strips
¼ cup olive oil in 2 parts: (2 tbsp., 2 tbsp.)

2 cups canned beef broth, low-salt variety
1 cup light dry red wine, like Chianti
    or Sangiovaise
2 bay leaves
(1 dozen white mushrooms, trimmed, rinsed,
    halved) – added near conclusion of recipe
1 cup boiling water, if necessary

DUMPLINGS:

3½ cups fresh bread, in coarse crumbs (a mix
    of wheat and white bread)
3 tbsp. water
2 eggs or ½ cup egg substitute, lightly beaten
1 medium-size onion, finely chopped

1 tbsp. fresh finely chopped parsley
½ tsp. ground mace
¼ tsp. salt
¼ tsp. black pepper

Have ready: a large heavy skillet and a large deep ovenproof casserole pan with a cover.

Prepare the STEW. Combine flour, salt and pepper in a medium-size bowl. Toss beef pieces in flour mixture, a small bunch at a time, until they are well coated. Set aside.

Heat 2 tablespoons olive oil in a large heavy skillet over moderate heat. Cook onions and peppers, stirring occasionally, until softened. Remove onions mix from pan with a slotted spoon and transfer them to a large ovenproof casserole with cover. Add remaining olive oil to skillet and increase to high heat. Cook the coated beef in hot oil a batch at a time, until browned on all sides. As beef browns, remove and add beef to casserole with onions mix.

Pour beef broth into skillet and stir over moderate heat, scraping the bottom and sides of the pan to loosen any leavings. Add this broth to the casserole along with wine and bay leaves. Cover casserole and cook in preheated oven at 325° for 2 hours.

As the casserole cooks, Prepare the DUMPLINGS. Pour bread crumbs into a medium-size bowl and add just enough water to moisten. Add beaten eggs, plus salt, pepper, parsley, onion and mace; mix thoroughly. Season with more salt and pepper if desired. Roll the mix between the palms of your hands and form balls, 2 inches in diameter.

After 2 hours, remove casserole from oven and stir in the mushrooms. Stir in, 1 cup boiling water, if needed. Scatter dumplings evenly over the surface of the stew so that they are partially submerged. Return stew to oven and continue to cook, covered, for an additional 30 minutes. Remove bay leaves and discard before serving. Serves 6.

STEW OF SCALLOPS, ZUCCHINI AND CANNELLINI
[A Cooking Hint: In the actual preparation, place all of the required ingredients and utensils atop your work counter.]

24 large sea scallops (about 1½ lbs.), rinsed in cold water, drained

2 tbsp. olive oil

½ cup white wine, like Chablis

2 medium-size zucchini, rinsed, trimmed,
    cut lengthwise into slivers (mandoline-sliced)

4 scallions with some greens, chopped

juice of 1 lemon

¼ cup fresh cilantro, minced

1 tbsp. Dijon mustard

1 tsp. ground cumin

1 can (1 lb.) cannellini beans, rinsed in cold water, drained

salt and freshly ground black pepper to taste

cilantro sprigs for garnish

Have ready: a large skillet.

Place scallops in a large bowl; squeeze juice from 1 lemon over them and sprinkle with cilantro, cumin, mustard, pepper and salt. Toss to coat thoroughly.

Heat 2 tablespoons olive oil in a large skillet at moderate-high. Cook marinated scallops in hot oil about 3 minutes on each side. Pour wine over scallops and heat thoroughly for an additional minute. Transfer scallops to a bowl; set aside.

Add a little more oil to skillet, if needed; cook zucchini and scallions at moderate-high for 2-3 minutes, tossing the vegetables and scraping bottom of skillet with a spatula. Return scallops and juices to skillet; add rinsed and drained cannellini and toss to mix thoroughly. Heat through for an additional 3-4 minutes. Serve directly out of skillet; garnish with sprigs of cilantro. Serves 4.

GUMBO

6 live blue crabs, water to cook crabs
2 whole chicken legs
$\frac{1}{4}$ cup olive oil, divided (2 tbsp., 2 tbsp.)
$\frac{1}{2}$ cup all-purpose flour
1 large yellow onion, finely sliced
1 large green bell pepper, trimmed, deseeded, finely sliced
1 large red bell pepper, trimmed, deseeded, finely sliced
4 links chorizo sausage, cut into chunks
1 lb. okra, trimmed, sliced
2 bay leaves
$\frac{1}{2}$ tsp. salt
$\frac{1}{2}$ tsp. freshly ground black pepper
cayenne pepper to taste
4 cups water (or enough water to cover)
$1\frac{1}{2}$ cups white rice in 3 cups water

Have ready: a large pot; a large skillet; tongs; a wooden mallet.

Half-fill a large pot with water and bring to a boil over high heat. With tongs, add crabs to boiling water and cook until their color brightens, about 5 minutes. Drain and set crabs aside to cool.

Heat 2 tablespoons olive oil in large skillet over high heat. Sauté chicken on all sides until light brown, 3-4 minutes per side. Remove chicken to a large pot.

Heat remaining 2 tablespoons olive oil in same skillet. Sprinkle flour on oil to form a paste, stirring continuously, until paste is tan in color, about 15 minutes. Remove skillet from heat and mix in half of the sliced onion and peppers. Set skillet aside.

Clean crabs by removing large shell and the inside gills. Add the cleaned crabs to the chicken pot. Stir in sausage, okra, remaining sliced onion and peppers and bay leaves. Add enough water to cover, about 4 cups, and bring to a boil. Reduce heat and simmer, covered, for 1 hour.

Slowly stir $\frac{1}{2}$ cup of hot gumbo broth into the skillet containing the flour paste and vegetables. Stir to eliminate any lumps. Pour this mixture back into the gumbo pot, stirring continuously. Season with salt, black pepper and cayenne, to taste. Simmer until vegetables dissolve into a thick stew, about 3 hours.

(Meanwhile, during last half-hour of cooking, prepare white rice by simmering $1\frac{1}{2}$ cups white rice in 3 cups boiling water for 25 minutes, or until water is absorbed.)

Remove chicken from pot and discard skin and bones; return chicken meat to pot. Remove crabs and break them up with a wooden mallet; return crab pieces to pot. Skim off any surface fat from pot. Discard bay leaves. Serve gumbo into individual bowls over white rice. Serves 6-8.

ARROZ CON POLLO

*[A Cooking Hint: Preheat broiler or oven prior to roasting, baking or broiling.
Accurate temperatures provide accurate results.]*

a 3-3½ lb. chicken, cut into serving pieces; or
    2-4 chicken legs, 2-4 thighs,
    one chicken breast, split (each half, cut in
    half) and a pair of wings
¼ cup (plus 1 tbsp.) olive oil, in 2 parts
    (¼ cup, 1 tbsp.)
½ tsp. black pepper
1 tsp. salt
⅛ tsp. cayenne pepper, or to taste
1 large onion, coarsely chopped
3-4 garlic cloves, minced
1½ cups low-salt chicken broth (for Homemade
    Chicken Broth, see page 81)
1 can (1 lb.) plum tomatoes, mashed with a fork
½ cup white rice
½ cup brown rice

½ cup water (more salt/pepper if needed)
½ cup white wine
¼ tsp. red pepper flakes (optional, to taste)
¼ tsp. ground saffron
2 bay leaves
1 red bell pepper, deseeded, sliced into strips
1 green bell pepper, deseeded, sliced into strips
1 yellow bell pepper, deseeded, sliced
    into strips
1 orange bell pepper, deseeded, sliced
    into strips
1 doz. baby bella mushrooms, trimmed, rinsed,
    leave whole, or halve them

Preheat oven 350°.

Have ready: a large skillet, a large 9x15-inch ovenproof casserole pan (with cover, or foil
to cover).

Season chicken pieces with salt and black/cayenne peppers. Heat ¼ cup olive oil in a large
skillet over moderate heat. Add chicken, a few pieces at a time, and cook, turning once, until
golden brown, about 5 minutes on each side.

Remove chicken to a large 9x15 ovenproof pan. Add onion and garlic to the skillet and cook
until softened, about 3 minutes. Add broth, water, wine, pepper flakes, saffron, bay leaves,
tomatoes and rice. Season with more salt and pepper (if needed) and bring to a boil. Pour this
liquid mixture over the chicken in the pan. Cover the pan with its own cover (or make a cover
with aluminum foil). Bake in preheated oven, at 350° for 25 minutes, until rice is tender and
chicken is done.

Meanwhile, heat remaining 1 tablespoon olive oil in skillet; add all of the peppers and cook
for 5 minutes, tossing peppers to cook, until they are just tender. You may wish to cook them in
batches. Transfer peppers to the chicken and rice casserole and serve at once. Serves 4-6.

SPICY POT ROAST AND TRIMMINGS

[A Cooking Hint: Before commencing a cooking project, maintain a reminder list for food purchases and preparation scheduling.]

3 lbs. beef chuck roast

2 tsp. ground cumin

1 tsp. ground coriander

1 tsp. Hungarian paprika

$\frac{1}{2}$ tsp. salt

$\frac{1}{2}$ tsp. freshly ground black pepper

3 tbsp. olive oil

2 large onions, thinly sliced

5 garlic cloves, chopped

3 large carrots, pared, cut into 2-inch chunks

6 small Red Bliss potatoes, scrubbed, halved

2 cups dry red wine, like Burgundy or Cabernet Sauvignon

1 cup prepared tomato sauce

$\frac{1}{2}$ cup balsamic vinegar

$1\frac{1}{2}$ cups low-salt beef stock

$\frac{1}{2}$ cup white raisins

2 tsp. brown sugar

Preheat oven to 250°.

Have ready: a large Dutch oven.

Combine cumin, coriander, paprika, salt and pepper and sprinkle all over roast. Pour 3 tablespoons olive oil into a large Dutch oven and set over medium-high heat. Brown the meat in the hot oil on all sides, about 5 minutes a turn. Once the meat is nicely browned, set roast aside on a large platter.

Put onions and garlic into the same Dutch oven and cook over medium heat for about 5-6 minutes until onions are translucent and slightly caramelized. Add carrots and potatoes and turn up heat to medium-high.

Pour in red wine, tomato sauce, vinegar and beef stock. Bring to a boil; then, reduce heat and cook for 5 minutes. Turn heat off and add raisins and brown sugar.

Return the roast to the Dutch oven and cover tightly. Make certain roast is submerged in juices and vegetables half-way up its sides. If needed, add more beef stock. Place Dutch oven into preheated 250° oven and cook for 3 to $3\frac{1}{2}$ hours, checking halfway through the cooking that there is enough liquid in the pot. (Add more beef stock, if needed.)

When the roast is "fork tender", remove from oven and allow it to rest for $\frac{1}{2}$ hour. Then, slice meat on a platter. Remove vegetables with juices to another platter. Pour sauce over sliced meat and serve with the vegetables. Serves 4-6.

ROASTED CORNISH HENS WITH ROSEMARY AND WINE

(This entire dinner, hens and vegetables, may be simultaneously prepared and roasted in the oven at 425°. Place the roasting pan on a rack in the center of the oven. On an overhead rack, in the same oven, place the three 5x7-inch pans plus the foil package. Mushrooms exit after 6-8 minutes; Asparagus after 8 minutes; Carrots after 15 minutes; and Potatoes after 25 minutes. Remove Cornish hens after 50-55 minutes of roasting.
Transfer all of the roasted vegetables to the large roasting pan with the roasted hens, surrounding the hens with sections of assorted roasted vegetables.)

2 Cornish hens

1 cup dry red wine, like Chianti or Sangiovaise

$\frac{1}{4}$ cup olive oil

2 tbsp. rosemary leaves, chopped

1 tsp. cracked black pepper

$\frac{1}{4}$ cup *lite* soy sauce

juice of 1 lemon

4 garlic cloves, minced

salt to taste

Preheat oven to 425°.
Have ready: a large roaster pan 14x18x3$\frac{1}{2}$; brush bottom of pan with olive oil.

In a small bowl, combine wine, oil, *lite* soy sauce, lemon juice, rosemary, minced garlic, salt and cracked pepper. Lay hens breast-side up, in oiled roaster pan and brush them with half of the wine/oil mix. Reserve remainder of dressing. Roast hens for 30 minutes at 425°. Then, brush hens with remainder of dressing and return to oven for another 20-25 minutes (or until meat thermometer inserted in thickest part of thigh registers 175°); a total of 50-55 minutes.
Serves 4-6 directly from the roaster pan.

. . . .

ROASTED YUKON GOLD POTATOES

2 lbs. tiny potatoes (like Yukon Gold),
    scrubbed, halved or quartered (Place cut
    potatoes in bowl of cold water as you
    prepare basting sauce.)

1 small white onion. chopped

$\frac{1}{4}$ cup slivered sun dried tomatoes

$\frac{1}{2}$ green bell pepper, deseeded, cut into thin
    slices (Finely chop other half and reserve.)

$\frac{1}{4}$ cup olive oil

$\frac{1}{2}$ tsp. black pepper

$\frac{1}{4}$ tsp. salt

1 tsp. dried oregano

$\frac{1}{4}$ tsp. cayenne pepper

Preheat oven 425°.
Mix potatoes, onions, sliced peppers and sun dried tomatoes in a bowl. Combine oil, salt, oregano and black/cayenne peppers and pour over potato mix. Toss to mix thoroughly. Pour into 5x7 pan and roast in oven for 25-30 minutes. Garnish with chopped green pepper. Serves 4-6.
(Recipe continues on following page)

(Recipe continued from page 124)

ROASTED CARROTS WITH BALSAMIC VINEGAR

10-12 fresh slender carrots, pared, leave whole (if carrot is thick, halve lengthwise)
$\frac{1}{4}$ cup olive oil
2 tbsp. balsamic vinegar
$\frac{1}{4}$ tsp. black pepper
salt to taste

    Preheat oven 425°.
    Lay whole carrots in a 5x7 pan. Blend oil, pepper. vinegar and salt. Brush carrots with this mix and roast them in the oven at 425° for 15 minutes, until just tender and lightly browned. An inserted toothpick, should slip out easily. Serves 4-6.

ROASTED GARLIC-ASPARAGUS

12-15 thick spears asparagus, trim bottom ends, rinse, drain
$\frac{1}{4}$ cup olive oil
6-8 garlic cloves, leave whole
$\frac{1}{4}$ tsp. black pepper
salt to taste

    Preheat oven to 425°.
    Lay asparagus spears in a 5x7 pan. Scatter garlic cloves over asparagus. Make a mix with oil, salt and pepper and brush this mix over asparagus and garlic. Roast in preheated oven at 425° for 8-10 minutes. Serves 4-6.

ROASTED WHITE MUSHROOMS AND RED PEPPERS

1 dozen-15 white small-medium mushrooms, trimmed, rinsed, drained
1 small red bell pepper, deseeded, chopped
$\frac{1}{4}$ tsp. black pepper
dash of salt
2 garlic cloves, minced
$\frac{1}{4}$ cup olive oil

    Preheat oven to 425°.
    Cut 2 sheets aluminum foil 9x12 (double them). Lay mushrooms, garlic and red pepper on the foil; bring up the sides to create a package. Drizzle oil, pepper and salt mix over the mushrooms, pepper and garlic and form a bundle with the foil, leaving top of package opened. Roast in preheated oven at 425° for 6-8 minutes. Serves 4-6.
(Conclusion of: ROASTED CORNISH HENS WITH ROSEMARY/WINE)

HAM AND POTATO IN SWISS

6 all-purpose potatoes, peeled, thinly sliced; set aside in a bowl of cold water

1 large onion, thinly sliced

6 slices boiled ham (about 4x6 inches), cut into long strips

1 cup ricotta

½ tsp. salt

¼ tsp. freshly ground black pepper

2 tbsp. unsalted butter or Smart Balance spread

3 cups low-fat milk (or use low-fat evaporated milk)

4-6 slices Swiss cheese (about 4x6 inches), cut into long strips

1 tbsp. fresh parsley, minced

4-6 large slices seeded rye bread; cut each in half

more butter or Smart Balance to spread on rye bread

Preheat oven to 375°.

Have ready: a buttered 2-quart casserole dish.

Butter bottom and sides of 2-quart casserole dish. Alternately layer potatoes, onion, ham and ricotta in the prepared casserole dish. Season each layer with salt and pepper to taste. Dot top layer with 2 tablespoons butter or Smart Balance; pour milk over the top. Bake casserole in preheated oven at 375° for 1 hour to 1 hour 15 minutes, until potatoes are tender. Insert a toothpick into potatoes to test for tenderness.

Arrange Swiss cheese strips in a lattice design on top of casserole. Continue baking until top is slightly browned, about 15-20 minutes. Lightly toast pieces of rye bread. Butter the toast. Insert edges of toasts into surface of casserole. Sprinkle with parsley. Serves 5-6.

A Housewarming with Friends.

VEAL/EGGPLANT PARMAGIANO

[A Cooking Hint: To oil or grease pans or skillets, spray or lightly coat with canola oil or olive oil; or Smart Balance spread. You will use less fat and enjoy a healthier recipe.]

6 veal cutlets, pounded thin

2 eggs or $\frac{1}{2}$ cup egg substitute

2 cups finely ground unseasoned Italian bread crumbs

salt, freshly ground black pepper, to taste

$\frac{1}{2}$ cup olive oil, divided ($\frac{1}{4}$ cup, $\frac{1}{4}$ cup)

1-2 eggplants, each about $3\frac{1}{2}$ inches in diameter; cut each lengthwise
    in $\frac{1}{4}$-inch-thick slices (about 10-12 slices)

2 cups homemade marinara sauce (see page 393 ff); or use packaged brand

2 tbsp. olive oil

6 slices prosciutto, very thinly sliced

2 tbsp. fresh parsley, chopped

6 fresh basil leaves

$\frac{1}{2}$ cup Parmesan cheese, grated

$\frac{1}{2}$ lb. mozzarella cheese, shredded

Preheat oven to 350°.
Have ready: a 9x13x3-inch baking pan; and a large skillet.

Pour bread crumbs on a flat plate.
In a shallow bowl, beat eggs (or egg substitute) with salt, pepper and chopped parsley, until foamy. Dip each veal cutlet in beaten egg and then, dredge in bread crumbs.

Over medium-high, heat $\frac{1}{4}$ cup olive oil in a large skillet. Fry breaded veal cutlets, one at a time, until golden, about 3 minutes on each side. Drain cutlets on paper towels.

Drain skillet of oil and wipe bottom of skillet with paper towel; over medium heat warm fresh $\frac{1}{4}$ cup olive oil in skillet. Fry eggplant slices, a couple at a time for 2-3 minutes on each side, until golden. Drain on paper towel. Add additional oil to skillet as needed, until all eggplant slices are cooked.

Cover bottom of 9x13x3 baking pan with $\frac{1}{2}$ cup of tomato sauce; sprinkle sauce with 1 tablespoon Parmesan cheese. Lay cooked cutlets in the pan, overlapping them to fit in the pan. Spoon another $\frac{1}{2}$ cup sauce over cutlets and sprinkle with 2 tablespoons Parmesan cheese. Top each cutlet with a layer of prosciutto, followed by a layer of overlapping eggplant (use all of the slices). Spoon remainder of sauce over pan; sprinkle remainder of Parmesan and the shredded mozzarella. Bake casserole in preheated oven at 350° for 30 minutes, until mozzarella has melted and is golden in color. Lay basil leaves over top of casserole. Cut into wedges when serving. Serves 4-6. Serve with a side of POTATO GNOCCHI (see page 217) or RICOTTA GNOCCHI (see page 217).

RED PEPPERS, ARTICHOKES AND SAUSAGES WITH FETTUCCINI

2 tbsp. olive oil

4 garlic cloves, chopped

4-5 links sweet Italian sausage with fennel, cut into 2-inch chunks

2 cups whole artichoke hearts, unseasoned, frozen or canned; drained
   (If artichokes are frozen, simmer them in water as directed on
   package, *before* commencing with this recipe.)

4 sweet red peppers, deseeded; each quartered, lengthwise

6 baby bella mushrooms, rinsed, drained, sliced

$\frac{1}{2}$ cup pitted oil-cured olives

1 tbsp. dried oregano

3-4 fresh basil leaves

$\frac{1}{4}$ tsp. freshly ground black pepper

$\frac{1}{2}$ tsp. salt

a pinch of hot red pepper flakes (Wear plastic gloves when handling hot pepper.)

$\frac{1}{2}$ cup dry white wine, like a Pinot Blanc

1 lb. fettuccini

$\frac{1}{2}$ cup Asiago cheese, grated

4-5 sprigs basil, for garnish

Have ready: a large skillet with a cover; a large pasta pot.

Start to boil salted water in a large pasta pot.

In a large skillet, over medium-high, brown garlic and sausage chunks in olive oil.
As sausages cook, add quartered peppers and mushrooms to the skillet. With the aid of a thin
spatula, move sausages and vegetables in skillet to prevent sticking; continue to cook for a total
of 4-5 minutes. Lower heat to medium; stir 1 can (or cooked and drained) artichoke hearts, wine,
olives, all spices and herbs. Cook for 2-3 minutes longer. Cover pot and turn off heat.

As you cook the ragout, and when the pasta water comes to a boil, add fettuccini and cook
al dente as directed on package. Drain pasta and prepare portions on 4-5 dinner plates. Spoon
sausage/vegetable ragout over each portion of fettuccini. Garnish with a generous serving of
grated Asiago cheese and a sprig of basil. Serve immediately. Serves 4-5.

BEEF AND BROCCOLI
(Serve with a side of steamed white rice.)

1 lb. flank steak, thinly sliced across the grain

1 egg

1 tbsp. dry white wine

1 tsp. *lite* soy sauce

1 tsp. cornstarch

1 tbsp. peanut oil

dash of salt

$\frac{1}{8}$ tsp. freshly ground black pepper

3 cups broccoli florets, rinsed, drained

$1\frac{1}{2}$ tsp. cornstarch mixed with 1 tbsp. cold water

$\frac{1}{4}$ cup canola oil for wok frying

SAUCE:

3 tbsp. *lite* soy sauce

1 tbsp. dry white wine

1 tsp. sesame oil

$\frac{1}{2}$ tsp. honey

$\frac{1}{4}$ cup chicken broth (Prepare by mashing
    1 low-salt chicken bouillon cube into $\frac{1}{4}$ cup boiling water.)

We Welcome Fargo to our Table of Plenty. Photo: C. Celenza

Have ready: a large wok.

Prepare the marinade by combining egg, wine, soy sauce, cornstarch, peanut oil, salt and pepper. Lay sliced flank steak in a shallow bowl and pour marinade over beef. Allow to marinate for 30 minutes.

Combine all of the sauce ingredients in a small bowl and set aside.

In a wok (or deep skillet) over high heat, warm $\frac{1}{4}$ cup canola oil. When very hot, add beef with marinade and stir-fry for 30 seconds, until beef changes color. Remove beef from heat and drain on paper towels. Make sure oil in wok is still hot (add a little more oil if needed). Add broccoli to wok and stir-fry for 20 seconds. Remove broccoli from heat and drain on paper towels.

Drain oil from wok. Reheat wok and add sauce ingredients. Bring sauce to a boil over high heat. Add beef and broccoli, stirring for about 10 seconds to warm the ingredients. Stir in cornstarch paste and stir until sauce thickens. Serve with steamed rice which you may prepare beforehand. (Keep rice warm, over hot water.) Serves 2.

VEAL AND PEPPERS IN A WINE SAUCE

2 tbsp. olive oil
2 lbs. boneless veal cubes
1 small onion, chopped
$1\frac{1}{2}$ cups prepared tomato sauce
1 large carrot, shredded
4 Italian green fryer peppers, deseeded,
    quartered lengthwise
6 porcini mushrooms, trimmed, rinsed, sliced

1 tbsp. dried oregano
1 bay leaf
$\frac{1}{2}$ tsp. salt
$\frac{1}{4}$ tsp. freshly ground black pepper
$\frac{1}{2}$ cup light red wine,
    like Chianti or Sangiovaise
seasoned toasted bread crisps, Bowtie pasta
    as accompaniments

Have ready: a large heavy skillet with cover.
In a large, heavy skillet, lightly brown onion and veal in olive oil at moderate heat, scraping bottom of pan to prevent sticking. Lower to simmer; stir in tomato sauce, peppers, carrots, mushrooms, herbs and spices. Cover pot and cook to simmer for 30 minutes. Stir in wine and continue to cook stew for another 10 minutes. Serve with seasoned bread crisps and a side of Bowtie pasta. Serves 4.

PASTA E SARDE

2 tbsp. olive oil
1 large onion, chopped
1 long Italian green pepper, deseeded, chopped
1 can (6 oz.) tomato paste,
    dissolved in $1\frac{1}{2}$ cup hot water
1 doz. fresh sardines, heads and bones removed
$\frac{1}{4}$ cup dried oregano
$\frac{1}{4}$ cup pignola (pine nuts)

$\frac{1}{4}$ cup golden raisins
freshly ground black pepper to taste
a pinch of hot pepper flakes
$\frac{1}{2}$ cup chopped pitted black olives
salt to taste
1 lb. spaghetti, linguine or bucatini
$\frac{1}{2}$ cup fine bread crumbs

Have ready: a large skillet, a pasta pot.
Sauté pepper and onion in oil in a large skillet at medium heat and cook until softened, about 4-5 minutes. Add and stir in diluted tomato paste and sardines and cook until fish flakes and turns white on inside, 3 minutes more. Add oregano, pignola, raisins, olives, black pepper, hot pepper flakes and salt to taste.
Bring a large pasta pot of water to a boil. Cook pasta al dente, as directed on package. Remove sardine sauce from burner and place in a large serving bowl. Drain pasta; add pasta to bowl with sardines sauce and toss to mix thoroughly. Divide pasta/sauce among 4-5 bowls; sprinkle bowls with bread crumbs. Serves 4-5.

WARM CREAMY PASTA, CHICKEN AND BROCCOLI

3-4 cups broccoli florets, rinsed in cold water, drained. Place broccoli florets in steamer strainer and set aside.

$2\frac{1}{2}$-3 cups cooked boneless chicken breasts and thighs, thinly sliced into strips (*NOTE: below)

1 lb. whole wheat penne rigati, salad-size

1 large celery stalk, with greens, finely chopped

1 large carrot, pared, shredded

1 small red onion, finely chopped

$\frac{1}{2}$ cup sweet red pepper, deseeded, finely chopped

$\frac{1}{2}$ cup sweet green bell pepper, deseeded, finely chopped

4 small white mushrooms, trimmed, finely chopped

$\frac{1}{4}$ cup parsley, finely chopped

$\frac{1}{2}$ cup grated Parmesan cheese

2 tbsp. extra virgin olive oil

3 tbsp. flour

2 tbsp. red wine vinegar

2 cups sour cream (low-fat available)

$\frac{1}{2}$ cup light mayonnaise

$\frac{1}{2}$ tsp. freshly ground black pepper

$\frac{1}{4}$ tsp. salt

extra Parmesan cheese for garnish (about $\frac{1}{2}$ cup or more, to taste)

12-15 cherry tomatoes (or assorted tiny tomatoes, heirloom variety)

*NOTE: Simmer boneless chicken breasts and thighs in 1 cup water for 20-25 minutes, until cooked. Drain chicken from stock; slice into strips. (Save stock to add to pasta cooking liquid.)

Have ready: a large steamer with a basket and a cover; a 9x15x3-inch rectangle or oval serving platter.

1) In a very large bowl (non-acidic reacting preferred), prepare as directed above and combine the following: celery, carrot, onion, red and green peppers, mushrooms, parsley, chicken strips and Parmesan. Set aside.

2) Prepare the sauce in a small pot (non-acidic reacting). Warm olive oil and stir in flour, salt, black pepper and Parmesan to make a thick paste. Stir in sour cream, mayo, red wine vinegar. Set aside.

3) Set 4 cups water to boil in bottom of steamer pot. When water boils, stir in pasta and cook uncovered for 5 minutes. Then, as pasta cooks, lay steamer basket of broccoli florets on top of cooking pasta; cover with lid and continue to boil 4-5 minutes longer.

Remove entire steamer from burner; remove cover. Set aside broccoli and drain pasta into a colander; then pour pasta into mixing bowl with vegetables. Stir in warm creamy sauce; toss pasta, chicken, vegetables to mix thoroughly in the sauce.

Transfer the warm salad into a large 9x15x3 platter. Around the edge of this platter, arrange cooked broccoli florets. Halve cherry tomatoes and scatter then over top of warm salad. At serving time, garnish entire platter with extra grated Parmesan. Serves 4-6.

*NOTE: If not serving within an hour, withhold cherry tomatoes and cheese garnish. Lightly lay a sheet of foil over salad and keep in a warm place. Just before serving, warm covered platter thoroughly in oven at 250° for 5-7 minutes. At serving, garnish with cherry tomato halves and extra Parmesan.

131

RIGATONI WITH MEATBALLS AND BROCCOLI RABE

(You will need a very large steamer pot with basket and cover; a colander; and a heat-resistant platter. This recipe can be enjoyed in less than 30 minutes as long as you prep the items in advance. Trim and rinse the broccoli rabe; rinse the ceci; mix, form and brown meatballs; peel garlic; etc.)

2 lbs. broccoli rabe (rapini), trimmed, rinsed, drained

1 lb. rigatoni pasta (whole wheat preferred)

1 can (1 lb.) ceci, rinsed, drained

6 garlic cloves, peeled, leave whole

1 sweet red pepper, washed, cored, deseeded, sliced into slivers

$\frac{1}{4}$ cup extra-virgin olive oil

12-15 tiny meatballs (See recipe below)

$\frac{1}{2}$ lb. smoky mozzarella, cut into $\frac{1}{2}$-inch cubes

1 cup shredded Asiago cheese

$\frac{1}{4}$ tsp. black pepper

$\frac{1}{2}$ tsp. salt

a pinch or two of hot pepper flakes

1 doz. cherry or grape tomatoes, halved

1 doz. pitted black olives, coarsely chopped

MEATBALLS: (about 12-15)

2 tbsp. olive oil

$\frac{1}{2}$ lb. ground beef round

$\frac{1}{2}$ lb. ground lean pork

$\frac{1}{4}$ cup staled Italian bread, coarsely grated

1 tbsp. chopped parsley

$\frac{1}{4}$ cup prepared tomato sauce or catsup

1 egg, beaten or $\frac{1}{2}$ cup egg substitute

salt, black pepper to taste

Prepare MEATBALLS:

In a 1-quart bowl, thoroughly mix all ingredients for meatballs. Using a tablespoon, form tiny meatballs. Heat 2 tablespoons olive oil in a large skillet at 320° and lightly brown meatballs all over for 3-4 minutes. Set them in a 9x15x3-inch heat-resistant platter; stir in ceci. Lightly lay a sheet of foil over the platter and set in preheated oven at 250° to keep warm. *Continue with the recipe.*

Fill the steamer basket with broccoli rabe, garlic and slivered red pepper. Set aside.

Pour 3 cups water at bottom of steamer; add 1 teaspoon salt to water. Bring water to a rapid boil; add and stir in the pasta; lay the steamer of vegetables on top of the pasta. Lay cover on top of steamer and continue to cook pasta and vegetables for 7 minutes (or 1-2 minutes less than directed on pasta package, for al dente).

After 7 minutes, remove entire pot from stove; lift vegetable basket off pasta and set aside. Drain pasta in a colander, saving 1 cup pasta liquid; pour pasta into the 9x15 heat-resistant platter of meatballs and ceci. Scatter 1 cup pasta liquid, olives, mozzarella cubes, some of the Asiago cheese, salt and pepper over the pasta/meatballs/ceci mixture and toss to mix. Move the entire pasta/meatball/ceci mixture to one-half of the large platter; pour vegetable contents of steamer basket into the space created in the 9x15 platter. Scatter cherry tomato halves over entire surface of platter; sprinkle remaining Asiago cheese and olive oil over surface. Serve immediately, while very warm. Serves 4-5.

RIGATONI AND BROCCOLI IN RICOTTA AND GORGONZOLA

4 thin slices lean prosciutto

$2\frac{1}{2}$-3 cups uncooked rigatoni pasta (about 10 oz.)

about 2 lbs. broccoli rabe (rapini), trimmed, rinsed; drained

4 garlic cloves, peeled

1 red bell pepper rinsed, deseeded, sliced into $\frac{1}{2}$-inch strips

2 tbsp. olive oil

1 tsp. salt

$\frac{1}{4}$ tsp. freshly ground black pepper

15 oz. part-skim ricotta

$\frac{1}{2}$ lb. gorgonzola cheese, crumbled

$\frac{1}{4}$ tsp. hot red pepper flakes (Careful when handling hot peppers.)

Have ready: a 15-inch pasta serving bowl; a large colander; a large steamer with basket.

Lightly sauté prosciutto; set aside on a paper towel. If you are using a large steamer pot with a basket, pack prepared rapini, garlic cloves and red pepper in the basket and set aside on counter. Pour 3 cups water into bottom half of steamer. Bring steamer to a boil; pour pasta into boiling water and stir pasta to prevent sticking. Cover steamer and cook pasta for 4-5 minutes in boiling water. While pasta is cooking, remove steamer cover and insert entire basket of vegetables over pasta. Replace steamer cover and continue to boil contents of steamer for another 7-8 minutes. Have a large colander waiting in sink.

Remove steamer pot from burner to set on counter. Remove cover from steamer. Empty vegetables from basket into large pasta serving bowl. Empty and drain rigatoni into colander; add pasta to serving bowl with vegetables. Sprinkle with salt and pepper and drizzle olive oil over entire filled serving bowl.

Spoon 15 ounces of ricotta over pasta/rapini mix and with 2 large spoons, toss contents of pasta bowl to coat pasta and vegetables with ricotta. Crumble cooked prosciutto over the dish; garnish with crumbled gorgonzola and sprinkle with hot pepper flakes (to taste). Serve immediately. Crusty Italian bread and a glass of red wine, like Montepulciano d'Abruzzo make a satisfying accompaniment. Serves 4.

MANICOTTI IN RAGOUT

Reprinted from: From the Table of Plenty: Food for the Body, Manna for the Soul
by Marion O. Celenza, page 312.

(Make your own Manicotti shells. They're simple to prepare. As directed in the recipe, prepare the shells a day in advance, and fill them on the serving day. Once you've tasted homemade Manicotti shells, you'll realize 30 minutes of your time and talent was worth it. Arrange the meat in the ragout on a separate platter and serve along with the Manicotti. Delicioso!)

(Prepare Manicotti shells on day before. Stack with waxed paper between each and refrigerate. Prepare sauce a day or two in advance and refrigerate. Heat sauce thoroughly before serving. Complete Manicotti early on the serving day and arrange in casserole dish. Bake as directed. Or prepare completely, without sauce on pasta, and freeze up to two weeks.)

MANICOTTI SHELLS:

$1\frac{1}{4}$ cups water

5 eggs

$1\frac{1}{4}$ cups flour

$\frac{1}{4}$ tsp. salt

FILLING:

2 lbs. ricotta

8 oz. mozzarella cheese, chopped fine

$\frac{1}{2}$ cup grated Parmesan cheese

2 eggs beaten or egg substitute

$\frac{1}{2}$ tsp. salt

$\frac{1}{4}$ tsp. black pepper

1 tbsp. chopped parsley

$\frac{1}{2}$ cup olive oil- enough to continuously coat pan

$\frac{1}{2}$ cup Parmesan cheese for garnish, at serving

RAGOUT SAUCE (see page 395); set aside in refrigerator.

SHELLS: In a 2-quart mixing bowl, beat eggs, flour, water and salt until smooth (use electric mixer). Pour $\frac{1}{2}$ cup light olive oil in a small bowl. Gently dip wad of paper toweling into oil and wipe the bottom of a 5-inch Teflon or non-stick pan. Wipe the pan with oil before each pouring of batter. Pour 2 tbsp. batter into pan, turning pan quickly to spread batter evenly over bottom of pan. Cook over medium heat until top of shell is dry, but bottom is not brown (a minute may do it). Turn shells out onto a wire rack to cool and keep them separate. Continue making shells until all the batter is used. As shells cool, waxed paper should be used to separate them, as you form stacks.

FILLING: In a 2-quart bowl, combine all filling ingredients and mix until blended. Spoon about $\frac{1}{4}$ cup of this filling into center of each shell and roll up. Spoon some sauce onto bottom of a 9x15x2-inch Pyrex or heat-resistant pan, which has been coated with olive oil. Arrange manicotti on Pyrex pan, seam-side down, in a single layer. At this point you may wish to wrap the pan in plastic and freeze; or refrigerate with plastic wrap until needed (within 2 days.)

AT BAKING TIME: Preheat oven to 350° and bake casserole uncovered, for 30 minutes. Meanwhile, the sauce should be heated thoroughly and spooned over manicotti at serving time, along with more cheese. Serves 6-8.

TUNA NOODLE CASSEROLE

1 lb. medium shells pasta

1 tbsp. olive oil

1 medium-size onion, chopped

1 cup white mushrooms, rinsed, sliced

1 can (10 oz.) cream of mushroom soup

2 cans (5 oz.) solid tuna in water , drained

1 large celery stalk, trimmed, finely chopped

1 small carrot, pared, finely chopped

1 cup frozen peas

$\frac{1}{2}$ tsp. dill weed

$\frac{1}{4}$ tsp. garlic powder

$\frac{1}{8}$ tsp. cayenne pepper

$\frac{1}{8}$ tsp. freshly ground black pepper

$\frac{1}{8}$ tsp. salt

$\frac{1}{4}$ cup evaporated milk, fat-free available

$\frac{1}{2}$ cup Parmesan cheese, grated

$\frac{1}{4}$ cup unseasoned bread crumbs

Preheat oven to 350°.

Have ready: a large 9x12 casserole dish, coated with olive oil.

Cook pasta al dente, according to directions on package. In a large skillet, add oil; over medium heat, cook onion until soft. Add sliced mushrooms, celery and carrot. Reduce heat and cook mushroom mix until vegetables are tender, about 5 minutes. Add and stir to combine, all remaining ingredients except bread crumbs. Add cooked/drained pasta and toss to mix.

Pour into oiled casserole dish. Sprinkle top with crumbs. Bake casserole, uncovered, in a preheated oven at 350° for 15 minutes or until bubbly. Serves 6.

A Thanksgiving Day Dinner.

SAL-MAC AND CHEESE

1 tbsp. olive oil

2 tbsp. all-purpose flour

$1\frac{1}{2}$ cups low-fat evaporated milk

$\frac{1}{4}$ tsp. salt

$\frac{1}{4}$ tsp. freshly ground black pepper

1 tbsp. Worcestershire sauce

2-3 shakes Tabasco sauce

2 cups sharp Cheddar cheese, shredded

$\frac{1}{2}$ cup Parmesan cheese, grated

1 lb. elbow macaroni, cooked al dente, according to direction on package, drained

1 can ($14\frac{1}{2}$ oz.) salmon; remove skin and bones; crumble into pieces with a fork

1 cup fresh plum tomatoes, rinsed, chopped

4 basil leaves, chopped

more Parmesan for garnish

Preheat oven to 350°.

Have ready: a 3-quart casserole baking dish, coated with olive oil.

Heat 1 tablespoon olive oil in a saucepan over medium-low heat. Whisk in flour; add milk, salt, pepper, Worcestershire and Tabasco sauces. Stir continuously over heat for a few minutes until mixture is smooth. Add cheeses and cook, stirring, until cheese is melted and mixture is thick and creamy. Remove from heat.

In a large mixing bowl, combine cooked elbow macaroni and cheese sauce. Stir in crumbled salmon, tomatoes and basil. Transfer this mixture to the large oiled baking dish. Garnish with additional grated Parmesan. Bake casserole in preheated oven at 350° for 30-35 minutes, until surface is lightly browned. Serves 6.

Our Family Celebrates a Wedding with Aunt Susie and Uncle Frank Colantuono. Photo: A. Colantuono

PASTA WITH BROCCOLI, PROSCIUTTO AND SMOKY MOZZARELLA

1 lb. penne rigati
2 cups small broccoli florets, rinsed, drained
3-4 baby bella mushrooms, trimmed, rinsed, sliced thin
½ lb. smoky mozzarella, cut into 1-inch cubes
¼ cup pitted Kalamata olives, chopped
6-8 cherry or grape tomatoes, halved
6-8 basil leaves for garnish

SAUCE:
¼ cup olive oil
2 tbsp. minced, deseeded red bell pepper
2 tbsp. minced, deseeded green bell pepper
1-inch piece chili pepper, minced (Wear plastic gloves when you use hot pepper.)
2 garlic cloves, minced
2 tbsp. finely chopped red onion
2 very thin slices prosciutto, chopped (use scissors)

½ cup mayonnaise (low-fat available)
1 cup sour cream (low-fat available)
½ tsp. dried thyme
1 tsp. dried basil
1 tbsp. fresh Italian parsley, minced
¼ tsp. freshly ground black pepper

Have ready: a large pasta salad bowl; a pasta pot.

Prepare the SAUCE. In a skillet, cook minced green, red and hot peppers, onion and garlic in oil at medium heat until tender, about 2-3 minutes. Add chopped prosciutto and sauté for 1 minute. Remove from heat. Combine mayonnaise and sour cream in a medium-size bowl. Blend thoroughly all herbs, black pepper and sautéed oil mixture into the creamy mix.

Meanwhile set pasta pot to boil. Cook penne rigati al dente, according to directions on pasta package. Add broccoli florets to pasta pot during last 6 minutes of cooking. Drain pasta and broccoli when pasta is cooked al dente, about 8 minutes. Pour cool water over pasta/broccoli in colander and drain thoroughly.

Transfer cooked pasta and broccoli into a large pasta salad bowl. Add sliced mushrooms and smoky mozzarella cubes, to pasta/broccoli. Pour prepared sauce over cooked pasta mix and toss to combine. Garnish with chopped olives, halves of cherry tomatoes and basil leaves. Serves 4-5.

FRANKFURTERS WITH FRUIT SAUCE
(This recipe, with its touch of "The Islands" is contributed by Enid Lopes.)

$\frac{1}{2}$ cup light brown sugar, packed

$1\frac{1}{2}$ tbsp. all-purpose flour

$\frac{1}{2}$ tsp. dry mustard

$\frac{3}{4}$ cup apricot nectar

$\frac{1}{4}$ cup cider vinegar

$\frac{1}{2}$ cup raisins

$\frac{3}{4}$ lb. beef frankfurters, sliced into rounds

1 lb. noodles

Have ready: a 2-quart saucepan.

Combine all ingredients, except frankfurters, in a 2-quart saucepan. Bring to a boil; reduce heat and simmer until sauce thickens, about 4-5 minutes. Add and stir in frankfurter rounds and cook for another 5 minutes. Serve over cooked noodles. Serves 4.

A Golf Outing Supper. Photo: L. Curro

NANA'S MAC AND CHEESE WITH BEEFBALLS

BEEFBALLS:

2 tbsp. olive oil

1 lb. double-chopped beef chuck
(meat should be finely ground)

$\frac{1}{2}$ cup fine unseasoned bread crumbs

1 tbsp. fresh parsley, minced

1 tbsp. onion, minced

1 egg beaten, or $\frac{1}{4}$ cup egg substitute

1 tsp. mustard spread

1 tsp. catsup

$\frac{1}{4}$ tsp. black pepper

dash of salt

Heat olive oil to medium-high, in a large skillet. Mix all ingredients for beefballs and form 1-inch meatballs. Brown beefballs for 4-5 minutes in hot oil on all sides, about 2 minutes on each side. Transfer to a plate and set aside. Makes about 12-14 beefballs.

MAC AND CHEESE:

1 tbsp. olive oil

2 tbsp. all-purpose flour

$1\frac{1}{2}$ cups low-fat evaporated milk

$\frac{1}{2}$ tsp. salt

$\frac{1}{4}$ tsp. freshly ground black pepper

1 tbsp. Worcestershire sauce

a couple or 3 shakes Tabasco sauce

2 cups sharp Cheddar cheese, shredded

$\frac{1}{2}$ cup Parmesan cheese, grated

1 lb. elbow macaroni, cooked al dente,
according to directions on package, drained

1 cup fresh plum tomatoes, rinsed, chopped

4 basil leaves, chopped

more Parmesan for garnish

Preheat oven to 350°.

Have ready: a skillet for beefballs; a 3-quart casserole baking dish, coated with olive oil.

Prepare cheese sauce and assemble. Heat 1 tablespoon olive oil in a saucepan over medium-low heat. Whisk in flour; add milk, salt, pepper, Worcestershire and Tabasco sauces. Stir continuously over heat for a few minutes until mixture is smooth. Add cheeses and cook, stirring, until cheese is melted and mixture is thick and creamy. Remove from heat.

In a large mixing bowl, combine elbow macaroni and cheese sauce. Stir in tomatoes and basil and beefballs. Transfer this mixture to the large oil-coated baking dish. Garnish with additional grated Parmesan. Bake casserole in preheated oven at 350° for 30-35 minutes, until surface is lightly browned. Serves 6.

SEAFOOD RISOTTO

2 tbsp. olive oil

1 small onion, chopped

2-3 garlic cloves, finely chopped

1 celery stalk, chopped

2-3 plum tomatoes, chopped with juice

1 dozen cherrystone clams, brush-scrubbed
(store on ice)

1 dozen mussels, brush-scrubbed,
remove beards (store on ice)

1 dozen jumbo shrimp in shell, rinsed
(store on ice)

2 cups water

1 cup white wine, like Pinot Grigio or Antinori

1 cup Arborio rice

1 tsp. crushed fennel seeds

1 tbsp. parsley, finely chopped

$\frac{1}{2}$ tsp. salt, or to taste

$\frac{1}{4}$ tsp. freshly ground black pepper

$\frac{1}{4}$ cup Parmesan cheese, grated

Have ready: a large stock pot.

In a large stock pot, heat 2 tablespoons olive oil. Add onion, garlic, celery and tomatoes and cook over medium heat for 4-5 minutes until onion is golden and tender. Stir in 1 cup rice and pour water and wine into the pot. Mix thoroughly. Cover pot and bring to a boil; then simmer gently for 12-15 minutes.

Add prepared mussels, clams, and shrimp in shells. Bring to boil; then, cover pot and simmer seafood risotto for another 5-7 minutes, or until clams and mussels open and rice is tender. Remove any clams and mussels which haven't opened and discard. Stir in fennel seeds, parsley, cheese, salt and pepper. Transfer to serving bowl and serve immediately. Provide small bowls to discard seafood shells. Serves 4.

A Wedding Party. Photo: S. Barbarotto

PASTA FRITTATA

[A Cooking Hint: To oil or grease pans or skillets, spray or lightly coat with canola oil or olive oil; or Smart Balance Spread.]

4 eggs or 1 cup egg substitute

1 cup ricotta

1 cup mozzarella, shredded

$\frac{1}{4}$ cup Parmesan cheese

$\frac{1}{2}$ tsp. salt

$\frac{1}{4}$ tsp. freshly ground black pepper

$\frac{1}{2}$ lb. thin pasta, like spaghetti or vermicelli

4 tbsp. olive oil, divided: (1, 2, 1 tablespoons)

1 red bell pepper, deseeded, sliced in thin strips

1 green bell pepper, deseeded, sliced in thin strips

1 onion, thinly sliced

Have ready: a 10-inch skillet with cover; a 10-inch flat plate; a large spatula.

In a large bowl, beat eggs (or egg substitute) with ricotta. Add mozzarella, Parmesan, salt and pepper and beat to combine. Set bowl aside.

Cook pasta in a large pot with enough water to cook al dente, according to directions on pasta package. Drain pasta in a colander; then return pasta to pot in which it was cooked. Add egg/ricotta mixture and toss to coat thoroughly. Set aside.

Heat 1 tablespoon olive oil in a 10-inch skillet over medium heat. Add and sauté peppers and onion until soft, about 7-8 minutes. Set aside.

Heat 2 tablespoons olive oil in same skillet over medium heat. Swirl pan to coat the pan with oil. Pour in pasta/egg mixture and distribute evenly over the pan. Cover skillet and cook for 3-4 minutes. Reduce heat to low and cook frittata until a brown crust forms at bottom, about 12-15 minutes. Remove cover and loosen the crust with spatula and continue to cook frittata until crust is crisp, 3-5 minutes longer. Loosen the crust with spatula, once more.

Place a 10-inch flat plate over the frittata in the skillet and carefully invert the frittata onto the plate. With spatula, scrape bottom of skillet to remove any leavings; add and swirl the remaining 1 tablespoon olive oil and return the oiled pan to the burner at medium heat. Slip the frittata, crust-side-up into the pan and cook the other side following the same directions as before. This time, the frittata should be cooked through in 8-10 minutes. When bottom is crusty, turn the pasta frittata out on a warm serving plate. Garnish with sautéed peppers and onions and serve warm. Serves 4.

WARM PASTA AND SOY BEAN CASSEROLE

12-15 1-inch turkey meatballs
(See MEATBALLS recipe, below*);
or, 4 Breaded Chicken or Turkey cutlets,
sliced into $\frac{1}{2}$-inch strips (Recipe: p. 46);
or, 8-10 Battered jumbo Shrimp
(Recipe: p. 176)
10 oz. salad-size pasta, like: mezza-ziti,
mezza-mezzani, medium shells
1 lb. (about 2 cups) cooked soy beans –
edible variety (sold in produce dept.)

$\frac{1}{2}$ cup each: red bell pepper,
green bell pepper; 2 tbsp. poblano,
deseeded, chopped
2-3 garlic cloves, minced
1 small red onion, finely chopped
4-6 sun dried tomatoes, sliced into strips
4-6 small white mushrooms, washed, quartered
1 tbsp. olive oil

*MEATBALLS:
1 lb. finely ground turkey
$\frac{1}{2}$ cup fine bread crumbs
1 tbsp. fresh parsley, chopped

1 egg, beaten or $\frac{1}{4}$ cup egg substitute
salt, black pepper, to taste

DRESSING:
2 tbsp. extra-virgin olive oil
black pepper and salt to taste
2 tbsp. white wine vinegar
dash of cayenne
2 tbsp. fresh lemon juice

$\frac{1}{4}$ cup fresh cilantro, chopped
$\frac{1}{2}$ cup low-fat mayonnaise
1 tbsp. grated fresh ginger
$\frac{1}{2}$ cup pitted Kalamata olives, chopped
$\frac{1}{2}$ cup Asiago cheese, grated

Have ready: a well-oiled skillet; a 5x7 baking pan; a large heat-resistant salad bowl.
STEP 1: You may Prepare TURKEY MEATBALLS a day in advance. In a medium-size bowl, combine ground turkey, crumbs, parsley, salt, pepper and beaten egg (or egg substitute). Form 1-inch meatballs and brown them on all sides in a well-oiled skillet over medium heat. Transfer to a bowl; set aside; or refrigerate until the next day. At serving preparation, cover lightly; reheat thoroughly in oven at 375°, 12-15 minutes.
Or, Prepare BREADED CHICKEN/TURKEY CUTLETS; or, JUMBO SHRIMP a day in advance.
STEP 2: Preheat oven to 375° $\frac{1}{2}$ hour before serving.
STEP 3: On serving day, rinse and drain soy beans; pour into a large heat-resistant salad bowl.
STEP 4: Prepare VEGETABLES. In a bowl, combine: all chopped peppers, onion, garlic, mushrooms and sun dried tomatoes. Toss vegetables with 1 tablespoon olive oil. Pour them into a 5x7 baking pan. Cover pan lightly with aluminum foil. Cook in preheated oven at 375° for 10-12 minutes. STEP 5: As the vegetables cook in the oven, thoroughly reheat in oven: meatballs (or Cutlets or Shrimp). ALSO, Prepare DRESSING. In a small bowl, blend all dressing ingredients, except cheese. Set aside.
STEP 6: Meanwhile, Prepare PASTA to cook al dente. Drain and pour pasta into salad bowl with soybeans. Add pan of cooked vegetables; drizzle dressing all over the bowl, and toss to mix thoroughly. Garnish salad surface with Meatballs (or Cutlets or Shrimp); generously garnish surface of salad with Asiago cheese. Serve immediately while warm. Serves 4-5.

RED BEAN SOUP AND DUMPLINGS
(A One-Pot Supper in the Tradition of St. Thomas, Virgin Islands,
as prepared by Enid Lopes.)

1 lb. dried kidney beans, soaked overnight in
    enough water to cover;
    or 4 cups (about 2 lbs.) canned kidney
    beans, rinsed in cold water and drained
8 cups water
1 tsp. salt
$\frac{1}{2}$ lb. ham hocks, pig tails, fresh pork
$\frac{1}{4}$ cup canned tomatoes
1 medium onion, chopped

DUMPLINGS:
1 cup flour
1 tsp. granulated sugar
$\frac{1}{4}$ cup cornmeal (yellow or white)
1 tbsp. shortening
water

1 firm, ripe plantain, cut into $\frac{1}{2}$-inch rounds
1 small bouquet: fresh thyme, parsley,
    celery stalks/greens
sugar to taste (optional)

Cousin Tina at a table by a California Shore. Photo: T. Miller

Have ready: a large soup pot with a cover; a large mixing bowl.

Soak dried beans overnight. Then, rinse beans in water. Pour beans and 8 cups water into a large soup pot. Add rest of ingredients except plantain and sugar. Cover pot and simmer soup for 2 hours or until beans are just tender. Add plantain rounds (and sugar) and dumplings during last 10 minutes of simmering the soup.

If you are using *canned* kidney beans, simmer pork, onion, tomatoes, herb bouquet and salt in water for 1 hour. Add canned beans, plantain (sugar) and Dumplings during last 10 minutes of cooking the soup.

In any case, <u>Prepare DUMPLINGS</u> as you cook the soup. Combine all Dumpling ingredients in a large bowl, to make a stiff dough. Knead dough lightly; roll dough on a board sprinkled with cornmeal. Cut dumplings into ovals, or diamond shapes. Drop them into the pot of simmering soup during last 10 minutes. Makes about 6 dumplings. Serve soup and dumplings over rice. Serves 8.

SVICKOVA (CZECH SAUERBRATEN)

(Margaret Citterbart's heirloom recipe has long been celebrated at her son, Bill's table. Bill and his son, William III are the renown Cherry Lane Litho of Plainview, N.Y., our printing craftsmen.) (May be prepared a day in advance and refrigerated. Re-heat to warm thoroughly before serving. Flavor is enhanced when prepared in advance.)

a 5 lb. Silver Tip beef roast (or Eye Round)
3-4 slices bacon
2 medium-to-large onions, coarsely chopped
1 celery knob (4 to 5 inches in diameter),
   coarsely chopped in $\frac{3}{4}$-inch dice
3 parsley roots, trimmed, chopped
2 large carrots, pared, chopped
1 lemon, rind and pith removed;
   then, halve the lemon

1 bay leaf
10 allspice
20 black peppercorns
6 whole cloves
$\frac{1}{4}$ tsp. thyme leaves
1 tsp. salt
$\frac{1}{2}$ tsp. pickling spice
   (with cinnamon and hot pepper removed)
1 can (1 lb.) beef broth
$1\frac{1}{2}$ cups water; $\frac{3}{4}$ cup water (divided)
1 pt. (2 cups) heavy cream
3 to 4 tsp. white vinegar
1 tbsp. all-purpose flour

Have ready: a large Dutch oven with a cover.

Over medium heat cook 2 slices bacon in a large Dutch oven; add beef and brown meat on all sides, adding another slice or two of bacon to the pot as roast is browning. Add coarsely chopped onions and celery knob to pot and cook for 3-4 minutes. Add and brown chopped carrots and parsley roots cooking for several minutes, careful not to burn. Pour beef broth and $1\frac{1}{2}$ cups water into the pot. Squeeze lemon halves and stir juice and lemon halves into gravy. Stir in all spices and salt. Reduce heat to low; cover pot and cook roast for $2\frac{1}{4}$ to $2\frac{1}{2}$ hours.

Remove meat from Dutch oven; cool meat; then, cut meat into $\frac{3}{4}$-inch serving slices. Set aside on a platter.

Strain the juices from the pot, pressing on the vegetables to remove all the liquid. (You may strain the gravy from the vegetables using cheesecloth or a food mill.) Set gravy aside in a bowl.

Return mashed vegetables to pot; add and mix $\frac{1}{4}$ cup water into vegetables; again strain liquid from vegetables; pour liquid into the small pot of gravy. Then, return all the liquid to the Dutch oven and heat on low. Discard vegetable residue.

In a small bowl, pour $1\frac{1}{2}$ cups heavy cream and slowly stir in 3 teaspoons white vinegar. Cream will thicken slightly. Add this liquid mix slowly to the heating gravy in the Dutch oven until incorporated.

Stir in and thoroughly blend 1 tablespoon flour to remaining $\frac{1}{2}$ cup heavy cream.

Through a strainer, add and stir in the bowl of flour and cream mixture into the hot gravy. Gravy will thicken. If gravy is too thick, add a little milk; if too thin, add more of the flour paste mixture. Adjust seasoning to taste; add more salt and vinegar, if needed.

Return sliced meat to gravy in Dutch oven and heat on low. Serve with Bread Dumplings. See recipe on page 145. Serves 5-6.

BREAD DUMPLINGS

4 cups all-purpose flour
1 tsp. salt
1 tsp. baking powder
2 eggs
2 cups milk
8 slices white bread (firm textured); cut into $\frac{1}{4}$-inch cubes

Have ready: a lightly buttered 9x12x1$\frac{1}{2}$-inch pan; wooden spoons; a 6-qt. Dutch oven.

Lightly oil pan with butter or shortening; spread bread cubes over buttered pan. Carefully, lightly toast bread cubes under broiler, to a light tan, about 1 minute.

Pour flour, salt and baking powder into a large mixing bowl; make a well in center of this mixture and beat in eggs. Add and stir in milk a little at a time using a wooden spoon, until mixture becomes a stiff dough (about 5-6 minutes). Dough will look pasty but fairly firm and glossy. Stir in bread cubes, a handful at a time. Dough will become quite stiff.

Fill a large pot with water and bring to a rapid boil. Liberally dust dough and your hands with flour. Scoop out dough, a handful at a time and form oval dumplings with your hands. (You will form about 5 dumplings.)

Drop dumplings into the boiling water. Dumplings will sink to bottom of pot; then, rise to surface. Cook them for 12-15 minutes; then, turn dumplings over and cook for 12-15 minutes longer. Check center of 1 dumpling for doneness, by slicing dumpling in half. If not cooked through, return to pot of boiling water and continue to cook them for another couple of minutes.

Remove dumplings, one at a time and slice each in half. Using ordinary white sewing thread, (or a Dumpling Cutter, if available), cut dumplings into $\frac{1}{2}$-inch slices. (A serrated-edge knife will also do the job.) Serve dumpling slices from a serving plate, to accompany the sauerbraten.

FOOD FOR THE COMMON FOLK
or: "A REALITY MENU COOKBOOK"

During my Act I, my pre-teen grammar school years, unplanned and unintentionally, I had commenced to create my first menu cookbook, MENU LOG: A COLLECTION OF RECIPES AS COORDINATED MENUS. Even as a child, traditionally raised in a food oriented atmosphere, I had been challenged to develop new recipes. I kept a diary, a black and white soft cover composition notebook, into which I documented my innovative recipes. To this day, my ideas for recipes reside in several notebooks tucked in a corner of the Corian kitchen counter.

I come from a large and prolific Italian family. My grandparents, both sides, immigrated to New York from Naples at the turn of the 20th century. My Father was one of nine surviving children; my Mother was the middle child in a family of six (out of eleven) surviving children. Her own Mother had passed on when my grandmother was only 40. Grandpa Vincenzo remarried and two additional children were added to Mama's family. Most of my aunts and uncles had maintained the tradition of raising their own large families.

Another Italian tradition is the love and sharing of "Good Home Cooking". Most of my aunts and uncles upheld that tradition, as well as my father's eldest brother, Uncle Raphael, a priest who had shared our home while he served his assignments for the Archdiocese of New York. His seasonal hobby was food-related: hunting deer, pheasants and rabbits at a sister's and a brother's farms in New Jersey. My modest immigrant heritage speaks through our simple, common-folk traditions and is demonstrated in the food gardens we continue to grow around our home gardens and small (or large) farms. Our simple menus, for the most part, range from "expanded peasant" recipes to "everyday nouveau". My healthy recipes are developed in graphic detail. The recipes suggest alternate ingredients, with less fat, less salt, less sugar.

During my Act II, and as I've lived my marriage and my profession, (as well as motherhood and parental caretaking), I've continued to "feed the people" through my documented recipes. However, it wasn't until my Act III, the after-retirement years, that my cookbooks have been published and shared. They relate the story of my long rewarding life.

I invite folks to share in the bounty, prepared by a home-cook, to serve at kitchen and dining room tables, at the picnic table, by the barbeque or on a grassy backyard knoll.

Recently after one of my speaking engagements at a senior club, a member approached me to sign his newly purchased cookbook. Having listened to my lengthy lifetime story, he had believed that my Act III definitely had script-potential for an exciting "TV reality show"- for old folks.

Sansone Farm Market in Hopewell, New Jersey.
Photo: I. Lang

146

Dinner Menus

by season:

Fall-Winter

Spring-Summer

Summer-Fall

Happy Thanksgiving Day from the Smaldone Family! Photos: J. Ingrilli

147

> **SPINACH AND WHITE BEAN SOUP**
> **MEDALLIONS OF PORK WITH RED PEPPERS**
> **BAKED POLENTA**
> **STIR-FRIED VEGETABLES**
> **BROWN SUGAR CAKE**

SPINACH AND WHITE BEAN SOUP

1 large onion, chopped

3 celery stalks, chopped

2 large carrots, pared, chopped

1 tbsp. olive oil

6 cups water

1 qt. packaged low-sodium vegetable broth

1 can (1 lb.) cannellini beans, rinsed in cool water, drained

1 large ripe tomato, chopped, with juice

1 tsp. dried thyme

1 tsp. dried oregano

$\frac{1}{2}$ tsp. black pepper

1 bay leaf

1 cup ditalini pasta

4 cups fresh baby spinach, chopped

Heat olive oil in a large stock pot and lightly brown onion and celery. Scrape bottom of pot to remove leavings. Pour water and vegetable broth into the stock pot. Add carrots, chopped tomato with juice, thyme, oregano, black pepper and bay leaf. Cover the pot and bring to a boil.
Then, reduce to simmer for 20 minutes. Stir in pasta and continue to cook for another 10 minutes. Stir in chopped spinach and cannellini beans and simmer for another 3 or 4 minutes.
Before serving soup, remove bay leaf and discard. Serves 6-8.

MEDALLIONS OF PORK WITH RED PEPPERS

1 large red pepper, deseeded, thinly sliced

1 onion, thinly sliced

1 small Chile pepper, deseeded, minced (Wear plastic gloves when handling hot pepper.)

3 large garlic cloves, minced

2 lbs. pork cutlets, each cut in half

1 cup all-purpose flour

$\frac{1}{2}$ tsp. black pepper

2-3 tbsp. olive oil

$\frac{1}{2}$ cup dry white wine

Spread flour on a sheet of waxed paper; sprinkle black pepper over flour. Heat oil, over medium heat in a skillet; dredge pork cutlets in flour mix and sauté in oil on both sides, about 2 minutes on each side. Remove cooked medallions to a plate lined with paper towels. Sauté red pepper, Chile, onion and garlic in the same skillet until lightly browned. Scrape bottom of pan frequently while cooking. Add cutlets and stir in wine and continue to cook for 1-2 minutes. Transfer cutlets and sauce to a large oven-proof platter. Lightly lay a sheet of aluminum foil over platter. Place platter in a very low oven, at 200° to keep warm. Serve with polenta or rice. Serves 6.

3 Generations of Sansones/Langs/Roccos, hosted by Irene and Ray Lang.
Photos: I. Lang

BAKED POLENTA

1 tbsp. olive oil

$\frac{1}{2}$ cup chopped onion (about 2 medium-size onions)

6 cups water; or 3 cups water and 3 cups low-sodium chicken broth

$1\frac{1}{2}$ cups yellow cornmeal

$\frac{1}{2}$ tsp. salt, or to taste

$\frac{1}{4}$ tsp. black pepper

2 tbsp. Parmesan cheese, grated

$\frac{1}{2}$ lb. part-skim mozzarella, coarsely chopped

$\frac{3}{4}$ cup low-fat milk

Preheat oven to 350°.

Lightly grease a 2-quart shallow baking pan.

Heat oil in a large, wide saucepan; cook onion in hot oil over medium heat, until golden, about 5 minutes.

In a separate bowl, combine cornmeal, salt, pepper and half the liquid. Whisk together to blend completely. Add to the saucepan with the onion and cook the polenta, stirring constantly, until mixture boils. Slowly stir in remaining liquid. Continue to cook polenta, stirring until mixture is very thick and smooth, about 2 minutes. Add the grated Parmesan.

Pour half of the polenta into the prepared greased 2-quart baking pan. Spread half of the shredded mozzarella over the polenta. Top with remaining polenta and remainder of mozzarella. Pour milk over the top. Bake in preheated oven at 350° for about 25 minutes, or until polenta is browned and bubbly. Allow polenta to stand for 10 minutes before serving. Then, spoon portions onto plates; or cut into squares and serve with a spatula. Serves 6.

The McCabe Family. Photo: J. McCabe

STIR-FRIED VEGETABLES

[A Cooking Hint: Do not overcook any vegetables; especially: carrots, celery, green beans, peas, broccoli, asparagus, spinach, peppers, Brussels sprouts.]

2 tbsp. peanut oil

3 garlic cloves, minced

1 tbsp. sesame seeds, plus 1 tbsp. for garnish

2 celery stalks, trimmed, chopped

1 cup button mushrooms, rinsed, drained

1 large leek, trimmed, sliced thin

1 small can baby corn, drained

1 medium-size zucchini, rinsed, sliced into rounds

1 small red bell pepper and 1 mild Chile pepper, deseeded, chopped

about 6 oz. Chinese cabbage leaves, rinsed, shredded

2 tbsp. *lite* soy sauce

1 tbsp. hoisin sauce

1 tsp. sesame oil

$\frac{1}{4}$ cup sherry

2 tsp. cornstarch blended into 6 tbsp. water

Have ready: a large wok or skillet.

Heat oil in wok until it is almost smoking. Lower heat slightly; add garlic and sesame seeds and stir-fry for 30 seconds. Add celery, corn, mushrooms, leek, zucchini, red pepper, Chile pepper and Chinese shredded cabbage. Stir-fry for 4-5 minutes or until cabbage and zucchini are softened.

In a small bowl, combine soy sauce, hoisin sauce, sherry, sesame oil, cornstarch and water. Stir this sauce into the wok and bring to a boil. Cook, stirring, until sauce thickens and turns opaque and cook for 1 minute longer. Spoon vegetables into a warm serving platter; garnish with sesame seeds. Serves 6.

Enjoy the Bounty with some of Ron and Joan Gordon's clan. Photo: J.Gordon

BROWN SUGAR CAKE

[A Cooking Hint: A large piece of citrus peel placed in a box of brown sugar will keep it moist and lump free.]

4 large eggs or 1 cup egg substitute

2 cups brown sugar

$1\frac{1}{2}$ tsp. vanilla extract

$1\frac{3}{4}$ cups sifted all-purpose flour

$\frac{1}{2}$ cup dates, chopped

$\frac{1}{8}$ tsp. salt

Preheat oven to 350°.

Have ready: an ungreased 9x13-inch baking pan.

Combine eggs and sugar in a double boiler, over hot, not simmering or boiling, water. Cook, stirring frequently with a wooden spoon, until thick enough to coat the back of the spoon, about 20 minutes.

Stir in vanilla, flour, dates and salt. Pour batter into ungreased 9x13 pan. Bake in center of preheated oven at 350° for 20 minutes, or until an inserted toothpick removes clean. Cool cake in pan; cut into squares. Serves 6.

Uncle Emil and Aunt Louise Orlando and Family. Photo: L. Orlando Kloenne

TUSCAN BEAN SOUP

ITALIAN FLAG SALMON FILLETS

ROASTED SWEET POTATOES

BRUSSELS SPROUTS AND TOMATOES

RED WINE AND HONEY MUSTARD DRESSING (see page 377)

CHOCOLATE FUDGE PIE

TUSCAN BEAN SOUP

[A Cooking Hint: Dried beans have a pantry life of up to 2 years. However, the older they are, the longer they must be soaked before using.]

(1. Prior to using in a recipe, dried beans are usually pre-soaked overnight, in water, at least twice the amount of the beans. 2. Or, tenderize the beans by covering them in a pot of cold water; then, bring the pot with beans to a boil and simmer for 2 minutes. Remove them from heat and allow beans to stand, tightly covered, for 1 hour. 3. Or, use preprocessed beans which require no soaking (read directions on package). 4. Or use canned/cold-water rinsed beans. However, some nutrients are wasted in each aspect of the preparation.)

1 lb. pkg. cannellini beans; soak overnight, or according to package directions; or: use 1 lg. can, about 20 oz.; rinse and drain

8 cups water, part of which may be Homemade Chicken Stock (see page 81); or: 1 can (15 oz.) low-sodium chicken broth

3 slices Canadian bacon, slivered

2 tbsp. olive oil

2 lg. celery stalks, with greens

1 small red onion, chopped

4-6 garlic cloves, chopped

1 large carrot, pared, shredded

1 doz. grape (or cherry) tomatoes, rinsed, halved

1 cup freshly shelled peas (or frozen peas)

½ cup orzo

1 cup ditalini pasta

1 tbsp. dried oregano

¼ cup chopped parsley

1 tsp. each: dried marjoram, thyme

½ tsp. freshly ground black pepper

1 tsp. salt (or to taste)

Have ready: a large soup pot with a cover.

Heat 2 tablespoons olive oil in a large soup pot. Lightly brown slivers of Canadian bacon, chopped onion and garlic. Pour in 10 cups water; scrape bottom of pot to loosen leavings. Cover with lid and bring pot to boil. Stir in soaked and drained beans, shredded carrot and chopped celery; simmer for 30 minutes. Add and mix: orzo, ditalini, peas, cherry tomato halves, herbs and spices. Cover pot and continue to simmer soup for 10 more minutes. Serves 6-8.

NOTE: This soup can be frozen for later use.

ITALIAN FLAG SALMON FILLET
(Prepare sauces in advance; freeze portions until needed.)

2 salmon fillets (total weight: about $2\frac{1}{2}$ lbs.); remove skin; with tweezers,
　　remove any obvious bones (*NOTE: below)
2 tbsp. olive oil
2 tbsp. olive oil for pan
salt to taste
freshly ground black pepper to taste
1 tbsp. dill weed

2 cups RED PEPPER SAUCE (see page 396)
1 cup PESTO SAUCE (see page 398)

　　If sauces have been prepared in advance, and frozen, remove containers from freezer on day or two before; refrigerate to soften.

　　*NOTE: Removing skin from the fish is easier if the fish is partially frozen. Start at short end of fillet and gently pull off skin with aid of a small knife.

　　Preheat broiler.
　　Line a baking pan, 9x12x3 with aluminum foil and brush bottom of foil-lined pan with olive oil.
　　Brush salmon with olive oil and place in pan. Sprinkle salmon with salt, pepper and dill weed. Set pan 5 inches below broiling element. Broil fish in preheated broiler for 3-5 minutes, depending upon thickness. Remove pan from oven. Turn off broiler; turn on oven to 400°.
　　Spread 2 cups Red Pepper Sauce in pan *under* salmon fillets; spread Pesto Sauce in pan *over* the fillets. Place pan in preheated oven at 400° and roast salmon and sauces for 15 minutes, until fish easily flakes, but is barely cooked in middle, and sauces are heated through. Serve fish with sauces from pan. Serves 4.

Sunday Brunch at Home.

ROASTED SWEET POTATOES

2 large or 4 small sweet potatoes, rinsed under cold water; use vegetable brush on skin

1 tbsp. fresh parsley, chopped

4 tbsp. red onion, minced

1 tbsp. Hungarian paprika

Preheat oven 400°.

Roast whole sweet potatoes on a baking pan in middle of oven at 400° for 1 hour to 1½ hours, depending on size. Remove from oven. Lay them on serving dish. If they are large, cut each in half lengthwise; if they are small, cut a gash across top of potato skin and gently squeeze each end of potatoes with your fingers to enable creamy sweet potato to "puff" out of its skin.

Sprinkle tops of sweet potato with minced red onion, parsley and paprika. Return them to oven for 5 more minutes. Serves 4.

BRUSSELS SPROUTS AND TOMATOES
[A Cooking Hint: Do not overcook any vegetables; especially: carrots, celery, green beans, peas, broccoli, asparagus, spinach, peppers, Brussels sprouts.]
[A Cooking Hint: Over-cooking Brussels sprouts will cause them to have a strong and unpleasant flavor. If fresh, steam them in a small amount of salted water for 3 minutes; then cook them, covered, for 3 to 8 minutes longer until tender (according to size).]

2 cups fresh Brussels sprouts, trimmed, rinsed, halved
1 cup cherry tomatoes, rinsed, halved
4 large garlic cloves, minced

Red Wine and Honey Mustard Dressing (see page 377)

In a small bowl thoroughly mix dressing ingredients. Set aside or refrigerate until needed. Remove from refrigerator about 1 hour before using. Shake well before using.

Simmer Brussels sprouts in 1 cup water for 12 minutes. Drain. Transfer to a serving bowl; add tomatoes and minced garlic. Drizzle dressing over sprouts mixture; toss gently. Serve when sprouts are warm or at room temperature. Serves 4.

CHOCOLATE FUDGE PIE

$\frac{1}{2}$ cup butter or Smart Balance spread, softened

$\frac{1}{2}$ cup granulated sugar

3 large eggs, separated; or $\frac{3}{4}$ cup egg beaters and 3 portions *Just Whites*,
    dried egg whites

$\frac{1}{2}$ cup all-purpose flour

2 oz. (2 squares) unsweetened chocolate, melted and cooled

1 tbsp. vanilla extract

$\frac{1}{4}$ cup cherry preserves

1 cup heavy cream for whipping, whipped (at high speed), until soft peaks are formed; or
    1 cup frozen non-dairy whipped topping (fat-free available)

Preheat oven to 325°.

Grease and flour an 8-inch pie-pan.

In a mixing bowl, cream butter with sugar. Lightly beat egg yolks or egg substitute and add to butter/sugar mix. Add flour, chocolate and vanilla extract and mix thoroughly.

In another bowl, beat egg whites until stiff, but not dry. (Or, follow directions on package for dehydrated egg whites.) Fold into the batter.

Spread about one-fourth of batter evenly over bottom of an 8-inch prepared pie pan. Spread cherry preserves on top, spreading not quite to edge of pan. Cover with remaining batter.

Bake pie in preheated oven at 325° until surface of pie feels firm but texture feels soft, about 30 minutes. Do not overbake. Set pie on a rack to cool at room temperature. Serve with whipped cream. Serves 5-6.

A 50th Anniversary.

> **ZUPPA DI POLPETA**
> **(MAMA'S VEGETABLE BEEFBALL SOUP)**
>
> **CHICKEN ADOBO**
> **SPINACH, PORTOBELLOS AND BACON**
> **SPICY SALAD DRESSING (see page 381)**
> **APPLE-PEAR GALETTE**

SPINACH, PORTOBELLOS AND BACON

10 oz. baby spinach, rinsed, trimmed, drained
2 Portobellos, washed, drained, each sliced into $\frac{1}{2}$-inch thick pieces
1 medium-size red onion, thinly sliced
4 plum tomatoes, rinsed, sliced into rounds
3 strips lean pork bacon, cooked just until crisp, drained on paper towels

Spicy Salad Dressing (see page 381)

    Prepare Spicy Salad Dressing. Refrigerate dressing until 1 hour prior to serving. Shake or stir thoroughly before using.
    In a large salad bowl, combine spinach, Portobello slices, sliced onion and tomato rounds. Refrigerate salad until serving. Then, sprinkle dressing over salad; toss to mix thoroughly. Crush the bacon strips and sprinkle over salad bowl. Serves 6.

Bermuda Holiday.

ZUPPA DI POLPETA

[A Cooking Hint: "How to Skin a Tomato"
1) wash tomato
2) immerse tomato in boiling water for 1 minute
3) remove tomato from boiling water and plunge it into cold water.]

BEEFBALLS:

1 lb. double -chopped beef chuck
    (meat should be finely ground)
$\frac{1}{2}$ cup fine bread crumbs
1 tbsp. fresh parsley, minced
1 tbsp. onion, minced
    (reserve 1 tablespoon onion from
    1 large onion in "soup" recipe)

1 tsp. mustard spread
1 tsp. catsup
$\frac{1}{4}$ tsp. black pepper, dash of salt
1 egg beaten, or $\frac{1}{4}$ cup egg substitute

SOUP:

remainder of large onion used to prepare
    "beefballs", chopped
2 large garlic cloves, minced
$\frac{1}{4}$ cup olive oil
2 carrots, pared, chopped
2-3 plum tomatoes, skinned, mashed
1 large celery stalk, chopped
1 small sweet red pepper and

    $\frac{1}{2}$ long Italian green pepper,
    deseeded, chopped
3-4 small white mushrooms, rinsed,
    trimmed, chopped
1 small fennel bulb, trimmed, chopped

1 large all-purpose potato, pared, cubed
1 cup escarole, chopped bite-size,
    packed tightly
$\frac{1}{2}$ tsp. black pepper
1 tsp. salt, or to taste
1 tsp. dried oregano
1 bay leaf
1 cup barley
$\frac{1}{2}$ cup ditalini pasta
10-12 cups water
1 can (1 lb.) red kidney beans, rinsed in
    cold water, drained

1) Prepare "BEEFBALLS" by combining finely ground beef, crumbs, parsley, minced onion, mustard, catsup, salt, pepper, and egg in a bowl. The mixture should be thickly creamed and smooth. Form 1-inch meatballs with the aid of a teaspoon and your hands. You will probably form 16-18 balls. Set aside.

2) Prepare SOUP. In a large soup pot over medium heat, lightly brown chopped onion, garlic, celery and fennel in hot oil. Stir and scrape bottom of pot frequently. Brown beefballs, on all sides, 6 at a time, for a few minutes. Transfer meatballs as they cook, to a bowl. After all of the meatballs are cooked, return them to soup pot; pour 10-12 cups water into soup pot. Add and stir in carrots, chopped tomato and juice, potatoes, mushrooms, herbs and spices and barley. Cover and raise heat under pot. Bring pot to a boil; then, lower to simmer for 30 minutes. Stir in ditalini pasta, kidney beans and escarole and continue to simmer soup for an additional 8-10 minutes.

    Remove pot from burner; taste soup and adjust spices as needed. Remove and discard bay leaf before serving. Serves 6-8.

CHICKEN ADOBO

4 whole chicken legs/thighs and 2 chicken breasts, split,
    rinsed in cold water; patted dry with paper towels

ADOBO SAUCE:
$\frac{1}{2}$ cup white vinegar
$\frac{1}{2}$ cup *lite* soy sauce
4 bay leaves
$\frac{1}{2}$ tsp. freshly ground black pepper
$\frac{1}{4}$ cup fresh cilantro, minced
6 garlic cloves, minced
1 tbsp. olive oil

Have ready: a 9x12x3-inch flame-resistant roasting pan; a large platter.

In a 9x12x13-inch roasting pan (which fits over a large surface burner), combine prepared chicken legs/thighs and breast halves, vinegar, soy sauce, bay leaves, pepper and 2 teaspoons of minced garlic. Place pan over high heat and bring to a boil. Then, reduce heat to simmer and cook chicken uncovered, turning chicken, often, for 25 minutes. Chicken should be tender, clear juices running from the thigh when pricked with a fork.
    Transfer chicken parts to a platter. Strain the cooking liquid in the pot, to remove fat. Set bowl of liquid aside.
    Return the roasting pan to high heat; add the olive oil and remaining minced garlic. When oil is hot, return chicken to roasting pan and sauté chicken on both sides until browned, about 3 minutes per side. Add reserved liquid and minced cilantro and simmer for 5-10 minutes.
    Remove chicken pieces to a large serving platter. Pour the sauce over chicken and serve. Serves 6.

Ahida, José and Family in Santo Domingo. Photos: A. Molina

APPLE-PEAR GALETTE

CRUST:
2 cups all-purpose flour
$\frac{1}{2}$ tsp. salt
1 tbsp. granulated sugar
2 tbsp. less than 1 cup butter or Smart Balance spread
a little more than $\frac{1}{3}$ cup ice water

FILLING:
2 large Granny Smith apples, peeled, cored
3-4 Bartlett pears, peeled, cored
juice of 1 lemon
$\frac{1}{2}$ cup cranberry raisins
$\frac{1}{3}$ cup dark brown sugar
1 tbsp. flour
1 tsp. ground cinnamon
1 tsp. coriander
$\frac{1}{2}$ tsp. ground nutmeg
2 tbsp. butter or Smart Balance spread
1 tbsp. granulated sugar mixed with 1 tbsp. ground cinnamon

Whipped cream or Vanilla ice cream

Preheat oven to 425°.

Have ready: a 10-inch round pizza pan or a 9x12-inch baking sheet, lightly greased.

Prepare CRUST. In a medium-size bowl, mix together: flour, salt and sugar. Add cold butter and cut into dough with a pastry cutter or 2 forks, until dough is crumbly and the texture is pea-like. Slowly add ice water just until dough comes together. Loosely gather dough into a ball and wrap it in plastic wrap; refrigerate dough while you prepare FILLING.
Thinly slice apples and pears. Place fruit in a bowl. Add cranberry raisins, lemon juice, brown sugar, flour and spices. Toss the mixture together.
Remove dough from refrigerator. Gently pat dough onto a lightly greased round pizza pan or a 9x12 rectangular baking sheet. (You can also roll out dough on a board, with a rolling pin.)
Lay fruit on a dough-covered pan, in overlapping circles or rows; then, fold the pastry up and around the edges to create a rim, pinching the dough together as it meets. Dot top of galette with butter and sprinkle with cinnamon-sugar.
Bake galette in a preheated oven at 425° for about 45-50 minutes; or until lightly browned and crisp on the bottom. Cool to room temperature and serve with a dollop of whipped cream or vanilla ice cream. Serves 6.

> **SAUSAGE LENTIL SOUP**
> **VENISON ROAST**
> **POTATOES IN SWISS**
> **GREEN BEANS AND PEPPERS**
> **CHOCOLATE ANGEL CAKE**

SAUSAGE LENTIL SOUP

2 tbsp. olive oil

4 links spicy Italian sausage with fennel; remove casing, chop sausage into small pieces

12 cups water

1 pkg. (1 lb.) brown lentils, picked over, rinsed in colander and drained

2-3 garlic cloves, minced

1 small onion, chopped

1 large celery stalk with greens, chopped

1 large carrot, pared, chopped

$\frac{1}{4}$ cup sun dried tomatoes, chopped

1 small sweet red pepper, deseeded, chopped

1 small poblano pepper, deseeded, chopped (Wear plastic gloves when using hot pepper.)

3-4 ripe plum tomatoes, chopped

2-3 bay leaves (leave whole)

1 tbsp. oregano

1 tsp. salt (to taste)

$\frac{1}{2}$ tsp. black pepper

$\frac{1}{4}$ cup brown rice

$\frac{1}{4}$ cup orzo

$\frac{1}{2}$ cup tiny shells pasta

In a 6-quart soup pot with a lid, lightly brown chopped sausage in 2 tablespoons olive oil. Add onion and garlic, scraping bottom of pot to prevent sticking. Pour 12 cups of water into the pot and add lentils, celery, carrot, sun dried and plum tomatoes, all peppers, herbs, spices and brown rice.

Cover pot and bring to a boil. Simmer soup gently for $1\frac{1}{2}$ hours, stirring occasionally. If serving soup within the day, add orzo and tiny shells to the soup during the last 10 minutes of cooking. (Or, cook the pasta separately on the day of serving, to add to the soup.) This soup freezes well, without the pasta. Add pasta before serving. Remove bay leaves and discard before serving. Serves 8-10.

VENISON ROAST
(You may substitute a 5 to 7-pound eye round Beef Roast.)

1 boneless venison roast, 5-7 lbs.

6 garlic cloves, slivered

$\frac{1}{4}$ cup peppercorns

4 tbsp. mustard dressing

2 cups catsup

$\frac{1}{2}$ tsp. salt

$\frac{1}{2}$ tsp. freshly ground black pepper

1 lg. onion, sliced

1 red bell pepper, deseeded, sliced vertically

1 green bell pepper, deseeded, sliced vertically

1 orange bell pepper, deseeded, sliced vertically

Preheat oven to 350°.

Have ready: a large roasting pan with ovenproof handles, about 13x14x3 x$\frac{1}{2}$-inches; aluminum foil.

Make 1 dozen $\frac{1}{2}$-inch deep slits around the roast. Insert peppercorns and garlic slivers into the slits. Lay the meat in the roasting pan.   Combine catsup and mustard. Spread this mixture all over the roast; sprinkle salt and pepper over the roast.
Cover the roast with slices of peppers and onions. Make a tent with a large sheet of aluminum foil. Cover the pan with foil and bake the roast with onions and peppers for 2-2$\frac{1}{2}$ hours, until tender. Baste the roast with its own juices several times as it cooks. Allow the roast to rest for 15 minutes before slicing. Serve with its own gravy and vegetables. Serves 8.

Marie and Neil Restaino and Family celebrate Christmas. Photo: N and M Restaino

POTATOES IN SWISS

1 small onion, finely sliced
2 lbs. all-purpose potatoes, peeled, thinly sliced
2 tbsp. olive oil
$\frac{1}{2}$ cup shredded Finlandia Swiss cheese

$\frac{1}{4}$ tsp. salt
$\frac{1}{4}$ tsp. freshly ground black pepper
2 eggs or $\frac{1}{2}$ cup egg substitute
2 cups sour cream (fat-free available)
$\frac{1}{4}$ tsp. nutmeg

Preheat oven to 325°.

Have ready: a greased 2-quart, shallow ovenproof dish.

Grease sides and bottom of a 2-quart, round, shallow ovenproof dish with olive oil. Mix sliced potatoes and onions in a bowl. Arrange half of the potato-onion mix to line the inside of the oiled dish. Sprinkle with shredded cheese. Overlap remaining onions/potatoes to make an attractive top layer. Sprinkle with salt and pepper.

In a bowl, whisk eggs, sour cream and nutmeg until blended. Pour over potatoes; drizzle remaining 1 tablespoon of olive oil over dish. Bake in a preheated oven at 325° for 1 hour and 15 minutes, or until bubbly, and potatoes are tender. Allow to rest for 10 minutes before serving. Serves 6.

GREEN BEANS AND PEPPERS

$1\frac{1}{2}$ lbs. green beans, ends trimmed
1 red bell pepper, deseeded, cut into strips
1 yellow bell pepper, deseeded, cut into strips
2 tbsp. honey mustard
2 tbsp. balsamic vinegar

2 tbsp. *lite* soy sauce
2 tbsp. olive oil
freshly ground black pepper and salt, to taste
$\frac{1}{4}$ cup chopped fresh dill

Cook beans in boiling water to cover until tender, about 5-6 minutes. Drain in colander. Transfer to a large serving bowl. Place peppers in a colander and slowly pour a quart-pot of boiling water over them. Drain and transfer peppers to the large bowl to combine with green beans. Set aside.

In a small bowl, blend mustard, vinegar and soy sauce. Whisk in olive oil and season with salt and pepper. Pour this sauce over the vegetables; toss well. Sprinkle with dill and toss again. Serve warm or at room temperature. Serves 4-6.

CHOCOLATE ANGEL CAKE

[A Cooking Hint: Place pans with cakes, pies, cookies on a rack in the "center" of the preheated oven to circulate heat around filled pan.]

2 egg whites or 2 portions of *Just Whites* 100% pure dried egg whites;
    (refer to directions on container)
$\frac{1}{2}$ cup granulated sugar
2 tbsp. all-purpose flour
$1\frac{1}{2}$ cups shredded coconut
$\frac{1}{2}$ cup semisweet chocolate morsels
$\frac{1}{2}$ cup sliced almonds with skins
1 pkg. (22 oz.) devils food cake mix
1 pkg. (4 oz.) instant chocolate pudding
4 eggs or 1 cup egg substitute
$\frac{3}{4}$ cup low-fat milk
$\frac{1}{2}$ cup Amaretto liqueur or almond liqueur
$\frac{1}{3}$ cup canola oil

confectioners' sugar
maraschino cherries
slices from 1 navel orange
shredded coconut

Preheat oven to 350°.

Have ready: Grease and flour a 10-cup fluted tube pan.

Beat egg whites until foamy. Add sugar, a tablespoon at a time and beat until mixture forms stiff, shiny peaks. Fold in almonds, coconut, morsels and flour. Set aside.
In a large bowl, combine cake mix, pudding mix, eggs, milk, liqueur and oil. Beat with an electric mixer at medium speed for 2 minutes. Pour half of this batter into a prepared pan. Evenly spoon egg white mixture over batter in pan; then top with remaining chocolate batter.
Bake cake in center of preheated oven at 350° for 50-55 minutes or until cake tests done. Cool in pan for 20 minutes. Remove from pan and complete cooling on wire rack. Garnish with confectioners' sugar and maraschino cherries and orange slices. Sprinkle with shredded coconut. Serves 8-10.

GERMAN POTATO SOUP
SAUSAGE AND CHEDDAR MEATLOAF
VEGETABLE PIEROGI
NUTTY APPLES AND ICE CREAM

GERMAN POTATO SOUP

3 quarts water (12 cups); or, 2 quarts water and
    1 quart low-salt chicken stock
    (You may make your own chicken stock;
    see page 81)
6 large all-purpose potatoes (about 3 lbs.),
    peeled, diced
1 large onion, diced

1 tbsp. olive oil
1 tbsp. Hungarian paprika
2 cups sour cream; bring to room temperature
$\frac{1}{2}$ cup chopped Italian parsley
$\frac{1}{2}$ tsp. black pepper
1 tsp. salt
2 strips lean bacon

8-10 oz. narrow egg noodles

Have ready: a 6-quart soup pot with lid.

Add diced potatoes and parsley to 3 quarts of water (or water mixed with chicken stock). Bring to a boil; cover pot and reduce heat to simmer for 15 minutes. Add noodles and simmer for 10 minutes longer, without lid, stirring frequently.

Meanwhile in a small skillet, over medium heat, sauté onion and bacon in oil until bacon crisps and onion browns, about 5-7 minutes. Remove bacon to drain on paper towels. Slightly cool onion; stir in paprika, salt and pepper; add this mixture to soup pot.

Stir 1 cupful of soup broth into sour cream, stirring until smooth. Crumble bacon and stir into the soup. Add the sour cream to the pot of soup, stirring until smooth. Set soup aside to thicken as it rests, and to allow the flavors to meld. Taste and adjust seasonings, if necessary. Serves 8-10.

SAUSAGE AND CHEDDAR MEATLOAF

2 lbs. ground sirloin

1 lb. spicy Italian pork sausage, removed from
    casing and crumbled

1 cup toasted rye bread, coarsely crumbled

2 eggs or $\frac{1}{2}$ cup egg substitute, beaten

$\frac{1}{2}$ tsp. salt

$\frac{1}{4}$ tsp. black pepper

$\frac{1}{2}$ cup catsup

1 cup corn flake crumbs

2 tbsp. olive oil for pan

$\frac{1}{4}$ cup spicy mustard

$\frac{1}{4}$ cup finely chopped Italian parsley

1 onion, finely chopped

$1\frac{1}{2}$ cups grated sharp Cheddar cheese, divided

3 strips lean bacon, cooked crisp, drained
    on paper towels, crumbled

2 hard-cooked large eggs, chopped

Preheat oven 350°.

Have ready: line inside of 10x15x4-inch baking pan with aluminum foil; brush pan with olive oil; 2 sheets waxed paper.

In a large mixing bowl, thoroughly combine ground sirloin, sausage, bread crumbs, beaten eggs, onion, salt, pepper, catsup and mustard. In a separate bowl, combine parsley, 1 cup Cheddar (reserve remaining $\frac{1}{2}$ cup), chopped hard cooked eggs and crumbled bacon.

Lay a large sheet of waxed paper on a work board. Spread 1 cup corn flake crumbs over the waxed paper. Pour meat mixture over the board/waxed paper/crumbs. Lay another sheet of waxed paper over the meat mixture and with a rolling pin, roll this mix into a rectangle, about 1-inch thick.

Remove top sheet of waxed paper and spread the egg and bacon mix all over the top of the flattened meat. Roll up the meat like a jelly roll, peeling back the remaining waxed paper as you go. Shape the ends of the roll with your hands to form a neat cylindrical form, entirely enclosing the bacon and egg mixture.

Lay the meatloaf, seam side down in the prepared baking pan. Sprinkle the meatloaf with remaining $\frac{1}{2}$ cup Cheddar cheese. Bake meatloaf in preheated oven at 350° for 60-70 minutes, until cooked through and browned. Serve hot. Serves 6.

VEGETABLE PIEROGI
*[A Cooking Hint: Add 1 tablespoon oil to butter when pan-browning,
to prevent butter from burning.]*

DUMPLINGS:

2 cups fresh plain yogurt	1 tsp. salt
1 egg, lightly beaten or $\frac{1}{4}$ cup egg substitute	$2\frac{1}{4}$ cups all-purpose flour (water)

FILLING:

1 very large potato ($\frac{1}{2}$-$\frac{3}{4}$ lb.)	$\frac{1}{2}$ tsp. salt
5 tbsp. butter or Smart Balance spread, and 1 tbsp. olive oil	$\frac{1}{4}$ tsp. black pepper sour cream at serving
1 onion, chopped	
1 cup peas (fresh, if available; or, use frozen peas, defrosted)	
1 lb. white mushrooms, trimmed and minced	

Prepare the DUMPLING DOUGH. Lightly heat yogurt, egg, and salt together with an electric mixer. Slowly add flour and continue to beat until smooth. Knead dough on a floured board, until smooth. Add water, one teaspoon at a time, only if needed to smoothen out the dough; it should feel like pizza dough. Form dough into a ball; wrap it in a clean kitchen towel; set it aside in a cool place for 2 hours.

Meanwhile, Prepare the FILLING. Peel and quarter the potato(es). Place them in a small pot and cover with cold water. Bring pot to a boil; lower heat and simmer until very tender, about 15-20 minutes. Drain potatoes. Whip the potatoes with 1 tablespoon butter until fluffy and creamy. Set aside.

Melt 2 tablespoons butter in a skillet over medium heat. Add onion and sauté until translucent, about 5 minutes. Add remaining 2 tablespoons butter/oil to skillet. Add mushrooms, peas, salt and pepper and sauté until mushrooms are tender and any residual water from the vegetables evaporates, about 5 minutes. Remove the mixture from skillet and set aside to slightly cool. Mix and blend vegetables into the mashed potatoes.

Bring a large pot of salted water to a boil.

Meanwhile, roll out dough $\frac{1}{8}$-inch thick. Cut into 3-inch rounds with a cookie cutter or rim of a glass. Spoon 1 heaping teaspoon of mashed potato filling on one side of the circle. Fold the other side over the filling so the pierogi resembles a half moon. Press edges together; seal pierogi with tines of a fork (or between your thumb and index finger).

Lower heat under boiling pot to simmer gently. One by one, add the pierogi to the simmering water and cook them in batches of 4-6 until cooked through, about 5-6 minutes. (I prefer to use 2 pots of simmering water, simultaneously.) Remove pierogi with a slotted spoon and drain on paper towels. Keep them warm in a serving bowl, while cooking remaining pierogi. Serve with sour cream. Makes about 25-30 pierogi; serves 5-6.

NUTTY APPLES AND ICE CREAM

[A Cooking Hint: Rinse all vegetables and fruits prior to eating them. This means berries, oranges, apples and melons, as well. Drain greens and berries thoroughly. Gently pat-dry berries with paper towels.]

6 medium-to-large Golden Delicious apples, cored

5 tbsp. butter or Smart Balance spread, softened;
    (additional butter for bottom of baking pan)

$\frac{1}{4}$ cup sugar

$\frac{1}{4}$ cup honey

$\frac{1}{2}$ cup shelled pistachio nuts

$\frac{1}{2}$ cup pignola (pine nuts)

$\frac{1}{2}$ cup chopped walnuts

$\frac{1}{2}$ cup cranberry raisins

$\frac{1}{2}$ tsp. ground cloves

$\frac{1}{2}$ tsp. ground cinnamon

2 tsp. brandy

Vanilla ice cream or whipped cream or whipped topping
    (fat-free available), at serving time

Preheat oven to 350°.

Butter bottom of a 9x12-inch baking pan.

Cream 4 tablespoons of butter with sugar and honey in a mixing bowl. Add all of the nuts, raisins, cloves, cinnamon and brandy. Chop all of the ingredients together to resemble a paste.

Stuff each cored apple with the nut mixture. Stand them, stem end down, in the baking pan. Rub skin of each apple with remaining 1 tablespoon butter and sprinkle any remaining nut mixture over the apples.

Bake apples in preheated oven at 350°, until soft, about 35-40 minutes. An inserted toothpick should easily slip in and out of cooked apple. Serve apples warm with vanilla ice cream or whipped cream or whipped topping (fat-free available). Serves 6.

THE MOST SCRUMPTIOUS TURKEY SOUP
CORNBREAD CAKES WITH FENNEL SAUSAGES, RAISINS AND PISTACHIOS
GREENS STIR-FRY
BLUE ANGEL PUFF

CORNBREAD CAKES WITH FENNEL SAUSAGES, RAISINS AND PISTACHIOS

2 cups packaged cornbread stuffing

4-5 links Italian fennel sausages,
    cut into narrow rounds (*NOTE: below)

1 large onion, finely chopped

1 large carrot, pared, trimmed, finely chopped

1 large celery stalk, trimmed, finely chopped

1 large garlic clove, minced

1 red bell pepper, deseeded, finely chopped

2 tbsp. olive oil

$\frac{1}{2}$ cup pistachio nuts, finely chopped

$\frac{1}{2}$ cup golden raisins

1 tbsp. fresh parsley, minced

$\frac{1}{4}$ tsp. cinnamon

$\frac{1}{2}$ tsp. ground cumin

1 tsp. ground coriander

$\frac{1}{2}$ tsp. dried thyme

freshly ground black pepper to taste

2 eggs, beaten or $\frac{1}{2}$ cup egg substitute

1 cup less-salt chicken broth, boiling hot

*NOTE: Freeze uncooked sausages for several hours; you will find that frozen sausages slice more evenly.

Preheat oven to 375°.

Have ready: a 9x12-inch ovenproof glass pan, generously greased with butter or Smart Balance spread.

In a large skillet cook sausage rounds, onion, garlic, carrot, pepper and celery in 2 tablespoons olive oil over moderate-low heat, stirring occasionally for 4-5 minutes, until sausages are cooked and vegetables are softened. Add pistachios, raisins, parsley, spices and herbs, cooking for 1 minute longer.

Transfer this mixture to a very large bowl. Add and combine cornbread stuffing, beaten eggs and hot broth and blend the mixture thoroughly. With your hands and a large serving spoon, form 3-inch patties. Lay the patties in a well-buttered 9x12 ovenproof, casserole dish. Bake the patties in preheated oven at 375° for 20 minutes. Makes 8-10 patties.

THE MOST SCRUMPTIOUS TURKEY SOUP

(In the olden days, when folks enjoyed "home cookin", my Mom would provide "doggie bags" for our Thanksgiving guests (usually aunts, uncles, and cousins). Her live-in family hardly ever had leftovers, leftover for us.

After the Cook's baton had been passed on to her only daughter, ME, I made sure that we had leftovers from the Thanksgiving meal. I roasted two turkeys (Tom Turkey was roasted on Thanksgiving Day; Teddy Turkey performed for the weekend following the actual feast.) We were provided with the feast for the day, the leftovers to share for sandwich wraps and turkey loaf or meatballs, and a couple of gallons of the most scrumptious turkey soup (prepared from the turkey carcass).

Now, you may ask, if turkey soup was the primary motive for roasting two birds, why not use the Turkey Day bird's carcass for a couple of gallons of scrumptious soup? Because Mama packed up carcass #1 for her own gallon of scrumptious soup.)

leftover carcass from a 10-14 lb. turkey

12 cups (3 qts.) water

about 2 cups chopped leftover
    dark and light turkey meat

2 large yellow onions, coarsely chopped

2 large celery stalks, pared, trimmed,
    coarsely chopped

2 large carrots, pared, trimmed,
    sliced in narrow rounds

1 large LI potato, pared, chopped
    into small chunks

4-5 small mushrooms, cleaned,
    coarsely chopped

$\frac{1}{4}$ cup each: minced sweet red pepper,
    green pepper

1 can (15 oz.) corn kernels

$\frac{1}{2}$ cup fresh parsley, chopped

3 ripe Italian plum tomatoes, skin removed,
    chopped (Immerse plum tomatoes in
    boiling water for 1 minute; remove from
    water and peel off skin with fingers.)

1 tbsp. black peppercorns

$\frac{1}{2}$ tsp. black pepper

3 bay leaves

1 tsp. dried thyme

1 tsp. dried crushed sage

1 tsp. salt (to taste)

$\frac{1}{2}$ cup uncooked white rice

1 tbsp. olive oil

Remove turkey scraps in bite-size pieces from turkey carcass to a small bowl. Remove and discard gristle and loose bones from carcass. Prepare vegetables as listed in ingredients and transfer onions, celery, carrots, potato, mushrooms, red and green peppers to a large bowl. Pour 12 cups water into a large stock pot with cover; add the trimmed turkey carcass. Cover the pot and bring to a simmer. Simmer the turkey bones for 1 hour, occasionally skimming off the foam.

Return soup pot to counter and remove carcass from pot. Use a strainer to remove any remnants of bones from the pot. To the pot, add and stir in the bowl of prepared vegetables. Cover the pot and return it to the stove burner. Bring the soup pot to a full boil. Add rice; cover the pot and lower to simmer for 30 minutes. Stir in parsley, bay leaves, thyme, sage, salt, peppercorns, black pepper, tomatoes, corn kernels and cooked turkey pieces. Continue to simmer the soup for another 10 minutes. Remove and discard bay leaves before serving. Serves 12 hearty portions.

Lamb Chops, Pears in Fontina, page 286

Rigatoni, Meatballs and Broccoli Rabe, page 132

Sole Amandine on a Bed of Mushrooms, Peppers, Asparagus, page 259

Polynesian Roasted Pork, page 212

Cornish Game Hens, Rosemary and Wine, page 124

Cheddar Cheese Meatloaf, page 166

Not Just Another Stuffed Veal Cutlet, page 208

Artichokes Stuffed with Prosciutto, Provolone and Olives, page 218

Flounder Kiev, page 197

Manicotti, page 134

Beef Stew with Dumplings, page 119

Salmon Stuffed Potatoes, page 77

Spicy Crusted Tuna Steaks, page 279

Mediterranean Roasted Stuffed Peppers, page 284

Pasta, Chicken and Broccoli, page 131

Potato Vegetable Roast, page 213

GREENS STIR-FRY

2 tbsp. peanut oil
2 garlic cloves, minced
1 lb. bok choy, rinsed, drained, shredded
10 oz. baby spinach
2 cups snow peas, trimmed, rinsed, drained
1 celery stalk, trimmed, chopped
1 green bell pepper, cored, deseeded,
   finely sliced

1 tsp. star anise, ground
$\frac{1}{4}$ cup water
$\frac{1}{2}$ tsp. salt
1 tbsp. sesame oil
1 tbsp. ginger soy sauce

Have ready: a large wok or a skillet with a cover.

Heat peanut oil in a large wok or skillet. Add garlic and stir-fry for 30 seconds. Stir in salt, star anise, bok choy, spinach, snow peas, celery and green pepper. Stir-fry the salad for 3-4 minutes. Drizzle water over greens; cover and cook for 3-4 minutes. Remove cover and stir in ginger soy sauce and sesame oil. Mix greens together thoroughly. Transfer the greens to a warm serving platter. Serves 6.

....

BLUE ANGEL PUFF

$\frac{1}{2}$ cup butter or Smart Balance spread
1 cup granulated sugar
2 eggs, separated or 2 portions egg whites
   and $\frac{1}{2}$ cup egg substitute
$\frac{1}{2}$ cup all-purpose flour
1 tsp. baking powder

$\frac{1}{4}$ tsp. salt
$\frac{1}{3}$ cup evaporated milk (fat-free available)
1 tsp. lemon extract
$1\frac{1}{2}$ cups fresh blueberries, lightly floured
(*NOTE: below)

*NOTE: Be sure to gently and thoroughly pat-dry blueberries. Scatter them over a large plate and sprinkle all over with 2 tablespoons flour. Set aside.

Preheat oven to 350°.

Have ready: 10-inch tube pan, greased and floured.

Cream together butter (or Smart Balance spread) and sugar until light and fluffy. Beat in egg yolks (or egg substitute). Combine milk and lemon extract. Sift dry ingredients; add to creamed mixture alternately with milk/lemon extract. Beat egg whites until stiff; fold into batter. Gently fold in floured blueberries. Pour batter into greased and floured 10-inch tube pan and bake in preheated oven at 350° for 35-40 minutes, or until cake springs back when touched lightly. Serves 8.

171

> ### GREENS AND BEANS SOUP
> ### CHICKEN TANDOORI
> ### COUSCOUS SALAD
> ### SPINACH BALLS
> ### BABA AU RHUM

GREENS AND BEANS SOUP

$\frac{1}{2}$ cup dried white beans, rinsed, picked over
   and soaked overnight in water to cover
2 tbsp. olive oil
1 garlic clove, minced
1 onion, minced
1 small fennel bulb, trimmed, minced
4 celery stalks, cut into small chunks
2 cups escarole, rinsed, shredded
2 cups green cabbage, rinsed, shredded
2 cups green beans, cut into small pieces
2 all-purpose potatoes, pared and cubed

12 cups (3 qts.) homemade chicken broth
   (see page 81);
   or packaged less-salt chicken broth
$\frac{1}{4}$ cup Italian parsley, chopped
$\frac{1}{4}$ cup fresh basil leaves, chopped
1 tsp. salt, or to taste
$\frac{1}{2}$ tsp. freshly ground black pepper
1 cup Parmesan cheese, grated;
   more Parmesan cheese at serving

Have ready: a medium-size sauce pan with a cover; a large soup pot with a cover.

Rinse soaked and drained beans and put them in a medium-size sauce pan with water to cover; cover with lid; bring to a boil over high heat. Reduce heat to medium and cook until beans are tender, about 30 minutes. Drain and set aside.

Warm olive oil in a large stock pot over low heat. Add garlic, onion and fennel and sauté until softened, about 10 minutes. Add celery, escarole, cabbage, green beans, potatoes, the pot of tender white beans and chicken broth. Cover pot and bring to a boil. Reduce heat and simmer for 1 hour. Stir in parsley, basil, salt and pepper and simmer for 30 minutes longer. Stir in Parmesan cheese. Garnish with more cheese at serving. Serves 6-8.

CHICKEN TANDOORI
(Start recipe evening before serving.)

3 whole chicken legs/thighs, and 2 chicken breasts, split;
    rinse in cool water; pat dry with paper towels
1 tsp. salt
1 cup plain yogurt (fat-free available)
2 tbsp. fresh lemon juice
1 tbsp. grated lemon rind
1 tbsp. white vinegar
4 garlic cloves, minced
2 tsp. fresh ginger, minced
1 tbsp. Garam Masala (see page 387)
$\frac{1}{4}$ cup olive oil

On day before serving, rub salt all over the pieces of chicken. Set the chicken in a large bowl. In a small bowl, combine yogurt, lemon juice, lemon rind, vinegar, garlic, ginger and Garam Masala. Pour over the chicken. Cover the bowl with plastic wrap and marinate chicken in refrigerator overnight, turning once.

One hour before serving, remove chicken from refrigerator and preheat oven to 500° (a very hot oven). If using a charcoal grill, light the coals.

Remove chicken from marinade and drizzle each piece with olive oil. Discard marinade. Roast in pan until juices run clear when thigh is pricked with fork, about 35-40 minutes. If grilling, set chicken parts on preheated grill, turning the chicken 4 or 5 times, until juices run clear, about 30 minutes. Serves 6.

Gather the Family to Celebrate with Delores and John Mazzola.
Photo: D. Mazzola

COUSCOUS SALAD

1½ cups dry couscous, 2½ cups water
¼ tsp. black pepper, salt to taste
¼ cup olive oil
¼ cup fresh lemon juice
2 large tomatoes, chopped with juice
1 medium-size zucchini, halved lengthwise,
    thinly sliced

½ cup fresh basil, shredded
1 large onion, thinly sliced
½ cup chopped pitted Kalamata olives
1 cup feta cheese, crumbled

Have ready: a medium-size serving bowl; plastic wrap.

In a 2-quart saucepan, bring 2½ cups water to a boil; stir in dry couscous. Cover pot. Remove pot from burner and allow covered pot of couscous to stand 5 minutes.
    Spoon into a serving bowl. Stir in pepper, salt, olive oil and lemon juice. Add zucchini, tomatoes, basil, onion and olives. Cover bowl with plastic wrap and refrigerate overnight.
    Just before serving, stir in feta cheese. Serves 6.

SPINACH BALLS

10 oz. baby spinach, rinsed, chopped, steamed
    in ½ cup water for 30 seconds; drained
2 cups packaged crumbled cornbread stuffing
1 onion, finely chopped

4 eggs, beaten or 1 cup egg substitute
½ cup butter or Smart Balance spread, melted
½ cup Parmesan cheese, grated

Preheat oven to 375°.

Have ready: a 9x12 baking sheet.

Squeeze water from steamed spinach with your hands. Combine all ingredients with drained spinach in a large bowl. Form the mixture into 2-inch balls with your hands and place them on a baking sheet. Bake them in preheated oven at 375° for about 20 minutes. Serve very warm. Serves 6.

BABA AU RHUM
[A Cooking Hint: Do not pre-sift flour unless specified in recipe.]

1 pkg. granulated yeast

$\frac{1}{3}$ cup warm milk

$2\frac{1}{2}$ cups sifted flour

$\frac{1}{2}$ cup butter or Smart Balance spread, softened

$2\frac{2}{3}$ cups granulated sugar

6 eggs or 2 eggs plus 1 cup egg substitute

$5\frac{1}{2}$ cups water

$\frac{1}{2}$ cup dark rum

Candied fruits for garnish

Have ready: a 10-inch Bundt pan or Savarin mold, buttered; a clean linen/cotton cloth.

Dissolve yeast in milk in a large non-metal bowl. Stir in $\frac{1}{2}$ cup of flour. Cover bowl with a towel and set aside in a warm place to rise for 30 minutes.

Beat 7 tablespoons of the butter in an electric mixer or blender. Beat in 2 tablespoons of the sugar and 2 tablespoons of the flour. Beat in the eggs, one portion at a time.

Beat the remaining flour into the risen yeast mixture; then, beat in the butter/egg mixture to make a thick dough-like batter. Butter a large baba or savarin mold or a Bundt pan with the remaining butter and spoon the batter into the mold. It should fill it halfway. Cover the mold with a clean cloth and set aside to rise until the dough reaches the top of the mold.

Preheat oven to 350°.

Bake baba for about 40 minutes, until browned on top. While the baba is baking, combine remaining sugar with the water in a saucepan and boil until syrupy and reduced by half way. Remove from heat and stir in rum.

When baba is baked, remove from oven and spoon rum syrup over it, allowing syrup to saturate the baba completely.

Cool baba completely. Then, unmold and garnish with candied fruit before serving. Serves 8-10.

FOR STELLA AND RAYMUND WU

HOT AND SOUR SOUP

SWEET AND SOUR BATTERED SHRIMP

CUMIN RICE AND PEPPERS

CURRIED GREEN BEANS

CHINESE NEW YEAR CAKE (NIAN GAO)

SWEET AND SOUR BATTERED SHRIMP

2 doz. large raw shrimp, shelled, cleaned,
    rinsed in cold water, drained

2 tbsp. fresh gingerroot, grated

1 garlic clove, minced

3 scallions with greens, thinly sliced

3 tbsp. sherry

2 tsp. sesame oil

1 tbsp. *lite* soy sauce

Enough canola oil for deep-frying, about 1 cup

4 scallions, with greens,
    each finely sliced lengthwise for garnish

BATTER:

6 egg whites or 6 portions dried egg whites
    mixed with water
    (see directions on package)

6 tbsp. cornstarch

4 tbsp. all-purpose flour

SAUCE:

$\frac{1}{4}$ cup tomato paste

$\frac{1}{4}$ cup white wine vinegar

$\frac{1}{4}$ cup *lite* soy sauce

juice from 1 lemon (about 2 tbsp.)

1 tbsp. grated lemon zest

$\frac{1}{4}$ cup brown sugar

1 green bell pepper, cored, deseeded and
    cut into thin matchsticks

$\frac{1}{2}$ tsp. chili sauce

2 cups packaged low-salt vegetable stock

1 tbsp. cornstarch

    Have ready: a large skillet.

    Place prepared shrimp in a large dish. Blend ginger, garlic, scallions, sherry, oil and soy sauce in a small bowl. Spread this sauce over the shrimp. Cover plate with plastic wrap and marinate shrimp in refrigerator for 30 minutes.

    Prepare BATTER by beating egg whites in a bowl until thick and foamy. Fold in flour and cornstarch to form a light batter.

    Place all SAUCE ingredients into a sauce pan and bring to a boil. Reduce heat to simmer for 10 minutes. Remove shrimp from marinade and dip them into batter to coat. (Discard remaining marinade.)

    Heat canola oil in a large skillet almost to smoking. Reduce heat and fry shrimp for 3-4 minutes until crisp. Serve shrimp with sauce; garnish with scallions. Serves 4-6.

HOT AND SOUR SOUP

[A Cooking Hint: Read recipe before you commence. Arrange all ingredients in separate small bowls as directed. This recipe is not as involved as you may think.]

$\frac{1}{2}$ lb. lean pork loin; freeze the pork for 1 hour until firm; with a sharp knife shred pork into $\frac{1}{4}$-inch slices

6 dried shitake mushrooms, coarsely chopped

4 fresh small white mushrooms, coarsely chopped

$\frac{1}{4}$ cup bamboo shoots, shredded

$\frac{1}{4}$ cup chopped scallion bulbs with some greens; 1 scallion finely chopped, for garnish

$\frac{1}{4}$ cup broccoli stems, splintered

$1\frac{1}{2}$ tbsp. *lite* soy sauce

$2\frac{1}{2}$ tbsp. cornstarch, (water)

2 tbsp. sesame oil, 1 tbsp. canola oil

1 tbsp. sherry

3 tbsp. red wine vinegar

5 cups chicken broth (low-salt if using packaged broth); or (see page 81 for recipe)

6 oz. fresh bean curd (tofu), cut into 1-inch chunks

1 tsp. freshly ground black pepper

2 eggs, lightly beaten, or $\frac{1}{2}$ cup egg substitute

Have ready: a large wok or large skillet (wide and shallow).

Arrange in separate small bowls as follows:

Bowl 1: shredded pork, 1 tbsp. soy sauce, $\frac{1}{2}$ tbsp. cornstarch, 1 tbsp. sesame oil, 1 tbsp. sherry; stir thoroughly

Bowl 2: chopped shitake and white mushrooms

Bowl 3: shredded bamboo shoots, splintered broccoli stems, chopped scallion bulb

Bowl 4: chicken broth

Bowl 5: 3 tbsp. red wine vinegar, $\frac{1}{2}$ tbsp. soy sauce

Bowl 6: 2 tbsp. cornstarch dissolved in 3 tablespoons water

Bowl 7: Tofu

Bowl 8: black pepper and 1 tbsp. sesame oil

Bowl 9: beaten egg

Bowl 10: scallion for garnish

Heat wok or a large skillet over high heat. Add 1 tablespoon canola oil. When oil is hot, add shredded pork mixture, stirring to separate strands of pork.

Add all mushrooms, bamboo shoots, broccoli stems and scallion bulb. Stir fry for 1 minute; add chicken broth; lower heat to simmer. Add vinegar and remaining soy sauce and simmer for 5 minutes.

Dissolve remaining 2 tablespoons of cornstarch in 3 tablespoons water. Stir this mixture into the broth. When it is thickened, add tofu and bring mixture to a boil. Remove pan from heat and add black pepper and remaining tablespoon of sesame oil.

Pour beaten eggs into wok in a thin stream, stirring and blending them gently in a circular motion so the eggs do not "cook". Cover the pan and allow to rest for 1 minute. Sprinkle with scallion garnish and serve immediately. Serves 4-5.

CUMIN RICE AND PEPPERS

2 tbsp. olive oil

4 scallions with some greens, finely chopped

4 garlic cloves, minced

1 small red bell pepper, cored, deseeded, finely chopped

1 small green bell pepper, cored, deseeded, finely chopped

$2\frac{1}{2}$ cups prepared chicken stock (see "How to Prepare Chicken Stock", page 81; or use packaged low-salt chicken stock)

1 cup long-grain rice

2 tsp. cumin seeds

1 tsp. dried oregano

$\frac{1}{2}$ tsp. freshly ground black pepper

salt, to taste

In a 2-quart sauce pot with cover, cook scallions, garlic and chopped peppers in olive oil over moderate heat for 5 minutes, until vegetables are softened. Scraping bottom of pot to loosen food particles, stir in chicken stock and rice, cumin, oregano, pepper and salt. Cover pot; raise heat to boil; then, lower to simmer for 20-25 minutes, until liquid is absorbed and rice is fluffy. Do not overcook. Transfer to serving bowl. Serves 4-6.

CURRIED GREEN BEANS

1 lb. green beans, rinsed, trimmed, cut into 1-inch pieces

2 tsp. butter or Smart Balance spread, cut into bits

1 tsp. curry powder

salt and fresh ground black pepper, to taste

$\frac{1}{2}$ cup water

Steam green beans, covered, in $\frac{1}{2}$ cup water for 5-7 minutes; do not overcook. Beans should be slightly firm to the bite. Drain beans; leave them in cooking pot. Dot with butter (or Smart Balance); sprinkle with curry powder, salt and pepper. Replace cover on pot and allow beans to rest for 5 minutes. Serves 4-6.

CHINESE NEW YEAR CAKE (NIAN GAO)
(Or any time of year.)

2 large eggs, separated, or 2 egg whites and $\frac{1}{2}$ cup egg substitute

$1\frac{1}{3}$ cups glutinous rice flour

$\frac{1}{3}$ cup evaporated milk, fat-free available

$\frac{1}{4}$ cup butter or Smart Balance spread

$\frac{1}{2}$ cup granulated sugar

1 tbsp. baking soda

1 cup dried fruits, chopped (like a mix of dried apricots, dried pitted prunes,
dried peaches and pears)

1-inch piece crystallized ginger, minced

Preheat oven to 350°.

Have ready: an 8-inch square cake pan, well-greased with canola oil and dusted with flour.

Beat egg whites until stiff. Set aside. Cream butter (or Smart Balance) with sugar and baking soda at the same time. Add egg yolks (or egg substitute) and mix thoroughly. Stir in $\frac{1}{2}$ cup of rice flour. Stir and mix in half of the milk. Repeat in 2 additions, mixing another $\frac{1}{2}$ cup rice flour and remainder of milk; then stir in remainder of rice flour.

Stir in dried fruits and ginger and carefully fold in beaten egg whites to the batter.
Pour the batter into the prepared greased and floured pan and bake in preheated oven at 350° for 40-45 minutes. Serve warm in thin slices. Serves 6-8.

A Birthday Party with Stella and Raymond Wu and Family.
Photo: the Wu's

179

BAKED BUTTERNUT SQUASH SOUP

HONEY-ORANGE DUCK

STUFFING ON THE SIDE

BROCCOLI SLAW

MOCHA AMARETTO CHEESECAKE

BAKED BUTTERNUT SQUASH SOUP

[A Cooking Hint: Prepare Homemade Chicken Stock by simmering legs and wings of chicken in 6 cups water in a 4-quart pot with a cover for 35-40 minutes. Remove chicken meat from legs and wings and stir the meat into the soup. It will make a hearty addition. Or add chopped celery and mayo to the chicken meat for a delicious chicken salad sandwich.]

4 lbs. butternut squash
(about 2 butternut squash), pared, deseeded, cut into $\frac{1}{2}$-inch cubes

2 large carrots, pared, cut into $\frac{1}{2}$-inch pieces

1 large onion, thinly sliced

4 tbsp. butter or Smart Balance spread

6 cups chicken broth (see "How to Prepare Chicken Stock", page 81; or use packaged low-sodium chicken broth)

2 tbsp. dark brown sugar

$\frac{1}{2}$ tsp. ground mace

$\frac{1}{2}$ tsp. ground ginger

$\frac{1}{8}$ tsp. cayenne pepper

1 tsp. salt

$\frac{1}{4}$ tsp. black pepper

2 tbsp. fresh lemon juice

1 pt. sour cream for garnish

$\frac{1}{4}$ cup fresh chives, minced, for garnish

Preheat oven to 400°.
Have ready: a food processor and a $4\frac{1}{2}$-quart soup pot; aluminum foil.

Place butternut squash, carrots, and onion in a roasting pan. Dot vegetables with butter. Pour $1\frac{1}{2}$ cups chicken broth over the vegetables and sprinkle with brown sugar. Cover pan tightly with foil and bake vegetables in preheated oven at 400° for 35 minutes, until tender.

Remove pan from oven and place the vegetables and any cooking liquid in a large $4\frac{1}{2}$-quart soup pot. Stir in remaining $3\frac{1}{2}$ cups broth, mace, ginger, cayenne, pepper and salt. Bring to a boil. Reduce heat and simmer, uncovered, for 10 minutes. Stir in lemon juice.

In a food processor, purée soup in small batches, one cupful at a time, until smooth. Return purée to pot; taste soup and adjust seasonings. Heat the soup thoroughly. When serving, ladle into bowls; garnish each bowl with a dollop of sour cream and a sprinkling of chives. Serves 6.

HONEY-ORANGE DUCK WITH STUFFING ON THE SIDE
(Start this recipe early on the day of serving.)

1 duck (about 5 lbs.), well-rinsed, patted dry with paper towels
1 tablespoon salt (*NOTE: below)

GLAZE:
$\frac{1}{2}$ cup Kentucky bourbon
$\frac{1}{2}$ cup honey

$\frac{1}{4}$ cup orange juice
$\frac{1}{4}$ cup olive oil

"STUFFING ON THE SIDE"
4 cups coarsely crumbled packaged cornbread
    stuffing; or, coarsely grate your own
    staled corn bread
$\frac{1}{2}$ cup deseeded chopped red bell pepper
$\frac{1}{2}$ cup deseeded chopped green bell pepper
2-3 strips bacon, cooked crisp; drained
1 small onion, chopped
4-5 small white mushrooms, chopped
2 tbsp. olive oil

$\frac{1}{4}$ tsp. black pepper
pinch of cayenne pepper
$\frac{1}{4}$ cup chopped cilantro
1 tbsp. ground sage
$\frac{1}{4}$ cup cranberry raisins, chopped
$\frac{1}{4}$ cup orange juice
$\frac{1}{4}$ cup hot water
2 eggs beaten or $\frac{1}{2}$ cup egg substitute

*NOTE: Trim away any visible fat and any loose skin from duck. Prick the skin all over with a fork. Salt the duck inside and out. Place duck in a large bowl; cover and refrigerate duck for several hours.

Have ready: a 9x12x1$\frac{1}{2}$-inch olive oil-greased pan; a large roasting pan with a rack.

<u>Prepare "STUFFING on the SIDE"</u>. Mix all stuffing ingredients in a large bowl. Scoop serving size spoonfuls of stuffing and form patties with your hands. Lay them side by side on an oil-greased 9x12 pan. As the duck roasts, bake the patties at 375° for 20-25 minutes until light golden brown.

<u>Prepare to ROAST the DUCK</u>. Preheat oven to 375°. Place rack in center of oven. Rinse duck in cold water; pat dry with paper towels. Blend bourbon, honey, orange juice and oil in a small bowl. Lay duck on rack of a large roasting pan. Brush duck with half of the honey-bourbon mix. Roast duck in preheated oven at 375° for about 2 hours, turning it frequently, and basting it with honey-bourbon mix. During last 20-25 minutes, you may add the tray of stuffing patties to the upper rack in the roasting oven to roast for 20-25 minutes.

Duck is cooked when thigh juices run clear when pricked with a fork and meat thermometer registers 165°. Serves 4-6.

CAPONATA

1 large eggplant or 2 small, about $1\frac{1}{2}$ lbs., pared, cut into 1-inch cubes
$\frac{1}{2}$ cup olive oil
2 onions, sliced thin
1 cup celery, diced
2 cups Italian plum tomatoes, chopped
2 tbsp. capers
1 tbsp. pignola (pine nuts)
8-10 pitted black Sicilian olives, chopped
$\frac{1}{4}$ cup red wine vinegar, 2 tbsp. sugar
$\frac{1}{2}$ tsp. salt
$\frac{1}{4}$ tsp. black pepper

    Have ready: a large fry pan; a 4-qt. saucepan with a cover; a small saucepan; a large serving bowl.

    Sauté cubed eggplant in heated olive oil in a frying pan until eggplant is softened and browned. Remove cooked eggplant to a 4-quart saucepan.

    To the frying pan, add sliced onions, adding a little more oil if needed, and sauté until onions are soft and golden. Do not burn them. Add diced celery and chopped plum tomatoes. Simmer onions, celery, tomatoes for 15 minutes; add capers, pine nuts and chopped olives. Set aside.

    In a small saucepan, combine red wine vinegar, sugar, salt and pepper and cook for a minute or two. Then, combine the celery/onion/tomato mix and the sauce (in the small saucepan) with the cooked eggplant. Cover this pan and allow the mixture to barely simmer over very low heat for 20 minutes to blend the flavors. Allow caponata to cool in a bowl; then, chill it in refrigerator before serving. Serve with toasty crusts of Italian bread. Serves 6 as a side dish.

Hank del Percio treats the family to an Italian cruise. Photos: H. del Percio

BLACK FOREST CHEESECAKE

CRUST:

1 cup quick oats (uncooked)

1 cup tiny crunchy wheat or oatmeal cereal squares, crushed

$\frac{1}{3}$ cup butter or Smart Balance spread, melted

$\frac{1}{4}$ cup firmly packed brown sugar

FILLING:

2 8 oz.-packages low-fat cream cheese, softened

$\frac{2}{3}$ cup granulated sugar

1 tsp. vanilla extract

2 eggs or $\frac{1}{2}$ cup egg substitute

1 cup dark chocolate morsels, at least 60% cacao, melted; melt chocolate in top of small
     double boiler, over hot simmering water, stirring frequently

$\frac{1}{4}$ cup heavy cream

1 can (21 oz.) cherry pie filling

1 cup whipped cream or low-fat whipped topping

Preheat oven to 350°.

Have ready: a greased 9-inch springform pan.

Thoroughly combine oats, cereal squares, melted butter and brown sugar. Press mixture on bottom and sides of greased 9-inch springform pan. Bake in preheated oven at 350° for 15 minutes. Cool.

Beat cream cheese, granulated sugar and vanilla at medium speed of electric mixer until fluffy. Add eggs (or egg substitute) one portion at a time, beating well after each. Stir in chocolate and heavy cream. Pour into prepared crust. Bake cheesecake at 350° for 1 hour, or until center is almost set. Cool cake completely in pan; then remove rim of pan. Chill in refrigerator for several hours. Spread cherry filling over top of cake; spoon dollops of whipped cream over cherries. Serves 12.

CARROT AND EGGPLANT POTAGE
CECI AND PROSCIUTTO
OVEN-ROASTED BEEF SIRLOIN
GRILLED VEGETABLES
COCONUT LAYER CAKE

CARROT AND EGGPLANT POTAGE

2 tbsp. olive oil

2 lg. yellow onions, chopped

6 garlic cloves, minced

1 eggplant, about $1\frac{1}{2}$ lbs., peeled, deseeded, chopped

6 lg. carrots, pared, chopped

1 lg. celery stalk with greens, chopped

2 all-purpose potatoes, pared, chopped

1 sweet red pepper, deseeded, chopped

1 can (8 oz.) diced tomatoes

24 oz. low-salt chicken broth; or (see page 81 for Homemade Chicken Broth)

6 cups water

1 tsp. salt, or to taste

1 tsp. black pepper

1 tsp. dried thyme, extra for garnish

Have ready: a large soup pot with a cover; a food processor to purée vegetables.

Heat oil in a large soup pot. Lightly brown onions and garlic (about 3-4 minutes). Add chopped eggplant and cook until softened, about 10 minutes. Stir in 6 cups water, chicken broth, celery, carrots, potatoes, red pepper and 1 can of diced tomatoes. Bring pot to a boil; cover and simmer soup for 15 minutes, until vegetables are tender. Stir in salt, pepper and thyme and continue to cook soup, covered, for 30 minutes. Cool slightly.

Remove about 2 cups of vegetables from pot. Set aside. Purée remaining pot of vegetables and soup in food processor. Return purée to large pot. Blend in 2 cups of unpuréed vegetables. Season with additional salt and pepper, if desired. Cover pot and heat soup thoroughly. Garnish each bowl with thyme at serving. Serves 6-8.

CECI (CHICK PEAS) AND PROSCIUTTO

2 tbsp. olive oil

1 medium onion, thinly sliced

2 garlic cloves, minced

1 small red bell pepper, deseeded,
    cut into thick strips

¼ lb. prosciutto, shaved (about 6-8 slices),
    cut into sections with scissors

1 can (20 oz.) ceci, rinsed, drained

1 can whole artichoke hearts in water,
    drained, halved

6 large basil leaves, shredded

1 tsp. dried oregano

½ tsp. freshly ground black pepper

salt to taste

Have ready: a flat, wide dish with a raised edge.

Heat oil at medium-high in a large skillet to cook onion, garlic and red pepper strips for 2-3 minutes until softened. Stir in prosciutto to cook for about 1 minute. Add ceci and artichokes and cook for another 2-3 minutes until warmed through. Sprinkle with salt, pepper and oregano and toss to thoroughly combine. Pour into a flat wide dish with a raised edge. Garnish with shredded basil. Serve warm. Serves 6.

....

OVEN-ROASTED BEEF SIRLOIN

1 sirloin tip roast, about 3-4 lbs.

SPICE RUB:

2 tsp. freshly ground black pepper

2 tsp. ground cumin

1 tsp. salt

2 tsp. ground coriander

1 tbsp. Hungarian paprika

hot red pepper flakes, to taste

1 tbsp. brown sugar

Preheat oven to 350°.

Have ready: line a small roasting pan with aluminum foil.

Combine all dry seasoning ingredients in a large enough bowl to fit the roast. Place roast in the bowl and rub the spices all over the beef. Lay the roast in the pan to cook in a preheated oven at 350° for 45 minutes to 1 hour, or until the roast registers an internal temperature of 130°-135° for medium-rare. Remove roast from oven and allow to rest for 15 minutes before slicing.

GRILLED VEGETABLES

[A Cooking Hint: Any hard vegetable can be French fried.
Try a tempura batter: a mix of flour and water.]

4-5 large Idaho potatoes, scrubbed, cut into $\frac{1}{2}$-inch slices, lengthwise (do not pare)

2 doz. slender asparagus, trimmed, each cut into 2-3 pieces

2-3 Portobello mushrooms, rinsed, patted dry, cut into $\frac{1}{2}$-inch slices, horizontally

2-3 garlic cloves, minced

4-6 plum tomatoes, rinsed, each cut into 4 wedges

$\frac{1}{2}$ cup sharp Cheddar cheese, shredded

DRESSING:

$\frac{1}{4}$ cup olive oil

2 tbsp. balsamic vinegar

1 tsp. dried oregano

$\frac{1}{4}$ tsp. freshly ground black pepper

salt to taste

Have ready: a large 12-inch grill pan with handle AND an ovenproof serving tray, 9x12-inches.

Blend Dressing ingredients. Pour oil, balsamic vinegar, oregano, pepper and salt in a small bowl.

Place cut potatoes in a large bowl. Lay asparagus and mushrooms on large flat dish. Sprinkle with garlic. Brush asparagus/mushrooms with oil mix. Set aside. Pour remaining oil mix over potatoes and toss to coat. Quarter the plum tomatoes and set aside in a bowl. Shred Cheddar cheese in a small bowl and set aside.

Preheat grill pan on heated stove burner for 1-2 minutes.

Pour potatoes into grill pan and cook on heated stove burner at medium-high heat for 10-12 minutes, until tender, frequently tossing potatoes with a Teflon spatula. Transfer potatoes to a large ovenproof platter. Cover with a sheet of foil to keep warm.

Lay prepared asparagus/Portobello into hot grill pan. Grill vegetables, tossing them frequently for 3-4 minutes, until asparagus are barely tender. Transfer asparagus and mushrooms to platter with potatoes. Scatter plum tomato wedges over platter of vegetables. Sprinkle with Cheddar cheese and serve. If not serving immediately, lay a sheet of aluminum foil loosely over the platter and keep it in a warm oven. Serves 4-6.

COCONUT LAYER CAKE

1 pkg. (22 oz.) yellow cake mix

1 pkg. (4 oz.) vanilla instant pudding mix

$1\frac{1}{3}$ cups low-fat milk

4 eggs, beaten or 1 cup egg substitute

$\frac{1}{4}$ cups canola oil

2 cups flaked coconut

1 cup chopped walnuts

COCONUT CREAM CHEESE FROSTING

4 tbsp. butter or Smart Balance spread

2 cups flaked coconut

1 pkg. (8 oz.) low-fat cream cheese

2 tsp. low-fat milk

$3\frac{1}{2}$ cups confectioners' sugar, sifted

$\frac{1}{2}$ tsp. vanilla extract

Preheat oven 350°.

An Afternoon Tea.

Prepare the cake layers. Grease and flour three 9-inch layer pans.

Blend cake mix, pudding mix, milk, eggs and oil in a large mixer bowl. Beat at medium speed of electric mixer for 4 minutes. Stir in coconut and walnuts. Pour batter evenly into 3 greased and floured 9-inch layer pans. Bake at 350° for 35 minutes. When done, an inserted toothpick will remove clean. Cool in pans 15 minutes; remove and cool on rack.

Prepare Coconut Cream Cheese Frosting while cake cools. Melt 2 tablespoons butter or (Smart Balance) spread in skillet. Add coconut and stir constantly over low heat until golden brown. Spread coconut over paper towels to cool. Cream 2 tablespoons butter (or Smart Balance spread) with cream cheese. Add milk; beat in sugar gradually. Blend in vanilla and stir in $1\frac{3}{4}$ cups coconut. Spread frosting on tops of each cake layer. Stack the layers and sprinkle with remaining coconut. Serves 6-8.

SAUSAGE MINESTRONE

CHICKEN WITH ONIONS AND OLIVES

FRESH BEET SALAD

SWEET POTATO POUND CAKE

SAUSAGE MINESTRONE

2 tbsp. olive oil

4 links sweet Italian sausage with fennel, chopped in small chunks (Sausage will chop easier if slightly frozen.)

10-12 cups water

1 large yellow onion, chopped

3 ripe plum tomatoes

1 cup prepared tomato sauce

1 large celery stalk with greens, chopped

1 large carrot, pared, sliced into narrow rounds

$\frac{1}{2}$ cup fresh or frozen peas

4 small fresh white mushrooms, cleaned, chopped

$\frac{1}{2}$ cup fresh cauliflower florets, chopped

$\frac{1}{2}$ cup fresh broccoli florets, chopped

$\frac{1}{2}$ cup fresh green beans, trimmed, cut into small sections

$\frac{1}{4}$ cup frozen corn kernels

$\frac{1}{4}$ cup canned ceci, rinsed in cold water

$\frac{1}{4}$ cup fresh minced Italian parsley

1 tbsp. dried oregano

1 tsp. salt, or to taste

$\frac{1}{2}$ tsp. black pepper

2 bay leaves

1 cup tiny seashells pasta

$\frac{1}{2}$ cup Parmesan cheese, grated; more Parmesan cheese at serving

Have ready: a large soup pot with a cover.

At medium heat, in a large soup pot with a cover, lightly brown sausage chunks and chopped onion in 2 tablespoons olive oil. Stir bottom of pot to remove any leavings. Pour 10 cups water into the soup pot, stirring the bottom of the pot. In a small sauce pan, bring 2 cups water to a boil. Drop in 3 plum tomatoes and allow to simmer for 1 minute. Remove tomatoes to a small bowl with cold water, and with fingers, peel off skin. (Do not discard small pot with hot water.) Mash tomatoes with a fork and return them to small pot of hot water; add this pot of mashed tomatoes in water to the large soup pot.

Add and mix all of the vegetables: chopped celery, sliced carrot, chopped mushrooms, cauliflower, broccoli, green beans, peas, ceci and corn kernels. Stir in herbs and spices. Stir in tomato sauce. Cover pot and bring to a boil; then simmer soup for 30-35 minutes. During the last 10 minutes, add pasta and continue to simmer the soup.

Remove pot of minestrone from burner and stir in grated Parmesan. Before serving, remove and discard bay leaves. Sprinkle additional Parmesan over each serving, if desired. Serves 8-10.

CHICKEN WITH ONIONS AND OLIVES

$\frac{1}{2}$ cup olive oil in 2 parts: $\frac{1}{4}$ cup, $\frac{1}{4}$ cup

2-3 large onions, sliced, about 3 cups

1 chicken, about 3-4 lbs., rinsed well in cool water, patted dry with paper towels,
    and cut into 8 pieces

$\frac{1}{4}$ cup white vinegar

$\frac{1}{4}$ cup black peppercorns

1 tsp. allspice

3 bay leaves

$\frac{1}{2}$ cup pimiento-stuffed olives, chopped

$\frac{1}{2}$ tsp. salt, or to taste

$\frac{1}{2}$ tsp. freshly ground black pepper

enough water to cover

    In a large skillet, over medium heat, sauté onions in $\frac{1}{4}$ cup of olive oil until soft, about 6-7 minutes. Add chicken pieces and cook until browned all over, about 3 minutes per side.

    In a small bowl, whisk together the remaining $\frac{1}{4}$ cup of olive oil and vinegar. Add this mix to the skillet. Add peppercorns, allspice, bay leaves, chopped olives, salt and ground pepper. Stir well to combine.

    Add just enough water to cover chicken in skillet. Cook and simmer until chicken is opaque near the bone and the sauce thickens slightly, about 30 minutes. Serves 5-6.

A High School Senior Picnic in the Snow. Photo: C. Celenza

FRESH BEET SALAD

15-18 small-medium fresh beets, trimmed, scrubbed, steamed, peeled and sliced
  Beets should be uniform in size. If steaming, be certain to use a large enough pot
  surface to spread beets in one or two layers. Water in bottom of pot should reach
  at least half-way up the side of pot. Steamed beets will cook between
  30 and 40 minutes, depending on size. (Small-medium size: 25-30 minutes.)
  Or, you may pressure cook beets: 12 minutes (small) to 18 minutes (large).
  Or, use 4 cups sliced canned or jarred unseasoned beets in water. Drain water.

3 heads endive, trimmed, rinsed, quartered in strips

1 small head radicchio, trimmed, leaves separated, rinsed and drained

$\frac{1}{2}$ cup packaged glazed walnut halves

$\frac{1}{2}$ cup pitted oil-cured olives

$\frac{1}{2}$ cup red onion, chopped

$\frac{1}{4}$ cup red wine vinegar

2 tbsp. extra-virgin olive oil

1 tbsp. Dijon mustard spread

salt and freshly ground black pepper

3 cups green leaf lettuce, rinsed, drained (use whole leaves)

$\frac{1}{2}$ cup bleu cheese, crumbled

  Line a large glass salad bowl with green leaf lettuce. Over the green leaf arrange whole leaves
of radicchio. Set aside.
  In a large bowl, combine cooked sliced beets, chopped onion,
glazed walnut halves and chopped pitted olives. Set aside.
  Whisk oil, red vinegar, mustard, salt and pepper in a small bowl.
Pour over bowl of onions and beets and toss to coat thoroughly.
Carefully pour beet mixture into lettuce lined salad bowl; sprinkle with
crumbled bleu cheese. Serve warm or at room temperature. Serves 6.

A Garden Party.

SWEET POTATO POUND CAKE

CAKE:
3¼ cups all-purpose flour
2 tsp. baking powder
½ tsp. baking soda
½ tsp. ground nutmeg
½ tsp. salt
½ cup low-fat milk

1 tsp. vanilla extract
8 oz. butter or Smart Balance spread,
    at room temperature
1 cup granulated sugar
1 cup brown sugar
4 large eggs or 1 cup egg substitute
2 cups cooked fresh sweet potatoes, mashed;
    or, use frozen sweet potato chunks,
    cooked, mashed

GLAZE:
½ cup buttermilk
½ cup granulated sugar
1¼ tsp. cornstarch
4 tbsp. butter or Smart Balance spread, cubed

¼ tsp. baking soda
1 tsp. vanilla extract
½ cup chopped pecans, for garnish

Preheat oven to 350°.

Have ready: a 10-inch tube or Bundt pan, greased and floured.

Prepare the CAKE. In a medium-size bowl, combine and whisk together: flour, baking powder, baking soda, nutmeg and salt. In a small bowl, combine milk and vanilla.
In a large bowl, beat butter, 2 sugars until lightly and fluffy. Scrape down sides of bowl. Add eggs one at a time, beating well after each addition. Add mashed sweet potatoes and mix until batter is combined. (Don't worry if batter looks a little curdled.)
With mixer on low speed, add half of the flour mixture. Beat just enough to incorporate the flour. Then, add half of the milk mixture; continue to beat on low until well-blended. Add remaining flour, followed by remaining milk. Beat on low to allow batter to become thick and smooth.
Pour batter into prepared tube or Bundt pan and bake cake in center of preheated oven at 350° for 60-75 minutes, or until an inserted toothpick in center of cake removes clean. Cool the cake in its pan for 20 minutes. Run a thin knife around the edge to loosen the cake; then, invert carefully, onto a wire rack.
Meanwhile, Prepare the GLAZE. In a medium-size saucepan, combine buttermilk, sugar, butter, cornstarch and baking soda. Place over medium heat and bring it to a gentle boil. Remove from heat immediately; stir thoroughly and set pot aside to cool at room temperature.
Add vanilla and stir well. Set the cake on a large cake plate. Spoon glaze over the warm cake. Sprinkle cake with chopped pecans. Cool completely before serving. You may wish to absorb residue glaze around cake on cake plate. Use paper towels and discard.
Serves 8-10 slices.

CABBAGE SOUP
FLOUNDER KIEV
PAPRIKA RICE
MINTY GREEN BEANS
CHOCOLATE-CHERRY PUDGEL

CABBAGE SOUP

10 cups water, plus 1 cup water

1 head green cabbage, rinsed, trimmed, shredded

1 large onion, thinly sliced

1 Granny Smith apple, peeled, cored, thinly sliced

1 cup prepared tomato sauce

2 lbs. short ribs and a beef shin bone

1 tsp. salt, to taste

$\frac{1}{2}$ tsp. freshly ground black pepper

1 tsp. Hungarian paprika

juice of 1 lemon

grated rind of 1 lemon

Have ready: a large soup pot with cover.

In a large soup pot with a cover, combine 10 cups water, shredded cabbage, onion, apple, tomato sauce, short ribs, beef bone and spices. Cover pot and bring to a boil. Then, simmer soup for 1 hour, skimming occasionally.

Add another 1 cup water into which you stir lemon juice and lemon rind. Continue to simmer soup, uncovered for 30 minutes longer.

Remove shin bone; skim off fat. Taste soup and adjust seasonings. Serves 6-8.

Tina, children and family celebrate Cliff and his life as husband, father, son and friend.
Photo: T. Miller

FLOUNDER KIEV

[A Cooking Hint: Clean fish or shell fish by dipping pieces of fish in cold salted water; then, pat dry with paper towels. Don't use running water.]

6 large fillets of flounder

FILLING:
1½ cups unseasoned bread crumbs
1-2 garlic cloves, minced
1 tbsp. fresh parsley, minced
1 tsp. dried thyme
¼ tsp. freshly ground black pepper
a couple shakes of Tabasco sauce
1 large egg, beaten or ¼ cup egg substitute
1 tbsp. olive oil
¼ cup warm water (or more)

1 cup flour for coating
1 cup unseasoned crumbs for coating
2 large eggs, beaten or ½ cup egg substitute
canola oil for sautéing fish rolls

Hank went fishing for his dinner. Photo: H. del Percio

6 small metal skewers

Have ready: a large skillet.

Pour about ¼-inch canola on bottom of skillet. Set aside.

Prepare the FILLING. In a bowl combine 1½ cups crumbs, garlic, parsley, thyme, pepper and Tabasco. In a small bowl, beat 1 tablespoon olive oil and 1 egg (or ¼ cup egg substitute) into ¼ cup warm water. Gradually add egg and water mixture to crumb mix, blending thoroughly. Add more warm water, 1 tablespoon at a time to crumb mix if too dry. Equally divide the filling into 6 portions. Lay fillets on a glass board and pack a portion of the crumbs mix over each fillet. Carefully roll each fillet starting at one narrow end, enclosing filling. Secure roll-ups with a small metal skewer.

Beat 2 eggs (or egg substitute) in a wide-mouth dish with a rim. Spread flour on a sheet of waxed paper; spread crumbs on another sheet of waxed paper. Heat the oil in the skillet to moderate, about 340°.

Dredge each roll-up in flour to coat; then dip into beaten egg (or egg substitute); cover each with crumbs and sauté fish in heated oil, turning them to cook on all sides, for 6-7 minutes. Remove to paper towels to drain. Serves 6.

197

PAPRIKA RICE

$3\frac{1}{2}$ cups water or low-salt chicken stock

$1\frac{1}{2}$ cups brown rice

2 tsp. Hungarian paprika

1 tbsp. parsley, finely chopped

$\frac{1}{2}$ tsp. salt

Bring water (or chicken stock) to boil in a 3-quart pot with a cover. Slowly stir in rice; add salt, stirring as pot returns to a boil. Cover pot and simmer rice for 45 minutes. Remove pot from burner; stir in parsley and paprika. Replace cover and allow rice to sit for 5-10 minutes. Transfer to serving bowl. Serves 6.

MINTY GREEN BEANS

1 lb. fresh green beans, trimmed, rinsed

2 tbsp. fresh mint leaves, minced

$\frac{1}{4}$ cup red onion, finely chopped

DRESSING:

1 tbsp. white vinegar

2 tbsp. extra-virgin olive oil

1 tsp. Dijon mustard

Have ready: a vegetable steamer; a serving bowl.

Cook green beans in a steamer pot with a couple of inches of water. Bring to a boil and steam beans for 4 minutes, until just tender. Meanwhile, in a small bowl, blend mustard, vinegar and oil. Drain beans and pour into a serving bowl. Drizzle green beans with mustard dressing; sprinkle mint and onion over green beans and toss to mix until well-combined. Serves 6.

Happy 50/50/25. Chip, Steve and John go back a long way.

CHOCOLATE-CHERRY PUDGEL
(Prepare a day in advance.)

1 pkg. (3 oz.) cherry gelatin

1 cup pitted cherries, chopped

1 pkg. (3 oz.) dark chocolate pudding (not instant)

1 pint heavy cream, whipped; or 1 pint Greek-style plain yogurt;

    or a 1-pint container non-dairy cream topping (fat-free available)

6 or more fresh Bing cherries with stems, for garnish

Have ready: 2 1-qt. bowls; 4-6 individual pint-size dessert serving glasses; a sheet of waxed paper.

Prepare gelatin as directed on package. Cool to room temperature; stir in chopped cherries. Divide gelatin-cherries mixture into 4-6 (8-oz.) dessert glasses. Refrigerate glasses for at least 4-6 hours or overnight, until firm.

Prepare chocolate pudding as directed on package. Spoon into a bowl and place a sheet of waxed paper directly on surface of cooked pudding. Allow to rest for 1 hour; then, refrigerate the bowl of pudding to completely chill.

A couple of hours before serving, whip heavy cream to soft peaks (or use yogurt or non-dairy topping). Just before serving, remove glasses of gelatin and bowl of pudding from refrigerator. Spoon 2 tablespoons whipped cream (or yogurt, or non-dairy topping) over each glass of gelatin. Remove waxed paper from surface of pudding. Spoon equal amounts of pudding into each dessert glass (over gelatin and cream). Top each glass with a dollop of whipped cream (or yogurt, non-dairy topping). Garnish each with Bing cherries. Serves 4-5.

A Christmas Buffet with Paula and Fred.

> ## SWEET POTATO SALAD
> ## STUFFED CHICKEN BREASTS SURPRISE
> ## BROCCOLI IN WINE
> ## CINNAMON STRAWBERRIES

SWEET POTATO SALAD

4-5 small baked sweet potatoes
$\frac{1}{4}$ cup low-fat mayonnaise
1 tbsp. mustard spread
1 cup celery, chopped (about 2-3 stalks)
1 small red bell pepper, deseeded, finely chopped
1 cup fresh pineapple, $\frac{1}{2}$-inch dice
2 scallions, finely chopped
$\frac{1}{2}$ cup chopped pecans
salt and freshly ground black pepper, to taste
finely chopped fresh dill weed, for garnish

Preheat oven to 400°.

Have ready: a large serving bowl; foil to wrap sweet potatoes.

Wrap sweet potatoes in foil and bake in a preheated oven at 400° for about 1 hour.
Unwrap; cool completely in refrigerator. Peel sweet potatoes and cut into 1-inch chunks.

In a large bowl, combine cool sweet potatoes, celery, red pepper, scallions, pineapple and nuts.
In a small bowl, blend mayonnaise, mustard, salt and pepper. Add this dressing into the sweet
potato mixture and toss gently. Cover the bowl and refrigerate for 1 hour to blend the tastes.
Sprinkle with chopped dill weed. Serves 4-5.

STUFFED CHICKEN BREASTS SURPRISE

4-6 chicken breast halves; remove skin, rinse in cold water,
    pat dry with paper towels
4-6 shaved slices of prosciutto
1 can (14 oz.) unseasoned artichokes, chopped
$\frac{1}{2}$ cup dried cranberries
4-6 thin slices Gruyere cheese
salt and freshly ground black pepper, to taste
$\frac{1}{4}$ cup olive oil; more olive oil for the pan
1 cup fine bread crumbs
2 tbsp. fresh Italian parsley, minced

Preheat oven to 375°.

Have ready: a 9x12x3-inch baking pan, lightly coated with olive oil.

Lay a sheet of waxed paper on a glass board. Spread a mix of bread crumbs, mixed with salt, black pepper and minced parsley. Cut a 4-inch slit along side of each chicken breast half, forming a deep pocket.

Place 4-6 slices of prosciutto on the board and lay a slice of Gruyere cheese over the prosciutto; sprinkle 1-2 tablespoons dried cranberries over the prosciutto/cheese. Pack 1 portion of the chopped artichokes on top of each of the 4-6 pieces of chicken breast halves; roll up each portion of the prosciutto/cheese/cranberry raisins mix and stuff one portion into the pocket of each piece of chicken.

Brush stuffed chicken with olive oil and thoroughly coat each in the crumbs mix. Lay prepared stuffed chicken on an oil-coated 9x12 pan. Bake chicken in preheated oven at 375° for 35-40 minutes, or until juices run clear when chicken is pierced with a thin knife. Serves 4-6.

Christmas with the Dircks Family.

BROCCOLI IN WINE

about 4 cups broccoli florets, rinsed, drained
2 scallions, trimmed, chopped
2 tbsp. fresh Italian parsley, chopped
2 tbsp. olive oil
2 oz. anchovies, chopped
$\frac{1}{2}$ cup Parmesan cheese, grated
1 doz. pitted black olives
salt, freshly ground black pepper, to taste

3 cups dry red table wine

    Have ready: a large skillet with a cover.

    In a large skillet, sauté scallions, parsley and broccoli in olive oil for 2 minutes. Stir in anchovies, cheese, olives, salt and pepper (to taste). Cook over medium heat for 3 minutes longer. Pour wine over the broccoli mix and continue the cooking, partly covered, over medium heat until wine evaporates, another 3-4 minutes. Serves 4-6.

CINNAMON STRAWBERRIES

2 lbs. fresh strawberries, trimmed, rinsed, drained,
    gently patted dry with paper towels
juice of 1 lemon
$\frac{1}{4}$ cup brown sugar
1 tsp. ground cinnamon
1 pt. heavy cream for whipping
1 tsp. vanilla extract
$\frac{1}{4}$ cup Macadamia nuts, chopped

    Have ready: 4-6 fruit compote dishes.

Mary, Melissa and Grandma Vicky display their Easter Lamb Cake. Photo: V. O'Moore

    Pour prepared strawberries in a large bowl; sprinkle with lemon juice, brown sugar and cinnamon. Gently toss; refrigerate strawberries while you whip the cream (to which you have added vanilla); form soft peaks.
    When serving, spoon portions of cinnamon strawberries into compote dishes. Garnish with a dollop of whipped cream; sprinkle with chopped Macadamia nuts. Serves 4-6.

CHOPPED SALAD
LEMON-OIL DRESSING (see page 379)
A HONEY OF A CHICKEN
SESAME NOODLES
PICKLED MUSHROOMS
COUPE MARRONS

CHOPPED SALAD

1 large head lettuce (Boston, Iceberg or Salad Bowl), rinsed, drained, chopped
1 large ripe beefsteak tomato, chopped, drained
1 cucumber, pared, deseeded, coarsely chopped
2 celery stalks, finely chopped
1 Spanish onion, diced
2 Italian fryer peppers, deseeded, thinly sliced in rings
2 sweet red pimientos, deseeded, thinly sliced in rings
1 tbsp. capers, rinsed, drained
$\frac{1}{4}$ cup green and black olives, pitted, chopped
5 flat oil-packed anchovy fillets, coarsely chopped

Lemon-Oil Dressing (see page 379)

Prepare salad dressing in advance.
Refrigerate dressing until 1 hour before serving.

In a large salad bowl, combine prepared lettuce, cucumber, celery, onion, all peppers, capers, olives and anchovies. Add tomatoes and gently toss salad to integrate the ingredients. Drizzle Lemon-Oil Dressing over salad. Serve in individual bowls. Serves 4-5.

A HONEY OF A CHICKEN

[A Cooking Hint: Preheat broiler or oven prior to roasting, baking or broiling.
Accurate temperatures provide accurate results.]

1 chicken (2½-3 lbs.), rinsed in cold water, patted dry with paper towels

SAUCE:

⅓ cup *lite* soy sauce

¼ cup peanut oil

1 tbsp. sesame oil

1 tbsp. sherry

2 tbsp. honey

1 garlic clove, minced

¼ tsp. salt

½ tsp. finely grated fresh ginger

2 tsp. five-spice powder

Preheat oven to 425°.

Have ready: a roasting pan with enough air space to fit the chicken.

Mix all of the sauce ingredients in a small pot and bring to a boil. Then, reduce heat to simmer and cook for 5 minutes. Set aside.

Lay chicken in roasting pan and roast in preheated oven at 425° for 10 minutes. Remove pan from oven; brush chicken all over with sauce. Reserve leftover sauce. Replace pan with chicken into oven and lower oven temperature to 350°. Continue to roast for 25-30 minutes until chicken skin is golden brown and when juices run clear when thigh is pricked with small skewer. Occasionally brush chicken with reserved sauce as it roasts. Remove from oven and allow chicken to rest for 10 minutes before carving. Serves 4-5.

Babcia's Easter Brunch. Photos: M. Mascolo

SESAME NOODLES

1 lb. fresh Chinese Egg noodles (spaghetti-like long strands)
$\frac{1}{4}$ cup sesame oil

2 slender cucumbers, peeled, seeded, cut into fine julienne
2 scallions with some greens, trimmed, minced
$\frac{1}{4}$ cup cilantro, finely chopped

SAUCE:
1 tsp. tahini (sesame seed paste)
$\frac{1}{3}$ cup peanut butter
$1\frac{1}{2}$ tsp. white vinegar
2 tsp. Hunan pepper sauce
1 tsp. fresh rcd Chile pepper, deseeded, minced
    (Wear plastic gloves when you handle hot peppers.)
2 tbsp. sugar
1 cup canned low-sodium chicken broth; or dissolve 1 chicken bouillon cube
    into 1 cup boiling water
$\frac{1}{2}$ tsp. freshly ground black pepper

   Boil noodles in a large pot of water until tender, about 5 minutes. Drain; cool thoroughly in cold water; drain again. Toss noodles with sesame oil. Cover and refrigerate for 1 hour.
   In a large bowl, combine tahini, peanut butter, vinegar, Hunan pepper sauce, Chile, sugar, chicken broth and pepper. Add the cold noodles and toss well. Add cucumber, scallions and cilantro; toss well and serve. Serves 4-5.

The Przybyszewski Family enjoys Babcia's Brunch. Photos: M. Mascolo

PICKLED MUSHROOMS

2 lbs. white mushrooms, trimmed, rinsed,
    quartered or halved
1 lb. shitake mushrooms, trimmed, rinsed,
    quartered or halved
$\frac{1}{4}$ cup sweet red pepper, deseeded, minced

1 tsp. salt
$\frac{1}{2}$ tsp. freshly ground black pepper
$\frac{1}{4}$ cup fresh lemon juice
$\frac{1}{2}$ cup olive oil
1 cup fresh Italian parsley, minced

    Half-fill a large pot with water; bring to a boil. Meanwhile, in a large bowl, dissolve salt in lemon juice. Add black pepper. Slowly whisk olive oil into the juice mix, until all of the oil has been added. Stir in parsley. Cover bowl and refrigerate.

    When pot of water boils, add white and shitake mushrooms. Blanch for 10 seconds. Immediately, drain water from mushrooms through a colander and refresh mushrooms under cold running water. Continue to rinse until mushrooms have cooled. Drain thoroughly and pat dry mushrooms with paper towels.

    Stir mushrooms into bowl with lemon/parsley vinaigrette. Cover bowl and refrigerate for 1 hour before serving. This dish will keep well in refrigerator, up to 3 days. Serves 4-6.

COUPE MARRONS

$1\frac{1}{2}$ doz. chestnuts, scored, steamed
    for 40 minutes; then, peel skin

SAUCE:
$\frac{1}{2}$ cup dark corn syrup
1 cup Amaretto liqueur
$\frac{1}{2}$ tsp. nutmeg
$\frac{1}{2}$ cup brown sugar
1 tsp. almond extract
1 tbsp. ground cinnamon
1 cinnamon stick

Vanilla Ice Cream

    Have ready: a 1-quart jar with screw-on lid.

    With a small sharp knife, cut a cross on flat surface of each chestnut. Steam scored chestnuts in boiling water for 40 minutes. Drain water; peel off skin from chestnuts. Place chestnuts in a bowl. Set aside.

    In a sauce pot with a cover, combine corn syrup, Amaretto, brown sugar, ground cinnamon, nutmeg, cinnamon stick and almond extract. Cover pot and bring to a boil; then, simmer sauce for 2 minutes.

    Drizzle hot syrup over shelled chestnuts in bowl; toss to mix thoroughly. Spoon chestnuts and syrup into a 1-quart glass jar with a screw-on lid. Store in refrigerator until needed, up to 1 week. If serving on preparation day, cool sauce in refrigerator for an hour or two. Serve in dessert bowls over vanilla ice cream. Serves 8.

ARUGULA, HEIRLOOM TOMATOES, WALNUTS
OLIVE OIL AND BALSAMIC VINEGAR DRESSING (see page 376)
NOT JUST ANOTHER STUFFED VEAL CUTLET
RIGATONI AND MUSHROOMS
ALMOND ORANGE TORTA

ARUGULA, HEIRLOOM TOMATOES, WALNUTS

4 cups arugula, trimmed, rinsed, drained

3-4 heirloom tomatoes, such as Brandywine, Celebrity, sliced $\frac{1}{2}$-inch thick

1 dozen basil leaves, rinsed, drained

$\frac{1}{2}$ lb. smoky mozzarella, thinly sliced, about 6-8 slices

$\frac{1}{2}$ cup pitted Kalamata olives

$\frac{1}{2}$ cup glazed walnut halves

freshly ground black pepper, to taste

Olive Oil and Balsamic Vinegar Dressing (see page 376)

Have ready: a large round flat glass dish, about 15 inches wide.

Prepare dressing in advance. Refrigerate until 1 hour prior to serving.

Lay a bed of arugula over a large, flat glass dish. Slice tomatoes, horizontally and arrange them over the plate. Arrange smoky mozzarella slices on top of tomatoes. Tuck basil leaves between slices of tomato and mozzarella. Scatter olives and walnuts over the salad. Grind black pepper over the mozzarella; drizzle Olive Oil and Balsamic Vinegar Dressing over the salad. Serve with a spatula and serving spoon to individual salad plates. Serves 6.

NOT JUST ANOTHER STUFFED VEAL CUTLET
(Greek style; try recipe with pork cutlets.)

8-10 veal cutlets, each about 3x5 inches, pounded thin

2 large eggs, beaten, or $\frac{1}{2}$ cup egg substitute

1 cup seasoned Italian bread crumbs

2 large red onions, each cut into 4-5 chunks

1 dozen bay leaves

2 tsp. olive oil to coat the pan

STUFFING:

$\frac{1}{4}$ lb. prosciutto, finely chopped

$\frac{1}{4}$ lb. Genoa salami, finely chopped

$\frac{1}{4}$ lb. mortadella, finely chopped

$\frac{1}{4}$ lb. Fontina cheese, finely chopped

$\frac{1}{4}$ cup fresh parsley, minced

$\frac{1}{4}$ cup pignola (pine nuts)

$\frac{1}{3}$ cup golden raisins, soaked in hot water to cover, for 30 minutes, drained

1 large egg, or $\frac{1}{4}$ cup egg substitute

Preheat oven to 400°.

Have ready: a 9x12x3-inch baking pan, coated with olive oil.

Prepare the STUFFING. In a large bowl, combine prosciutto, salami, mortadella and Fontina cheese. Add parsley, raisins and pignola; add 1 beaten egg and mix thoroughly. Set aside.

In a shallow bowl, lightly beat 2 eggs. Spread bread crumbs over a sheet of waxed paper. Lay out the veal cutlets, flat, on a glass board. Divide the stuffing among the cutlets, placing a portion of stuffing in center of each cutlet. Roll up each cutlet; dip each into beaten eggs and roll and coat each into the crumbs.

Lay stuffed cutlets in 2 rows, lengthwise, in a 9x13x3-inch oil-coated pan, allowing 1 inch between each rolled cutlet. In the spaces between the roll-ups, tuck in 1 chunk of onion and 1 bay leaf. Roast the pan of stuffed veal cutlets in a preheated oven at 400° for 8 to 10 minutes; turn over each and continue to cook for an additional 8 to10 minutes. Do not overcook. Transfer veal and onions to a serving platter. Discard bay leaves. Serves 6.

Melville Fire Chief Bob Reiser and wife, Kathleen enjoy a
fire department party. Photo: R. Reiser

RIGATONI AND MUSHROOMS

[A Cooking Hint: Add a tablespoon of olive oil (or other vegetable oil) to the pasta water to prevent sticking, especially with lasagna.]

1 lb. rigatoni pasta

$\frac{1}{4}$ cup olive oil

2 cups sliced assorted mushrooms (include porcini, baby bella, shitake in the mix)

1 long spicy Italian green pepper, deseeded, chopped

6 scallions with greens, trimmed, chopped (divided: 4 scallions in recipe; 2 for garnish)

$\frac{1}{2}$ lb. marscapone cheese

$\frac{1}{2}$ cup grated Pecorino Romano cheese

$\frac{1}{2}$ tsp. salt

$\frac{1}{4}$ tsp. freshly ground black pepper

(extra Pecorino Romano cheese for garnish)

Prcheat skillet to 320°.

Heat olive oil in skillet; sauté sliced mushrooms, chopped Italian pepper and chopped scallion bulbs in hot oil for 2-3 minutes. (Set aside chopped scallion with some greens for garnish.)

Add mascarpone and $\frac{1}{2}$ cup Pecorino Romano cheese to skillet and continue to stir the pot. Sprinkle and mix salt and ground black pepper into the pan. In 2-3 minutes you should have achieved a thick, creamy mushroom sauce.

Meanwhile, set the pasta pot to a full boil and cook the rigatoni al dente as you prepare the sauce. Keep the sauce warm, stirring continuously. Drain the cooked pasta and decant into a large platter. Pour sauce over the pasta and thoroughly toss with serving utensils. Over the dish, sprinkle more Pecorino Romano cheese and chopped scallions, for garnish. Serves 4-6.

The Last Supper.

209

ALMOND ORANGE TORTA

[A Cooking Hint: Pith from citrus will easily be removed after the unpeeled orange is first placed in a hot oven for a few seconds and then plunged into cold water.]

$1\frac{1}{2}$ cups all-purpose flour
$\frac{1}{2}$ cup finely ground almonds with skin
1 tsp. baking powder
$\frac{1}{2}$ tsp. ground cinnamon
$\frac{1}{4}$ tsp. salt
$\frac{1}{4}$ tsp. ground cloves
1 large egg, at room temperature or $\frac{1}{4}$ cup egg substitute
whites from 3 large eggs at room temperature or
     3 portions of *Just Whites* (dried egg whites, refer to directions on package)
1 cup granulated sugar
1 tsp. vanilla extract
$\frac{1}{2}$ cup fresh orange juice
$\frac{1}{2}$ cup canola oil
2 tsp. grated orange peel
confectioners' sugar

4 large navel oranges, sliced into $\frac{1}{2}$-inch rounds; cut each slice in half

Preheat oven to 325°.

Have ready: a 9-inch spring-form pan, lightly oiled and floured.

In a large bowl, combine flour, almonds, baking powder, cinnamon, cloves and salt. Set aside. Beat whole egg and egg whites in a large mixing bowl at high speed until light. Gradually, beat in sugar until mixture is foamy and very pale, about 5 minutes. At low speed, gradually beat in orange juice, grated peel and vanilla. Beat in canola oil in a slow and steady stream.

Gently fold dry ingredients into egg mixture, just until blended. Mixture will be thin. Spread batter evenly into prepared lightly oil and floured spring-form pan.

Bake cake in a preheated oven at 325° for 40-45 minutes, or until inserted toothpick removes clean. Cool cake in pan on wire rack. Then, loosen cake from sides of pan with a spatula or thin flat knife. Transfer cake to serving plate. Just before serving, sprinkle cake with sifted confectioners' sugar. Serve cake wedges with orange slices. Serves 8.

MESCLUN AND HEIRLOOM TOMATOES
RASPBERRY VINAIGRETTE (see page 383)
POLYNESIAN ROASTED PORK
POTATO-VEGETABLE ROAST
CREAMY RICE PUDDING WITH FRUITS

MESCLUN AND HEIRLOOM TOMATOES

3-4 cups mesclun greens, rinsed, drained
1 dozen tiny heirloom tomatoes
$\frac{1}{2}$ cup chopped walnuts
$\frac{1}{2}$ cup chopped gorgonzola cheese

Raspberry Vinaigrette Dressing (see page 383)

Prepare Raspberry Vinaigrette Dressing a few hours before serving and refrigerate. Remove from refrigerator 1 hour before using.

In a large salad bowl, combine mesclun, tomatoes, walnuts and gorgonzola. Cover lightly with plastic wrap and refrigerate until serving. At serving time, spoon dressing over salad; toss gently to blend thoroughly. Serve immediately. Serves 6.

POLYNESIAN ROASTED PORK
(Use fresh fruits, if possible.)

6 center-cut boneless loin pork chops, 1-inch thick
2 tbsp. olive oil
$1\frac{1}{2}$ cups finely ground corn flake crumbs

SAUCE:
$\frac{1}{2}$ cup Asian plum sauce
$\frac{1}{2}$ cup *lite* ginger-soy sauce
2 tbsp. Chinese mustard

1 cup fresh red apple sliced with skin
1 cup fresh peach slices with skin
1 cup sliced fresh Bartlett pears
1 cup 1-inch chunks of fresh pineapple
$\frac{1}{2}$ cup whole cashews

Preheat oven to 375°.

Have ready: brush a 9x15x3-inch, non-stick baking pan with olive oil.

In a small bowl, blend plum sauce, ginger-soy sauce and Chinese mustard. Set aside.

Combine all fruits and nuts in a large bowl; set aside.

Lay a sheet of waxed paper on a board. Brush boneless pork chops on both sides with olive oil. Coat them with cornflakes crumbs and lay them in a greased 9x15x3-inch baking pan to bake in preheated oven at 375°.

After 10 minutes, remove pan from oven. Brush uncooked tops of chops with sauce mix. With a spatula, turn the chops over; brush the browned side with the sauce mix. Return pan to oven and continue to bake the chops for 10 minutes longer. Remove tray from oven; arrange all fruits and nuts around inside of the pan. Brush tops of fruit and chops with sauce; with spatula, turn them over again, and brush again with additional sauce and return tray to the oven for another 5 minutes or until meat thermometer registers 145° (safe cooking) when inserted in center of chop. (Use all of the sauce.) Serves 6.

POTATO-VEGETABLE ROAST

2 lbs. tiny California potatoes, scrubbed,
   halved or quartered
2 large sweet potatoes, pared,
   cut into 2-inch chunks
2 cups broccoli florets, rinsed, drained
2-3 carrots, pared, cut into 1-inch rounds
6 sun dried tomato halves, cut into strips
1 large yellow onion, thinly sliced

$\frac{1}{4}$ cup olive oil
$\frac{1}{2}$ tsp. freshly ground black pepper
1 tbsp. dried oregano
1 tsp. "salt-no salt" (see page 376)
6 large basil leaves, leave whole, rinsed
2 bay leaves
(more olive oil to drizzle)

Preheat oven to 375°.

Have ready: a 9x15x3-inch roasting pan, brushed with olive oil.

In a large bowl, combine potatoes, sweet potatoes, broccoli, carrots, onion and sun dried tomatoes. In a small bowl, blend olive oil with oregano, basil, pepper and "salt-no-salt". Pour this mix over bowl of vegetables; toss them with 2 spoons to mix thoroughly. Pour the mixture into the prepared 9x15-inch pan. Lay 2 bay leaves on vegetables, across surface of pan. Roast the vegetables in a preheated oven at 375° for 35-40 minutes, until potatoes are tender; do not overcook. Drizzle a tablespoon or two of olive oil over the pan. Before serving, remove and discard bay leaves. Serves 6.

Eva with Grandma Paula and Grandpa Fred.

CREAMY RICE PUDDING WITH FRUIT

$\frac{1}{2}$ cup short grain white rice
2 eggs or $\frac{1}{2}$ cup egg substitute
3 cups hot evaporated milk (fat-free available)
($\frac{1}{4}$ cup golden raisins – optional)
$\frac{1}{4}$ tsp. salt

1 tbsp. butter or Smart Balance spread
1 tsp. vanilla (or 1 tsp. lemon extract; or 1 tsp. orange extract)
1 tsp. lemon or orange rind, grated
2-4 tbsp. granulated sugar
1 tsp. (heaping) ground cinnamon or ground nutmeg
(more spice for garnish)

$\frac{1}{2}$ pt. heavy cream, whipped;
    or a container (8 oz.) frozen whipped topping (fat-free available)
(1 tbsp. liqueur, Cherry Heering or Chambord – optional)
$\frac{1}{2}$ cup strawberries, rinsed, drained, sliced;
    or $\frac{1}{2}$ cup red grapes, rinsed, drained, halved;
    or $\frac{1}{2}$ cup blueberries, rinsed, drained
1 pineapple spear and an orange half-slice for garnish, for each serving
$\frac{1}{2}$ cup crumbled macaroon cookies (optional)

Have ready: a 2-qt. double boiler; individual dessert glasses.

Pour enough water in bottom half of a 2-qt. double boiler; set to boil. In top half of the double boiler, pour 3 cups evaporated milk and salt and heat on a second stove burner until milk is barely hot. (You will see tiny bubbles form around the edge of the milk.) Stir in rice, egg (or egg substitute), (and raisins) and set this pot into the bottom half of the double boiler with the heating water. Lower the heat under the double boiler to a gentle roll, and cook the rice mix, uncovered, stirring frequently, for 20-25 minutes. Milk should become absorbed into the rice; add more water to bottom pot, if necessary. *(Pot of rice must steam in hot water throughout this procedure.)*
When rice is cooked tender, remove both pots from the burner. Remove pot of rice mix to work counter. Add and blend: 1 tbsp. butter (or Smart Balance), 1 tsp. extract, 1 tsp. rind, 2-4 tbsp. sugar and 1 tsp. spice.
Cool to just warm. At this point, if serving a warm pudding, stir in a fruit selection and/or crumbled cookies and liqueur. Fold in the whipped cream. Spoon portions into dessert glasses; garnish each serving with a sprinkling of spice and a pineapple spear/orange half-slice.
If serving chilled, refrigerate the prepared pudding in the pot for 1-2 hours. At serving time, prepare portions into dessert bowls; garnish each portion with berries and crumbled cookies. Sprinkle with spice; garnish with pineapple spear/orange half-slice. Serves 6.

ZUCCHINI SLAW
PORK CUTLETS PARMAGIANO WITH TOMATO MUSHROOM SAUCE
POTATO GNOCCHI or RICOTTA GNOCCHI
ARTICHOKES STUFFED WITH PROSCIUTTO, PROVOLONE AND OLIVES
ICE CREAM TORTONI

ZUCCHINI SLAW

2 pounds (about 3-4 medium) zucchini, trimmed; cut each zucchini crosswise into 3-inch
    segments; julienne the segments down to the seeded core (discard the seeded core);
    place zucchini strips into a large bowl. (*NOTE: below)

4-6 plum tomatoes, deseeded, diced

1 tsp. garlic minced

$\frac{1}{4}$ cup white wine vinegar

2 tbsp. extra-virgin olive oil

$\frac{1}{4}$ tsp. salt, or to taste

$\frac{1}{4}$ tsp. freshly ground black pepper, or to taste

8 large basil leaves, shredded

$\frac{1}{2}$ cup pignola (pine nuts)

Shaved sharp provolone cheese for garnish

   *NOTE: "Julienne" is a French term for cutting vegetables, usually into tiny matchsticks.
To "julienne", slice the vegetable as thinly as possible (less then $\frac{1}{8}$-inch), using a knife or a
"mandoline". Lay the strips on top of each other and cut across into strips, as thinly as possible.

   Place julienned zucchini in a large bowl; gently stir in tomato quarters and minced garlic;
add vinegar, olive oil, salt and pepper, carefully tossing to coat vegetables evenly. Stir in shredded
basil. (The slaw can be made up to this point, several hours in advance.) Cover and refrigerate.
Just before serving, stir in pine nuts; shred provolone over each portion. Serves 6.

PORK CUTLETS PARMAGIANO WITH MUSHROOM TOMATO SAUCE

6 pork cutlets, 3x6 inches; do not pound thin
2 eggs, beaten or $\frac{1}{2}$ cup egg substitute
2 cups fine corn flake crumbs
$\frac{1}{2}$ tsp. freshly ground black pepper, dash of salt
$\frac{1}{2}$ cup finely chopped parsley
$\frac{1}{2}$ cup grated Pecorino Romano cheese
1 lb. smoky mozzarella, thinly sliced
olive oil to brush cutlets and for bottom of pan
more shredded Pecorino Romano cheese for garnish, about $\frac{1}{2}$ cup

3 cups Tomato Mushroom Sauce (see page 392)
    or: simmer 2 cups sliced white mushrooms into prepared Marinara Sauce for
    5 minutes. (You will use half the sauce for Pork Cutlets and remaining sauce for Gnocchi.)

Preheat oven to 375°.

Have ready: a large skillet; a 9x15x3-inch baking pan.
Lay a large sheet of waxed paper on a board. Spread a mix of corn flake crumbs, black pepper, salt and grated cheese on waxed paper. In a large deep plate beat eggs with parsley. Dip each cutlet into egg mix; then coat with crumbs mix on both sides. Sauté cutlets for 2 minutes on each side in preheated oiled skillet at 300°. Transfer cutlets to a 9x15x3-inch baking pan. Lay 1-2 thin slices of smoky mozzarella over each cutlet. Bake in preheated oven at 375° for 10 minutes. Lower oven to 300°; remove pan from oven and spoon $1\frac{1}{2}$ cups Tomato Mushroom Sauce over the cutlets. Garnish with remaining shredded Pecorino Romano and return to oven for another 10-12 minutes. Serve Pork Cutlets Parmagiano with sauce and a side of Gnocchi in sauce. Serves 5-6.

Angela, Rudy and Joseph Palumbo share their happpy day.
Photo: A. Palumbo

POTATO GNOCCHI

(If you prefer, some specialty food stores carry freshly made Gnocchi.)

3 lbs. all-purpose potatoes, boiled in jackets
$\frac{1}{2}$ cups all-purpose flour
1 tsp. salt
$\frac{1}{4}$ tsp. black pepper
3 eggs beaten
1 cup Parmesan cheese, grated

SAUCE:
Tomato Mushroom Sauce (see page 392)
more grated Parmesan cheese for garnish

Have ready: a 6-qt. pot of lightly salted water to cook gnocchi; a large slotted spoon; a floured board.

Boil potatoes in jackets, until tender, about 20-30 minutes. While hot, peel off skin from potatoes and press through a ricer. Combine flour, seasonings, eggs and cheese into the potatoes. Add more flour (up to a cupful) if dough is not firm enough to hold together. Mix the ingredients thoroughly. Divide dough into 4 sections; on a floured board, roll each section into $\frac{1}{2}$-inch thick long ropes. Cut each rope into 1-inch pieces; roll little pieces of potato dough off the tines of a fork, off the pebbly side of a cheese grater, or off a gnocchi board. (*NOTE: below.)

Fill a 6-quart pot with salted water and bring to boil. Drop gnocchi into boiling water a bunch at a time, until they float to top of pot (within minutes). Skim them off the top of the pot with a large slotted spoon and pour them into a serving bowl. Spoon Tomato Mushroom Sauce over gnocchi; garnish with grated Parmesan. In this menu, serve gnocchi as a side for Pork Cutlets.

*NOTE: At this point you may spread formed gnocchi over a semolina-sprinkled baking sheet(s) and freeze the tray(s), uncovered, for 2-3 hours. When frozen, divide gnocchi into several small plastic bags and quickly refreeze, up to 2 weeks. When serving, proceed as directed in recipe, above. Serves 5-6 as a side dish.

RICOTTA GNOCCHI

2 cups all-purpose flour
1 lb. (16 oz.) whole milk ricotta
4 large eggs, beaten

1 cup grated Parmesan cheese
1 tsp. salt
$\frac{1}{4}$ tsp. black pepper
1 tsp. nutmeg

In a large bowl, combine ricotta, beaten eggs, Parmesan, all spices. Work in 2 cups flour, a cupful at a time, to form a soft dough. Add more flour if dough is sticky. At this point in the recipe, continue to follow same directions for POTATO GNOCCHI (above). Serves 5-6 as a side dish.

ARTICHOKES STUFFED WITH PROSCIUTTO/PROVOLONE/OLIVES

5-6 large globe artichokes (With a sharp knife, cut off about $\frac{1}{2}$-inch across base of
    artichokes; chop off about 1-inch across tops of leaves, removing sharp points.)
2 cups water (or more), divided: about 1 cup for the pot; $\frac{1}{4}$ cup for stuffing;
    $\frac{1}{2}$ cup for roasting pan
juice of 2 lemons

STUFFING:

1 cup unseasoned coarse Italian bread crumbs

4 strips prosciutto, chopped

5-6 whole garlic cloves; 5 garlic cloves,
    chopped

$\frac{1}{4}$ cup fresh Italian parsley, chopped

1 small sweet red pepper, deseeded, chopped

1 small green pepper deseeded, chopped

1 cup provolone cheese, cubed

$\frac{1}{4}$ cup Parmesan cheese, grated

$\frac{1}{2}$ cup pitted black olives, chopped

salt and black pepper, to taste

$\frac{1}{2}$ cup olive oil, in two parts

Preheat oven to 425°.

Have ready: a large, wide pot with a cover; a 12-inch round or a 9x12x4-inch baking pan, coated with olive oil (and $\frac{1}{2}$ cup hot water); a serving platter.

Trim artichokes as directed above. Spread leaves from choke, careful not to break the artichoke. With kitchen shears, snip off sharp points of the choke and discard. Rinse artichokes under cool water and stand them up in a wide pot with a cover, adding enough water to reach 1 inch at bottom. Sprinkle artichokes with lemon juice. Cover the pot and bring to boil. Then, simmer artichokes for 15 minutes.

Meanwhile, Prepare STUFFING in a bowl. Combine bread crumbs, chopped garlic, chopped peppers and prosciutto, grated cheese, cheese cubes, salt, pepper, parsley and olives. Sprinkle one-quarter cup each: olive oil and hot water over stuffing ingredients, and thoroughly mix with 2 spoons or your hands.

After 15 minutes, remove pot of artichokes from burner; drain water from pot. Stuff and pack cavities of artichokes, and between the leaves, with stuffing mix. Stand stuffed artichokes in a well-oiled baking pan, to which $\frac{1}{2}$ cup hot water has been added. Sprinkle remainder of olive oil ($\frac{1}{2}$ cup) over each artichoke in pan. Press one garlic clove into center of each artichoke. Roast them in preheated oven at 425° for 20-25 minutes, until tender; or until you can easily remove one of the outer leaves with your fingers. Transfer artichokes to serving plate; pour residual liquid from pot over each artichoke. Serve them warm. Serves 5-6.

ICE CREAM TORTONI

10 foil or paper muffin-pan liners (2½-inch cups)

10 2-inch chocolate chip cookies (see page 366 for recipe; or use packaged cookies)

1 pint Vanilla Bean Ice Cream, slightly softened, low-fat available

1 cup whipped cream, or frozen non-dairy whipped topping, thawed

¼ cup mini semisweet chocolate morsels

2 tbsp. almond liqueur (like Amaretto), or ½ tsp. almond extract

¼ cup finely chopped almonds with skin

Insert liners into muffin cups. Insert 1 chocolate chip cookie at bottom of each liner.
Set aside. In a medium bowl, fold whipped topping into ice cream. Stir in chocolate morsels and liqueur. Spoon and divide the mixture into cookie-lined, paper-lined muffin cups. Sprinkle tops of tortoni with chopped almonds. Freeze them for 30 minutes or until firm; or until serving time. Can be frozen up to 2 months. Serves 10.

50/50-25 at the Harvard Museum of Natural History. Photo: F. Barbarotto

ESCAROLE SALAD
VINAIGRETTE DRESSING (see page 383)
SHRIMP WITH SCALLIONS, LONG-GRAINED RICE
STUFFED PEPPERS
HEAVENLY ORANGE RICOTTA CAKE
ICED TEA WITH ORANGE

ESCAROLE SALAD

3 cups of escarole (from center of head), trimmed, rinsed, drained, chopped

2 heads Belgian endive, trimmed, rinsed, drained, finely sliced lengthwise

2 yellow tomatoes, rinsed, halved, cut into $\frac{1}{4}$-inch slices

2 oz. (1 tin) flat anchovies, chopped

$\frac{1}{2}$ cup pitted black olives, sliced

Vinaigrette Dressing (see page 383)

Have ready: a large salad bowl, chilled in refrigerator for 1 hour.

Prepare Vinaigrette Dressing in advance and refrigerate. Remove dressing from refrigerator 1 hour prior to serving.

In a large salad bowl, combine chopped escarole and sliced endive. Spread anchovies and olive slices over salad; toss to mix. Line the edge of salad bowl with half-moons of yellow tomatoes. Cover bowl lightly with plastic wrap and refrigerate salad until serving. Shake or stir dressing thoroughly; spoon over salad. Gently toss salad, trying not to disturb the "edge of tomatoes". Serves 4-5.

SHRIMP WITH SCALLIONS

[A Cookimg Hint: Clean fish or shellfish by "dipping" pieces in cold, salted water; then, pat dry with paper towel. Do not use running water.]

2 lbs. medium shrimp, rinsed in cold water, shelled, patted dry with paper towels
4 tbsp. canola oil
2 tbsp. soy sauce
2 tbsp. dry sherry

2 tbsp. sugar
6 slices fresh ginger ($\frac{1}{4}$-inch thick)
1 bunch scallions, trimmed, cut into 2-inch lengths

Have ready: a large wok or skillet; a warm platter.

In a small bowl, mix together: soy, sherry and sugar. Set aside.

In a large wok (or skillet), heat 2 tablespoons oil until very hot. Add 3 slices of ginger and stir-fry for 1 minute. Add half of the scallions, half of the shrimp and half of soy mixture and stir-fry quickly, until shrimp turn pink, about 3-5 minutes. Remove to a warm platter; discard ginger.

Return wok to heat and warm remaining 2 tablespoons oil until very hot. Add remaining ginger, shrimp, scallions and soy mixture and stir-fry as before. Add to previously cooked shrimp and mix. Serve over steamed white long-grained rice. Serves 4-5.

STUFFED PEPPERS

1 doz. green or red Italian frying peppers, deseeded, cored, rinsed, drained
6 slices artisan white bread, crusts removed (stale the crusts for future grating)
6 flat anchovy fillets

3 large garlic cloves
3 tbsp. Parmesan cheese, grated
$\frac{1}{4}$ cup fresh Italian parsley
$\frac{1}{2}$ cup olive oil, divided: $\frac{1}{4}$ cup, $\frac{1}{4}$ cup

Preheat oven to 375°.

Have ready: a food processor; line a 9x12 baking sheet with foil.

Tear bread into small pieces and place in a bowl. In a food processor, combine bread with anchovies, garlic, Parmesan and parsley. Turn on machine and slowly pour in $\frac{1}{4}$ cup olive oil. Stop the machine to check the mixture. Texture of bread should resemble coarse crumbs and should be fairly moist. Add 1-2 tablespoons water to moisten, if needed.

Loosely stuff the peppers with the bread mix; do not pack too tightly. Arrange stuffed peppers on baking sheet. If you have leftover stuffing, form tiny patties and tuck in patties around the peppers. Moisten peppers by sprinkling them with remaining olive oil. Bake in preheated oven, at 375° for 35-45 minutes, until peppers are browned and have begun to collapse. If necessary, add a little more water to bottom of pan to keep it wet. Serves 4-5.

HEAVENLY ORANGE RICOTTA CAKE

1 pkg. (22 oz.) yellow cake mix
3 eggs or $\frac{3}{4}$ cup egg substitute
1 cup low-fat ricotta
1 cup evaporated milk (fat-free available)
$\frac{1}{3}$ cup orange juice

1 tbsp. grated orange rind
1 tsp. cinnamon
$\frac{1}{2}$ cup dried cranberries,
     soaked in 1 tbsp. Grand Marnier (or brandy)
$\frac{1}{2}$ cup chopped walnuts

Preheat oven to 350°.

Have ready: a 10-inch Bundt pan, generously greased and dusted with flour.
In a large bowl, combine cake mix, eggs (or egg substitute), milk, orange juice, rind, cinnamon and ricotta and beat at medium speed for 2 minutes. Stir in nuts and soaked dried cranberries.
Pour batter into prepared greased/floured Bundt pan and bake cake on rack in center of the preheated oven, at 350° for 40-45 minutes, or until inserted toothpick tests clean. Cool cake in pan for 15-20 minutes. Remove cake from pan and thoroughly cool. Store, loosely covered, in refrigerator. Serve with Iced Tea with Orange. Serves 8.

....

ICED TEA WITH ORANGE

Brew tea for 6 servings. Pour 6 cups boiling water into a large heat-tempered pitcher. Steep 6-8 packets of Earl Grey Orange Pekoe Tea in boiling water for 3-5 minutes. Allow pitcher of tea to come to room temperature. Just before serving, add 1 cup fresh orange juice to the pitcher. At serving, add ice to glasses; pour Tea with Orange into the glasses; garnish each glass with a half-slice of a navel orange and a sprig of fresh mint. Add sugar to taste, if desired.

A Swim Party.

A SUMMER BARBEQUE

SPINACH SALAD WITH FONTINA

RASPBERRY VINAIGRETTE (see page 383)

PIGS AND RIBS

SAUSAGES AND RIBS

CUCUMBER SALAD

WARM POTATO SALAD

BLUEBERRY-LEMON TART

SPINACH SALAD WITH FONTINA

10 oz. baby spinach, rinsed, drained

6 plum tomatoes, quartered

1 cup raspberries or red grapes, rinsed, drained

½ cup glazed walnut halves

½ lb. Fontina cheese, chopped in small cubes

Raspberry Vinaigrette (see page 383)

Have ready: a large glass salad bowl.

Prepare Raspberry Vinaigrette. Store in refrigerator until 1 hour before using. Stir and shake well before serving.

In a large salad bowl, combine baby spinach, plum tomatoes, grapes, nuts and Fontina cheese. Shake or stir dressing thoroughly. Drizzle dressing over salad; toss to thoroughly mix. Serves 6.

Cousins Lou & Jim Sansone at the Family Reunion on the Farm. Photo: I. Lang

PIGS AND RIBS (For a Barbeque)

6-8 loin pork chops, $\frac{1}{2}$-inch thick
1-2 rack(s) of pork ribs (about 4-4$\frac{1}{2}$ lbs.)
3 pans 9x15 (to marinate racks of pork ribs and pork chops)

BARBEQUE SAUCE:

1 tbsp. olive oil
1 onion, chopped
2 cups prepared tomato sauce
1 cup red wine vinegar
1 tbsp. garlic powder
$\frac{1}{4}$ tsp. freshly ground black pepper

$\frac{1}{4}$ tsp. cayenne pepper
$\frac{1}{4}$ tsp. sweet paprika
1 tsp. salt
$\frac{1}{2}$ cup packed dark brown sugar
2 tbsp. Worcestershire sauce

BOURBON SAUCE:

1 cup of BBQ sauce (see recipe above)
$\frac{1}{4}$ cup orange marmalade
2 tbsp. bourbon

Have ready: three 9x15-inch pans.
1.) Prepare BBQ SAUCE and BOURBON SAUCE. Combine ingredients for each sauce in 2 small saucepans, simmer for 5 minutes. Set aside.

2.) Preheat the Grill to 175°, a slow grill. Lay pork chops on the grill, 5 inches above heat. Cover the grill and slow cook chops for about 10 minutes on each side. Baste chops with Bourbon Sauce. Cover grill and continue to cook chops for another 5 minutes on each side. Place chops in a 9x15 pan; baste them again; cover lightly with a sheet of foil and keep in a warming oven.

3.) Repeat a similar procedure with 2 racks of ribs. Baste ribs with Barbeque Sauce. Grill the basted racks of ribs 15 minutes on each side; baste them again and continue to grill at low temperature for another 30-40 minutes, turning them frequently. Serves 8.

A Couple of Cousins Reunions at the Hopewell Farm.

SAUSAGES AND RIBS (Oven-Cooked)

[A Cooking Hint: Before cutting sausages into chunks or rounds, refrigerate them after sautéing the sausages. Or freeze uncooked sausage links. Then, slice into rounds or cut in chunks when frozen. Proceed to sauté as directed in recipe. Another help: prick casing around sausages with tines of a fork before cooking to allow air release and to prevent casing from shrinking.]

1 doz. sausages (Select from: Italian pork sausages, spicy turkey sausages,
    spicy chicken sausages)
1 rack pork spare ribs, about $2\frac{1}{2}$ lbs.

BARBEQUE SAUCE:

1 cup catsup
1 tbsp. white vinegar
$\frac{1}{4}$ cup orange juice
$\frac{1}{4}$ tsp. salt
$\frac{1}{4}$ tsp. freshly ground black pepper
$\frac{1}{4}$ tsp. Tabasco

$\frac{1}{4}$ tsp. whole cloves
1 tbsp. Worcestershire sauce
$\frac{1}{4}$ cup dark molasses
$\frac{1}{4}$ tsp. garlic powder
$\frac{1}{4}$ tsp. dry mustard
1 tbsp. olive oil

Preheat oven to 350°.

Have ready: two 9x15-inch grill pans.

Prepare BARBEQUE SAUCE. Combine all sauce ingredients in a small sauce pot and simmer for 5 minutes. Keep sauce warm; set aside.

Set sausages on grill pan. Bake in preheated oven at 350°, 35-45 minutes, frequently basting sausages with Barbeque Sauce and turning them often. Lay a loose sheet of foil over sausages and keep them warm.

Lay the rack of ribs on a grill pan; baste with Barbeque Sauce on both sides of ribs; turn rack of ribs several times to cook until tender, about 40-50 minutes. Serves 6-8.

CUCUMBER SALAD
(This salad may be prepared a day or two in advance and refrigerated.)

6 medium-to-large slender cucumbers, peeled, deseeded and cut into sticks (julienne);
    or shave-slice the cucumbers

1 large red onion, thinly sliced

1 tsp. honey mustard

1 tsp. salt

¼ cup olive oil

½ cup granulated sugar

2 tbsp. fresh dill, minced

½ cup red wine vinegar

2 tsp. sweet paprika

Have ready: a non-metallic colander; a large non-metallic bowl.

Place cucumbers in a non-metallic colander; sprinkle salt over them, mixing well with your hands. Allow to stand 2 hours.

Gently squeeze water out of cucumbers with your hands. Return cucumbers to colander.

In a large non-metal bowl, whisk together: sugar, vinegar, mustard and oil. Add cucumbers and mix; mix in onion. Cover bowl and refrigerate for 2 hours. Add dill and paprika and mix well. Serves 6-8.

Our Sansone cousins.

WARM POTATO SALAD

[A Cooking Hint: Start potatoes to cook in boiling salted water, rather then cold water.
Drain them immediately. Cover them lightly with a clean dish towel (to keep them warm).
Never place a lid on the pot or potatoes will get soggy.]

2 lbs. Red Bliss potatoes (do not pare), quartered
5 cups water
$1\frac{1}{4}$ tsp. salt, divided (1 tsp., $\frac{1}{4}$ tsp.)
$\frac{1}{4}$ lb. thick-sliced bacon, cut into $\frac{1}{2}$-inch pieces
2 cups prepared chicken broth; Recipe for Homemade Chicken Broth (see page 81)

3 tbsp. all-purpose flour
2 tsp. dry mustard
2 tbsp. granulated sugar
1 tsp. celery seeds

$\frac{1}{3}$ cup cider vinegar
$\frac{1}{2}$ cup scallions, finely chopped
$\frac{1}{4}$ tsp. freshly ground black pepper

Place potatoes in a medium-size pot with 5 cups cold water and 1 teaspoon salt. Bring to a boil over high heat; reduce to simmer 8-10 minutes. Drain.

Meanwhile, fry bacon in a skillet over medium heat until crisp. Drain on paper towels. Reserve bacon fat.

In a medium-size saucepan, heat $1\frac{1}{2}$ tablespoons of bacon fat. Sprinkle flour on bacon fat and whisk them together to form a paste (the roux). Cook, whisking continuously, to cook the flour for 2-3 minutes.

Slowly whisk chicken broth into the roux and continue to whisk until smooth and thickened, about 2 minutes.

In a small bowl, mix together; mustard, sugar, celery seeds and vinegar. Add this mixture to the sauce and bring to a boil. Reduce heat and simmer until slightly thickened, 5-10 minutes.

Pour the sauce over the potatoes. Add bacon, scallions, pepper and $\frac{1}{4}$ teaspoon salt. Toss and serve warm. Serves 6.

Baby Merika listens to Great-Grandma Herta. Photo: I. Lang

227

BLUEBERRY-LEMON TART

$\frac{1}{2}$ cup butter or Smart Balance spread

1 pkg. (22 oz.) lemon cake mix

3 tbsp. cold water (2 times: for cake mix AND for blueberry filling)

1 pt. blueberries, rinsed, drained

$\frac{1}{2}$ cup granulated sugar

2 tbsp. all-purpose flour

$\frac{1}{8}$ tsp. salt

confectioners' sugar for garnish

Preheat oven to 400°.

Have ready: a 9-inch spring-form pan.

In a large bowl, with a pastry blender or 2 knives (used as a pair of scissors), cut butter into the cake mix until the mixture resembles coarse crumbs. Add 3 tablespoons cold water, tossing with a fork to mix. Set aside $1\frac{1}{4}$ cups of this mix for crumble topping.

With your hand, knead the cake mix mixture remaining in the bowl until it holds together. Pat this mixture onto bottom and $\frac{3}{4}$-inch up the sides of a 9-inch spring-form pan; set aside.

Reserve about $\frac{1}{4}$ cup blueberries for garnish. In a 2-quart saucepan over medium heat, warm remaining blueberries with sugar, flour, salt and 3 tablespoons water until mixture comes to a boil, stirring constantly. Spoon blueberry mixture over cake mix in pan; sprinkle crumble topping over top.

Bake the tart in preheated oven at 400° for 35 minutes or until top is golden. Cool tart in pan on wire rack for 10 minutes. Remove sides of spring-form pan; cool tart 20 minutes longer. Just before serving, garnish with reserved blueberries and sprinkle with confectioners' sugar. Serve warm or cool. Makes 8-10 servings.

Yummy!

STUFFED TOMATOES
SALMON FILLETS VINAIGRETTE
BAKED MACARONI, SPINACH AND CHEESE
STUFFED MUSHROOMS WITH ANCHOVY
PEACH SORBET
SNICKERDOODLES

STUFFED TOMATOES

4 large ripe tomatoes, rinsed, tops removed
¼ cup olive oil
2 small onions, chopped
2 garlic cloves, minced
2 sweet Italian sausage links, chopped (It will be easier to chop sausage if partially frozen.)
1 ripe tomato, peeled, deseeded, chopped (see page 402 "How to Remove Skin from Tomato")
2 tbsp. fresh basil leaves, chopped
½ cup corn flakes crumbs

Preheat oven to 250°.

Have ready: a lightly greased 9x12 shallow baking pan.

With a small spoon, scoop out seeds from the whole tomatoes. Try not to discard pulp.
Set aside.
Warm olive oil in a large skillet oven medium heat. Add onions and garlic and cook until onion is translucent, about 4-5 minutes. Stir in chopped sausages, chopped tomato and basil and sauté until sausages are cooked, about 5 minutes. Remove pan from burner and set aside to cool.
Divide the filling equally among the 4 tomatoes. Sprinkle tops of tomatoes with corn flake crumbs, about 2 tablespoons for each tomato. Stand the tomatoes in prepared 9x12 pan and cover with aluminum foil. Bake tomatoes until softened and hot throughout, about 30-40 minutes, depending on size of tomatoes. Serves 4.

SALMON FILLETS VINAIGRETTE

4 sections of salmon fillets, about $\frac{1}{2}$ lb. each section

VINAIGRETTE:

1 tbsp. white wine vinegar

juice of 2 oranges (about 1 cup)

juice of 2 limes (about $\frac{1}{4}$ cup)

juice of 2 lemons (about $\frac{1}{4}$ cup)

$\frac{1}{4}$ cup olive oil

$\frac{1}{4}$ cup fresh cilantro, finely chopped

salt and freshly ground black pepper, to taste

slices of oranges, limes, lemons for garnish

Preheat oven to broil.

Have ready: a broiling pan; a wide dish with a raised edge.

Whisk to combine vinegar, juices, oil, salt and pepper in a small bowl. Stir in cilantro. Lay salmon fillets in a wide dish with a rim. Pour vinaigrette over salmon and marinate fillets for 30 minutes, turning them once.

Lay marinated fillets on a broiling pan and broil them 5-6 minutes per side. Drizzle 1 tablespoon of remaining vinaigrette over each portion. Garnish with citrus slices. Serves 4.

....

BAKED MACARONI, SPINACH AND CHEESE

$\frac{1}{2}$ lb. (about $2\frac{1}{2}$ cups) elbow pasta, uncooked

2 cups low-fat milk

2 tbsp. olive oil

3 tbsp. flour

$\frac{1}{4}$ tsp. freshly ground black pepper

$\frac{1}{4}$ tsp. nutmeg

salt to taste

$\frac{1}{2}$ lb. (8 oz.) light Swiss cheese, shredded

10 oz. pkg. baby spinach, rinsed, drained

$\frac{1}{4}$ cup Parmesan cheese, grated

Hungarian paprika for garnish, to taste

Preheat oven to 375°.

Have ready: a 9x12-inch casserole dish, greased with oil.

Bring a large pot of water to boil. Cook pasta 2 minutes less than package directs. Combine cooked pasta with baby spinach; set aside.

In a saucepan, heat milk over medium heat to a simmer. (Do not boil.)

Meanwhile, warm olive oil in a large pot over medium heat. Whisk in flour and cook until bubbly. Do not burn. Slowly pour milk into pot and whisk continuously until mixture is thick and bubbly, about 3-4 minutes. Do not boil.

Remove from burner; add pepper, salt, nutmeg and Swiss cheese. Stir until cheese is completely melted and smooth. Immediately pour cheese mixture over pasta and spinach. Combine thoroughly.

Pour into a greased 9x12-inch casserole; top with grated Parmesan cheese. Sprinkle with paprika. Bake in preheated oven at 375° for 35 minutes. Serve immediately. Serves 6.

STUFFED MUSHROOMS WITH ANCHOVY

12 large white mushrooms, trimmed, rinsed, drained; remove stems (Mince stems and set aside.)

2 tbsp. olive oil

2 shallots, minced

1 large garlic clove, minced

1 strip bacon, minced

6 anchovy fillets, minced

2 tbsp. fresh parsley, minced

$\frac{1}{2}$ cup coarse bread crumbs

dash of salt

$\frac{1}{4}$ tsp. freshly ground black pepper

1 cup dry white wine

juice of 1 lemon

Preheat oven to 350°.

Have ready: a 9x12 baking dish, coated with olive oil.

Warm 2 tablespoons olive oil in a large skillet. Add minced shallots, garlic and bacon and sauté for 3 minutes. Add minced mushrooms stems and cook slowly until tender, about 7-8 minutes. Stir in minced anchovies, parsley and 2 tablespoons crumbs to make a moist and pliable mixture. Season with salt and pepper.

Divide the stuffing mixture among the 12 large mushroom caps. Lay mushrooms in 9x12 prepared casserole dish. Sprinkle each mushroom with more crumbs and drizzle remaining 1 tablespoon olive oil over them.

Pour wine and lemon juice into a small sauce pot and set over medium-high heat to burn off alcohol, about 4-5 minutes. Carefully pour wine mix into the baking dish and bake mushrooms in preheated oven at 350° until crumbs are golden, about 15 minutes. Serves 4-5.

Fish in Pond.

PEACH SORBET

[A Cooking Hint: How to Skin a Peach:
1. wash peach
2. immerse peach in boiling water for 1 minute
3. remove peach from boiling water and plunge it into cold water
4. peel off skin with fingers]

8 ripe peaches, peeled, halved, pitted and cut into chunks
1 can (11 oz.) peach nectar
$\frac{3}{4}$ cup granulated sugar
$\frac{1}{2}$ tsp. freshly grated lemon peel

Have ready: a food processor or blender; a 2-quart metal pan.

Purée all ingredients in batches in a food processor or blender. Pour into a shallow 2-quart metal pan. Cover and freeze for about 3 hours or until firm.

With a blunt knife, break frozen mixture into chunks and process in batches in a food processor or blender until slushy. Pack in a 2-quart freezer container and freeze at least 2 hours or until firm. Scoop into dessert glasses. Serves 4-5.

....

SNICKERDOODLES

1 cup butter or Smart Balance spread, softened
1 cup granulated sugar
2 tsp. cream of tartar
$\frac{1}{2}$ cup brown sugar
1 tsp. baking soda
2 large eggs or $\frac{1}{2}$ cup egg substitute
$\frac{1}{4}$ tsp. salt
$2\frac{3}{4}$ cup all-purpose flour
2 tbsp. granulated sugar, 2 tsp. cinnamon

Preheat oven to 400°.

Have ready: 3 ungreased cookie sheets.

In a large bowl, thoroughly mix: butter, sugars, eggs. Sift flour into the mixture and add cream of tartar, baking soda and salt. Stir to combine into a stiff batter.

Shape dough into 1-inch balls. Roll balls into a mixture of 2 tablespoons sugar and 2 teaspoons cinnamon. Place 2 inches apart on ungreased baking sheets, about 24 cookies per sheet. Bake in preheated oven at 400° for 8-10 minutes. These cookies puff up at first; then, flatten out. Makes about 6 dozen cookies.

EGG AND BACON SALAD ON A BED OF GREENS

HONEY MUSTARD DRESSING (see page 377)

GRILLED SEA SCALLOPS KEBABS

FLORENTINE PENNE

LUSCIOUS FRUITS

EGG AND BACON SALAD ON A BED OF GREENS

4-6 large eggs, hard-cooked
2 cups Romaine lettuce, rinsed, drained, chopped
2 cups arugula, rinsed, drained, chopped
4-6 plum tomatoes, rinsed, quartered lengthwise
4 Kirby cucumbers, pared, sliced in rounds
$\frac{1}{2}$ lb. Swiss cheese, cut into $\frac{1}{2}$-inch cubes
3 strips lean bacon, cooked, drained on paper towels

Honey Mustard Dressing (see page 377)

Prepare Honey Mustard Dressing. Store in refrigerator until 1 hour prior to serving. Lay a bed of chopped Romaine lettuce mixed with chopped arugula. Arrange tomato sections over the salad. Scatter Kirby rounds and Swiss cheese cubes. Crush drained cooked bacon and sprinkle over salad dish. Sprinkle salad with Honey Mustard Dressing. Gently toss salad and serve. Serves 4-6.

Uncle Emil and Aunt Louise Orlando's Children and Spouses enjoy a Family Luncheon.

GRILLED SEA SCALLOPS KEBABS

12 8-inch wooden skewers
2 dozen large basil leaves
2 dozen thin slices prosciutto
2 lbs., about 24 large sea scallops, rinsed in cold water, drained and patted dry
    with paper towels

Soak 1 dozen 8-inch wooden skewers in water for 30 minutes. Lay a slice of prosciutto on a cutting board. Place one basil leaf at one end of the slice of prosciutto and lay a sea scallop on the basil leaf. Wrap the prosciutto around the scallop and basil, tucking in the sides. Repeat this procedure with each scallop, basil leaf and slice of prosciutto. Thread two scallop packets onto each skewer.

Grill kebabs on an open grill over medium-hot coals until prosciutto begins to brown and sizzle, 2-5 minutes for each side. Yields 1 dozen kebabs. Serves 4-6.

FLORENTINE PENNE

a 12 oz. pkg. whole wheat penne pasta
2 tbsp. olive oil
$\frac{1}{2}$ lb. fresh sliced white mushrooms
1 cup pitted oil-cured olives, chopped
10 oz. pkg. fresh baby spinach, rinsed, drained

$\frac{1}{2}$ cup sun dried tomatoes, cut into slivers
6 garlic cloves, minced
$\frac{1}{2}$ cup pignola (pine nuts)
$\frac{1}{2}$ cup Asiago cheese, grated, for garnish

Have ready: a large skillet; a large serving bowl.

Cook pasta for 2 minutes less than as directed on package; drain. While pasta is cooking, heat olive oil in a large skillet and sauté mushrooms, olives, garlic, sun dried tomatoes and pignola for 10-12 minutes until mushrooms are cooked. Add and stir in spinach to this mixture. Combine cooked and drained pasta with the sautéed vegetables and cook for an additional 4-5 minutes. Pour into a large serving bowl. Serve hot with a sprinkling of grated Asiago cheese. Serves 6.

LUSCIOUS FRUITS
[A Cooking Hint: Rinse all vegetables and fruits prior to eating; this means berries, oranges, apples and melons as well. Drain greens and berries thoroughly. Gently pat-dry berries with paper towels.]

FRUIT TRAY: (Use a large 15-inch glass dish/tray.)
2 golden delicious apples (rinsed, cored, cut in slices 1-inch thick, *1 hour before serving*)
18-20 large strawberries, trimmed, rinsed, drained, gently patted dry with paper towels
6 small bunches black grapes, rinsed, drained, patted dry with paper towels

CHOCOLATE DIP:
1 pkg. (6 oz.) Ghiradelli dark chocolate morsels
1 tsp. butter or Smart Balance spread
2 tbsp. orange liqueur like Grand Marnier (or: 1 tbsp. orange extract)

Have ready: a small double boiler (2 pots); or 2 pots which will fit one into the other.

Prepare chocolate for dipping 2-3 hours before serving.
Pour enough water into bottom pot of double boiler for lower portion of top pot to rest. Pour 6 ounces dark chocolate morsels into top pot; add butter and liqueur. Place the filled double boiler on the stove burner and bring water to a boil. Lower heat to simmer to melt the chocolate in top pot. Stir the chocolate mix occasionally. Remove pots from burner.
When chocolate cools, or about 1 hour prior to serving, dip strawberries into chocolate and arrange them on a large glass tray. You may wish to form a circle of strawberries around the edge of the platter.
Chocolate-dipped apple slices should follow, arranged around the interior circle of the platter.
Dip small bunches of grapes into chocolate mixture. Mound them in center of platter.
Keep platter at a cool room temperature or, refrigerate on lowest shelf, uncovered. Caffé espresso is a delicious accompaniment. Serves 6-8.

HAWAIIAN SPINACH SALAD
ASIAN DRESSING I (see page 382)
SEA SCALLOPS WITH ROASTED RED PEPPERS
PENNE WITH ZUCCHINI
ORANGE-CRANBERRY CHEESECAKE

HAWAIIAN SPINACH SALAD

10 oz. pkg. baby spinach, rinsed, drained
1 can (12 oz.) Mandarin orange segments, drained; reserve juice to incorporate
    into dressing
1 cup fresh (or canned) pineapple chunks
$\frac{1}{4}$ cup flaked coconut
$\frac{1}{4}$ cup pimiento olives, chopped

Asian Dressing I (see page 382)

Prepare Asian Dressing I. Substitute orange juice and rind
for lemon juice and rind. Refrigerate dressing until 1 hour prior
to using.
In a decorative salad bowl, combine baby spinach, Mandarin
oranges, pineapple chunks, flaked coconut and olives. At
serving, sprinkle dressing over bowl; toss to mix. Serves 6.

SEA SCALLOPS WITH ROASTED RED PEPPERS
[A Cooking Hint: "How to Roast Peppers", see *NOTE below.]

2 large sweet peppers, roasted
2 lbs. snow peas, trimmed, rinsed, drained
2-3 tbsp. olive oil
2 lbs. large sea scallops, about 24 scallops,
    rinsed in cold water, drained,
    patted dry with paper towels
$\frac{1}{4}$ cup shallots, finely chopped
2-3 large garlic cloves, finely chopped

1 tsp. dried thyme
$\frac{1}{4}$ tsp. hot pepper flakes
2 tbsp. anisette (or ouzo)
2 tbsp. olive oil
2 tbsp. lemon juice
salt and freshly ground black pepper to taste
$\frac{1}{2}$ cup fresh parsley, finely chopped

Have ready: a large non-stick skillet.

Cut peeled, deseeded roasted peppers into $\frac{1}{2}$-inch cubes. Heat oil in a large non-stick skillet. Add snow peas to skillet and cook and stir over medium heat for 2 minutes. Add scallops, cubed peppers, chopped shallots, garlic, thyme, salt and pepper(s). Cook, stirring and tossing over high heat until scallops are cooked through. Do not overcook. Sprinkle with lemon juice and anisette; sprinkle with parsley. Serve from skillet. Serves 6.

*NOTE: "How to Roast Peppers"
(1) If you're roasting more than 2 peppers, preheat oven to 450°. Lay 4-6 peppers on a cookie sheet lined with a sheet of foil. I remove the seeds before I roast the peppers, by coring the peppers and removing the stem with the ribs and seeds. Insert a clove of peeled garlic into the cavity of each pepper. Roast peppers 15-20 minutes on each side (turn twice). The skin will char. Remove the tray from the oven; wrap the peppers in the foil, and allow them to steam, covered, until they're cool enough to handle. Then, you can peel off the skin (starting from blossom end). You may serve them (with the garlic) as a whole pepper or sliced into strips.

(2) OR: If you're roasting 1 or 2 peppers, use a long-handled fork and char the peppers over an open flame, turning them every 2-3 minutes, until skins are charred. Then, proceed to remove skin as in Method (1). Also, cut off ends and discard seeds and ribs.

(3) OR: Broil peppers by laying them on a cookie sheet lined with foil as in Method (1). (You may remove seeds before broiling.) Broil in preheated broiler-oven about 3 inches from heat, turning peppers every 5 minutes for 20 minutes or so, until skins are charred. Proceed as directed in Method (1). (If preparing Chiles, use protective gloves.) IN ANY CASE, DO NOT LEAVE PROCEDURE UNATTENDED.

PENNE WITH ZUCCHINI

1-1½ lb. penne pasta
¼ cup olive oil
2 large garlic cloves, minced
1 small onion, minced
4 strips thinly sliced prosciutto, finely chopped
a sprinkling of hot red pepper flakes
4 small zucchini, scrubbed, julienne (Do not pare.)
2 tomatoes, chopped, with juice
¼ cup fresh Italian parsley, minced
1 tbsp. olive oil
½ cup fresh basil leaves, torn
1 tsp. salt
½ tsp. freshly ground black pepper
1 cup freshly grated Pecorino Romano cheese

Have ready: a large skillet.

Cook garlic in olive oil over medium heat in a large skillet until garlic is golden, about 2-3 minutes. Add onion and red pepper flakes and cook until onion is soft, about 3-4 minutes longer. Add prosciutto and zucchini. Partially cover pan and cook zucchini mixture until barely soft, about 4-5 minutes. Stir in tomatoes and cover pan. Reduce heat to very low and cook for 5 minutes.

Meanwhile boil penne in a large pasta pot with lots of lightly salted water, until al dente (according to directions on package); drain.

Add parsley, basil, salt and pepper and 1 tablespoon olive oil to the sauce and stir well to mix thoroughly.

Pour sauce into a large pasta serving bowl. Add cooked penne and toss. Sprinkle Pecorino Romano cheese over bowl and serve immediately. Serves 6.

Our Lady of Mercy Food Pantry, Hicksville, NY.
Photo with permission: Jim Reilly

ORANGE-CRANBERRY CHEESECAKE
(A low-fat cheesecake recipe.)
[A Cooking Hint: Dipping citrus fruit in hot water before squeezing,
will double and triple the amount of juice the fruit yields.]

2 8 oz. pkg. low-fat cream cheese

1 lb. low-fat ricotta

1$\frac{1}{2}$ cups granulated sugar

4 large whole eggs, beaten;
   or 1 cup egg substitute; or a combination
   of both (1 cup), beaten

3 tbsp. cornstarch

3 tbsp. all-purpose flour

1$\frac{1}{2}$ tbsp. orange juice

1 tsp. grated orange peel

1 tsp. orange extract

$\frac{1}{2}$ cup canola oil,
   or Smart Balance spread, melted

1 pt. fat-free sour cream

TOPPING: ORANGE-CRANBERRY SAUCE:

1 pkg. (12 oz.) fresh cranberries,
   rinsed, drained

1 cup orange juice

1 cup granulated sugar

1 tbsp. Grand Marnier liqueur

1 tbsp. grated orange peel

Have ready: a 9-inch spring-form pan, greased with canola oil.

Prepare TOPPING. In a 2-quart sauce pot with a cover, combine cranberries, orange juice and sugar. Stir in liqueur and peel; stir to dissolve sugar. Cover the pot and bring to a boil; then, simmer for 10 minutes, stirring occasionally. Remove from burner; cool and pour into a container with a cover. Refrigerate sauce to gel for at least 1-2 hours.

Preheat oven to 325°.

Meanwhile, Prepare the CHEESECAKE. Grease a 9-inch spring form pan. Using electric mixer, in a 4-quart bowl, beat cream cheese with ricotta cheese at high speed. Gradually, beat in sugar and eggs (or egg substitute). At low speed, beat in cornstarch, flour, orange juice and peel, and orange extract. Add oil (or melted Smart Balance spread) and sour cream. Beat until smooth. Pour batter into the greased 9-inch spring-form pan. Bake cake on rack in center of preheated oven at 325° for 1 hour, 10 minutes, or until firm around the edges. Turn off oven. Allow pan to stand in oven for 2 hours. Then, remove cake from oven and let it cool completely, at least 2 hours. Do not remove sides of pan; run a thin knife around edge of cheesecake to loosen cake. Refrigerate the cake for 3 hours; wrap in plastic if storing longer in refrigerator.

Two hours before serving cake, remove from refrigerator. Spoon chilled Cranberry-Orange Sauce over the cheesecake to cover and return it to refrigerator for another hour. Do *not* cover. Before serving, again run a thin knife around cake and sides of pan. Then, release the clasp from the pan and remove sides of the pan. (This cake may be frozen at this point, to serve at a later date.) This cheesecake takes about 7 hours to prepare, from start to finish. Serve with espresso. Serves 12.

> ### SLAW WITH PINEAPPLE AND GRAPES
> ### CHICKEN AND SAUSAGE STEW WITH CHEESE POLENTA
> ### ROASTED VEGETABLES
> ### CHOCOLATE FUDGE RIBBON CAKE

SLAW WITH PINEAPPLE AND GRAPES

2 cups shredded green cabbage
2 cups shredded red cabbage
1 small red onion, chopped fine
1 celery stalk, chopped fine
$1\frac{1}{2}$ cups fresh pineapple in small chunks
1 cup red seedless grapes

DRESSING:
$\frac{1}{2}$ cup light Miracle Whip dressing
$\frac{1}{4}$ cup cider vinegar
2-3 tbsp. fresh lemon juice
2 tbsp. extra-virgin olive oil
$\frac{1}{2}$ tsp. salt
$\frac{1}{4}$ tsp. freshly ground black pepper
1 tbsp. granulated sugar

6 large cabbage leaves as a base

   In a large salad bowl, combine green cabbage, red cabbage, celery, onion, pineapple and grapes. In a small bowl, blend Miracle Whip, vinegar, lemon juice, oil, salt, pepper and sugar. Pour over vegetables/fruits in the salad bowl. Toss with 2 large serving spoons to thoroughly coat salad with dressing. Serve in individual salad bowls. Line each bowl with a leaf of cabbage; spoon portions of slaw salad into bowl. Serves 6.

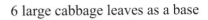

CHICKEN AND SAUSAGE STEW WITH CHEESE POLENTA

$\frac{1}{2}$ cup all-purpose flour

$\frac{1}{2}$ tsp. salt

$\frac{1}{4}$ tsp. black pepper

4 chicken legs (remove skin); rinse in cold water, pat dry with paper towels

4 chicken thighs (remove skin); rinse in cold water, pat dry with paper towels

3 chicken breasts, split (remove skin)

5-6 links sweet Italian sausages, each link cut in 1-inch diagonal slices (Sausage will cut easier if frozen.)

2 tbsp. olive oil

1 large yellow onion, sliced thin

1 small Chile pepper, deseeded, chopped (Wear plastic gloves with handling hot pepper.)

1 large green pepper, deseeded, chopped

6-8 Baby Bella mushrooms, rinsed, trimmed, halved

1 large can (about 29 oz.) tomatoes with juice

$\frac{1}{2}$ cup dry white wine, like Chardonnay

$\frac{1}{2}$ tsp. dried basil

$\frac{1}{2}$ tsp. dried oregano

1 bay leaf

$\frac{1}{4}$ cup fresh parsley, minced, for garnish

Have ready: a 6-qt. Dutch oven.

In a 9x12-inch clear plastic zip-lock bag, blend $\frac{1}{2}$ cup flour, $\frac{1}{2}$ tsp. salt and $\frac{1}{4}$ tsp. black pepper. Add 2-4 pieces of chicken into the plastic bag; shake the bag vigorously until pieces are well-coated. Transfer coated chicken to a tray and set aside. Continue this same procedure until all of the pieces of chicken are coated with flour mixture.

In a 6-quart Dutch oven, warm olive oil over medium heat. Add sausage slices to brown on all sides, about 3-4 minutes. Remove sausage from Dutch oven to a bowl. Set aside.

In drippings (add more oil if necessary), brown chicken pieces, 4-5 pieces at a time, on both sides; about 15-20 minutes (breast halves will cook longer then legs and thighs). Transfer chicken pieces to a plate as they brown.

Sauté onion, green pepper, Chile pepper and mushrooms about 3 minutes. Stir in tomatoes, plus juices, wine, herbs and spices. Return sausage pieces and chicken parts to the Dutch oven with the vegetables/sauce. Bring pot to a boil; reduce heat; simmer covered for 30 minutes. Meanwhile prepare Cheese Polenta (recipe on page 242). Garnish stew with minced parsley. Serve from the Dutch oven. Serves 6.

CHEESE POLENTA

2 tbsp. olive oil for pan
$\frac{1}{4}$ cup butter or Smart Balance spread
4 scallions, chopped
4 cups water, 1 tsp. salt
2 cups yellow cornmeal
$\frac{3}{4}$ cup Parmesan cheese, grated

Have ready: a 9x13x2-inch pan, coated with olive oil; a wide spatula.

In a 3-quart saucepan, over medium-high heat, melt butter; sauté scallions 2 minutes. Add water and salt. Bring pot to a boil; slowly add cornmeal, stirring continuously with whisk to prevent lumps.
Reduce heat to medium-low; cook polenta, stirring continuously, 10-15 minutes. Stir in cheese. Pour polenta into an oil-coated 9x13x2-inch pan; spread evenly.
Allow polenta to rest 10 minutes. Cut polenta lengthwise, into 4 equal strips; cut crosswise, into 6 equal sections. Use a spatula to serve Polenta with Chicken and Sausage Stew and a serving of the delicious sauce. Serves 6.

....

ROASTED VEGETABLES
[A Cooking Hint: Do not overcook any vegetables, especially: carrots, celery, green beans, peas, broccoli, asparagus, spinach, peppers, or Brussels sprouts.]

3 cups broccoli florets, rinsed, drained
6-8 white mushrooms, rinsed, halved
$\frac{1}{2}$ red bell pepper, $\frac{1}{2}$ green bell pepper, rinsed, deseeded, cut into strips
$\frac{1}{2}$ red onion, thinly sliced
3 large garlic cloves, halved
3-4 sun dried tomato halves, cut into strips
2 tbsp. each: olive oil, red wine vinegar
salt, black pepper to taste
3 large bay leaves
$\frac{1}{2}$ cup low-fat shredded sharp Cheddar cheese

Preheat oven to 425°.

Have ready: a 9x12x3-inch roasting pan lined with aluminum foil.
Toss all of the ingredients into a large bowl. Pour into the foil-lined pan and roast in preheated oven at 425° for 12-15 minutes. Serves 6.

CHOCOLATE FUDGE RIBBON CAKE

1 pkg. (22 oz.) chocolate cake mix
$1\frac{1}{3}$ cups milk (fat-free available)
$\frac{1}{2}$ cup canola oil
3 large eggs or $\frac{3}{4}$ cup egg substitute
1 pkg. (8 oz.) low-fat cream cheese, softened
2 tbsp. butter or Smart Balance spread, softened
1 tbsp. cornstarch
1 can (14 oz.) sweetened condensed milk (NOT evaporated milk)
1 egg or $\frac{1}{4}$ cup egg substitute
1 tsp. almond extract
confectioners' sugar for garnish, if desired

Preheat oven to 350°.

Have ready: grease and flour a 10-inch Bundt pan; a large cake plate.

Prepare chocolate cake mix as directed on package. *(Substitute milk, fat-free available, for water.)* Pour batter into a well-greased and floured 10-inch Bundt pan.

In a small bowl, beat cream cheese, butter and cornstarch until fluffy. Gradually, beat in condensed milk; beat in egg and almond extract, until smooth. Pour this mixture evenly over the chocolate cake batter in the Bundt pan.

Bake in center of preheated oven at 350° for 50-55 minutes, or until wooden toothpick inserted near center of cake removes clean. Cool cake 10 minutes; remove from pan onto cake plate and allow to cool thoroughly. Store covered, in refrigerator. (Dust with confectioners' sugar at serving time.) Serves 8-10.

A Night at the Museum. Photo: F. Barbarotto

GREENS SALAD

OLIVE OIL AND RED WINE VINEGAR DRESSING (see page 376)

SICILIAN SPAGHETTI

SALMON WITH SCALLOPS AND SHRIMP

CASSATA BOMBE

GREENS SALAD

[A Cooking Hint: Always chill salad vegetables before assembling salad; also chill salad plates.]

2 cups cicoria (dandelions), trimmed, rinsed, drained, chopped
4 cups baby arugula, trimmed, rinsed, drained
1$\frac{1}{2}$ cups packaged garlic croutons
2 large garlic cloves; mince 1 of the cloves and set aside
$\frac{1}{2}$ cup Parmesan cheese, grated

Olive Oil and Red Wine Vinegar Dressing (see page 376)

Have ready: a wooden salad bowl, coated with 1 tablespoon olive oil.

Prepare dressing in a cruet or a jar. Refrigerate until 1 hour prior to serving. Assemble salad just before serving. Rub 1 garlic clove in a large oil-coated wooden salad bowl. (Then, you may mince this garlic clove and add to the other minced clove.)
Pour prepared greens and croutons into the wooden bowl. Sprinkle with minced garlic. Just before serving, drizzle greens with Olive Oil and Red Wine Vinegar Dressing. Grate Parmesan over salad and toss and serve. Serves 5-6.

SICILIAN SPAGHETTI

[A Cooking Hint: Prior to serving pasta, warm individual pasta plates in hot water; or, if plates are ovenproof, warm them in "turned-off" preheated oven at 200°.]

1 lb. spaghetti, cooked al dente, just before serving

SAUCE:
2 tbsp. olive oil
2-3 large garlic cloves, chopped
1 small eggplant (about 6 inches long and $2\frac{1}{2}$ inches wide), pared, diced
6-8 ripe plum tomatoes, chopped with juice
2 Italian poblano peppers, trimmed, deseeded, thinly sliced
3-4 fresh basil leaves, chopped
1 tbsp. capers
4 anchovy fillets, minced
1 doz. pitted black olives, halved
$\frac{1}{2}$ tsp. salt
$\frac{1}{2}$ tsp. freshly ground black pepper
pinch of hot red pepper flakes (if poblanos are mild), to taste

    Heat olive oil in a 4-quart saucepot and brown garlic. Add diced eggplant, peppers, chopped tomatoes and juice and simmer for 30 minutes. Stir in basil, capers, anchovies, olives, salt and pepper(s). Cover pot and simmer sauce for 10 minutes until tastes are well blended.

    Meanwhile, set lots of lightly salted water to boil in a pasta pot. Cook spaghetti al dente, according to directions on package. Drain and transfer pasta to a large warm serving bowl. Ladle some of the sauce over the spaghetti and toss to coat thoroughly. Ladle remaining sauce over pasta in bowl. Serves 4-5.

Peek-A-Boo Party. Photo: F. Barbarotto

245

SALMON WITH SCALLOPS AND SHRIMP

4-5 portions of salmon fillets, each 4x5x$\frac{3}{4}$-inches; remove skin

1 lb. sea scallops and 1 lb. extra-large shrimp, shelled, rinsed, drained

2 tbsp. olive oil and 2 tbsp. olive oil for pan

1 jar (about 25 oz.) prepared marinara sauce

4-5 plum tomatoes, chopped with juice

4 garlic cloves, peeled, leave whole

4-5 porcini mushrooms, rinsed, sliced

1 can (14 oz.) unseasoned artichokes, drained, quartered

$\frac{1}{2}$ cup dry white wine, like Pinot Blanc

$\frac{1}{2}$ tsp. salt

$\frac{1}{2}$ tsp. freshly ground black pepper

$\frac{1}{4}$ cup fresh parsley, chopped

Preheat oven to 400°.

Have ready: a large skillet; a 9x13x4-inch heavy roasting pan, coated with olive oil.

Lightly brown garlic, scallops and shrimp on both sides in olive oil in a large skillet over medium heat. After 3 minutes, add artichokes and mushrooms. Cook seafood and vegetables, stirring often for another 2 minutes. Pour and stir marinara sauce and chopped tomatoes with juices into the skillet and gently simmer the sauce, uncovered for 10 minutes. Stir in wine, salt, pepper and parsley and simmer for an additional 2-3 minutes. Set aside.

Coat bottom of a large, heavy roasting pan with olive oil. Lay prepared portions of salmon fillets in pan; pour seafood/vegetable sauce over the salmon and roast in a preheated oven at 400° for 15-20 minutes, depending upon thickness of fish, or until salmon is barely translucent. Serves 4-5.

Tailgating at the Polo Match.

CASSATA BOMBE

1 pint vanilla bean ice cream
1 pint chocolate ice cream

FILLING:
$\frac{1}{2}$ cup heavy cream, whipped
$\frac{1}{4}$ cup confectioners' sugar
$\frac{1}{2}$ cup mixed candied fruits, in tiny dice
1 egg white, beaten stiff or 1 portion *Just Whites*
    (Prepare as directed on package for 1 portion of egg whites.)

Have ready: a $1\frac{1}{2}$-quart circular mold with a lid.

Prepare the filling. Whip heavy cream and stir in confectioners' sugar and diced candied fruits. Beat egg-white until stiff and fold it thoroughly into the whipped cream mixture.

It will be better if ice cream is somewhat softened. With a large spoon dipped in water, line the bottom and sides of a $1\frac{1}{2}$-quart circular mold with vanilla ice cream to a depth of $\frac{1}{2}$ inch; smooth the surface. Then, cover vanilla ice cream with a layer of chocolate ice cream.

Fill the hollow in the center with the cream/egg white mixture; smooth the top; cover the bombe with waxed paper and the lid of the mold. Freeze the mold until the cassata is very firm throughout, at least several hours.

To serve: have ready, a pot larger than the mold. Fill it with tepid water. Carefully dip the bombe in the covered mold into the tepid water, nearly to the mold's upper edge. Have a large serving plate, ready to accept the cassata bombe when you invert it onto the plate. Unmold the cassata onto the plate. Slice in wedges. Serves 4-6.

Happy Birthday, Dave! Photo: R. Bastien

HUMMUS AND CRUDITÉS
CHICKEN PAPRIKASH
SHREDDED POTATO PATTIES
BERRY PARFAIT

HUMMUS AND CRUDITÉS

Boston lettuce to line platter, bowl
$\frac{1}{2}$ cup sesame paste (Tahini)
2 large garlic cloves, finely chopped
$\frac{1}{2}$ cup lemon juice (or a little more)
$\frac{1}{2}$ tsp. salt
$\frac{1}{4}$ tsp. black pepper
1 lb. can chick peas, rinsed in cold water, drained
1 tbsp. olive oil
2 tbsp. Italian parsley, finely chopped

2 carrots, pared, cut into sticks
2 cups broccoli florets, rinsed, drained
3-4 celery stalks, trimmed, cut into strips
6 small pitas, quartered

   Have ready: a blender; a 12-inch serving platter for vegetables; a small bowl for Hummus; a bread basket for pitas.

   Spoon Tahini in a bowl and stir until the paste and its oil are well blended.

   Mix garlic, lemon juice, salt, pepper into a blender. With motor running, add chick peas, 1 tablespoon at a time; add olive oil and Tahini. This mixture should be creamy and smooth. Add a little more lemon juice or water if mix becomes too thick. Taste to adjust the seasoning.

   Spoon the dip into a serving bowl lined with lettuce. Sprinkle chopped parsley over hummus before serving. Accompany with a basket of fresh pita, quartered for dipping; and a lettuce-lined platter with cut-up raw and crisp carrot sticks, celery strips and broccoli florets. Serves 6 as an appetizer/salad.

CHICKEN PAPRIKASH

1 chicken, about 3 lbs., cut into serving pieces,
    rinsed in cold water, patted dry
    with paper towels
2 tbsp. olive oil
1 large onion, chopped
1 large tomato, peeled, deseeded, chopped
    (*NOTE: next column)
1 green bell pepper, deseeded, cut into strips
1 tbsp. Hungarian paprika
1 tsp. salt
$\frac{1}{4}$ tsp. black pepper
$\frac{1}{2}$ cup water
1 tbsp. flour
$\frac{1}{2}$ cup sour cream (fat-free available)

*NOTE: "How To Skin a Tomato"
1) wash tomato
2) immerse tomato in boiling water
    for 1 minute
3) remove tomato from boiling water and
    plunge it into cold water
4) peel off skin with fingers

Have ready: an ovenproof serving platter; an ovenproof casserole-size pot/bowl with a cover.

Heat oil in a large heavy casserole over moderate heat. Add chopped onion; cook over low heat, covered, for 10-15 minutes until onion is very soft, but not brown. Increase heat to moderate. Add pieces of chicken and cook, turning chicken occasionally for 10 minutes. Reduce heat to low. Add tomato and green pepper and stir in paprika, salt and black pepper. Add water and cook, covered for 20 minutes. Remove lid and continue to cook chicken for 10-15 minutes longer, stirring occasionally, until chicken is fork tender. Transfer chicken to a heat-resistant serving platter; keep warm in a low oven.

Stir flour into sour cream until well-blended. Add and stir this mixture into pan with tomato/pepper mix; cook for 4-5 minutes, stirring occasionally, until sauce thickens. Pour sauce over platter of warm chicken and serve at once. Serves 4-6.

SHREDDED POTATO PATTIES

6-8 medium-size all-purpose potatoes
8 tbsp. butter or Smart Balance spread

1 tsp. salt
$\frac{1}{2}$ tsp. black pepper

Have ready: a small heavy fry pan; a potato grater; a colander; a spatula.

Cook potatoes in boiling water until barely tender, about 15-20 minutes. (Time varies according to size; insert a toothpick into center of potato to test.) Drain potatoes in colander; allow them to cool. Peel potatoes with your fingers; coarsely grate them into a bowl. Sprinkle with salt and pepper. Heat 2 tablespoons butter in a small heavy fry pan over moderate heat. Divide grated potatoes into 6 portions. Add one portion of grated potatoes at a time to fry pan; stir until coated with butter. Spread potato mix over bottom of fry pan with a spatula, pressing them into a flat cake (patty). Fry each patty until brown/crisp on bottom. Turn and fry other side. Transfer patties to heat-resistant platter and keep them warm in a low oven, as you cook remaining patties, adding more butter to pan as you cook, as necessary. Serves 6.

BERRY PARFAIT

1 pt. blueberries, rinsed, thoroughly drained, gently patted with paper towel

$\frac{1}{2}$ pt. raspberries, gently rinsed, drained, patted with paper towel

1 pt. strawberries, trimmed, rinsed, drained, patted with paper towel, halved

1 large unpeeled navel orange, rinsed, patted dry with paper towel;

    sliced into 6 rounds; halve the slices

1 pt. plain Greek-style yogurt (fat-free available)

1 tbsp. cherry liqueur

2 tbsp. honey

$\frac{1}{4}$ cup dark chocolate covered almonds

    Have ready: an 8-inch glass pie plate with a rim.

    Spread blueberries over bottom of 8-inch glass pie plate. Spread strawberries; then, raspberries, over blueberries. Spoon 5 small mounds of yogurt around edge of plate, over berries; and 1 mound over center. Sprinkle cherry liqueur and drizzle honey over the fruit and yogurt. Scatter chocolate almonds over parfait; garnish rim of plate with half-moons of orange slices. Serves 6.

The Bride-to-Be Cuts the Cake.

BASKET OF VEGETABLES WITH BLEU CHEESE DIP

GRILLED STEAK AND PEPPERS

SPICY MUSHROOMS

LENTILS AND FRUITS

STRAWBERRY PIE GLACÉ

BASKET OF VEGETABLES WITH BLEU CHEESE DIP

[A Cooking Hint: Rinse all vegetables and fruit prior to eating; this means berries, oranges, apples, melons, pineapples, as well. Drain greens and berries thoroughly. Gently pat-dry berries with paper towels.]

1 cup broccoli florets, trimmed, rinsed, drained
1 cup cauliflower florets, trimmed, rinsed, drained
3 slender carrots, pared, rinsed, trimmed, cut into 2-inch lengths
3 celery stalks, rinsed, trimmed, cut into 2-inch lengths
1 dozen cherry or grape tomatoes, rinsed, drained, patted dry with paper towel
Basket of bread crisps

BLEU CHEESE DIP:
1 cup sour cream (fat-free available)
1 tbsp. prepared horseradish
$\frac{1}{4}$ tsp. freshly ground black pepper
1 tbsp. chives, minced
1 cup bleu cheese, chopped

Prepare BLEU CHEESE DIP. Blend all dip ingredients into a bowl. Cover bowl and refrigerate until serving. Arrange prepared raw vegetables around a 15-inch glass serving platter. Leave space in center of platter for dip bowl. Cover and refrigerate platter of vegetables until ready to serve. At serving, place dip bowl in center of vegetable platter; accompany vegetables with a basket of bread crisps. Serves 6.

GRILLED STEAK AND PEPPERS
(Begin preparation early on the day; or evening before.)

6 1-inch thick boneless beef sirloin strips
2 large red bell peppers, cored, deseeded, rinsed, sliced into 1-inch vertical strips
MARINADE:

grated rind from 2 oranges
1 cup fresh orange juice
2 tbsp. extra-virgin olive oil
1 garlic clove, minced

1 tbsp. cider vinegar
1 tbsp. *lite* soy sauce
$\frac{1}{4}$ tsp. dried hot pepper flakes
dash of salt

Have ready: a blender; an olive-oiled broiler pan or grill rack.

In a large shallow dish, arrange strip steaks in one layer. Spread red bell pepper slices over the beef. Using a blender, combine orange juice and orange zest, oil, garlic, vinegar, soy sauce, hot pepper flakes and salt. Blend until smooth. Pour this marinade over steaks/peppers, coating them thoroughly; allow the mixture to marinate, covered and refrigerated, overnight. (Discard marinade when ready to grill or broil steaks.)

Grill steaks and peppers on an oiled rack, set 5-6 inches over heating element for 7-8 minutes on each side for medium-rare; or broil steaks in a oiled broiler pan, set 4-5 inches under broiler element for 3-4 minutes on each side for medium-rare. Transfer steaks to serving platter. Serves 6.

SPICY MUSHROOMS

2 tbsp. peanut oil
3-4 garlic cloves, minced
4 scallions with some greens, chopped
1 lb. button mushrooms, rinsed, drained
6-8 shitake mushrooms, rinsed, drained
2 large Portobello mushrooms, rinsed,
    drained, sliced
1 tbsp. chili sauce

1 tbsp. *lite* soy sauce
1 tbsp. hoisin sauce
1 tbsp. red wine vinegar
small piece Thai pepper, minced
    (Use plastic gloves when handling
    hot peppers.)
1 tbsp. brown sugar
1 tsp. sesame oil
$\frac{1}{4}$ cup fresh parsley, minced

Have ready: a large wok or skillet; a serving platter.

Heat peanut oil in a wok until almost smoking. Reduce heat slightly; add garlic and scallions and stir-fry for 30 seconds. Add mushrooms, chili sauce, soy sauce, hoisin sauce, vinegar, Thai pepper and sugar and stir-fry for 4-5 minutes or until mushrooms are cooked through. Sprinkle sesame oil over mushrooms. Transfer to a warm serving platter; garnish with parsley and serve immediately. Serves 6.

LENTILS AND FRUIT

8 oz. brown lentils

4 cups water

2 tbsp. olive oil

1 large onion, finely chopped

2-3 large garlic cloves, minced

1 celery stalk, trimmed, finely chopped

3 fresh plum tomatoes, chopped with liquid

1 tart apple, cored, deseeded, coarsely chopped with skin

$\frac{1}{2}$ cup fresh pineapple, cubed (or use canned pineapple with juice)

chopped segments of 1 navel orange, skin and pith removed

1 tbsp. fresh parsley, minced

$\frac{1}{4}$ tsp. cayenne pepper

salt to taste

Have ready: a 4-quart saucepot with a cover; a large skillet.

In a 4-quart saucepot with cover, combine lentils with water. Cover pot and bring to a boil. Then, lower to simmer lentils for 35-40 minutes until lentils are tender.

Meanwhile, in a large skillet over moderate heat, cook onion, garlic, celery in olive oil until vegetables are tender. Continue to simmer; scrape bottom of pan to remove vegetable particles while stirring to add chopped tomatoes with juice. Cook for 5 minutes; add apple, pineapple and orange segments. Simmer this mixture for 5-7 minutes, or until apple is tender.

When lentils are cooked, drain them from pot and transfer to skillet with fruit mix. Reserve some of the lentil liquid to add to the lentil/fruit skillet, to maintain moisture. Stir in parsley, cayenne and salt. Fluff up the mixture; serve out of the skillet. Serves 6.

Good Friends gather around the table for a celebration.

STRAWBERRY PIE GLACÉ

1 baked pie shell (plain pastry) (see page 337): Pie Crust recipe; or, use your favorite
    recipe; or, use packaged unbaked pie crust, found in dairy section of supermarts

1 cup granulated sugar

3 tbsp. cornstarch

$\frac{1}{4}$ tsp salt

$\frac{3}{4}$ cup water

1 tsp. lemon juice

3 cups strawberries, trimmed, rinsed, drained, patted dry with paper towel;
    slice strawberries, except for 1 dozen to leave whole for garnish

1 cup heavy cream for whipping; or whipped cream in a can;
    or 8 oz. container non-dairy whipped topping (fat-free available)

Have ready: a 9-inch baked plain pastry pie shell, cooled to room temperature;
a small double boiler.

Combine sugar, cornstarch, salt, water and lemon juice in a saucepan. Pour into top pot of a double boiler; pour enough water in bottom half of double boiler to cover lower section of top half when pots fit into each other. Bring water in bottom half to a simmer and cook the sauce, stirring continuously until mixture thickens; continue to simmer sauce for 20 minutes. Remove top pot with sauce and allow to cool.

Arrange sliced strawberries in baked pie shell; arrange whole strawberries over top of pie. Pour sauce over berries in pie pan. Chill pie in refrigerator for several hours. Before serving, whip the cream until soft peaks are formed; garnish top of pie with whipped cream. Serves 6-8.

The Lang Family Celebrates Irene and Ray's 25th Wedding Anniversary.
Photo: I. Lang

A SUMMER FRUIT SALAD
APPLE CIDER DRESSING (see page 384)
CITRUS PORK
SPINACH ARTICHOKE PIE
RAINBOW OF SHERBETS

A SUMMER FRUIT SALAD
(Chill all fruits and lettuce in refrigerator prior to use.)

4-6 wedges watermelon, (3x5x1 inches each); remove rind
4-6 slices cantaloupe, (1-inch thick); remove rind
1 pt. raspberries, gently rinsed, drained, patted dry with paper towel
4-6 small bunches seedless green, red grapes, rinsed, drained,
    patted dry with paper towel
1 navel orange, rinsed, sliced into 4-6 rounds, each slice halved
1 dozen cherry or grape tomatoes, rinsed, patted dry with paper towel
a bed of chopped iceberg lettuce, rinsed, drained

Apple Cider Dressing, (see page 384)

Have ready: a 15-inch glass or ceramic platter.

Prepare Apple Cider Dressing in advance. Refrigerate dressing until 1 hour before serving.

Prepare each fruit as instructed above, several hours in advance. Refrigerate fruits in covered containers. Paper towel-dry raspberries and grapes and place in separate bowls.

When almost ready to serve, spread chopped lettuce over a large platter. Scatter tomatoes, grapes and raspberries over lettuce. Shake jar of dressing and drizzle 2-3 tablespoons of dressing over the platter. Arrange slices of melons and orange halves over the chopped lettuce mix. Serve immediately. Serves 4-6.

CITRUS PORK

4-6 boneless pork tenderloin, each $\frac{1}{2}$-inch thick, trim fat
$\frac{1}{4}$ cup spicy mustard spread
2 tbsp. honey
1 cup corn flake crumbs
salt, freshly ground black pepper, to taste
1 cup fresh orange juice
1 navel orange, sliced into thin rounds; halved
a sprinkling of ground cinnamon, to taste

Preheat oven to 400°.

Have ready: a 9x12-inch baking pan, coated with olive oil.

Spread corn flake crumbs over a sheet of waxed paper; sprinkle to taste, freshly ground black pepper and salt over the crumbs. Blend honey with mustard in a small bowl. With a knife spreader, coat both sides of tenderloin pieces with the honey-mustard mix; coat on both sides with corn flake crumbs. Lay pork in prepared baking pan. Drizzle $\frac{1}{2}$ cup orange juice over each dressed tenderloin. (Save remainder of juice.) Garnish pork in pan with orange slices, sprinkled with cinnamon.
Bake in preheated oven at 400° for 20-25 minutes until crumbs are golden. Remove pan from oven and drizzle leftover orange juice over pork. Serve hot. Serves 4-6.

Chow-Time!

SPINACH ARTICHOKE PIE

1 lb. baby spinach, trimmed, rinsed, drained
$\frac{1}{2}$ cup water
1 medium red onion, chopped
2 large garlic cloves, minced
1 tbsp. olive oil
2 (1 lb.) cans artichoke hearts in water, drained, quartered
16 oz. fat-free plain Greek-style yogurt
2 slices whole wheat bread, crumbled
$\frac{1}{4}$ cup low-fat Cheddar cheese, finely chopped

Preheat oven 350°.

Have ready: a 2-qt. baking dish, greased with olive oil.

Cook spinach in $\frac{1}{2}$ cup water for 30 seconds; drain thoroughly. Sauté onion and garlic in olive oil for 2 minutes. Combine onion/garlic with spinach. Fold in yogurt. Pour spinach mix into the oil-greased baking dish. Stuff the quartered artichokes into the top of the spinach mix. Sprinkle surface with bread crumbles and chopped Cheddar. Bake for 30 minutes in preheated oven at 350°. Serves 6.

RAINBOW OF SHERBETS

1 pt. orange sherbet
1 pt. raspberry sherbet
1 pt. lemon (or lime) sherbet (or both)
small jar chocolate fudge sauce
$\frac{1}{2}$ cup finely chopped walnuts
2 limes, rinsed, quartered

Arrange 2-inch balls of sherbets over a 12-inch serving dish with a 2-inch raised edge. Tuck wedges of lime between the balls of sherbet. Drizzle sherbet with chocolate fudge sauce. Sprinkle with chopped walnuts. Serve immediately. Serves 4-6.

TOMATO AND FENNEL SALAD
SOLE AMANDINE
ON A BED OF MUSHROOMS, PEPPERS AND ASPARAGUS
SWEET POTATO PIE

TOMATO AND FENNEL SALAD

3 large beefsteak tomatoes, rinsed, drained, sliced into $\frac{1}{4}$-inch rounds

2 large fennel bulbs, trimmed, rinsed, drained, sliced in $\frac{1}{4}$-inch rings

$\frac{1}{4}$ cup pitted Kalamata olives

$\frac{1}{4}$ cup pitted green Sicilian olives

salt and freshly ground black pepper, to taste

$\frac{1}{4}$ cup extra-virgin olive oil

6 large basil leaves, for garnish

Have ready: a 12-inch glass platter.

Arrange slices of tomatoes and rings of fennel in alternating circles over a 12-inch glass platter. Tuck in basil leaves between fennel and tomato slices. Scatter olives over the surface of the salad. Sprinkle with salt and pepper; drizzle with olive oil. Serves 6.

John's Georgetown U Dental School's 45th Reunion.

SOLE AMANDINE
ON A BED OF MUSHROOMS, PEPPERS AND ASPARAGUS

6 large fillets of sole, rinsed in cold water, patted dry with paper towels
1 cup fine bread crumbs
$\frac{1}{4}$ tsp. black pepper
dash of cayenne
2 tbsp. fresh parsley, finely chopped
1 cup toasted almonds, shaved
18 asparagus spears, trimmed, rinsed, drained
2 cups white mushrooms, trimmed, rinsed, drained, sliced
2 shallots, finely sliced
1 red bell pepper, cored, deseeded, rinsed, drained; finely sliced
1 green bell pepper, cored, deseeded, rinsed, drained; finely sliced
$\frac{1}{4}$ tsp. freshly ground black pepper, salt to taste
$\frac{1}{4}$ cup olive oil, divided
juice of 1 lemon
1 large lemon (or 2 medium) cut into wedges for garnish

Preheat oven to 375°.

Have ready: two 9x12x3-inch baking pans.

Grease bottoms of two 9x12x3 pans, each with 1 tablespoon of olive oil. Lay a sheet of waxed paper on a board and cover with breadcrumbs, shaved almonds, parsley, black pepper and cayenne. Coat both sides of 6 slices of sole with the crumbs mixture. Lay sole in a 9x12 oiled pan and bake in preheated oven at 375° for 10 minutes on each side, depending upon thickness of fish, for a total of 20-25 minutes.

Meanwhile toss mushrooms, shallots and red and green pepper slices in a bowl with 1 tablespoon olive oil, lemon juice and black pepper. Set aside. Lay all of the asparagus on one section of the second 9x12 pan. Sprinkle asparagus with remaining 1 tablespoon olive oil. Pour the bowl of seasoned mushroom mix into the rest of the baking pan. Bake vegetables in preheated oven at 375° for 20-25 minutes until pepper slices start to brown.

Serve sole on individual plates, over a bed of peppers, shallots, mushrooms and a side of asparagus spears. Garnish with a lemon wedge. Serves 6.

SWEET POTATO PIE

2 pounds sweet potatoes, peeled,
    cut into chunks
$\frac{1}{2}$ cup butter or Smart Balance spread, softened
1 tsp. ground cinnamon
$\frac{1}{4}$ tsp. ground ginger
$\frac{1}{4}$ tsp. ground nutmeg
1 cup packed brown sugar
2 tbsp. granulated sugar

$\frac{1}{2}$ tsp. salt
3 large eggs, or $\frac{3}{4}$ cup egg substitute, beaten
$\frac{1}{2}$ cup fresh orange juice
1 tbsp. grated orange peel
$\frac{1}{2}$ cup evaporated milk, fat-free available

1 unbaked 9-inch pie crust (Bake your own favorite recipe; or see recipe on page 336 ff;
    or, use packaged crust which you roll out to fit pan.)

Whipped cream for garnish

Preheat oven to 450°.

Prepare the pie crust in a 9-inch pan, crimping the edges of the crust around the pan. Set aside.

Meanwhile boil sweet potato chunks until soft, for 10-12 minutes. Drain.

In a large bowl, mash sweet potatoes; add butter, cinnamon, ginger, nutmeg, salt, sugars and beat until thoroughly mixed. Beat eggs until light; add them to the sweet potato mixture along with orange juice, peel and evaporated milk. Mix thoroughly.

Pour this filling into the pie shell. Bake in preheated oven at 450° for 10 minutes. Reduce temperature to 350° and continue to bake pie until the filling puffs up and is firm in the middle, about 30 minutes longer. Cool pie on a rack. Serve with whipped cream, if desired. Serves 6-8.

Geese at Dinner.

ZUCCHINI SOUP

SALMON BOMBAY

CRAB-STUFFED POTATOES

STEAMED BROCCOLI AND CARROTS

KEY LIME MERINGUE PIE
(Includes Low-Fat Version)

ZUCCHINI SOUP

2 tbsp. olive oil

1 onion, chopped

2 cups (1 lb. can) crushed tomatoes

6 cups water

3-4 small zucchini trimmed, rinsed, sliced in $\frac{1}{4}$-inch rounds

1 large all-purpose potato, peeled, cut into small cubes

1 small Italian green pepper, deseeded, chopped

1 tsp. salt, or to taste

$\frac{1}{2}$ tsp. freshly ground black pepper

1 tbsp. dried oregano

$\frac{1}{2}$ cup Parmesan cheese, grated

1 large egg, or $\frac{1}{4}$ cup egg substitute, beaten

3-4 fresh basil leaves, torn into tiny pieces

   In a large soup pot, warm oil over medium heat and sauté onion and green pepper until onion is soft and opaque, about 5 minutes. Add crushed tomatoes and simmer for 15 minutes until thickened. Stir in 6 cups water, potato, zucchini, salt, pepper and oregano. Bring to a boil; then, lower to simmer. Cover pot and continue to cook soup for 10-15 minutes, until potato is tender. Stir in beaten egg and cheese to cook for another 3-4 minutes. Float basil on top of soup. Taste soup and adjust herbs and spices, if needed. Serves 6.

SALMON BOMBAY

4-5 sections of salmon fillet (8 oz. each), about $\frac{3}{4}$-inch thick; skin removed

SPICE RUB:
$1\frac{1}{2}$ tsp. brown sugar
1 tsp. ground cumin
$\frac{1}{2}$ tsp. ground cinnamon
$\frac{1}{2}$ tsp. dried thyme
$\frac{1}{4}$ tsp. ground cayenne
$\frac{1}{2}$ tsp. salt
$\frac{1}{2}$ tsp. freshly ground black pepper

2 tbsp. olive oil

Have ready: a large non-stick skillet, brushed with 2 tablespoons olive oil.

Thoroughly blend all spices in a small bowl. Gently rub spice mix over both sides of the fish. Lay salmon fillets, flesh-side down in a large preheated oiled skillet. Cook fish at medium-high for 6 minutes, or until salmon is deeply golden and readily lifts from the surface of pan. Turn and cook other side until salmon is barely translucent in the center, about 6 minutes longer. Transfer to a warming tray. Serves 4-5.

An Orlando-Colantuono mini Cousins Reunion in Staten Island.

CRAB-STUFFED POTATOES

4-6 large Idaho baking potatoes
1 can (about 7 oz.) crabmeat
$\frac{1}{4}$ cup finely chopped sweet red pepper
3 scallions with greens, finely chopped (Reserve 2-3 tbsp. for garnish.)
$\frac{1}{4}$ tsp. salt
$\frac{1}{4}$ tsp. freshly ground black pepper
1 tbsp. finely chopped Italian parsley
1 tbsp. olive oil
Hungarian paprika for additional garnish

Preheat oven to 400°.

Bake large potatoes in preheated oven at 400° for about 1 hour 10 minutes. Remove potatoes from oven and lower oven temperature to 350°. Cut a large triangle of potato skin off the flat part of each potato and discard pieces of potato skin.
With a tablespoon, scoop out most of the cooked potato into a medium-size bowl. Set potato shells aside.
Add the can of crabmeat to potatoes in the mixing bowl. Mash with hand masher. Add and stir in finely chopped red pepper, chopped scallion bulbs, parsley, salt, pepper and olive oil. Mix thoroughly. (Reserve chopped scallion greens for garnish.)
Stuff each of the potato shells with equal portions of this mix. Sprinkle tops of stuffed potatoes with finely chopped scallions and paprika. Return prepared stuffed potatoes to oven at 350° for an additional 10 minutes. Serves 4-6.

STEAMED BROCCOLI AND CARROTS

4 cups broccoli florets, rinsed, drained
4-5 large carrots, pared, French-cut, 1-inch thick
2 tbsp. olive oil
salt and freshly ground black pepper to taste
1-2 cups water
lemon wedges for garnish

Have ready: a large steamer with a basket; a large serving platter.
Cook broccoli florets and cut carrots in 1-2 cups water in a large vegetable steamer with a basket. Place vegetables in the basket. Cover pot. Bring water to boil; then lower heat to steam for 4 5 minutes. Transfer basket of vegetables to a serving platter; drizzle with olive oil and sprinkle with salt and pepper to taste. Garnish with lemon wedges. Serves 4-5.

KEY LIME MERINGUE PIE

(If you live in the Florida Keys, pick 3 ripe limes from your Key Lime tree.)
[A Cooking Hint: When preparing meringue, have utensils absolutely free of grease;
egg whites must be at room temperature and free from any traces of yolks,
in order to whip and peak properly.]

CRUST: (for a 9-inch pie pan)
$1\frac{3}{4}$ cups graham cracker crumbs, or 1 packaged graham cracker crust for a 9-inch pie
$\frac{1}{4}$ cup granulated sugar
4 tbsp. butter or Smart Balance spread, melted

FILLING:
4 egg yolks at room temperature (Save whites for meringue.)
1 can (14 oz.) sweetened condensed milk *(Do not use evaporated milk.)*
$\frac{2}{3}$ cup freshly squeezed lime juice
1 tsp. freshly grated lime zest
$\frac{1}{2}$ tsp. lemon extract
(several lime peel twirls for garnish; save in plastic baggie)

MERINGUE TOPPING:
whites from 4 large eggs (saved from filling);
    or, use dried meringue powder, like *Just Whites* and follow instructions
$\frac{1}{4}$ tsp. cream of tartar
$\frac{1}{2}$ cup granulated sugar

Preheat oven to 350°.

Have ready: a 9-inch pie pan.

Prepare CRUST. Blend graham cracker crumbs with sugar in a medium-size bowl. Drizzle butter over the mix and toss with a fork or your fingers until mix is well combined. Press crust evenly into bottom of 9-inch pie pan. Bake crust for 5-7 minutes in preheated oven at 350°. (Do not brown edges of crust.) Remove from oven and cool completely on wire rack for at least 30 minutes.
Prepare FILLING. Beat egg yolks in a medium-size bowl for 4-5 minutes, until pale yellow and thick. Beat in condensed milk, lime juice, zest, lemon extract for 2 minutes. With a rubber spatula, spread filling evenly into cooled crust.
Prepare TOPPING. Beat egg whites until frothy. Add cream of tartar and $\frac{1}{4}$ cup sugar; beat until *soft* peaks are formed. Beat in remaining $\frac{1}{4}$ cup sugar, one tablespoon at a time until *stiff* peaks are formed. Spread meringue over lime filling in pie. With a spoon or rubber spatula, swirl meringue into fluffy peaks and valleys. Bake pie in preheated oven at 350° for 10-12 minutes. Meringue will very lightly brown. Refrigerate pie for 5-6 hours before serving. Garnish meringue topping with lime twirls before serving. Serves 6.

KEY LIME PIE
(Low-fat recipe.)

CRUST:
Follow recipe ingredients and instructions as stated on page 264.
<u>Exception:</u> Use Smart Balance spread instead of butter.

FILLING:
1 cup egg substitute
1 can (14 oz.) fat-free condensed milk (Do not use evaporated milk.)
$\frac{2}{3}$ cup freshly squeezed lime juice
1 tsp. freshly grated lime zest
$\frac{1}{2}$ tsp. lemon extract
Several twirls lime peel for garnish; save in plastic baggie.

Follow recipe instructions as stated on page 264.

MERINGUE TOPPING:
Follow recipe ingredients and instructions as stated on page 264;
      or, make the following adjustment:
      Instead of a Meringue Topping, bake lime pie in its crust in a preheated oven at 350° for 10-12 minutes. Cool on counter; then, refrigerate pie for 5-6 hours. Just before serving, spread and swirl 2 cups fat-free Whipped Topping over top of cold lime pie. Garnish with lime twirls. Serves 6.

Cruisin' and Eatin' on the *Michelangelo*.

265

"A SPECIAL MENU FOR MERCY"
CORN CHOWDER
TOMATO AND GREEN BEANS BREAD SALAD
FLEW IN FROM HAVANA
BROWN RICE AND BLACK BEANS
RUM CAKE

CORN CHOWDER

4 cups corn, cut from cob, or 4 cups frozen
    corn kernels (not cream-style)
2 medium-size potatoes, peeled, cut into
    $\frac{1}{2}$-inch cubes
1 small red onion, chopped
$2\frac{1}{2}$-3 cups water, divided
2 cups chicken stock;
    for Homemade Chicken Stock, see page 81;
    or, use low-sodium packaged chicken stock

2 tbsp. olive oil
2 tbsp. butter or Smart Balance spread
2 cups hot low-fat milk
2 cups evaporated low-fat milk,
    or low-fat half-and-half
1 tsp. salt to taste
$\frac{1}{2}$ tsp. coarsely ground black pepper
pinch of cayenne

Have ready: a food processor and a large double boiler.

Place corn in a large 4-quart soup pot with a cover. Over the corn, pour 1 cup water and chicken stock. Cover pot and simmer on low heat for 15 minutes. Watch the pot to prevent sticking or scorching. Add a little more water, if necessary.

Meanwhile boil cubed potatoes in $1\frac{1}{2}$ cups water until tender, about 10-12 minutes. In a small skillet, slowly cook chopped onion in a mix of 2 tablespoons olive oil and 2 tablespoons butter; cook until soft for about 10 minutes; do not brown. Add cooked onion, well-drained potatoes and hot milk to the pot of corn. Mix thoroughly. Process this mixture, one or two cupfuls at a time, in a food processor, running it at low speed for 1 minute, and another minute at high speed.

Pour the coarse purée in the top of a large double boiler. Set to boil. Season chowder with salt, coarsely ground black pepper and cayenne. Heat soup thoroughly over boiling water. When chowder is very hot, stir in 2 cups evaporated milk. Pour into a soup tureen and serve hot. Serves 6.

TOMATO AND GREEN BEANS BREAD SALAD

2 cups fresh tomatoes, deseeded, chopped
2 cups fresh green beans, cut into pieces,
    cooked al dente
1 small Chile, deseeded, minced (Wear plastic
    gloves when working with hot peppers.)
1 cup fresh basil, chopped
$\frac{1}{2}$ cup sharp provolone cheese, cubed
1 small red onion, thinly sliced

DRESSING:
1 large garlic clove, minced
$\frac{1}{4}$ tsp. salt
$\frac{1}{2}$ tsp. freshly ground black pepper
$\frac{1}{2}$ cup extra-virgin olive oil
2 tbsp. red wine vinegar

4 cups cubed Italian bread, lightly toasted;
    or use packaged croutons

    In a large salad bowl, combine bread cubes, tomatoes, green beans, Chile, onion, cheese cubes and basil. Refrigerate salad if not serving within 30 minutes. In a small bowl whisk together olive oil, vinegar, salt , pepper and garlic for the dressing. Thirty minutes before serving, drizzle dressing over the bowl of salad. Lay a sheet of waxed paper over the salad and allow to stand for 30 minutes, to blend flavors. Toss again. Serves 6.

BROWN RICE WITH BLACK BEANS

2 tbsp. olive oil
1 small onion, finely chopped
2 garlic cloves, minced
1 large celery stalk, trimmed, finely chopped
$\frac{1}{2}$-inch hot Chile pepper, deseeded, minced
    (Careful when handling hot peppers.)
$2\frac{1}{2}$ cups chicken stock (See page 81 "How to
    Make Chicken Stock";
    or, use packaged low-sodium stock.)

$\frac{1}{2}$ cup canned chopped tomatoes with juice
1 cup brown rice
1 tsp. ground cumin
$\frac{1}{2}$ tsp. freshly ground black pepper
$\frac{1}{2}$ tsp. salt, or to taste
1 small can (1 lb.) black beans,
    rinsed in cold water, drained
$\frac{1}{4}$ cup fresh cilantro, finely chopped

    In a 2-quart sauce pot, over moderate heat, cook onion, garlic, celery and Chile in olive oil until vegetables are tender. As you scrape bottom of pot to loosen vegetable particles, add and stir in tomatoes with juice, stock, rice, cumin, pepper and salt. Cover pot and raise heat to boil. Then, lower to simmer rice for 40-45 minutes or until liquid is almost absorbed. Stir in beans and cilantro. Transfer to serving bowl. Serves 6.

FLEW IN FROM HAVANA

1 roasting chicken, $4\frac{1}{2}$-5 lbs.; rinse in cold water, pat dry with paper towels
2 tbsp. olive oil
1 tsp. Hungarian paprika
$\frac{1}{2}$ tsp. coarsely ground black pepper
1 cup chicken broth; for Homemade Stock, see page 81; or, use packaged low-sodium
    chicken stock; or dissolve one chicken bouillon into 1 cup boiling water
$\frac{1}{2}$ cup sherry

Pins and Cook's string to truss chicken

SAUSAGE STUFFING:
3 cups packaged corn bread crumbs
3 sweet Italian sausages with fennel, lightly browned in a skillet
    over medium heat; slice into 1-inch rounds
$\frac{1}{2}$ cup raisins, soaked in boiling water for 15 minutes; drained
1 small tomato, chopped with juice
$\frac{1}{2}$ cup pignola (pine nuts)
$\frac{1}{2}$ cup spicy Sicilian green olives, pitted, chopped
1 small onion, chopped
$\frac{1}{2}$ cup pimiento-stuffed olives, sliced thin
1 tbsp. olive oil
2 large eggs, beaten, or $\frac{1}{2}$ cup egg substitute
1 cup boiling water
salt and black pepper, to taste

Preheat oven to 425°.

Have ready: a large roasting pan with a rack.

Celebrating with Mercedes' Family. Photo: T/M. Levitz

Prepare STUFFING. Place cooked sausage rounds into a large bowl. Add drained raisins.
Stir in corn bread crumbs, pignola, olives, onion, tomato, salt and pepper. Moisten with olive oil,
beaten egg (or egg substitute) and water, stirring to mix thoroughly. Stuff prepared chicken loosely with
this mixture.
    Reserve any stuffing which doesn't fit; form patties with leftover stuffing. (Place patties in a
greased pan and bake them in oven during the last 20 minutes of roasting the chicken.)
    Truss, then rub chicken with olive oil; sprinkle with paprika and coarsely ground black pepper.
Roast the chicken on rack in roasting pan in a preheated oven at 425° for 10 minutes. Add chicken broth
and sherry to the pan.
    Reduce oven temperature to 350°; roast and occasionally baste chicken, until juices run clear when
the thigh is pricked with a small skewer; cook about 40 minutes. Allow chicken to rest for 10 minutes
before carving. Serves 6.

RUM CAKE

1 pkg. (22 oz.) yellow cake mix
1 pkg. (4 oz.) instant vanilla pudding
1 tsp. ground cinnamon
4 large eggs or 1 cup egg substitute
¾ cup light rum
¾ cup canola oil
½ cup sliced almonds with skin
confectioners' sugar
cinnamon to sprinkle

Preheat oven to 350°.

Have ready: 9-inch tube pan, generously greased.

In a large bowl beat together for five minutes, until smooth: yellow cake mix, instant pudding, cinnamon, eggs, rum and canola oil. Sprinkle bottom of well-greased 9-inch tube pan with sliced almonds. Pour batter into prepared tube pan.

Bake cake in preheated oven at 350° for 45 minutes, or until inserted toothpick removes clean. Place cake in pan upright on rack for 5 minutes to cool. Turn cake onto a decorative serving dish. When completely cooled, and *just before serving*, dust cake with confectioners' sugar and a sprinkling of cinnamon. This cake is best when allowed to mellow for 2 or 3 days before serving. Serves 8-10.

Dorothy and John Sanson with a gathering of family. Photo: D. Sanson

---

MANHATTAN CLAM CHOWDER
(ITALIAN STYLE)

SHRIMP WITH FENNEL AND KALAMATA OLIVES
SPAGHETTI
ASPARAGUS AND EGGS
BLUEBERRY-PINEAPPLE PARFAIT

MANHATTAN CLAM CHOWDER
(Italian Style)

2 dozen cherrystone clams, shucked;
    reserve clam juice and clams, discard shells
2 strips thinly sliced prosciutto
2 tbsp. olive oil
1 large onion, minced
2-3 medium-size all-purpose potatoes, peeled,
    cut into $\frac{1}{2}$-inch cubes
1 carrot, pared, finely chopped
1 celery stalk, trimmed, finely chopped
$\frac{1}{4}$ cup trimmed green beans,
    chopped in small segments

$\frac{1}{4}$ cup fresh (or frozen) peas
4 large fresh ripe tomatoes, peeled, deseeded,
    chopped with juice (*NOTE: below)
6 cups water
1 cup dry white wine, like Chardonnay
1 tbsp. dried thyme
$\frac{1}{4}$ cup fresh parsley, minced
$\frac{1}{4}$ tsp. freshly ground black pepper
salt, to taste

*NOTE: [A Cooking Hint: "How to Skin a Tomato"]
1. wash tomato
2. immerse tomato in boiling water for 1 minute
3. remove tomato from boiling water and plunge it into cold water
4. peel off skin with fingers

Have fishery shuck clams. Reserve in container; reserve clam juice in another container.
    In a large soup pot, sauté prosciutto in olive oil, for 2-3 minutes. Remove prosciutto to paper towel to drain. Add minced onion to pot and sauté for 3-4 minutes, until tender.
    Rinse clams in several rinses of cold water; drain. Remove any sacs of waste from clams; chop each clam into 2-3 pieces and place in a small bowl. Strain clam liquid through a fine strainer; reserve in bowl.
    To a large soup pot with onion, add: cubed potatoes, chopped tomatoes and juice, chopped carrot, celery, green beans and peas. Stir in 6 cups water and 1 cup wine, herbs and spices. Bring pot to a boil; then, simmer for 5 minutes. Crush reserved crisped prosciutto and add to pot. Taste soup and adjust spices, if necessary. Serve with crispy crackers. Serves 6.

SHRIMP WITH FENNEL AND KALMATA OLIVES
(Use as an entrée or serve as a sauce over spaghetti.)

1 lb. medium shrimp, peeled, rinsed, drained

2 tbsp. olive oil

3 garlic cloves, minced

1 large fennel bulb, trimmed, halved;
   sliced thin

¼ cup water

¼ cup dry white wine, like Chardonnay

3 medium-size fresh ripe tomatoes,
   cubed (with juice)

½ cup pitted Kalamata olives, chopped

½ cup fresh parsley, chopped

2-3 large basil leaves, chopped

¼ tsp. salt

¼ tsp. freshly ground black pepper

a pinch of hot red pepper flakes

Sauté garlic in olive oil for 1 minute in a large skillet. Add sliced fennel and cook for 2 minutes. Add water and wine and cook for 3-4 minutes, until most of water is absorbed.

Add shrimp and cook for 2 minutes, stirring them, to cook all sides. Add tomatoes and olives and cook for another 3 minutes. Stir in salt, peppers and parsley. Garnish with chopped basil. Serve by itself or as a sauce over spaghetti. Serves 6.

. . . .

ASPARAGUS AND EGGS

[A Cooking Hint: Never cook eggs in boiling water; simply simmer them for desired consistency. Soft-boiled, 3 minutes; hard-cooked, 5-7 minutes. Adding a pinch of salt to water will prevent the yolk from escaping through a crack you may have inadvertently made in the egg shell.]

8 tbsp. butter or Smart Balance spread,
   softened

¼ cup tepid water

6 large eggs, hard-cooked, cooled

2-3 lbs. asparagus
   (about 3-4 spears for each serving),
   ends trimmed, rinsed, drained

salt

freshly ground black pepper

nutmeg

2 tbsp. olive oil

Cook's twine

Have ready: a tall asparagus pot with enclosed strainer and with a cover.

In a bowl, beat butter (or Smart Balance) until creamy. Slowly add tepid water, a few drops at a time, beating, as if making a mayonnaise. When the sauce becomes thick and creamy, set aside. Peel the hard-cooked eggs; set aside.

Using a thick Cook's twine, tie the asparagus in a bundle. Bring 1 inch of water to a rapid boil in a tall pot. Stand the asparagus in the strainer pot, into the water, tips up; cover the pot. Steam until tender, 2-5 minutes, depending on thickness of asparagus.

Remove asparagus from pot and lay the bundle on a serving platter. Cut the twine and discard. Halve the eggs and arrange them around the asparagus. Sprinkle salt, pepper and nutmeg over the platter; drizzle with olive oil. Serves 6.

BLUEBERRY-PINEAPPLE PARFAIT

1 pt. blueberries, rinsed, drained
2 cups fresh pineapple, cut in 1-inch cubes
2 tbsp. light rum
1 pt. vanilla bean ice cream
1 cup whipped cream or fat-free whipped topping
Bing cherries for garnish, rinsed, drained

Have ready: 6 tall parfait glasses.

Place cubed pineapple in a bowl; drizzle with rum; refrigerate for 30 minutes. Just before serving, have ready: 6 parfait glasses. Divide pineapple cubes into bottom of parfait glasses. Lay 1 heaping tablespoon vanilla ice cream over the pineapple. Then, divide prepared blueberries into the parfait glasses, on top of ice cream. Cover blueberries with another heaping tablespoonful of ice cream (use all of the ice cream). Add a dollop of whipped cream to top each parfait glass. Garnish with 2-3 Bing cherries. Serve immediately. Serves 6.

At the Senior Prom in the Waldorf.

CAESAR SALAD

CAESAR DRESSING

SWEET AND SOUR SOUP

TANDOORI SHRIMP

RICE AND SNOW PEAS

ALMOND-RAISIN RUGELACH

CINNAMON-CHOCOLATE-PECAN RUGELACH

CAESAR SALAD

1 large head or 2 small-medium heads Romaine lettuce, (about 3-4 cups);
 rinsed, drained, torn into bite-size pieces
2 strips crisply fried bacon, crushed
½ cup Parmesan cheese, grated
1 cup packaged croutons

DRESSING:
3 tbsp. white wine vinegar
4 anchovies, minced
3 tbsp. fresh lemon juice
¼ tsp. salt
1-2 garlic cloves, minced
¼ tsp. freshly ground black pepper, or more to taste
1 tsp. Dijon mustard
¼ cup egg substitute
1 tsp. Worcestershire sauce
½ cup extra-virgin olive oil

 In a large salad bowl combine Romaine lettuce, bacon, cheese and croutons. In a small bowl, combine olive oil, vinegar, lemon juice, garlic, mustard, Worcestershire sauce, anchovies, salt and pepper and egg substitute Whisk dressing until frothy, then creamy. Pour over Romaine lettuce mix in salad bowl. Toss quickly and serve. Serves 6.

SWEET AND SOUR SOUP

1 tbsp. olive oil
1 small onion, thinly sliced
2 garlic cloves, minced
$\frac{1}{4}$ cup chopped scallions with greens
1 tbsp. *lite* soy sauce
8 cups chicken broth (see page 81, "Homemade Chicken Broth");
    or, 2 qts. low-sodium packaged chicken broth
8 medium-size dried black mushrooms, trimmed, soaked in warm water until soft,
    (about 30 minutes); drained
$\frac{1}{2}$ cup canned bamboo shoots, shredded
1 cup fresh bean sprouts
1 small green Chile, deseeded, thinly sliced (Wear plastic gloves when handling hot peppers.)
$\frac{1}{2}$ lb. small shrimp, peeled, deveined, leave whole
2 tbsp. cornstarch
2 tbsp. cold water
$\frac{1}{2}$ tsp. salt
freshly ground black pepper to taste

In a large soup pot lightly brown onion, scallions and garlic in 1 tablespoon olive oil about 4-5 minutes. Stir in soy sauce. Scrape bottom of pot to loosen leavings. Pour 8 cups chicken broth into pot. Add mushrooms, bamboo shoots, bean sprouts, Chile and shrimp. Bring pot to a boil. Then, simmer for 5 minutes. As soup simmers, stir in 2 tablespoons cornstarch which has been blended into 2 tablespoons of water to create a paste. Stir in salt and pepper to taste. Simmer soup for 2 minutes longer. Serves 6.

A Night at the Pub.

TANDOORI SHRIMP
(You may start recipe evening before serving.)

2 lbs. jumbo or large shrimp, about 20-24 shrimp, shelled, deveined; leave tail on;
    rinse shrimp in cold water and pat dry with paper towels
4 tbsp. olive oil for basting the rack and shrimp
3 medium-size onions, each quartered
3 green bell peppers, deseeded, each quartered

MARINADE:

2 garlic cloves, minced

1 tbsp. fresh ginger, peeled, grated

3 fresh hot green Chiles, deseeded, minced

3 tbsp. lemon juice

2 tsp. horseradish

1 tbsp. fresh cilantro, chopped fine

1 tsp. mustard powder

1 tsp. dried thyme

1 tbsp. garam masala
    (see page 387 for recipe)

1 tsp. turmeric

    Before final preparation, fire up grill or preheat broiler.
    Have ready: 6-8 long, thin metal skewers; a large metal rack.

    Evening Before: Combine all marinade ingredients in a large ceramic (or glass) bowl. Add prepared shrimp and toss to thoroughly combine. Marinate shrimp at room temperature for 30 minutes; or refrigerate in sauce overnight.
    On Serving Day: Start up a covered charcoal grill to moderate-high. Or, preheat broiler. Lightly brush metal rack with oil. Alternately thread shrimp, pepper and onion sections on metal skewers; begin and end with green pepper chunk, followed by alternating shrimp/onion sections. Discard marinade. Each skewer should hold: 3-4 marinated shrimp, 2 pepper chunks, 2 onion sections. Lightly brush vegetables/shrimp with olive oil. Place skewers on rack. Barbeque or broil, turning skewers 2 or 3 times, until shrimp are opaque (about 5-6 minutes). Slide shrimp/ vegetables onto each serving plate. Serve with Rice and Snow Peas. (Recipe follows on page 276.) Serves 6.

At a Lake in Maine with Ruthie, Dr. Gill and Their Family. Photo: R. Bastien

RICE AND SNOW PEAS

1 cup long grain white rice

$2\frac{1}{2}$ cups water

2 tbsp. peanut oil

1 small onion, chopped

1 garlic clove, minced

$\frac{1}{4}$ cup scallions with some greens, chopped

2 cups snow peas, trimmed, rinsed, drained

1 tbsp. ginger soy sauce

$\frac{1}{2}$ tsp. salt

$\frac{1}{4}$ tsp. freshly ground black pepper

2 tbsp. balsamic vinegar

$\frac{1}{4}$ cup sherry

Have ready: a wok or a skillet.

Simmer 1 cup rice in $2\frac{1}{2}$ cups water for 20-25 minutes, or until water is mostly absorbed. Meanwhile, in a wok or skillet, heat peanut oil at moderate-high; sauté onion, scallions, garlic and snow peas for 3-5 minutes, until onion is lightly browned. Stir in ginger soy sauce, salt, pepper, balsamic vinegar and sherry. Combine snow peas mixture with cooked rice. Serves 6.

John's Georgetown U Dental School's 50th Reunion.

ALMOND-RAISIN RUGELACH
(Begin recipe on day before.)

1 lb. butter or Smart Balance spread, softened
2 cups sour cream, fat-free available
4 cups all-purpose flour
1 tbsp. cinnamon

5 tbsp. granulated sugar
1½ cups chopped almonds
1 cup raisins
8 tbsp. butter or Smart Balance spread, melted

In a large bowl beat together: butter, sour cream and flour until well combined. Form the dough into a ball; wrap in waxed paper; refrigerate overnight.

Next day, preheat oven to 350°.

Grease 2 large cookie sheets.

In a small bowl combine cinnamon, sugar, nuts and raisins. Divide dough ball into 6 equal pieces. On a lightly floured board, roll out 1 piece at a time to form a circle about 6 inches in diameter and about ¼-inch thick. Brush each circle with melted butter and sprinkle each circle with sugar-nut-raisin mixture. Cut each circle into 8 pie-shaped wedges and roll them up, starting with wide outer edge. Pinch closed and place them on greased cookie sheets. Bake for 30 minutes in preheated oven at 350°, until rugelach are lightly browned. Makes about 4 dozen.

....

CINNAMON-CHOCOLATE-PECAN RUGELACH
(Begin recipe on day before.)

1 lb. butter or Smart Balance spread, softened
2 cups sour cream, fat-free available
4 cups all-purpose flour
5 tbsp. granulated sugar

1 tbsp. cinnamon
1½ cups chopped pecans
1 cup mini-chocolate morsels
8 tbsp. butter or Smart Balance spread, melted

In a large bowl, beat together: butter, sour cream and flour until well combined. Form the dough into a ball; wrap in waxed paper; refrigerate overnight.

Next day, preheat oven to 350°.

Grease 2 large cookie sheets.

In a small bowl combine cinnamon, sugar, nuts and chocolate morsels. Divide dough ball into 6 equal pieces. On a lightly floured board, roll out 1 piece at a time to form a circle about 6 inches in diameter and about ¼-inch thick. Brush each circle with melted butter and sprinkle each with sugar-nuts-chocolate morsels mixture. Cut each circle into 8 pie-shaped wedges and roll them up, starting with wide outer edge. Pinch closed and place them on greased cookie sheets. Bake for 30 minutes in preheated oven at 350°, until rugelach are lightly browned. Makes about 4 dozen.

A MENU FOR THE RED HAT

CREAMY TOMATO AND VEGETABLE CHOWDER WITH SCALLOPS

CABBAGE SALAD

SPICY CRUSTED TUNA STEAKS

LATKES

BAKED APPLE CRUNCH

Musical Accompaniment:
J. S. Bach's Brandenburg Concerto #3 in G Major, "Allegro"

CREAMY TOMATO AND VEGETABLE CHOWDER WITH SCALLOPS

[A Cooking Hint: How to Skin a Tomato
1. wash tomato   2. immerse tomato in boiling water for 1 minute
3. remove tomato from boiling water and plunge it into cold water
4. peel off skin with fingers]

2 tbsp. olive oil

1 large onion, finely chopped

7 cups water (or 3 cups water and 4 cups
    low-sodium vegetable stock)

1 Chile pepper, deseeded, chopped (Wear
    plastic gloves with handling hot peppers.)

2 large carrots, pared, chopped

1 large celery stalk with greens,
    trimmed, chopped

1 cup green beans, cut into small pieces

½ cup fresh or frozen peas

3-4 plum tomatoes, peeled, chopped

2 cups prepared tomato sauce

½ cup barley

½ cup brown rice

1 tbsp. oregano

1 tsp. salt, or to taste

½ tsp. black pepper

1 can (12 oz.) evaporated milk,
    fat-free available

1 cup tiny maruzzelle (sea shells) pasta

2 cups bay scallops, rinsed, halved

Heat oil in a large soup pot with cover and cook onions until tender. Pour water and stock into pot; add Chile pepper, carrots, celery, green beans, peas, tomatoes, prepared tomato sauce, barley, brown rice, oregano, salt and pepper. Cover pot and bring it to boil. Then, lower heat and simmer for 30 minutes. Remove 2 cups *only* liquid from pot and pour into a 2-quart bowl. Whisk evaporated milk into soup liquid until blended.

Gradually pour this creamy tomato mix back into the soup pot. Stir to blend thoroughly. Stir in pasta. Cover pot; bring to a boil; then, lower heat to simmer soup for 6-8 minutes. During last 2 minutes stir in scallops. Taste soup to adjust spices, if necessary. Serve with bread crisps. Serves 6-8.

CABBAGE SALAD

3 cups green cabbage, shredded

3 cups red cabbage, shredded

1 large carrot, pared, shredded

1 large onion, finely chopped

$\frac{1}{2}$ cup red wine vinegar

$\frac{1}{4}$ cup extra-virgin olive oil

salt and freshly ground black pepper, to taste

Combine vinegar, olive oil, salt and pepper in a small bowl or jar and whisk until smooth. Combine shredded cabbages, chopped onion and shredded carrot into a large salad bowl. Pour vinegar and oil dressing over the vegetables and toss to coat thoroughly. Cover bowl with plastic wrap; refrigerate salad until well chilled, about 4-5 hours. Serves 6.

SPICY CRUSTED TUNA STEAKS

olive oil to brush grill pan

4-6 portions fresh tuna steaks,
   1-inch thick, remove skin

2 large Vidalia onions, thinly sliced

$\frac{1}{4}$ cup prepared horseradish

2 tbsp. olive oil

$\frac{1}{4}$ cup capers (*NOTE: below)

$\frac{1}{4}$ cup balsamic vinegar

juice of 1 lemon

juice of 1 lime

$\frac{1}{4}$ tsp. salt

2 tsp. cracked pepper

*NOTE: Capers are small buds from the evergreen bush, eg: Juniper. The berries are dried, pickled in vinegar brine or packed in salt.

You will need a large 15-inch grill pan with a handle.

Brush surface of grill pan with olive oil. In a small bowl, combine prepared horseradish, capers, pepper, salt, balsamic vinegar, lemon and lime juices and olive oil. Remove skin from tuna; rinse portions under cold water and pat dry with paper towels. Preheat a large oil-greased grill pan on stove burner set to medium-high.

Brush both sides of tuna portions with horseradish mix. Lay 2-3 pieces at a time on grill pan; add sliced onions and cook onions with tuna, at medium-high: 2-3 minutes on each side for rare; 3-4 minutes on each side for medium rare; 4-5 minutes on each side for "no pink". Suggestion: Slice each portion in $\frac{1}{4}$-inch biased cuts when serving with onions in sauce. Serves 4-6.

LATKES

6 potatoes, peeled and grated; use a food processor. Cut peeled potatoes in lengthwise
strips to fit in the food processor feed tube. Using medium-coarse shredding disk,
feed sections of potato into processor. Transfer grated potatoes into a large bowl.

1 large yellow onion, grated; cut onion into chunks and feed into food processor as instructed
above. Transfer grated onion to bowl with potatoes.

2 eggs, beaten or $\frac{1}{2}$ cup egg substitute

1 tbsp. parsley, finely chopped

$\frac{1}{2}$ tsp. salt

$\frac{1}{2}$ tsp. black pepper

1 tsp. baking powder

$\frac{1}{2}$ cup matzoh meal

Canola oil for frying

Have ready: a food processor; a large griddle or a large skillet, greased.

Combine grated potatoes with onion, parsley and beaten eggs. Mix together: salt, pepper,
baking powder and matzoh meal. Slowly stir the dry ingredients into the potato mix.

Heat oil in a large skillet or on a griddle. Drop the batter, a heaping tablespoon at a time
into the hot skillet and fry them for a minute on each side, until both sides are golden brown.
Serve immediately. Applesauce makes a tasty accompaniment. Serves 6.

Camping in the California Hills. Photo: T. Miller

BAKED APPLE CRUNCH

FILLING:
2 lbs. Granny Smith apples (about 8 apples), peeled, cored, sliced
$\frac{1}{4}$ cup granulated sugar
$\frac{1}{4}$ cup brown sugar
1 tsp. ground cinnamon
1 tsp. ground nutmeg
1 tsp. ground cloves

CRUNCH TOPPING:
$\frac{1}{2}$ cup all-purpose flour
$\frac{1}{4}$ cup granulated sugar
3 tbsp. butter or Smart Balance spread
1 tsp. vanilla extract
confectioners' sugar for garnish
melted dark chocolate for drizzling (In a small double boiler, melt 6 oz. dark chocolate
    morsels over simmering water; stir until smooth. Drizzle over top of crunch.)

Preheat oven to 350°.

Have ready: a 9-inch pie plate or a round casserole.

Prepare the FILLING. In large bowl, combine apples, sugars and spices. Stir to coat apples thoroughly. Spoon the filling into a 9-inch pie plate (or casserole) and set aside.
Prepare the CRUNCH. In a medium bowl, combine flour, sugar, butter and vanilla. Work the mixture between your fingers and crumble on top of apple filling. Bake in preheated oven at 350° on rack in center of oven for 1 hour, until golden. Drizzle with melted dark chocolate and garnish with confectioners' sugar. Best when served warm. Serves 6.

L.I. Red Hat Convention 2007.
Photo with permission: Queen Johanna Rose (Johanna Dyckman)

A TASTE OF CUBA

SPICY RICE AND BEANS SALAD

CUBAN PORK ROAST

MEDITERRANEAN ROASTED STUFFED PEPPERS

PINEAPPLE-RUM RAISIN ICE CREAM COMPOTE

SPICY RICE AND BEANS SALAD

1 cup cooked brown rice, at room temperature
1 can (1 lb.) less-salt corn kernels
1 can (1 lb.) less-salt dark red kidney beans
1 medium-size onion, thinly sliced
1 tbsp. red pepper, deseeded, minced
1 tbsp. cayenne or Chile pepper, deseeded, minced
    (Wear plastic cloves when handling hot peppers.)
1 tbsp. fresh cilantro, minced
$\frac{1}{2}$ tsp. salt
$\frac{1}{4}$ tsp. freshly ground black pepper
$\frac{1}{4}$ tsp. chili powder
1 tbsp. olive oil
1 tbsp. lime juice
Beds of Romaine lettuce

Richard Campo PC multi-tasks at Lunch.

Have ready: 4 individual glass salad bowls lined with Romaine lettuce.

Combine all of the ingredients (except lettuce) in a large bowl. Spoon servings of Rice and Beans into salad bowls lined with beds of Romaine lettuce. Serves 4.

Flowers
from the Garden of...

Mom's Garden

Love Grows Here

...MaryLou Mascolo

Mary Lou's

CUBAN PORK ROAST

4 lb. loin of pork, boned and tied

SPICE RUB: (Combine in a small bowl.)

3 tbsp. ground cumin

3 tbsp. chili powder

1 tbsp. prepared salsa

2 garlic cloves, minced

2 tbsp. olive oil and 2 tbsp. butter or
    Smart Balance spread (to make a paste)

$\frac{1}{2}$ tsp. each: ground allspice, ground cloves

1 tbsp. brown sugar

2 tsp. coriander

a sprinkling of salt

MARINADE: (Blend in a bowl.)

2 cups orange juice

$\frac{1}{2}$ cup lime juice

$\frac{1}{3}$ cup brown sugar

$\frac{1}{3}$ cup dark rum

1 garlic clove, minced

Have ready: a small roasting pan to fit the pork.

Rub all over pork: spice mix combined with oil/butter to form a paste. Baste with marinade. Place roast in bowl and allow to marinate in refrigerator for 2 hours. Then, allow to stand out of refrigerator for 30 minutes.

Preheat oven to 450°.

Lay prepared pork in pan to roast in a preheated oven at 450°. As soon as you place the pan in the oven, reduce oven temperature to 325° and roast the marinated boned loin of pork for 30 minutes per pound (about 2 hours for 4 pounds). Internal temperature will register 170° when done. During this time, baste the roast several times with its own juice. Remove from oven and allow to rest for 10-15 minutes before carving into thin slices. Serves 4-5.

Mercy's Party Never Ends. Photo: T/M. Levitz

MEDITERRANEAN ROASTED STUFFED PEPPERS

4 large red bell peppers, cut out stem
    and remove seeds

2 cups packaged cubed cornbread stuffing

1 lb. small shrimp, shelled, trimmed,
    rinsed and drained

½ cup sliced pepperoni, cut into strips

1 small onion, finely chopped

2 garlic cloves, minced

½ cup white raisins, chopped

¼ cup pignola (pine nuts)

¼ tsp. black pepper

1 tbsp. fresh parsley, minced

2 tbsp. olive oil
    (more olive oil to drizzle over peppers)

½ cup hot water (to cook shrimp and to use
    as stock in recipe)

Preheat oven to 450°.

Have ready: a 7x10x3-inch roasting pan (to withstand a high temperature), coated with olive oil.

In a large bowl, mix cornbread cubes, chopped onion, garlic, strips of pepperoni, pepper, parsley, raisins, pignola and 2 tablespoons olive oil. Set aside. Simmer cleaned shrimp in one half cup water for several minutes until pink. Drain shrimp liquid into a bowl. Remove 4-6 shrimp for garnish. Add rest of cooked shrimp to stuffing mix. Drizzle hot shrimp water, a little at a time, into the bowl of stuffing to moisten. Add a little more hot water, if needed.

Stuff each prepared red bell pepper with a portion of stuffing; garnish tops, each with a shrimp. Coat bottom of 7x10-inch pan with olive oil; lay stuffed peppers straight up in pan. Drizzle about 1 teaspoon olive oil over each pepper. Leave space around each pepper in pan. Roast peppers in preheated oven at 450° for 15 minutes. Reduce temperature to 400°; lay a loose sheet of foil over the pan and roast for 20 minutes longer. Pepper shells should be *just tender*. Remove from oven. Serve warm. Serves 4.

···

PINEAPPLE-RUM RAISIN ICE CREAM COMPOTE

½ pint heavy whipping cream, beaten into stiff peaks

1 pint vanilla bean ice cream

½ cup white raisins, chopped

¼ cup light rum

½ cup fresh ripe or canned pineapple, cut into 1-inch cubes

Have ready: four 1-cup dessert bowls.

Soak raisins in rum for 10 minutes. Empty ice cream into a bowl; soften by mashing. Fold into ice cream: rum-soaked raisins, cubed pineapple and whipped cream. Spoon into 4 dessert bowls. Serves 4.

BEANS AND BROCCOLI SOUP
LAMB CHOPS AND PEARS IN FONTINA
SWEET POTATO CROQUETTES
APPLESAUCE WALNUT LAYER CAKE

BEANS AND BROCCOLI SOUP

1 pkg. (1 lb.) cannellini beans, soaked
  overnight in enough cold water to cover
10 cups hot water
1 large onion, chopped
2 strips lean bacon
1 celery stalk with greens, trimmed, chopped
1 large all-purpose potato, pared, chopped
1-2 carrots, pared, cut into rounds
$\frac{1}{4}$ cup chopped sweet red pepper, deseeded
$\frac{1}{4}$ cup chopped sweet green pepper, deseeded

1 parsnip, pared, chopped
1-inch piece fresh ginger, minced
$\frac{1}{4}$ cup chopped Italian parsley
2 bay leaves
$\frac{1}{2}$ tsp. black pepper
1 tsp. salt
$\frac{1}{2}$ cup orzo
$\frac{1}{2}$ cup brown rice
2 cups tiny florets of broccoli, rinsed, drained

Have ready: a six-quart soup pot with a cover.

Rinse soaked beans; drain. Over medium heat, brown bacon in large soup pot. Add chopped onion to pot as bacon cooks. Remove bacon and drain on paper towels. Pour 10 cups hot water into soup pot, scraping bottom of pot to loosen onion leavings. To the pot, add: celery, potato, carrots, green and red peppers, parsnip, ginger, parsley and bay leaves. Cover pot and bring a rolling boil. Lower heat to simmer and cook beans mix for 1 hour until beans are tender. Turn up heat under pot to a slow boil and add rice, black pepper and salt. Lower to simmer and continue to cook soup for another 15 minutes. Stir in orzo and broccoli florets; continue to simmer for 10-12 minutes longer. Turn off heat under pot. Add and crumble cooked bacon to pot. Allow pot to sit on burner for a few minutes longer to blend the spices. Remove bay leaves and discard. Serve hot. This soup may be frozen and stored for several months. Serves 8-10.

LAMB CHOPS AND PEARS IN FONTINA

[A Cooking Hint: Add 1 tablespoon oil to butter when pan-browning to prevent butter from burning. When broiling steak or chops, brush both sides very lightly with olive oil to seal in juices.]

1 tbsp. butter or Smart Balance spread, for pan

1 tbsp. olive oil, for pan

6 loin lamb chops, 1-inch thick, trim fat

2 tbsp. olive oil

1 cup Fontina cheese, chopped in tiny cubes

(a sprinkling of paprika)

freshly ground black pepper

salt to taste

$\frac{1}{4}$ cup crushed dried rosemary

$\frac{1}{4}$ cup Grilling Spice for lamb chops (see page 316)

6 Bosc pears, halved, remove seeds; brush lightly with olive oil

Preheat oven to 400°; then, preheat broiler.

Have ready: a 9x12x1$\frac{1}{2}$-inch baking pan and a large 12-inch grill pan with ovenproof handle, lightly greased with butter and oil.

Brush cut side of pear halves with olive oil. Fill center of each pear with 1 tablespoon of chopped Fontina. Sprinkle paprika over tops of pears and cheese. Lay pear halves on prepared 9x12 pan. Roast pears in preheated oven at 400° for 15 minutes or until cheese starts to brown. Remove pan and lay a sheet of foil loosely over the pears. Keep them warm.

Trim most of the fat from lamb chops. Brush chops lightly with olive oil. Generously sprinkle chops with crushed rosemary, Grilling Spice and black pepper and a little salt.

Preheat broiler. Lay prepared chops on grill pan with oven-proof handle and place grill pan on oven rack 3-inches under heating element; broil about 5 minutes. Turn chops over to broil the other side for about 2-3 minutes, depending upon thickness of chops.

Remove chops from broiler and pack tops of each chop with 1 tablespoon chopped Fontina. Return chops to broiler and continue to cook them for 1-2 minutes longer, until cheese bubbles and starts to brown.

Do not overcook the chops. Lamb chops should be slightly pink with juices running. Internal temperature of chops for medium-rare is 140°-150°.

Serve immediately, accompanied by 2 warm Fontina pear halves. Serves 6.

SWEET POTATO CROQUETTES

5 medium-large sweet potatoes, pared, cut into chunks; boiled for 15-20 minutes, drained
   (Or, use microwaveable packaged frozen sweet potatoes, about 24 oz.;
     steamed according to directions.)
2 large all-purpose potatoes, pared, cut into chunks; boiled for 10-12 minutes; drained
1 egg beaten, or $\frac{1}{4}$ cup egg substitute
1 cup sharp Cheddar cheese, grated
1 tbsp. minced onion
1 tbsp. chopped parsley
$\frac{1}{4}$ teaspoon salt
$\frac{1}{4}$ tsp. black pepper
1 tsp. pumpkin pie spice (a mix of cinnamon, cloves, nutmeg, ginger, allspice)

$1\frac{1}{2}$ cups flour to coat croquettes
canola or corn oil for frying
extra pumpkin spice mix for garnish

   Have ready: a large skillet; a serving platter.

   Preheat oil in a large skillet to 320°. In a large bowl, rice sweet potatoes and potatoes while hot. Add and combine: minced onion, parsley, salt, pepper, spices, grated Cheddar, beaten egg. Pour flour to coat croquettes on a flat dish. With aid of a large serving spoon and your floured hands, scoop servings of the potato mix to form croquettes, the size of small fat knockwurst. Pack them firmly; roll them into flour to coat on all sides. Sauté them, 3-4 at a time on all sides, in preheated oil. Drain on paper towels; transfer to an oven-proof serving platter. Lightly sprinkle them with pumpkin spice mix. If not serving immediately, maintain them at room temperature; warm thoroughly at 250° for 15 minutes before serving. Serves 6.

APPLESAUCE WALNUT LAYER CAKE

*[A Cooking Hint: When making a cake, add $\frac{1}{2}$ – 1 cup unseasoned applesauce
or pure pumpkin instead of fat to a cake recipe to add moisture and
to reduce fat content. 1 cup applesauce or pumpkin = 1 cup oil.]*

1 pkg. (22 oz.) yellow cake mix

1 stick ($\frac{1}{2}$ cup) butter or Smart Balance
    spread, softened

1$\frac{1}{3}$ cups unseasoned applesauce

3 eggs or $\frac{3}{4}$ cup egg substitute

1 tsp. cinnamon

$\frac{1}{2}$ cup chopped walnuts

MOCHA FROSTING:

1 tbsp. instant coffee powder

6 oz. semisweet chocolate morsels

$\frac{1}{4}$ cup water

1 cup (2 sticks) butter or Smart Balance
    spread, at room temperature

3 egg yolks or $\frac{3}{4}$ cup egg substitute

2 cups confectioners' sugar, sifted

GARNISH: $\frac{1}{4}$ cup each: walnut halves, semisweet chocolate morsels

Preheat oven to 375°.

Have ready: 2 greased and floured 9-inch round cake pans; a large cake plate.

Prepare the CAKE. Combine cake mix, softened butter, applesauce, eggs and cinnamon into a large mixing bowl. Beat for 4 minutes at medium speed. Stir in chopped walnuts. Turn batter evenly into 2 9-inch greased pans. Bake in preheated oven at 375° for 30-35 minutes, or until inserted toothpick removes clean. Cool layers for 20 minutes in pans; turn onto racks to cool completely. Frost with MOCHA FROSTING when completely cooled.

Prepare FROSTING. Over low heat, cook chocolate, coffee powder and water in a small saucepot, stirring until smooth and creamy. Set aside to cool. Cream butter until light and fluffy. Beat in egg yolks one at a time. Beat in cooled chocolate mixture; then, beat in confectioners' sugar. Refrigerate frosting until it is thick enough to spread (several hours).

Assembling the CAKE. Place bottom layer on cake serving plate; frost layer with $\frac{1}{2}$ cup frosting; top with second layer. Frost top and sides of cake with remaining frosting. Garnish top outer edge of cake with walnut halves; sprinkle chocolate morsels in a circle on top, in center of cake. Refrigerate cake until an hour or two before serving. Serves 8.

ZUPPA DI RISO AL LIMONE

SHISH KEBABS ON THE GRILL

GREEN BEANS AND TOMATOES

ZIPPY CARROTS

PEACHY CRISP

ZUPPA DI RISO AL LIMONE

8 cups chicken stock (see page 81 for recipe); or
    use 2 qts. low-sodium packaged chicken stock
1 cup white rice
$\frac{1}{2}$ cup wild rice, rinsed and drained in several washings
2 egg yolks or $\frac{1}{2}$ cup egg substitute
$\frac{1}{4}$ cup Italian parsley, minced
juice of 1 lemon
$\frac{1}{2}$ cup Parmesan cheese, grated
$\frac{1}{4}$ cup water
salt, black pepper to taste
1 lemon finely sliced into rounds for garnish
more grated Parmesan cheese for garnish

Have ready: a large soup pot with a cover; a large soup tureen.

Bring 2 quarts chicken stock to a full boil; pour $\frac{1}{2}$ cup wild rice into rapidly boiling water and cook for 20 minutes. Stir in 1 cup white rice and continue to cook for 20 minutes longer.

Meanwhile, in a small bowl, beat egg yolks (or egg substitute) with juice of 1 lemon, Parmesan cheese and $\frac{1}{4}$ cup water, until well blended. Pour this mixture into a soup tureen and gradually pour the boiling rice soup into it, stirring continuously. Stir in parsley, salt and pepper (to taste). Soup will be thick. Float thin lemon rounds on surface of soup in tureen. Garnish with more Parmesan when serving. Serves 6.

SHISH KEBABS ON THE GRILL

MARINADE:

$\frac{1}{3}$ cup honey

2 tbsp. brown sugar

juice of 2 lemons

juice of 1 lime

1 tbsp. fresh ginger, grated

$\frac{1}{3}$ cup white vinegar

$\frac{1}{4}$ cup olive oil

1 green bell pepper, deseeded, diced

1 tsp. Tabasco sauce

1 tbsp. each: Worcestershire sauce, soy sauce

1 garlic clove, minced

$\frac{1}{4}$ tsp. each: ground cinnamon, ground cumin

$\frac{1}{2}$ tsp. curry powder

KEBABS:

3 lbs. boneless lamb, cut into 1-inch cubes

1 lb. sweet Italian sausage, cut into 1-inch slices

   (Freeze sausage before slicing; sausage slices better when partially frozen.)

12 white mushrooms, trimmed, rinsed, drained

2 red bell peppers, deseeded, cut into 2-inch squares

2 zucchini (about $\frac{1}{2}$ lb.) rinsed, cut into 1-inch rounds

2 onions, each cut into 4 wedges

1 pt. cherry tomatoes, rinsed, drained

Have ready: 6-8 metal skewers, each 12 inches long; a large, shallow baking pan, 9x15 inches.

Prepare MARINADE: Mix all marinade ingredients in a bowl.

Assemble the KEBABS: thread meat and vegetables on 6-8 metal skewers (each 12 inches long), alternating the ingredients.

Lay the skewers side-by-side on a shallow baking pan. Brush marinade over kebabs and turn them to coat thoroughly. Marinate kebabs at room temperature for 1 hour. Turn the kebabs and marinate them for 1 hour longer.

Fire up the charcoal grill. Cook the kebabs 5 inches above medium to medium-high heat for 10-15 minutes, basting frequently with marinade, and turning skewers as needed. Serves 6-8.

GREEN BEANS AND TOMATOES

2 tbsp. olive oil

4 garlic cloves, minced

4 small shallots, minced

4-5 plum tomatoes, chopped

1$\frac{1}{2}$ lbs. green beans, trimmed, rinsed,
    drained, each cut in half

2 tsp. fresh lemon juice

1 tbsp. dry red wine

$\frac{1}{2}$ tsp. salt

$\frac{1}{4}$ tsp. freshly ground black pepper

Warm oil in a 2-quart sauce pan over medium heat. Add garlic and shallots; lower heat and sauté until soft, about 3 minutes.

Add chopped tomatoes, green beans, lemon juice, wine, salt and pepper. Simmer until just tender, 3-5 minutes. Do not overcook. Serve immediately. Serves 6.

ZIPPY CARROTS
[A Cooking Hint: When preparing most vegetables, steam or pressure cook to help to preserve vitamins/nutrients.]

6-8 carrots, trimmed, pared

1 tbsp. fresh lemon juice

2 tbsp. olive oil

1 tsp. Hungarian paprika

$\frac{1}{2}$ tsp. ground cumin

$\frac{1}{2}$ tsp. salt

$\frac{1}{4}$ tsp. ground cinnamon

2 tbsp. fresh Italian parsley, minced

Place whole carrots in a steamer with a couple inches of cold water and bring to a boil. Steam them until carrots are tender, but not too soft, 8-10 minutes. Drain and cool them under cold water.

Meanwhile in a medium-size bowl, whisk lemon juice with olive oil to make a vinaigrette. Whisk in paprika, cumin, salt and cinnamon. Cut carrots into bite-size. Add them to the vinaigrette and toss to mix. Stir in parsley. Serves 6.

PEACHY CRISP

1 doz. ripe peaches, rinsed
$\frac{1}{3}$ cup all-purpose flour
1 tsp. almond extract
$\frac{1}{2}$ tsp. ground ginger
$\frac{2}{3}$ cup granulated sugar

TOPPING:
$1\frac{1}{2}$ cups all-purpose flour
$1\frac{1}{2}$ cups oats
$\frac{1}{4}$ tsp. salt, 1 cup brown sugar
1 cup chopped pecans
$\frac{1}{4}$ cup plus 2 tbsp. butter or Smart Balance
    spread, cut into bits,
    softened to room temperature

Preheat oven to 375°.

Grease a 9x13-inch baking pan with butter or (Smart Balance spread).

Cut peaches in half. (Do not remove skin.) Remove pits and cut each half into 4 wedges. Toss fruit with almond extract, sugar, flour and ginger. Transfer to baking pan.

In a medium-size bowl, combine all topping ingredients, working the mix with your fingertips until coarse crumbs are formed. Sprinkle crumbs over the peaches in pan.

Bake in preheated oven at 375° until filling bubbles and fruit is very soft, about 40-45 minutes. Serve warm. Serves 8-10.

Food Pantry at St. Hugh of Lincoln, Huntington Station, NY. Photos with permission: Jim Reilly

---

ZUPPA DI RISO E FAGIOLI
APRICOT/HONEY-GLAZED CHICKEN
ROASTED POTATOES, ONIONS, RED PEPPERS AND BLACK BEANS
CHOCOLATE APPLESAUCE CAKE

ZUPPA DI RISO E FAGIOLI

1 lb. (2 cups) white beans or cranberry beans
 (You may combine both; soak beans
 overnight in enough water to cover.
 Rinse beans in cold water prior to using.)
8 cups water
2 tbsp. olive oil
1 large yellow onion, chopped
1 celery stalk, with greens, chopped
2 large ripe tomatoes, peeled, chopped
(*NOTE: below)

1 tsp. salt, or to taste
½ tsp. freshly ground black pepper
⅛ tsp. crushed hot pepper flakes
¼ cup Italian parsley, minced
½ cup uncooked rice
½ cup Romano cheese; more Romano cheese
 at serving

*NOTE: To remove skin from a tomato:
1. wash tomato
2. immerse tomato in boiling water for 1 minute
3. remove tomato from boiling water and plunge it into cold water
4. peel off skin with fingers

Heat 2 tablespoons olive oil in a large soup pot with cover and lightly brown chopped onion and celery. Add peeled, chopped tomatoes, parsley, seasonings and crushed red pepper flakes. Cook for 2 minutes longer. Pour 8 cups water into pot; stir in the presoaked beans and rice into the pot; stir and scrape bottom of pot to remove leavings. Cover pot; raise the heat under pot to high and bring to a boil. Then, lower to simmer and cook soup, stirring occasionally, for 20-25 minutes. During last 5 minutes, as soup simmers, stir in Romano cheese. Serve with an additional garnish of Romano cheese. Serves 6.

APRICOT/HONEY-GLAZED CHICKEN

6-8 boneless, skinless, thick chicken breast halves, (about 1½-2 lbs.)

Rinse chicken in cold running water; pat dry with paper towels.

2 tbsp. olive oil

6 tbsp. apricot preserves

½ cup honey mustard

1 tsp. ground ginger

1 tbsp. honey

Preheat burner to medium-high.

Have ready: a large grill pan.

In a small bowl, blend mustard, honey, preserves and ginger.

Brush surface of grill pan with olive oil; brush prepared chicken with olive oil. Brush both sides of chicken breasts with apricot-honey mixture and lay chicken on preheated, oiled grill pan. Grill chicken at medium-high for 5 minutes; then lower heat to medium and continue to cook for 2-3 additional minutes. Turn over glazed chicken breasts; raise surface temperature to medium-high and repeat cooking procedure for other side. During cooking procedure, brush chicken with basting mixture frequently. Chicken is cooked when internal temperature registers 170° and juices run clear. Transfer chicken to oven-proof serving platter. If not serving immediately, cover platter with a sheet of aluminum foil and keep chicken in a low oven, 200°, up to 15 minutes. Serves 6.

A Sunday Dinner with the Taylor-Lopes Families. Photo: E. Lopes

ROASTED POTATOES, ONION, RED PEPPERS AND BLACK BEANS

6 medium-size all-purpose potatoes or Yukon
    gold potatoes, if available; chopped into
    2-inch cubes (do not pare)
2 large red bell peppers, deseeded,
    cut into 1-inch slices
1 large onion, thinly sliced
1 large can (22 oz.) black beans,
    rinsed in cold water, drained
$\frac{1}{2}$ cup chopped, pitted spicy black olives,
    for garnish

$\frac{1}{4}$ cup olive oil
1 tbsp. dried oregano
$\frac{1}{2}$ tsp. garlic powder
$\frac{1}{2}$ tsp. salt
$\frac{1}{4}$ tsp. black pepper
dash of cayenne pepper
$\frac{1}{2}$ cup coarse bread crumbs
a sprinkling of olive oil (about 1-2 tbsp.)

Preheat oven to 400°.

Have ready: a 9x12x3-inch roasting pan.

In a small bowl blend olive oil with oregano, salt, pepper, cayenne and garlic powder.

In a large bowl, toss cubed potatoes, onion and red peppers with olive oil mixture to coat thoroughly.

Transfer prepared vegetables to a 9x12x3-inch roasting pan and cook in a preheated oven at 400° for 20-25 minutes, until potatoes are starting to color. Remove pan from oven; stir in black beans. Garnish top of pan with chopped black olives and bread crumbs. Sprinkle with olive oil. Return pan to oven to cook 5 minutes longer. Potatoes should be tender (a toothpick will slide easily when inserted into potato cube). Serves 6.

Dr. Steve and Irene Restaino and their Family do Lunch on the Patio. Photo: S. Restaino

CHOCOLATE APPLESAUCE CAKE

[A Cooking Hint: Use substitutes to fit health needs: substitute apple sauce or pure pumpkin for butter/oil for added moisture and no additional fat.]

1 pkg. (about 22 oz.) devil's food cake mix
1 cup milk, fat-free available
$\frac{1}{2}$ cup applesauce
3 large eggs or $\frac{3}{4}$ cup egg substitute

GLAZE:
$\frac{1}{2}$ cup heavy whipping cream
4 oz. bittersweet chocolate, coarsely chopped
$\frac{1}{2}$ cup sliced almonds with skins, for garnish

Preheat oven to 350°.

Have ready: a 12-inch tube pan, greased and dusted with flour.

Prepare the CAKE. In a large mixing bowl, combine devil's food cake mix, milk, applesauce and eggs. Beat at low speed until moistened. Beat 2 minutes at high speed. Pour batter into prepared tube pan and bake cake in preheated oven at 350° for 45 minutes, or until a toothpick inserted in center of cake removes clean. Remove from oven and cool on rack for 20 minutes. Invert and remove cake to cake plate to cool completely.

Meanwhile Prepare the GLAZE. Heat cream in a small saucepan over medium heat until bubbles form around edges. Remove from heat; stir in chopped chocolate until melted. Cool glaze to room temperature. Spoon glaze over cake and spread over top and sides with a spatula. Garnish with a sprinkling of sliced almonds over top of cake. Allow cake to stand until glaze sets. Serves 8-10.

BUTTERNUT SQUASH CRAB SOUP

GREEK ISLES TILAPIA

MUSHROOMS STUFFED WITH PROSCIUTTO, SUN DRIED TOMATOES, OLIVES

ORZO WITH LEMON AND OLIVES

RICOTTA PIE

BUTTERNUT SQUASH CRAB SOUP

*[A Cooking Hint: Before preparing any recipe, read the procedure thoroughly.
Visualize the techniques and procedures required.]*

2 tbsp. olive oil
2 scallions, minced
2 tbsp. curry powder
½ tsp. ground coriander
1 tsp. dry mustard
½ tsp. ground cinnamon
½ tsp. brown sugar

6 cups chicken stock (see page 81 for recipe);
    or use low-sodium packaged chicken broth
4 cups butternut squash purée
    (about 3 lbs. butternut squash,
    pared, cubed; makes 4 cups purée)
1 cup corn kernels (canned or frozen)
1 lb. lump crabmeat
1 cup plain Greek yogurt
freshly ground black pepper and salt to taste

Have ready: a large soup pot; a food processor.

Warm olive oil in a large soup pot and lightly brown scallions. Add curry, coriander, dry mustard, cinnamon and brown sugar and cook for 1 minute. Stir in chicken broth and cubed butternut squash. Simmer for 10 minutes. With a large strainer, remove softened butternut squash from soup pot to a bowl.

In a food processor, purée the butternut squash, a portion at a time and return the purée to the soup pot. Add salt and pepper to taste; simmer soup gently for 30 minutes.

Stir in corn kernels and crabmeat. Cook to heat through, another 5 minutes. Stir in yogurt and serve. Serves 6.

GREEK ISLES TILAPIA

2 lbs. tilapia fillets (about 6-8 fillets), rinsed in
    cold water, patted dry with paper towels
salt, freshly ground pepper
1 cup plain Greek yogurt
½ cup low-fat mayonnaise
1 tbsp. fresh lemon juice

½ tsp. curry powder
3 tbsp. olive oil
6-8 white mushrooms, trimmed, rinsed,
    drained, sliced
1 large white onion, sliced thin
½ lb. seedless grapes
½ cup pitted Kalamata olives, chopped

Preheat oven to 350°.
Have ready: 6-8 small metal skewers.

    Sprinkle fish with salt and pepper. In a bowl, combine ½ cup yogurt, mayonnaise, lemon juice and curry powder. Spread this mixture over one side of fillets. Starting at thinner end, roll up and secure each fillet with a small metal skewer (or tie with white string). Place the tilapia rolls in a 7x9-inch baking dish and top with leftover yogurt mixture.
    Heat oil in a skillet over medium heat. Add mushrooms and onion and cook until softened, stirring frequently, about 5 minutes. Stir in grapes and heat through, about 1 minute longer. Pour over fish fillets; sprinkle with chopped olives. Bake fish in preheated oven at 350° until fish is cooked through, about 30 minutes. Serves 6.

ORZO WITH LEMON AND OLIVES

1¼ lbs. orzo
finely minced zest from 1 lemon
1 cup pitted oil-cured olives, chopped
3 cups arugula, rinsed, drained, chopped

¼ cup extra-virgin olive oil
1 cup feta cheese, chopped fine
salt and freshly ground black pepper to taste

    Boil orzo in a large pot of water until barely tender, about 7-8 minutes. Meanwhile, combine lemon peel, olives, arugula, oil and chopped feta in a large bowl and mix thoroughly. Set aside.
    Drain the pasta; transfer orzo to the large bowl and quickly toss with the olive mixture. Season with salt and black pepper. Serve immediately. Serves 6.

MUSHROOMS STUFFED WITH PROSCIUTTO, SUN DRIED TOMATOES, OLIVES

(Stuffed mushrooms have been a specialty at my dinner table. They can be served as appetizers, entrées or sides. Did you know that mushrooms are loaded with Vitamin D, besides, being low in calories? Of course, I'm not making any excuses for the olive oil and bread crumbs, which go into my stuffing recipes. And the variety of mushrooms extends beyond imagination: white buttons, large whites, cremini, Portobello and baby bella, chanterelles, shiitake, enoki, oyster, morels, porcini, truffles- to name only a few of the edible variety. Our modern green grocers, supermarkets and food specialty shops guarantee to remove any fears we may have regarding poisonous mushroom types. Unless you are a mycologist, avoid harvesting fungi from a mossy knoll in the woods.)

8-10 large white mushrooms for stuffing; rinsed; remove stems (trim, rinse and chop stems); set aside

1 cup unseasoned Italian bread crumbs

mushroom stems, chopped

4 thin slices prosciutto (divided, 2 + 2)

3-4 sun dried tomato halves, slivered

1 tsp. Chile pepper, deseeded, minced (Wear plastic gloves when using hot peppers.)

1 small Italian fryer pepper, deseeded, chopped

$\frac{1}{4}$ cup oil-cured olives, pitted, chopped

2 garlic cloves, minced

$\frac{1}{4}$ cup Asiago cheese, grated

1 tbsp. crushed rosemary leaves

$\frac{1}{4}$ tsp. freshly ground black pepper

$\frac{1}{4}$ tsp. salt

$\frac{1}{4}$ cup olive oil (in 2 parts)

(2-3 tbsp. hot water, as needed)

Preheat oven to 350°.

Have ready: a large ovenproof casserole dish to fit the mushrooms. Coat bottom of dish with 1 tablespoon olive oil.

In a bowl, mix crumbs, chopped stems, slivers of sun dried tomatoes, chopped Chile and fryer peppers, chopped pitted olives, minced garlic, Asiago cheese, herbs and spices. With a pair of scissors, cut 2 slices of prosciutto into small pieces and add to the mixture. (Save remaining 2 slices for garnish.) Sprinkle this mix with 2 tablespoons olive oil; add 2-3 tablespoons of hot water to dampen the mixture to hold together.

Stuff each mushroom with this crumb mix and pack stuffing firmly with your fingers. Lay stuffed mushrooms in oil-coated ovenproof casserole dish. Sprinkle remaining 1 tablespoon of olive oil over mushrooms. With scissors, cut remaining 2 slices of prosciutto, each into 5 pieces, about 1-inch each piece. Press a prosciutto square on top of each stuffed mushroom.

Bake casserole in preheated oven at 350° for 20 minutes. You may prepare this recipe early on the day and refrigerate, lightly covered with waxed paper. Then, bake the mushroom casserole just before serving. Add a green salad and some bread crisps for a satisfying luncheon dish. Serves 4. (Especially for Lynn and PJ.)

RICOTTA PIE

CRUST:

2¼ cups all-purpose flour

½ cup sugar

⅛ tsp. salt

½ cup butter or Smart Balance spread, chilled
and cut into small pieces

1 large egg plus 1 large egg yolk,
or ½ cup egg substitute

2 tsp. grated lemon peel

⅓ cup ice water

FILLING:

1 lb. whole milk ricotta

½ cup sugar

1 tbsp. all-purpose flour

4 large eggs, separated; or 1 cup egg substitute
and whites from 4 large eggs
(or 4 portions *Just Whites* - egg whites;
use according to directions on package)

¼ cup heavy cream or evaporated milk
(fat-free available)

¼ cup sour cream (fat-free available)

2 tbsp. candied orange peel, finely chopped

1 tsp. vanilla extract

¼ tsp. salt

2 tbsp. Marsala or Madeira wine

Prepare the CRUST. In a bowl, combine flour, sugar and salt. Use a fork or pastry blender to work in the butter, until mixture resembles coarse meal. Stir in whole egg and egg yolk (or egg substitute). Add lemon peel and drizzle in the ice water 1 tablespoon at a time, adding just enough cold water for the dough to come together in a ball. Knead dough briefly, on a floured board until smooth. Cover dough with plastic wrap and refrigerate.

Preheat oven to 350°.

Have ready: a buttered 10-inch tart pan with removable sides (rim).

Prepare the FILLING. Using a mixer or food processor, beat ricotta until smooth. Add sugar and flour and beat until smooth. Using a wooden spoon, stir in the egg yolks (or egg substitute), heavy cream, sour cream, vanilla , candied orange peel, sweet wine and salt.

In a separate bowl, beat egg whites (or dried egg white mix) until soft peaks form. Fold whites into the batter.

On a lightly floured board, roll out dough until it is ¼-inch thick. Press dough into the prepared tart pan. Pour in filling. Bake pie in a preheated oven at 350° for 50-60 minutes. Turn off oven; open oven door and leave pie inside for an additional 30 minutes. Serve at room temperature or refrigerated. Store covered in refrigerator if not serving within the day made. Serves 8.

> **SALAD OF ROMAINE, RED ONION AND FIGS IN PARMESAN**
>
> **PARMESAN CHEESE DRESSING (see page 381)**
>
> **STUFFED TURKEY CUTLETS**
>
> **PUMPKIN-TURKEY FRITTERS**
>
> **STEAMED SPINACH**
>
> **PEAR-HAZELNUT CRISP**

SALAD OF ROMAINE, RED ONION AND FIGS IN PARMESAN

4 cups Romaine lettuce, trimmed, rinsed,
   drained, cut into pieces

1 small red onion, finely sliced

4-6 fresh figs (Calimyrna, Brown Turkey or
   Kadota), in season, rinsed and quartered;
   or $1\frac{1}{2}$ cups seedless red grapes,
   rinsed, drained

Parmesan Cheese Dressing (see page 381)

6 plum tomatoes, quartered

$\frac{1}{4}$ cup pignola (pine nuts)

1 cup packaged herbed croutons
   (low-fat available)

$\frac{1}{4}$ cup shredded Parmesan cheese

Prepare Parmesan Cheese Dressing in advance. Refrigerate dressing until 1 hour before serving.

In a large salad bowl, combine Romaine lettuce, red onion, quartered figs, tomatoes and croutons. Sprinkle pignola and Parmesan over salad bowl. Cover lightly with waxed paper and refrigerate until needed. Just before serving, drizzle dressing over salad; toss and serve. Serves 6.

STEAMED SPINACH

1 lb. fresh spinach, trimmed rinsed, drained

a pinch of hot pepper flakes

6 large garlic cloves, halved

salt and freshly ground black pepper

2 tbsp. olive oil

2 tbsp. Parmesan cheese, shredded

Have ready: a large steamer pot with basket; 2 cups water.

Place prepared spinach in basket of steamer pot. Scatter garlic and pepper flakes over spinach. Pour 2 cups water in lower portion of steamer; bring to boil. Turn off heat. Count to 30 seconds. Remove steamer from burner. Count to 30 again. Transfer spinach mix to a serving bowl; drizzle with olive oil; sprinkle with Parmesan; season with salt and pepper. Gently toss and serve while hot. Serves 6.

STUFFED TURKEY CUTLETS
(May be prepared with thin chicken cutlets.)

6 turkey cutlets
2 eggs, beaten or ½ cup egg substitute
1 cup fine corn flake crumbs

1 tsp. ground sage
¼ tsp. freshly ground black pepper

Spread crumbs, pepper and sage on a sheet of waxed paper. Dip cutlets in egg to coat both sides. Coat turkey cutlets with crumb mix. Set aside.

STUFFING:

2 cups packaged, unseasoned corn bread
    for stuffing
½ cup finely chopped deseeded,
    sweet red pepper
½ cup finely chopped, deseeded,
    green bell pepper
1 small Chile pepper, deseeded, minced (Wear
    plastic gloves when handling hot pepper.)

1 celery stalk with greens, finely chopped
1 small onion, finely chopped
¼ cup fresh cilantro, finely chopped
1 cup shredded salami with peppercorns
1 egg, beaten or ½ cup egg substitute
½ cup hot water
1 tbsp. olive oil
freshly ground black pepper to taste

In a large bowl, mix all of the stuffing ingredients to make a moist stuffing. Set aside.

SAUCE:
3-4 cups Marinara Sauce (see page 393);
    or use 1 jar (20 oz.) prepared
    marinara sauce
1 tbsp. Gravy Master

¼ tsp. freshly ground black pepper
1 tbsp. olive oil
2-3 Portobello mushrooms, rinsed, sliced thin

Heat 1 tablespoon olive oil in a 2-quart saucepan. Sauté mushroom slices in oil for 3-4 minutes. Stir in prepared Marinara Sauce, Gravy Master and black pepper. Cover pot and gently simmer sauce for 5 minutes. Keep pot of sauce warm as you continue with recipe.

Preheat oven 375°.

Have ready: a 9x12x4-inch roasting pan. Coat bottom of pan with 2 tablespoons olive oil.
Pour 1 cupful sauce on bottom of 9x12 greased pan. Lay crumb-coated turkey cutlets in pan. Then, spoon about ½ cupful of stuffing in your hands and form a patty for each of the cutlets. Pack the patty firmly on top of each cutlet. Bake the cutlets in preheated oven at 375° for 15 minutes.
Remove pan from oven and pour remaining sauce over each "stuffed" cutlet; continue to roast turkey cutlets for an additional 10 minutes. Serves 6.

PUMPKIN-TURKEY FRITTERS

4 large all-purpose potatoes, pared, cut into
    chunks, boiled for mashing;
    or, use 4 portions instant potato flakes
    (follow directions on package)
1 can (1 lb.) solid pure pumpkin
2 cups cooked turkey, chopped (preferably
    from legs, wings)
2 cups Bisquick
2 eggs, beaten, or $\frac{1}{2}$ cup egg substitute
1 tsp. baking powder

1 tbsp. pumpkin pie spice
    (a blend of cinnamon, nutmeg, allspice,
    ginger, cloves)
$\frac{1}{4}$ cup parsley, minced
$\frac{1}{2}$ tsp. salt
$\frac{1}{4}$ tsp. black pepper
1 tbsp. brown sugar
canola oil for frying

Preheat a large skillet to 300°.
Have ready: a large ovenproof serving platter.
Mash hot boiled potatoes in a large bowl (or, use 4 portions "instant mashed potato" as directed). Empty can of pumpkin into bowl. Add and blend: cooked chopped turkey, Bisquick, baking powder, parsley and all spices. Add beaten eggs and mix thoroughly. Make a fairly smooth batter. Heat $\frac{1}{4}$ inch canola oil in a large skillet to 300°. Drop batter from a large serving tablespoon into the hot oil, frying 3-4 fritters at a time. Turn them over to lightly brown both sides. When cooked, transfer with spatula to paper towels to drain. Arrange them on an ovenproof platter. Keep them warm. Makes about 10-12 fritters. Serves 4-6.

PEAR-HAZELNUT CRISP

CRUMBLE MIX:
$\frac{3}{4}$ cup all-purpose flour
$\frac{1}{2}$ cup dark brown sugar
$\frac{1}{2}$ cup hazelnuts, finely chopped
6 tbsp. butter or Smart Balance spread,
    barely melted (but not hot)

COATING FOR PEARS:
$\frac{1}{2}$ cup granulated sugar
4 tsp. gingerroot, peeled, minced
1 tsp. ground cardamom
2 tbsp. all-purpose flour

6 large pears, cored, sliced thin, vertically
$\frac{1}{4}$ cup lemon juice
Preheat oven to 375°.
Have ready: a 9-inch square baking pan, greased.
Place sliced pears in a large bowl; sprinkle with lemon juice and toss to coat.
Prepare CRUMBLE. Combine flour, brown sugar, nuts in a medium-size bowl; with a fork, stir in melted butter to form large clumps. Set aside. Prepare COATING. Combine sugar, gingerroot, cardamom, 2 tbsp. flour in small bowl. Evenly coat pears with this sugar mix; turn into a greased 9-inch square pan; sprinkle Crumble evenly over top. Bake until golden brown in center of oven at 375° for 45-50 minutes. Serve warm or cool. Cut into 3x3-inch squares. Serves 6.

A THANKSGIVING DAY MENU
TURKEY CHILI SOUP
THANKSGIVING SALAD
APPLE CIDER DRESSING (see page 384)
ROASTED TURKEY WITH STUFFING
BUTTERNUT SQUASH CROQUETTES
GREEN BEANS AND RED PEPPERS AMANDINE
CHOCOLATE PUMPKIN BROWNIES

TURKEY CHILI SOUP

1 pkg. (1 lb.) red kidney beans (Soak beans overnight, in enough water to cover.)
1 turkey leg, 1 turkey wing, rinsed in cold water;
    OR substitute: turkey meatballs and turkey sausage (*NOTE: recipe page 305)

12 cups water
2 tbsp. olive oil
1 large yellow onion, chopped
4 garlic cloves, chopped
1 celery stalk, trimmed, chopped
1 large carrot, pared, chopped
1 can (1 lb.) tomato purée
3 ripe plum tomatoes, chopped
1 large, each: red pepper, green pepper and
    1-2 small Chile peppers, deseeded, chopped
    (Wear plastic gloves when handling hot
    peppers.)

$\frac{1}{2}$ cup brown rice
$\frac{1}{2}$ cup orzo
1 can (20 oz.) red kidney beans, rinsed, drained
1 tsp. salt (or to taste)
$\frac{1}{2}$ tsp. black pepper
2 tbsp. chili powder
$\frac{1}{4}$ cup fresh cilantro, finely chopped
$\frac{1}{4}$ cup fresh cilantro, finely chopped
    (for garnish)

Have ready: one large soup pot with a cover.

Rinse beans and soak them overnight, in enough water to cover. Next day, in a large soup pot, brown onion and garlic in 2 tablespoons olive oil. Scrape bottom of pot to remove leavings. Pour 12 cups water and rinsed turkey parts into the pot. Cover pot and bring to boil. Then, simmer turkey for 45 minutes. Transfer leg and wing to a glass board; remove meat from bones; transfer meat to a plate. (Discard skin and bones.)

To the soup pot, add to combine: celery, carrot, all peppers, chopped tomato and purée, all spices and $\frac{1}{4}$ cup cilantro. Stir in pre-soaked beans. Cover pot and bring to boil; then, simmer for 1 hour, until beans are tender. During last 25 minutes of simmering, add and blend into soup: brown rice and orzo. Continue to simmer soup, stirring occasionally. During last 10 minutes, stir in cooked turkey pieces. Taste soup and adjust spices, if necessary. Garnish with fresh chopped cilantro before serving. This soup freezes well. Serves 8-10. (Continued on following page)

(Continued from page 304)

*NOTE: TURKEY MEATBALLS AND TURKEY SAUSAGE
(An alternate recipe using turkey meat.)

4 links turkey sausage, cut into narrow rounds (Sausages slice smoothly if
    sliced when partially frozen.)

MEATBALLS:

1 lb. ground turkey meat	$\frac{1}{2}$ tsp. salt
$\frac{1}{2}$ cup fine bread crumbs	$\frac{1}{4}$ tsp. black pepper
1 tbsp. finely chopped parsley	1 egg or $\frac{1}{4}$ cup egg substitute
$\frac{1}{4}$ cup catsup	1 tbsp. olive oil
1 tbsp. finely chopped onion	

    In a medium-size bowl combine and blend all ingredients for turkey meatballs except olive oil. Form 1-inch meatballs. Refer to recipe for TURKEY CHILI SOUP. Using the same large soup pot, lightly brown turkey meatballs for a few minutes in hot oil at the same time you brown onion and garlic. (Do not overcook.) Remove meatballs to a plate; set aside. Lightly brown turkey sausage rounds for a few minutes in same pot, adding more olive oil if needed. Remove cooked sausage rounds to plate with meatballs. Add cooked meatballs/sausage rounds to soup during last 10 minutes of cooking soup.

. . . .

THANKSGIVING SALAD

1 lb. mixed salad greens, rinsed, drained	1 large carrot, pared, shredded
1 small head radicchio, trimmed,	1 apple, cored, chopped bite-size
rinsed, drained	$\frac{1}{2}$ lb. bleu cheese, chopped
2 celery stalks, trimmed, chopped	$\frac{1}{2}$ cup glazed walnut halves
1 doz. or more grape tomatoes, rinsed	

Apple Cider Dressing (see page 384)

    Have ready: a large salad bowl.

    Prepare Apple Cider Dressing in advance. Refrigerate dressing until 1 hour before serving. Mix all salad ingredients in a large salad bowl. Just before serving, add dressing; toss to mix thoroughly. Serves 6.

ROASTED TURKEY WITH STUFFING

[A Cooking Hint: Turkey Roasting Time Table is based upon a thawed, stuffed turkey.
For unstuffed turkeys, decrease cooking time by 1 hour.
Always check internal temperature with a meat thermometer.]

Turkey Roasting Times (Internal Temperature: 185° F)

Weight	Approximate Roast Time at 325°	
10-12 lbs.	$3\frac{1}{2} - 4\frac{1}{2}$ hrs.	
12-16 lbs.	$4\frac{1}{2} - 5\frac{1}{2}$ hrs.	Have ready:
16-20 lbs.	$5\frac{1}{2} - 6\frac{1}{2}$ hrs.	a large roasting pan with a rack.
20-24 lbs.	$6\frac{1}{2} - 7$ hrs.	For a 10-12 lb. turkey: 14x18x6-inch pan
24-30 lbs.	$7 - 8$ hrs.	

1 10-12 lb. turkey Remove any enclosed packaged turkey parts from its cavities.
    Rinse turkey with cold water, inside and outside; dry the bird with paper towels.
    Discard immediately paper and parts which you are not using in this recipe.
    Salt and pepper inside the breast cavity. Set turkey on a wood board to rest.

4-5 whole bay leaves
salt
freshly ground black pepper
$\frac{1}{4}$ cup olive oil

STUFFING (Fruit and Nuts Cornbread):

4 cups small-cubed stale cornbread or low-salt
    packaged cubed cornbread
2 cups dried prunes, dates and figs;
    remove any stems
1 cup sweet wine, like Madeira or Marsala
$\frac{1}{4}$ lb. prosciutto, chopped
1 cup pecans, finely chopped
$\frac{1}{4}$ cup olive oil

1 small onion, minced
1 cup Italian parsley, minced
1 cup celery and leaves, finely chopped
$\frac{1}{2}$ tsp. salt, or to taste
$\frac{1}{2}$ tsp. black pepper
2 tsp. dried thyme
1 tsp. each: rosemary, dried sage
$\frac{1}{2}$ cup pkg. low-salt chicken broth

    Prepare the STUFFING. In a saucepan, simmer dried fruit in sweet wine for 15 minutes.
Drain and chop. Place chopped fruit, prosciutto and pecans in a medium-size bowl; set aside.
Heat olive oil in a skillet and sauté onion for 4-5 minutes, until soft. Add parsley, celery, thyme,
rosemary, sage, salt and pepper and cook for 5 minutes. Transfer this mix to a large bowl; add
cubed cornbread, chicken broth and fruit mix and toss to combine. Allow to cool slightly.
Set rack in oven to lowest level. (Continued on following page)

(Continued from page 306)

Preheat oven to 325°.

Then, <u>STUFF the TURKEY</u> loosely with cornbread mix and continue with roasting the turkey. *(OR, if you prefer, bake the stuffing in a 9x12 metal pan or a greased Pyrex casserole at 350° for 20-25 minutes, until lightly browned.)*

<u>ROAST the TURKEY</u>. Set the turkey, breast-side-up, on the roasting rack of a large roasting pan (14x18x6-inch pan for a 10-12 lb. turkey). Allow enough space around the bird to permit heat to circulate. Generously brush the turkey with half of the $\frac{1}{4}$ cup of olive oil; season with salt and pepper and lay 4-5 large bay leaves on its breast and legs. Roast the turkey for 2 hours at 325°. Baste with remaining olive oil; increase oven temperature to 425°. Continue to roast for about 45 minutes longer, or until a meat thermometer registers 185° in the thickest part of the turkey's thigh.
Remove turkey from oven and allow to rest for 15 minutes before carving. Spoon out stuffing to a serving bowl. Serve with pan gravy. (*NOTE: recipe below.) Serves 6.

*NOTE: PAN GRAVY (2 cups)
3 tbsp. all-purpose flour, stirred into $\frac{1}{2}$ cup cold water
2-3 chicken bouillon cubes, mashed into 1 cup boiling water
salt, pepper to taste
$\frac{1}{4}$ cup dry sherry

After the roasted turkey has been transferred from the roasting pan to the carving platter, scrape the leavings from bottom of roasting pan (about 1 cup); stir in another cup of boiling water, into which 2-3 chicken bouillon cubes have been mashed/dissolved. Turn this liquid into a 1-quart saucepan; stir in floured water, salt, pepper and sherry to make about 2 cups or more of smooth pan gravy. Simmer the gravy, stirring until it thickens. Add more sherry, about 2 tablespoons, if gravy is too thick. Serve hot in a gravy boat to accompany carved turkey and stuffing.

BUTTERNUT SQUASH CROQUETTES

2 cups water
4 cups butternut squash, pared, cut into chunks
2 large all-purpose potatoes, pared,
    cut into chunks
1 egg beaten, or $\frac{1}{4}$ cup egg substitute
$\frac{1}{2}$ tsp. salt
$\frac{1}{4}$ tsp. black pepper

$\frac{1}{4}$ cup minced onion
$\frac{1}{2}$ tsp. ground ginger
1 tbsp. minced cilantro
1 cup finely chopped cured ham
$\frac{1}{4}$ cup grated sharp Cheddar cheese

about $1\frac{1}{2}$ cups all purpose flour, to coat
canola or corn oil for frying
powdered ginger for sprinkling

Preheat oil to in a large skillet to 300°.

Have ready: a large pot; a ricer; a large serving spoon; a large skillet.

Bring 2 cups water to boil in a large pot. Add butternut squash and potatoes to boiling water; bring to simmer for 10-12 minutes, or until potatoes are tender. Drain. Transfer vegetables to a large bowl.

Rice cooked, hot potatoes/squash. Add and combine onion, ham, cheese, cilantro, spices and egg. Mix thoroughly. Spread enough flour, at least 1 cup, onto a flat dish, to coat the croquettes.

With the aid of a large serving spoon, scoop the squash mix, and with your floured hands, form croquettes, the size of small, fat knockwurst. Pack the croquettes firmly; then, roll them into the flour to coat all sides.

Fry them, 3 or 4 at a time, on all sides, in preheated oil at 300°. I turn them twice more, to form 3-sided croquettes. Drain them on paper towels and transfer to an ovenproof serving platter. Lightly sprinkle with powdered ginger. If not serving immediately, maintain at room temperature and warm them thoroughly in oven at 250° for 20 minutes before serving. Serves 6.

GREEN BEANS AND RED BELL PEPPER AMANDINE

2 tbsp. olive oil
1 cup water
$1\frac{1}{2}$ lbs. fresh green beans, julienne-cut
1 small onion, finely sliced
2 large red bell peppers, deseeded, finely sliced, vertically
$\frac{1}{4}$ tsp. each: salt, freshly ground black pepper
$\frac{1}{4}$ cup shaved almonds with skins

Preheat 2 tablespoons olive oil to 300° in a 1-quart pot. Brown onion and almonds in oil, about 3-4 minutes. Set aside. Meanwhile, simmer julienne-cut green beans and red pepper slices in 1 cup water for 4-5 minutes, until just tender. Do not overcook. Drain vegetables and pour them into a serving bowl. Stir in salt, pepper and onion/nut mix. Serve warm. Serves 6.

CHOCOLATE PUMPKIN BROWNIES

1 pkg. brownie cake mix (1 lb. 4 oz.)
2 eggs, beaten or $\frac{1}{2}$ cup egg substitute
$\frac{1}{3}$ cup canola oil
$\frac{1}{3}$ cup evaporated milk, fat-free available
1 can (1 lb.) pure pumpkin
1 tsp. pumpkin pie mix (a combination of cinnamon, cloves, ginger, allspice, nutmeg)
1 cup miniature semi-sweet chocolate morsels, divided ($\frac{1}{2}$ cup, $\frac{1}{2}$ cup)

Preheat oven to 350°. (Dark-coated pan: preheat to 325°.)

Have ready: a 9x13-inch cake pan, greased with butter or Smart Balance spread.

Beat eggs, milk, oil, pumpkin and spices. Add and stir in brownie mix, a little at a time. Beat about 50 strokes, until well-blended and smooth. Stir in $\frac{1}{2}$ cup mini chocolate morsels. Pour batter into greased 9x13-inch baking pan. Sprinkle remaining $\frac{1}{2}$ cup mini morsels in vertical lines across the surface of batter.
Bake brownies in preheated oven at 350° for 25-28 minutes, or until inserted toothpick removes clean. Do not overbake. *Cool cake completely* before cutting portions. Then, cut cake *in pan* into small portions. Carefully remove brownies from pan with a spatula. Makes about 2 dozen small pumpkin brownies.

WHITE BEAN MINESTRONE
SALAD OF ARTICHOKE HEARTS, TOMATOES, OLIVES AND FETA
BALSAMIC VINEGAR AND OLIVE OIL DRESSING (see page 376)
LEG OF LAMB AND POTATOES IN OREGANO
A ROCKY ROAD CHOCOLATE CAKE

WHITE BEAN MINESTRONE
(Start this recipe about 8 hours before serving; this soup freezes well.)

1 lb. dried Great Northern or navy beans

2 tbsp. olive oil

1 large onion, chopped

3-4 garlic cloves, chopped

2 celery stalks with greens, chopped

2 carrots, pared, cut into narrow rounds

1 medium zucchini, diced

1 ripe tomato, chopped

10 cups water

1 tsp. salt, or to taste

$\frac{1}{2}$ tsp. black pepper

1 tsp. each: dried oregano, thyme

2 bay leaves

1 can (20 oz.) cannellini beans, rinsed, drained

1 can (1 lb.) corn kernels, rinsed, drained

Have ready: a 6-quart soup pot with a cover; a food processor.

Soak dried beans in cold water, overnight; then, rinse in cold water and drain.

In a 6-quart soup pot, lightly brown onion and garlic in 2 tablespoons olive oil. Add 10 cups of water, prepared beans, celery, carrots, zucchini and tomato. Cover pot and bring to a rolling boil. Reduce heat to simmer soup for 1 hour, and cook beans until tender. Add 1 can each of rinsed cannellini and corn kernels. Stir in herbs and spices. Cover pot and simmer soup for 20 minutes.

Transfer 4 cupfuls of soup solids to a 2-quart bowl. Slightly cool the remainder of the contents in the soup pot. With a food processor, purée the remaining solid contents in the soup pot, returning the purée to the same soup pot. Return and blend the 4 cups of vegetables to the same soup pot. Remove bay leaves and discard. Taste soup and adjust seasonings, as needed. Cover pot and heat thoroughly before serving.

This soup may be frozen in containers for a couple of months. Defrost in refrigerator. Serve hot. Serves 8-10.

SALAD OF ARTICHOKE HEARTS, TOMATOES, OLIVES AND FETA

2 cans (1 lb. each) artichoke hearts in water,
   drained, halved
6-8 ripe plum tomatoes, quartered

1 cup Kalamata olives, pitted
1 small red onion, finely sliced
1 cup feta cheese, chopped

Balsamic Vinegar and Olive Oil Dressing (see page 376)

   Prepare dressing in advance. Refrigerate dressing until needed. Remove dressing from refrigerator one hour before serving. Shake thoroughly before serving.
   Combine all salad ingredients in a large salad bowl. Just before serving, drizzle salad with dressing; toss to mix thoroughly. Serve in individual salad bowls. Serves 6.

LEG OF LAMB AND POTATOES IN OREGANO

4 lbs. all-purpose potatoes, peeled,
   thickly sliced, lengthwise
a 4 lb. boneless leg of lamb,
   rolled and tied, lengthwise
6 large garlic cloves, slivered
½ tsp. salt, or to taste

2 tbsp. dried oregano
1 tsp. peppercorns
2 tbsp. olive oil
juice of 2 lemons
more olive oil, salt, freshly ground black
   pepper, oregano for potatoes

Preheat oven to 300°.

Have ready: a large roasting pan, 13x15x4; a large ovenproof serving platter.

   Cut peeled potatoes in thick slices, lengthwise. Set them aside in a large bowl of cold water. Cut small slits on the surface of the meat. Rub lamb with olive oil; press garlic slivers and peppercorns into the slits. Sprinkle entire roast with salt and oregano. Put potatoes in a large bowl; sprinkle salt, pepper, oregano and olive oil over potatoes; toss to coat .
   Place roast in roasting pan. Pour seasoned potatoes around the meat. Squeeze juice from 2 lemons over entire pan. Roast in preheated oven at 300° for 45 minutes. Occasionally shuffle potatoes as they roast, adding a little water to bottom of pan, from time to time, to ensure pan is never dry.
   Check doneness of lamb with a meat thermometer. Medium-rare at 145°; well-done at 165°. Cook lamb to suit; remove pan from oven; allow to rest for 5 minutes. Slice meat and serve on a platter with roasted potatoes. Serves 6.

A ROCKY ROAD CHOCOLATE CAKE

1 pkg. (22 oz.) devil's food cake mix
1 pkg. (4 oz.) instant chocolate pudding
4 eggs or 1 cup egg substitute
1 cup low-fat mayonnaise
1 cup low-fat milk (fat-free available)
1 cup almonds, chopped
1 cup white raisins
1 cup miniature marshmallows
1 pkg. (6 oz.) semisweet chocolate morsels

confectioners' sugar

Preheat oven to 350°.

Have ready: 1 12-cup Bundt pan, greased and floured; a mixer.

In a small bowl, combine almonds, raisins, marshmallows and chocolate morsels. Set aside. In a large bowl with mixer at low speed, beat together cake mix, pudding mix, eggs, mayonnaise and milk until just blended. Increase speed to medium and beat for 2 minutes. Stir in nut mixture. Pour batter in prepared pan. Bake in preheated oven for 50 minutes, or until tester inserted in center of cake removes clean. Cool cake in pan for 15 minutes. Remove cake from pan; cool on rack. When cake is completely cooled, and just before serving, dust with confectioners' sugar. Serves 8-10.

Celeste and Pals wish Sister Crystal a very "Happy Birthday".
(Are those carrots and Brussels sprouts?) Photo: E. Lopes

TANGY ARUGULA AND BLACKBERRIES SALAD

RASPBERRY VINAIGRETTE DRESSING (see page 383)

SEASHELLS BY THE SEASHORE

STEAMED BROCCOLI

ICE CREAM CAKE (see pages 247, 340)

TANGY ARUGULA AND BLACKBERRIES SALAD

4 cups (about 10 oz.) arugula (rocket), rinsed, drained

1 small red onion, chopped

$\frac{1}{2}$ pint fresh blackberries (or raspberries), carefully rinsed, drained

$\frac{1}{2}$ cup ricotta salata, diced

Raspberry Vinaigrette (see page 383)

Have ready: a large salad bowl.

Prepare Raspberry Vinaigrette in advance. Refrigerate until 1 hour before serving. Blend thoroughly.

Combine arugula, onion, blackberries and ricotta salata in a large salad bowl. If not serving immediately, refrigerate salad. Spoon dressing on salad at serving; toss to coat thoroughly. Serves 4-5.

STEAMED BROCCOLI

Trim and rinse 1 large bunch of broccoli (4-5 stalks with florets). Pour 1 cup water in a steamer with basket. Add broccoli to pot; cover pot and steam broccoli for 4-5 minutes. Transfer to serving dish; drizzle with olive oil; salt and pepper to taste. Serve as a side dish. Serves 4-5.

SEASHELLS BY THE SEASHORE
(Prepare and freeze Stuffed Shells up to 2 weeks before serving.)

1 lb. jumbo pasta shells

2 large eggs, beaten, or $\frac{1}{2}$ cup egg substitute

2 lbs. ricotta

1 tbsp. fresh Italian parsley, minced

8 oz. mozzarella, small dice

$\frac{1}{2}$ tsp. salt, $\frac{1}{4}$ tsp. pepper

$\frac{1}{2}$ cup Parmesan cheese, grated

$\frac{1}{4}$ tsp. ground nutmeg

5-6 cups Marinara Sauce (see page 393)
   Prepare Marinara Sauce in advance; refrigerate; or prepare several weeks in advance and freeze. Thaw in refrigerator for 1 day prior to using.

1 lb. jumbo shrimp in shell, rinsed, drained

1 lb. sea scallops, rinsed, drained

1 tbsp. oregano

3-4 fresh basil leaves

1 can (1 lb.) unseasoned artichokes in water, halved

1 large red bell pepper, deseeded, thinly sliced

6 small-medium white mushrooms, trimmed, rinsed, halved

1 cup Asiago cheese, grated

   Preheat oven to 350°.
   Have ready: an 18x14x3$\frac{1}{2}$-inch roasting pan.
   Parboil jumbo shells as directed on package (about 7 minutes). Drain; rinse with cool water; drain again; set aside. In a 2-quart bowl, thoroughly combine ricotta, diced mozzarella, Parmesan, eggs, parsley and seasonings. Evenly spread 2 cups Marinara Sauce on bottom of a large, deep roasting pan. Stuff each parboiled jumbo shell with 1 tablespoon of cheese mixture. Arrange stuffed shells, side-by-side in one half of the pan.
   Pour 2 cups prepared sauce into a large bowl. Stir in scallops, shrimp in shell, mushrooms, artichokes, red pepper, oregano, basil. Pour the seafood mix into the vacant half of the roasting pan. Spoon remainder of sauce over stuffed shells. Sprinkle Asiago cheese over entire pan. Bake in preheated oven at 350° for 30-35 minutes, or until bubbly. Delicioso! Serves 4-5.

. . . .

ICE CREAM CAKE
(May be prepared and frozen up to 2 weeks in advance.)

See pages 247, 340 for recipes.

   Transfer to refrigerator 15 minutes prior to serving. Refreeze leftovers quickly.
Serves 8-10.

314

GRILLING, BROILING, BARBECUING
[A Cooking Hint: Season meat a couple of hours before cooking it. Then, pat meat dry with paper towels just before grilling or roasting.]

The Home Cook may prepare a meal within 30-60 minutes. Grilling or broiling the entrée with one of the suggested spice rubs or marinades, plus adding a salad and/or one or two sides, creates a tasty meal for one serving or four servings.

Both Grilling and Broiling are "dry-heat" methods of cooking. Cooking heat is conducted through the air from an open flame (Grilling) or a heating element (Broiling). The surface of the food is quickly browned, which helps to intermingle flavors and aromas. The fat literally falls away. Apply one of the suggested marinade/spice rubs to enhance the process of grilling/broiling.

"When to turn the chop, steak or fillet" is the most important technique for the Grill Cook to learn. Those grill marks are awfully attractive when timed correctly. Ideally, the Grill Cook should turn the chop (or steak etc.) *"once"*: grill on one side; turn over once and grill the other side; remove from grill. (Experience teaches best.) The Cook doesn't have the grill marks to concern about when you use the Broiling element in the oven. Nonetheless, the Cook must turn over the chops, steak or fillet, to cook both surfaces of the entrées. When grilling, set the cooking grate about 5 inches over the flame. When broiling, set the cooking rack about 2-3 inches below the heating element.

NOTE: Barbecuing, Grilling or Broiling are related: Barbecuing uses an open flame to cook; however, this method relies on wood or coals to produce the flame. And using a Grill Pan on a grate or stove surface burner is not "grilling", per se. The grill pan is the conductor of the heat; fat remains in the pan with the chops or steak. (Yet, those grill marks sure are good-looking!) An up-to-date MEAT THERMOMETER becomes an invaluable partner for Grill or Broiler cooking.

(Continued on page 316)

(Continued from page 315)

MARINADES AND RUBS FOR LAMB (Based on 4 servings.)

(<u>Accompaniment Suggestions for Lamb</u>: mashed potatoes, grilled asparagus
and a greens salad from this cookbook.)

For Lamb Chops and Kebobs

1.) 2 tsp. olive oil
$\frac{1}{4}$ cup dry vermouth
$\frac{1}{4}$ cup fresh parsley
2 garlic cloves, minced
$\frac{1}{4}$ tsp. salt
$\frac{1}{4}$ tsp. Hungarian paprika
$\frac{1}{4}$ tsp. freshly ground black pepper

Blend oil, vermouth and parsley and brush on both sides of chops. Mix garlic, salt, pepper and paprika; rub on both sides of chops. Grill or Broil on both sides to medium-rare.

2.) 2 tbsp. olive oil
$\frac{1}{4}$ tsp. salt
3-4 bay leaves
$\frac{1}{4}$ cup dry sherry
$\frac{1}{4}$ tsp. freshly ground black pepper

Blend oil and sherry and brush on both sides of chops. Mix salt and pepper and sprinkle on chops. Lay bay leaves over chops. Grill or broil on both sides to medium-rare. Discard bay leaves.

3.) 2 tbsp. olive oil
1 tsp. dried oregano
$\frac{1}{4}$ cup Parmesan cheese, grated
$\frac{1}{4}$ tsp. freshly ground black pepper

Brush lamb with olive oil. Blend cheese, oregano and pepper to coat lamb on all sides.

4.) 2 tbsp. olive oil
Kosher salt to taste
$\frac{1}{2}$ tsp. dried thyme
2-3 garlic cloves, minced
$\frac{1}{4}$ tsp. freshly ground black pepper
$\frac{1}{4}$ tsp. rosemary

Brush lamb with olive oil. Blend garlic, salt, pepper, thyme and rosemary to coat lamb on all sides.

For Lamb Roasts

1.) $\frac{1}{4}$ cup olive oil
$\frac{1}{4}$ cup fresh parsley, chopped
$\frac{1}{4}$ cup peppercorns
$\frac{1}{2}$ cup dry vermouth
6 garlic cloves, slivered
Hungarian Paprika

With a sharp knife, make slits all over the lamb roast. Press slivers of garlic and peppercorn into the slits. In a small bowl mix parsley, oil and vermouth; drizzle over meat; sprinkle with paprika. Roast lamb in preheated oven at 350°, 20 minutes per pound. Check with meat thermometer for doneness. A 4-4$\frac{1}{2}$ lb. boned, rolled and tied lamb will be ready in about 1 hour and 15 minutes for medium-rare.

2.) " Garam Masala" (see page 387). Sprinkle the mix of spices on a sheet of waxed paper. Roll lamb roast into spices to coat. (Continued on following page)

(Continued from page 316)

MARINADES AND RUBS FOR PORK (Based on 4 servings)
(<u>Accompaniment Suggestions for Pork Recipes</u>: roasted sweet potatoes or brown rice, broccoli florets and a salad with added fruit and nuts, from this cookbook.)

For Pork Chops

1.) 2 tbsp. olive oil   1 tsp. brown sugar
   1 tsp. each: onion powder, garlic powder   salt and black pepper
   1 tsp. each: dried oregano, dried basil
   ½ tsp. each: marjoram, rosemary, thyme
Brush pork with olive oil. Blend sugar, spices and herbs. Coat chops with this mix; slow-grill or broil chops on both sides. Internal juices will run clear when cut with knife.

2.) 2 tbsp. olive oil   Kosher salt and black pepper, to taste
   1 tsp. each: garlic powder, crushed sage leaves, mustard powder
   1 bay leaf, crushed
Brush pork with olive oil. Mix spices and herbs and rub on chops. Grill or broil chops on both sides. Internal juices will run clear when pierced with knife.

3.) 2 tbsp. olive oil   juice of 1 lemon
   2 tbsp. fresh dill, chopped   1 tbsp. honey
   ¼ tsp. cracked black pepper   ¼ tsp. Kosher salt   1 tbsp. mustard spread
Brush chops with olive oil and lemon juice on both sides. Blend mustard, honey, herb and spices and spread over both sides of chops. Grill or broil on both sides. Internal juices will run clear when pierced with a knife.

For Fresh Pork Roast

¼ cup olive oil   2 tbsp. balsamic vinegar
¼ tsp. freshly ground black pepper   ¼ tsp. cayenne
2 garlic cloves, minced
1 tsp. each: crushed sage leaves, onion powder, ground mustard
   Brush pork with a mixture of olive oil and balsamic vinegar. Combine rest of ingredients and rub over pork. Roast in preheated oven at 300°. A 4½ lb. boneless rolled pork roast will cook in 2½ to 3 hours. Check with meat thermometer for doneness.

For Roast Loin of Pork (8-10 chops)

¼ cup olive oil   2 tbsp. red wine vinegar
4 tbsp. fennel seeds   1 tbsp. cracked black pepper   ½ tsp. Kosher salt
   Cut halfway between each chop. Baste loin of pork with a mixture of oil and vinegar (baste between chops). Sprinkle with a mixture of fennel seeds, pepper and salt. Roast in preheated oven at 350°. For 4½ lb. pork loin roast, cook 2½-3 hours. Check with meat thermometer for doneness. (Continued on page 318)

(Continued from page 317)

MARINADE AND RUBS FOR BEEF (STEAKS AND ROASTS)
*[A Cooking Hint: When broiling steak or chops, brush both sides
very lightly with olive oil to seal in juices.]*

1.) 2 tbsp. olive oil
$\frac{1}{2}$ tsp. each: freshly ground black pepper, Kosher salt
1 tsp. each: Hungarian paprika, brown sugar
$\frac{1}{2}$ tsp. each: ground cumin, ground coriander
$\frac{1}{8}$ tsp. hot pepper flakes
Rub beef with olive oil. Blend remainder of ingredients and rub over beef. Grill or broil beef on both sides. Check with meat thermometer for desired doneness.

2.) $\frac{1}{4}$ cup dry Sherry   1 tbsp. olive oil
$\frac{1}{2}$ tsp. cracked black pepper $\frac{1}{8}$ tsp. cayenne
1 tsp. garlic powder   1 tbsp. *lite* soy sauce
1 tbsp. balsamic vinegar   1 tsp. honey
Mix all ingredients in a small bowl. Brush on both sides of beef. Grill or broil meat on both sides. Check with meat thermometer for desired doneness.

3.) 2 tbsp. olive oil
1 tsp. each: cracked black pepper, Hungarian paprika
1 tsp. each: onion powder, garlic powder
$\frac{1}{2}$ tsp. each: cayenne, dill weed, ground coriander
$\frac{1}{4}$ tsp. Kosher salt
Brush beef with olive oil. Mix remainder of ingredients and rub over meat. Grill or broil beef on both sides. Check with meat thermometer for desired doneness.

. . . .

PHILLY STEAK
(Use Rub #2 for this recipe.)

2-3 lbs., 1-inch thick flank steak for London Broil
#2 Rub
1 large onion, sliced thin   1 tbsp. olive oil
1 green pepper, cored, deseeded, sliced thin   4-5 ciabatta rolls
Marinate flank steak with Rub #2 for a couple of hours in refrigerator. Meanwhile, sauté sliced onion and pepper in olive oil over medium heat for 4-5 minutes, until lightly browned and tender. Broil steak 2-3 inches away from broiling element for 3 minutes on each side. Or, grill steak 5 inches over coals for 3-4 minutes on each side. Carve $\frac{1}{4}$-inch slices. Smother with sautéed peppers and onions (in oil) and serve in a ciabatta. (Continued on following page)

(Continued from page 318)

SCIVALETTA (LAMB SAUSAGE)
(This Lamb Sausage recipe was developed by Frank Scalavino's family of meat marketers, in the tradition of their Sicilian Italian heritage. We also thank the owners of *Meats Supreme, www.meatssupreme.com* for the following Home Cook's adaptation.)

<u>Recipe makes 10 lbs. thin sausage, LAMB or PORK.</u>

1. Chop 10 lbs. Lamb (from leg) or Pork Butt, using $\frac{3}{8}$-inch plate on chopper.
2. Flatly spread chopped Lamb (or Pork) over mixing table.
3. Season evenly with:
   (.10 lbs.) salt   (.20 lbs.) sharp provolone, cut in small chunks
   (.02 lbs.) black pepper $\frac{3}{4}$ head fresh parsley, rinsed, finely chopped
4. Mix thoroughly with your hands.
5. Using a hand funnel, push mixed and seasoned Lamb (or Pork) into end of pre-flushed Sheep Casing, after it has been secured onto end of funnel.
   Do Not Overfill *casing* or *it will tear.*
6. Form 8-inch or 10-inch rings with sausage in casing.
7. Insert 4.5-inch skewers into 4 opposite sides to secure sausage ring for grilling.
8. *You Are Ready to Grill…*

. . . .

SKILLET CHICKEN

4 boneless, skinless chicken breasts (about 6 oz. each)
2 tbsp. all-purpose flour $\frac{1}{4}$ tsp. salt
$\frac{1}{4}$ tsp. freshly ground black pepper   2 tbsp. olive oil

Have ready: a 12-inch skillet.
First, prepare sauces. Select from the recipes on page 320. Set aside.
Rinse chicken in cool water; pat dry with paper towels. On a sheet of waxed paper sprinkle a mix with flour, salt and pepper. Coat chicken breasts in this mixture. Set aside.
Heat 2 tablespoons olive oil in a large skillet. Add prepared chicken breasts and cook 5 minutes, turning once, until golden on outside and opaque at center. Remove chicken to an ovenproof plate; keep warm in a turned-off, low oven.
Simmer selected sauce in skillet as directed in each Sauce Recipe. Spoon over prepared chicken and serve. Serves 4. (Continued on page 320)

(Continued from page 319)

5 SAUCES FOR SKILLET CHICKEN

1.) Mustard Sauce

$\frac{1}{3}$ cup low-fat sour cream
$\frac{1}{4}$ cup low-sodium chicken broth
$\frac{1}{4}$ cup prepared mustard

$\frac{1}{4}$ tsp. freshly ground black pepper
1 tbsp. fresh dill, minced for garnish

Mix ingredients (except dill) and simmer in skillet for 1 minute. Spoon over prepared chicken breasts; garnish with minced dill. Serve with egg noodles and steamed broccoli spears.

2.) Garlic-Lemon Sauce

$\frac{1}{2}$ cup low-sodium chicken broth
2 garlic cloves, minced
$\frac{1}{4}$ tsp. freshly ground black pepper
1 tsp. capers and 1 tbsp. parsley, chopped- for garnish

2 tbsp. fresh lemon juice
1 tsp. olive oil

Mix chicken broth, garlic and pepper. Simmer in skillet for 2 minutes. Remove skillet from heat; stir in lemon juice and olive oil. Spoon over prepared chicken breasts; garnish with capers and parsley. Serve with brown rice and a tomato salad.

3.) Honey-Orange Sauce

$\frac{3}{4}$ cup orange juice
$\frac{1}{4}$ cup low-sodium chicken broth
1 tbsp. honey

1 tsp. dried rosemary
1 navel orange, peeled, sliced in segments
6-8 scallions, trimmed, sliced

Mix orange juice, chicken broth, honey and rosemary. Simmer in skillet for 2 minutes. Stir in peeled orange segments and sliced scallions; heat through. Spoon sauce over prepared chicken breasts. Serve with couscous and steamed carrot rounds.

4.) Spicy Tomato Sauce

1 can (1 lb.) chopped tomatoes
3 tbsp. cilantro, chopped
1 tsp. chili powder
$\frac{1}{2}$ tsp. ground cumin

$\frac{1}{2}$ cup Jack cheese, shredded, for garnish
$\frac{1}{4}$ cup pimiento olives, sliced, for garnish

Mash chopped tomatoes, cilantro, chili powder and cumin in a bowl. Pour into skillet and simmer for 3 minutes. Pour over prepared chicken breasts. Top chicken with shredded cheese and garnish with sliced olives. Serve with steamed corn on the cob and a greens salad.

5.) Wine Sauce

$\frac{1}{3}$ cup low-sodium chicken broth
$\frac{1}{2}$ cup dry white wine, like Chardonnay
$\frac{1}{4}$ tsp. dried thyme
$\frac{1}{8}$ tsp. freshly ground black pepper

1 tsp. olive oil
4 thin slices prosciutto, shredded,
 (cut with scissors)
4-6 plum tomatoes, chopped

Mix chicken broth, wine, thyme, pepper and oil in a bowl. Pour into skillet and simmer for 2 minutes. Stir in shredded prosciutto and chopped tomatoes. Spoon over prepared chicken breasts. Serve with mashed potatoes and steamed green beans.

(Concluded on following page)

(Continued from page 320)

USDA MEAT TEMPERATURE CHART
(Fahrenheit)

Revised May 24, 2011

(Meat is considered *safe* to consume at these Internal Cooking Temperatures)

BEEF, VEAL, PORK AND LAMB (Roasts, Chops, in thickest part) - 145°
(Allow 3 minutes "rest time" before carving or consuming.)

GROUND BEEF, VEAL, PORK AND LAMB - 160°
(No "rest time" required before consuming.)

CHICKEN, TURKEY - 165°

A Suckling Pig.

Shivaletta (Lamb Sausage).

321

ONLY ONE

Most of my menus have been written as directed for two, four, six servings. Cooking is a science. Recipe ingredients can be increased or decreased to suit a couple or a crowd _most of the time. At the conclusion of each of my recipes, you will find the suggested number of portions that this Cook has assigned to the recipe as printed. (I tend to be generous with my portions.)

On several occasions, especially when I've been Guest Speaker at senior groups, a club member (usually male) has requested that I write a "Cookbook for One". Immediately, my happy, carefree, cookbook-author demeanor collapses. I become tense, concerned, almost grandmotherly. These aren't commendable traits for cooks/authors of cookbooks.

I commence to envision this saddened fellow, alone at his supper table; or worse, sitting (or standing) at his kitchen counter, gazing forlornly and unappetizingly at an unopened can of chicken noodle soup, loaded with 850mg of sodium per serving. Or worse, planning to clamp his jaws on a fast-food greasy burger with over 1000 calories, most of them, fat.

There exists a small number of instructional modern "cookbooks for one". (See footnotes at end of essay.) Many, or most of my hundreds of recipes can easily be revised by the Home Cook to serve only one or two portions. It would be especially challenging if the Cook wished to prepare a stew, or to roast a turkey or an entire meat roast. With a little realistic ingenuity, the roasted turkey or loin of pork could easily be transformed into a turkey leg or a single 1-inch thick loin pork chop-in-bone. You can accomplish "cooking for one" portion of stew by preparing the entire recipe for a stew; removing one or two portions, and freezing the remainder of the stew in separate portions for other suppers. I am "one" at most suppertimes; I wouldn't think of denying myself any of my delicious entrées.

"Salads for One" are the easiest to prepare. There are so many inventive cold or warm salads to create. Grill one chicken cutlet (breaded or not); slice the grilled cutlet and arrange the slices over a greens salad which may also include: sliced tomato; crunchy vegetables like celery or carrot; fruit, such as red grapes or blueberries; and little chunks of creamy cheese _ and nuts. Drizzle a little homemade dressing from your refrigerator stock, and add a slice or two of artisan multi-grain bread.

Soups are best when you prepare for 10-12 portions, and freeze in 4-portion containers. (Don't forget to label the containers.) Defrost one package at a time in your fridge and you can add a delicious soup to your menu of weekly suppers (or lunch), four times a week, on alternating days.

Full-size cakes may be most difficult to prep for one portion. Not to concern yourself. Transform the cake recipe into 6 to 8 large muffins. Refer to a cake mix package to adjust the baking time. Then again, why select a cake for "dessert for one" if you're not giving a party? And a party shouldn't be for "only one".

~~~~~~~~~~~~~~~~

Suggested references for "cooking for one":
"The Pleasures of Cooking For One" by Judith Jones.
"Going Solo in the Kitchen" by Jane Doerfer

After-Dinner Treats

Cheese

Cakes and Pies

Cookies

Desserts and Sweets

The McMahon-O'Moore Families, Fr. Bill and Nancy Lanahan wish you a "Happy Thanksgiving".

THE CHEESE STANDS ALONE

Since ancient times, cheese has been defined as a food consisting of the curd of milk which has been separated from the whey. Although milk from various animals has been used to make cheese, milk from cows, sheep and goats is most common.

To make cheese, *casein*, milk's chief protein, is coagulated by enzyme action, by lactic acid, or by both. The many kinds of cheeses depend for their individual qualities on 1) the kind and condition of the milk, 2) the processes used in their making and 3) the method used and extent of, *curing*.

There are two main kinds of cheeses: *hard cheeses*, which improve with age, and *soft cheeses* which are made for immediate consumption. Hard cheeses include Cheddar (originally from England), Edam and Gouda (Holland), Emmental Gruyere (Switzerland) and Parmesan and Provolone (Italy).

Among the semisoft cheeses are Roquefort (France), American brick and Muenster (France, Germany). Soft cheeses may be fresh (unripened) e.g.: cream and cottage cheese; or may be softened by microorganisms in a ripening process that develops the flavor, e.g.: Camembert, Brie (France) and Limburger (Germany).

Cheese is a valuable source of protein, fat, insoluble minerals and when made from whole milk, vitamin A. The civilized world includes cheese for breakfast, lunch and dinner; as snacks and in desserts. Cheese has been a major food in my own family's Italian heritage. As a child, I had many opportunities to observe my Aunts Catherine and Margaret prepare "Farm cheese", Chevre-like, semi-soft creamy cheese wheels made from raw Jersey cow's milk and cultures, and aged with the aid of a cheese press, molds and cheesecloth.

My family has always considered cheese as a food staple. Our infant son's first word was "Cheese".

The following is a brief encyclopedia of our country's most popular of world cheeses. We can document over 650 different cheeses in the world. Listed are cheeses which I have enjoyed and have included in my recipes. In our modern society, most of these cheeses may be purchased at food specialty shops, international food shops and local super marts.

FYI: Always allow cheese to achieve room temperature before consuming it. And enjoy Wines and Beers with most cheeses. Note: very strong cheeses can mask the flavor of wine. The more acidic the cheeses, the sweeter the wine.

Suggestions:

With Strong Cheeses:	Gewurztraminer	Picolit
	Chateaneuf du Pape	
With Mild Cheeses:	Valpolicella	Claret
	Biancolella	
With Sharp Cheeses:	Sangiovaise	
With Hard Cheeses:	full boded wines like:	
	Tokay and Spanish Sherry	
With Tangy Cheese:	an old Sherry	

CHEESES FROM MANY NATIONS

DANISH CHEESES

BLUE CASTELLO: A blue-veined cheese with a buttery taste. It is rindless; the entire cheese is edible.

CREAM HAVARTI: a delicious, mild, creamy, semisoft cheese, laced with small to mid-sized holes. It is a table and a dessert cheese; serve with fruit and wine. Some Havarti, available with added dill, jalapeño, garlic or herbs.

FONTINA: Danish Fontina is pale yellow, semisoft, with a mild, sweet flavor (a derivative of Italian Fontina). A table cheese and a good sandwich cheese; goes well with a light wine.

SAGA: is a cross between blue cheese and brie. It is a creamy, mild, blue-veined cheese with a white-mold rind. A dessert cheese to be served with fruit and wine. Also used in salads and snacks on crackers.

SAMSOE: a relative of Swiss Emmental, it has a golden yellow color, covered in wax. It is mild and nutty; springy to firm and has scattered large holes.

ENGLISH CHEESES

CHEDDAR: an original English cheese. Fully cured, it is a hard, natural cheese. Comes with an artificial rind (if any). Color ranges from white to pale yellow. (Some cheddars add tint, creating a yellow-orange color.) It is made from cow's milk and has a slightly crumbly texture. Its taste becomes sharper as it matures.

CHESHIRE: one of the oldest English cheeses, dating back to the 12th century. It is firm and more crumbly than Cheddar. It is rich, mellow and slightly salty.

CLOTTED CREAM: it is a thick, rich creamy cheese, to be eaten with a spoon. It's served over fruit (like strawberries), scones, fish and vegetables.

LEICESTER: a natural hard cheese, it is rich though mild, with a flaky texture and a deep orange color. Excellent with fruit and beer.

STILTON: a blue-mold cheese with a rich and mellow flavor and a piquant aftertaste. It has blue-green veins and a wrinkled inedible rind. Milder than Roquefort, it is excellent for crumbling over salads or as a dessert cheese with a Port wine. Called "The King of Cheeses."

WENSLEYDALE WITH CRANBERRIES: made from cow's milk, a mild and crumbly cheese, with added blueberries and cranberries. (Continued on page 326)

(Continued from page 325)

FINNISH CHEESES

FINLANDIA SWISS: similar to Swiss Emmental; aged over 100 days, it is sharp, rindless and delicious. (One of my favorites!)

LAPPI: is a semisoft, semisweet cheese that slices smoothly. Good in recipes and to melt.

FRENCH CHEESES

BLEU d'AUVERGNE: similar to Roquefort but made from cow's milk and not quite as sharp; with blue veins and a tangy, spicy flavor of grasses and wild flowers.

BOURSIN (GOURNAY): a soft, spreadable natural cow's milk cheese, flavored with garlic, herbs, pepper or fruits.

BRIE: is the best known French cheese. Brie was one of the "tributes" which French subjects had to pay to their kings. Hence, Brie becomes known as "The Queen of Cheeses". "Real" French Brie is very different from the cheese exported to the United States. French Brie is unstabilized and is at its peak of flavor when the surface turns lightly brown. Stabilized Brie has a much longer shelf life and is not susceptible to bacteriological infections. As long as this cheese is pure white, it is not mature. Cutting unstabilized Brie before it is ripe will stop the maturing process; thus, the cheese will never develop properly. Exported Brie is stabilized and never matures. Brie is a great dessert cheese. It's exported as either a 1 or 2 kilogram wheel and is packaged in a wooden box. Brie should be served at room temperature.

CAMEMBERT: a soft-ripened white mold cheese. It is soft and creamy with an edible crust (like Brie).

CHANTAL: a French cheddar, although it is milder and less acidic than cheddar.

CHAUMES: made from cow's milk, this tangerine colored cheese is creamy and mild like butter, with a gold rind.

CHEVRES: made from goat's milk. These cheeses come in varied sizes and shapes: round patties, logs, drums, pyramids, etc.; their textures vary from soft, but firm like cream cheese, to very hard. They're excellent dessert cheeses or as snacks and used in cooking.

EMMENTAL: similar to Swiss Emmental. (See SWISS CHEESES)
(Continued on following page)

(Continued from page 326)

MUNSTER: is one of the few cheeses which ripen from the inside out. It is dark yellow with a strong flavor. Best served with dark bread and beer. Very different from domestic Munster which is a white, mild cheese.

PORT SALUT: a mild and pleasant dessert or table cheese, originally made by the Trappist monks. It is creamy and butter-like; yet firm enough to slice and goes well with fruit and light wine. Genuine Port Salut has an edible orange rind; imitations use a plastic, inedible rind.

ROQUEFORT: the most famous blue-mold cheese in the world. Made from sheep's milk, it comes from caves near the Spanish border. It is sharp and piquant. The blue mold is added to the curd by mixing it with powdered bread containing the Penicillium Roquefort mold. A dessert cheese in France, Americans prefer it in salads or dips.

VACHERIN MONT d'OR: a seasonal cheese, made from winter milk of cows who are brought down from their pastures for the season. A runny, gooey soft cheese with an inedible rind, can be spooned and spread. Used as a dessert cheese or as its own sauce.

GERMAN CHEESES

BAVARIAN BLUE: is crumbly and lightly acidic; excellent to add to salads.

BUTTERKASE: a mild, creamy cheese, perfect for sandwiches.

EMMENTAL: a similar characteristics as Swiss Emmental: (See SWISS CHEESES)

LIMBURGER: a soft-ripened cheese with a pungent odor. It has a thin crust, soft white texture. Processed constantly with brine. Goes well with red wine or beer.

TILSIT: a natural semi-soft cheese with a strong flavor and tiny holes. Good for slicing as a sandwich cheese. A robust wine or beer accompanies well.

GREEK CHEESES

FETA: is made from sheep's milk and has a strong, acidic flavor. Its texture is crumbly and white in color. Feta must be covered in a brine at all times; otherwise it will dry out and mold quickly. Used as an eating cheese and as a topping.

GRAVIERA: from Crete; it is made from sheep's milk. A firm, oily cheese, with a sweet taste of olives. (Continued on page 328)

(Continued from page 327)

HOLLAND CHEESES

EDAM: is a semisoft to hard matured cheese, depending on age. It is similar in flavor to Gouda, yet dryer and less creamy. Shaped in balls, the cheeses are coated in red, yellow or black wax.

GOUDA: is a semisoft to hard natural cheese, depending on age. It's pale yellow and slightly sweet and nutty. A very popular world cheese, serve it as a table cheese and a dessert cheese, with fruit and wine.

LEYDEN: is a bland part-skim, semi-soft to hard cheese, laced with caraway or cumin seeds.

SMOKED GOUDA: is a hardy cheese with an edible brown rind and a creamy, yellow interior which is slowly smoked in brick ovens. It comes shaped like a sausage and is a convenient snacking cheese. Great with beers.

IRISH CHEESES

CHEDDAR: similar to English CHEDDAR. (See ENGLISH CHEESES)

DUNBARRA: a soft, creamy cheese with an edible white rind.

KERRYGOLD DUBLINER: an aged cheese with a sweet, nutty flavor. Good to melt in sandwiches and to grate over pasta. Accompany with a rich stout.

ITALIAN CHEESES

ASIAGO: made from cow's milk in region of Veneto, Italy. Delicate taste when fresh; spicy and savory when aged.

CACIOCAVALLO: a hard cheese which is made from cow's milk throughout Italy. Usually shaped into a pear with upper end tied; the rind is thin and smooth; its color, white or straw.

FONTINA: a firm whole-milk slicing cheese made in Italy's Val d'Aosta. Its flavor is delicate, milky and slightly nutty. This cheese is easy to melt and is popular for fondues and au gratin dishes.

GORGONZOLA: a buttery, soft, blue-veined cheese (made with mold spores, Penicillium glaucum) with a pungent aroma; not as salty as bleu cheese. Made in Lombardy and Piedmont, Italy. (Continued on following page)

(Continued from page 328)

GRANA PADANO: a hard cheese from the Po Valley in Italy. It's an eating and a grating cheese with a pungent aroma, yet delicate flavor.

MASCARPONE: a thick cheese, like clotted cream; used mostly in desserts.

MOZZARELLA di BUFALA: a fresh, elastic cheese made from buffalo milk and cow's milk, and produced in various shapes. From Campania, Italy, it is sometimes Smoked (affumicata).

PARMESAN: a hard grating cow's milk cheese, used mostly as a grated cheese for topping.

PARMIGIANO REGGIANO: a hard cheese made from whole milk in the region of Emilia-Romagna. It is essential in Italian cuisine; good for grating.

PECORINO ROMANO: a hard cheese produced exclusively from sheep's milk in Latium and Sardinia, Italy. The taste has a piquant flavor and it is used as an eating or a grating cheese.

PECORINO SICILIANO: a hard compact cheese with a hearty aroma. It's made from sheep's milk in Sicily, Italy. Used for eating or grating.

PROVOLONE: produced throughout Italy, this is a hard cheese made from cow's milk and shaped in various oval and round forms; mild or sharp; smoked provolone is also available.

RICOTTA: made from whey collected from making other cheese and re-cooked. It is white, creamy and milky like cottage cheese; used in all parts of the meal, from appetizers to dessert.

RICOTTA SALATA: made when fresh Ricotta goes through its natural aging process; a firm pungent cheese suitable for eating or grating results. It is almost white in color.

SCAMORZA: this "drawn-curd" cheese from Molise, Abruzzo and Tuscany, can be plain or smoked. It is best served fresh, as it quickly hardens with age.

STRING CHEESE: an "accidental" cheese which is universally enjoyed. Legend has it that in a cheese factory in Naples, when mozzarella was first made, curds accidentally fell into a pail of hot water and took the form of string-like strips. Usually, made from sheep's milk, it is peelable and when peeled, forms into strings (or strips) from a larger cheese. (Continued on page 330)

(Continued from page 329)
NORWEGIAN CHEESES

GJETOST: a hard cheese made from goat's milk. It has a sweet caramel taste and is deep tan in color. This is a dessert cheese and should be sliced paper-thin. Enjoy in place of candy.

JARLSBERG: "Baby Swiss"; it has the consistency, texture and hole formation of Swiss Emmental; its flavor is nuttier and sweeter. Used as table cheese, dessert cheese or in sandwiches. Good with wine or beer.

SWEDISH CHEESES

GRADDOST: very mild, creamy and tasty. Laced with small holes; it makes an excellent dessert cheese and goes well with fruit and wine.

HERRGARDOST: a pale yellow cheese, shaped into wheels and has a few small holes. Similar to Gouda.

VASTERBOTTEN: a rich, full-flavored, dry-textured, celebration cheese, it is a tangy, bittersweet, hefty cheese made in 40-pound wheels.

SPANISH CHEESES

AFUEGA'L PITU: an ancient cow's milk cheese from Austurias, it's a soft cheese made by lactic coagulation and molded by hand in a conical shape.

CABRALES: a renowned Spanish blue cheese from Austurias. It's made from a blend of raw cow's, goat's and sheep's milk. It has a creamy texture and an earthy and powerful aroma and taste. Enjoy with a fruity red wine.

GARROTXA: a semisoft cheese made from pasteurized goat's milk, with a grey rind and a nutty flavor.

MANCHEGO: from La Mancha region, it's made from pasteurized sheep's milk and has a salty, nutty flavor. Cheese is white or pale yellow and has a grayish rind and a spread of holes.

NAKED GOAT: made with raw goat's milk; a simple aged cheese, rich, creamy and full-bodied.

RONCAL: a hard beige cheese with a grayish rind from Navarre. It is made from sheep's milk and has a rich, oily and nutty flavor. (Continued on following page)

(Continued from page 330)

SWITZERLAND CHEESES

EMMENTAL: most commonly referred to as "Swiss Cheese", it's a creamy cow's milk cheese with large holes, which are created in the process of fermentation. It is a much copied cheese. It is used as a table cheese, fondue dessert cheese and a sandwich cheese.

GRUYERE: made from cow's milk, it is a hard cheese, similar to Emmental, but with a smaller hole formation. It has a chewy texture and develops tiny cracks as it ages. Traditionally, a Fondue cheese, it is also an excellent sandwich cheese and melts evenly for fondues.

RACIETTE: is a mild pale yellow hard cheese with an inedible crust and a firm texture. A good melting cheese.

TILSITER: a natural cheese with a rich Swiss flavor. It is enjoyed melted; or chunked and served with beer.

USA CHEESES

BRICK: an old Wisconsin brick cheese with a nutty and tangy taste.

CHEDDAR: similar to English Cheddar.

COLBY: a bland, mild and mellow cheese with a lightly sweet taste. Good for shredding or melting and used in recipes.

MONTEREY JACK: has a semisoft texture with a bland flavor. When young, it is often blended with jalapeños or herbs. As it ages it develops a rich, savory flavor and can be grated.

VERMONT CAMEMBERT: a pale yellow, mild and creamy cheese with a moldy rind. As it ages, it turns yellow-orange and develops more body and an earthy flavor.

BIBLIOGRAPHY

Cheeses.com
CONCISE COLUMBIA ENCYCLOPEDIA (Columbia U. Press)
EHOW.com
Hugh Johnson's POCKET ENCYCLOPEDIA OF WINE, Fireside
igourmet.com
wikipedia.org
WINES OF ITALY, Sheldon Wasserman, Stein and Day

AFTER-DINNER TREATS

Additional *DESSERT RECIPES*

from ALL ARE WELCOME TO THIS TABLE
(Dinner Menus)

FONDUES
("They're Ba-a-a-ck!")

<u>Suggestions for Entertaining with FONDUES</u>

Use a wooden spoon to stir the FONDUE.

Recommended Brandies and Wines: Kirsch, Cognac, dry White Wines,
Applejack, Dry Sherry, Madeira, Lager Beer.

Use only natural cheeses, not pasteurized.

Stock your Breadbasket with Crusty 1-inch cubed Italian or French Breads,
Rye and Pumpernickel Breads, Artisan breads with seeds and Dried Fruits.

Serve each guest a heat-proof handled fork. Spear the bread on the soft side;
dip bread into the well-heated cheese mixture.

Serve Fondues with Fresh Fruits. Fruit selections of Avocados, Bananas, Apples,
dipped into lemon juice, or other citrus juices, will prevent discoloration of the fruit.

Serve Fondues with an accompaniment of whole Cranberry Sauce or Applesauce.

Most important: Never allow the Fondue to boil or burn.

- -

FONDUE (as an Appetizer)

1 lb. Gruyere (or Emmenthaler) cheese; or a combination of both, coarsely shredded
1 garlic clove, minced
1 tsp. cornstarch
½ cup Kirsch
2 cups Sauterne or Sherry
1 tsp. powdered nutmeg

    Blend shredded cheese and minced garlic in a medium-size bowl. Blend Kirsch and cornstarch in another small bowl. Set both bowls aside. Pour Sauterne in a medium-size saucepan and heat uncovered, over moderate-high. When wine in saucepan shows tiny bubbles on its surface and starts to foam, add shredded cheese, mixed with minced garlic, a little at a time, stirring continuously. *Do not allow the Fondue to boil.* Continue to add cheese until you feel a slight resistance to the spoon as you stir. While continuing to stir the pot, slowly add Kirsch mixture until mix thickens; stir in nutmeg.
    Transfer Fondue to a heat-proof heavy pan and place the fondue pan over a warming candle in a metal base; or in a fondue pot; or in a chafing dish; or electric skillet (on low heat). Serve with a breadbasket of cubed Italian or French bread. (Continued on page 334)

(Continued from page 333)

SANTA FE FONDUE

2 cups Spanish Sherry
1 lb. Cheddar cheese, shredded
1 small jalapeño, deseeded, minced (Wear plastic gloves when handling hot peppers.)
½ cup Brandy
1 tbsp. fresh cilantro, minced
1 tbsp. prepared salsa

Heat Sherry in a medium-size pot uncovered, over moderate-high heat. When wine bubbles and becomes foamy, add shredded Cheddar and minced jalapeño a little at a time, stirring continuously. *Do not boil.* Continue to add cheese until you feel a slight resistance to the spoon as you stir. As you stir the cheese mixture, and as it thickens, add Brandy, cilantro and salsa. Transfer Fondue to a fondue pot over a warming candle; or to a chafing dish; or to an electric skillet (on low heat). Serve with tortilla chips, taco chips.

FONDUE IN THE ALPS

1 lb. Fontina, Gruyere or Bleu cheese, finely chopped
1 scallion, minced
1 tsp. cornstarch
1 tsp. cinnamon
½ cup dry Sherry
2 cups Lager Beer

Blend chopped cheese with minced scallion in a medium-size bowl. In a small bowl, blend cornstarch and cinnamon into Sherry. Set aside. Pour Lager Beer into a medium-size saucepot, and heat uncovered, over moderate-high. When liquid shows tiny bubbles on the surface and begins to foam, gradually add the cheese mix, stirring continuously. *Do not allow Fondue to boil.*
Continue to add cheese until you feel a slight resistance to the spoon as you stir, until mixture thickens. Stir Sherry mixture into the Fondue. Transfer Fondue to a fondue pot to set over a warming candle; or a chafing dish; or an electric skillet (on low heat). Serve with cubed pumpernickel bread, hearty rye bread and chunks of soft pretzels. (Continued on following page)

(Continued from page 334)

FONDUE (as a Dessert)

CHOCOLATE FONDUE

$\frac{1}{2}$ cup heavy cream (a little more if Fondue is too thick)
12 oz. dark chocolate, chopped, or morsels
1 tbsp. liqueur, like: Amaretto, Kahlua, Bailey's Irish Cream, Grand Marnier

Pour cream into a 1-quart saucepan and simmer over medium heat. Do not boil. Add chocolate in small batches, stirring until melted, before adding next batch. When all chocolate is incorporated, add liqueur. Be sure to cook over moderate heat and *do not allow chocolate to boil.* (This type of Fondue can easily burn.) If Fondue becomes too thick, add additional cream, one tablespoon at a time. Stir gently to incorporate. Transfer Fondue to a fondue pan or a chafing dish over a warming candle in a metal base; or a small electric skillet (on low heat). Serve with any or all of the following: strawberries, banana chunks, dried apricots, fresh apple slices, pretzel rods, biscotti.

CHOCOLATE MOCHA FONDUE

6 oz. dark chocolate, chopped, or morsels
$\frac{1}{4}$ cup low-fat evaporated milk
2 tbsp. coffee
$\frac{1}{4}$ cup tiny marshmallows
$\frac{1}{2}$ tsp. Rum

Combine all ingredients in a saucepan, over hot water (a double boiler arrangement). Stir chocolate mixture until smooth. Turn off heat. Transfer sauce to a fondue pan or a chafing dish over a warming candle in a metal base; or a small electric skillet (on low heat). Serve with banana chunks, pineapple spears, navel orange slices, cubes of pound cake.

A 50th College Reunion.

PIE CRUST RECIPES
*[A Cooking Hint: When pre-baking pastry crust, place another
pie pan directly on the crust in its pan.]*
RICH PASTRY

$\frac{3}{4}$ cup chilled unsalted butter
   or Smart Balance spread, diced
$2\frac{1}{4}$ cups all-purpose flour
2 tbsp. granulated sugar

1 large egg or $\frac{1}{4}$ cup egg substitute
(1 tbsp. grated lemon rind) optional

Combine chilled, diced butter (or Smart Balance), flour and sugar in a bowl. Use a pastry cutter or cut with 2 knives until mixture has texture of coarse meal. Beat in egg (or egg substitute); work with a fork or your fingers until smooth. Form into a ball; wrap in waxed paper (or plastic wrap) and refrigerate for 1 hour, until firm. Cut dough in half. Roll each half on a floured pastry board to prepare bottom and top crust for 1 pie. You may wish to use top half of pastry shell as a lattice-crust top. In that case, with a pastry cutter, cut 1-inch strips of pastry dough in crisscross on top of fruit pie. Proceed as directed in Pie Recipe. Makes: pastry for 9-inch, 2-crust pie.

SPICY APPLE PIE
(Prepare Pie Crust in advance. See above recipe for top/bottom pie crusts
for a 9-inch Rich Pastry Crust.)

FILLING:

4 cups apples, peeled, cut into $\frac{1}{2}$-inch slices,
   discard pits
   (Suggestions for Apple Variety):
   Granny Smith, Greening, Cortland,
   Empire or a combination of varieties.
$\frac{1}{2}$ cup raisins, soaked in 2 tablespoons
   rum for 30 minutes

$\frac{1}{2}$ cup walnuts
3 tbsp. cornstarch
$\frac{1}{2}$ cup brown sugar
2 tbsp. lemon juice
2 tbsp. combined: cinnamon, nutmeg,
   allspice, cloves

Preheat oven to 400°.
In a large bowl combine all ingredients for apple pie filling. Allow fruits, nuts and spices to stand for 10 minutes. Stir to mix, again.
Since you have prepared pie crust in advance, roll $\frac{1}{2}$ of prepared dough ball on a floured board. With a pastry crimper or a pastry wheel, cut out a10-inch circle of rolled dough for bottom crust, to fit into a 9-inch pie pan.
Wrap the rolled dough around the rolling pin and unroll it onto the 9-inch pie pan. Gently fit the dough into the pan with your floured fingers, allowing for a 1-inch edge of dough around the pan. Fill and pack the crust-lined pan with the apple mixture, pressing the apples into place.
Roll out the top crust onto the floured board, to form a 10-inch circle. With a sharp knife or a pastry wheel, cut 10 1-inch strips of dough. Arrange 5 strips across the filled pie pan, going from east to west; then, criss-cross the remaining 5 strips to go from north to south. Pinch and press the pastry edges of the lower crust and top lattice together. Sprinkle latticed top crust with granulated sugar. Bake pie in center of preheated oven at 400° for 10 minutes. Lower temperature to 350° and continue to bake pie for 25-30 minutes, or until bubbly, and crust is lightly browned. Serve warm or at room temperature. Serve pie portions, each with a wedge of Cheddar cheese (optional).
Serves 6-8.

PLAIN PASTRY CRUST

*[A Cooking Hint: When pre-baking pastry crust, place another pie
pan directly on the crust in its pan.]*

½ cup butter or Smart Balance spread   ¼ tsp. salt

2½ cups all-purpose flour   5 to 7 tbsp. ice water

   Add butter (or Smart Balance) to flour mixed with salt. Use a pastry cutter or cut with 2 knives until mixture has texture of coarse meal. Add ice water. Form into a ball with hands; if dough crumbles, add 1-2 tablespoons water. Knead on floured board until smooth. Wrap dough ball in waxed paper or plastic wrap and chill in refrigerator for 1 hour or longer. Then, proceed as directed in recipe. Makes pastry for a 9-inch, 2-crust pie.

BLUEBERRY PIE

(Prepare pie crust in advance. See recipe (above) for top/bottom pie crusts
for a 9-inch Plain Pastry Crust.)

FILLING:

2 pts. blueberries, rinsed, thoroughly drained;   confectioners' sugar for garnish
   gently pat blueberries with paper towels   ¼-½ cup blueberries, rinsed,

1 cup granulated sugar   drained, patted dry

1 tbsp. lemon juice

2 tbsp. cornstarch or small pearl tapioca

   Prepare pie crust in advance. Cut dough ball in half; roll ½ of prepared dough on a floured board to make a 10-inch circle to fit into a 9-inch pie pan with a 1-inch fluted edge.
   Combine filling ingredients and pour into the crust-lined 9-inch pie pan, spreading the filling evenly across the bottom of the pan.
   Roll out top crust with remaining half of dough ball. Wrap the circle of dough around the rolling pin and unroll the dough over the fruit-filled pie pan. Join the top and bottom crusts by pinching edges of crust together with your fingers; or use a pastry crimper. With a small knife, cut a large letter "B" in center of top crust.
   Bake pie in center of preheated oven at 400° for 10 minutes; lower temperature to 350° and continue to bake for 20-25 minutes until crust starts to brown. Serve warm or at room temperature. Serves 6-8.

Suggestions:

   1) After pie is baked and thoroughly cooled, and just before serving, sift confectioners' sugar over entire top surface of pie crust. Pour blueberries over top center of pie.

   2) Or, at serving, add a small ball of Vanilla Bean ice cream along side each pie portion.

BASIC PASTRY CRUST FOR TARTS (SWEET PASTRY DOUGH) (PASTA FROLLA)

SINGLE CRUST: 9-inch tart pan with
  removable fluted sides.
$1\frac{1}{3}$ cups all-purpose flour
3 tbsp. granulated sugar
$\frac{1}{2}$ tsp. salt
grated rind of 1 lemon or 1 orange

1 stick ($\frac{1}{2}$ cup) cold unsalted butter
  or Smart Balance spread, cut into bits
1 large egg, lightly beaten
  or $\frac{1}{4}$ cup egg substitute
1 tsp. vanilla extract
($\frac{1}{4}$ cup puréed almonds) optional

In a bowl, whisk together: flour, sugar, salt, rind and blend in the butter (or Smart Balance), until mix resembles coarse meal. Add egg (or egg substitute) and vanilla and thoroughly mix together until egg is incorporated. Turn the mixture onto a floured board and knead dough lightly with your hand to distribute egg. Form a disk. Chill dough wrapped in plastic, for at least 1 hour or overnight. Allow dough to stand at room temperature until softened to roll. Roll out dough $\frac{1}{8}$-inch thick on a floured board. Fit dough into a 9-inch tart pan with a removable rim, and crimp the edge. *Chill the pie shell for 30 minutes before filling.*

CHERRY ALMOND TART

1 recipe for single-crust sweet pastry (see above)
$\frac{1}{2}$ cup cherry preserves
3 large eggs or $\frac{3}{4}$ cup egg substitute
$\frac{1}{4}$ cup granulated sugar

1 pkg. (7 oz.) almond paste
$\frac{1}{2}$ cup flour
$\frac{1}{2}$ cup sliced almonds
(confectioners' sugar for dusting tart, optional)

Preheat oven 350°. Spread cherry preserves on bottom of prepared single crust "pasta frolla". In a bowl with an electric mixer, beat eggs (or egg substitute) until foamy; gradually beat in granulated sugar. Crumble almond paste into egg mixture and beat egg mixture until well combined. Fold in flour thoroughly, but gently. Spread this mix evenly over preserves; sprinkle with sliced almonds. Bake the tart in lower portion of preheated oven at 350° for 35-40 minutes, or until golden, and firm in center. Allow to cool in pan on a rack for 10 minutes. Remove rim; let tart cool completely on the rack. Dust with confectioners' sugar, if desired. Serves 6-8.

DOUBLE-CRUST PASTA FROLLA

$2\frac{1}{2}$ cups all-purpose flour
$\frac{1}{3}$ cup granulated sugar
$\frac{1}{2}$ tsp. salt
freshly grated rind of 1 lemon or 1 orange

$1\frac{1}{2}$ sticks cold unsalted butter or $\frac{3}{4}$ cup
  Smart Balance spread; cut into bits
1 large whole egg, plus 1 egg yolk ;
  or $\frac{1}{2}$ cup egg substitute
1 tsp. vanilla extract

In a large bowl whisk together: flour, sugar, salt, rind and blend in butter (or Smart Balance), combining the mixture until it resembles a coarse meal. In a small bowl, whisk together whole egg and yolk (or egg substitute) and vanilla. Add egg mixture to flour mixture and toss until egg is incorporated. Turn mixture onto a floured board and knead lightly with your hand. Form dough into 2 disks, one slightly larger than the other. Chill dough, wrapped in plastic, for at least 1 hour or overnight. Allow to stand at room temperature until softened but still firm enough to roll. Makes 2 crusts; good for cheese-filled pastry cakes with top crust.

PUSH-PASTRY PIE SHELL

*[A Cooking Hint: When pre-baking pastry crust, place another
pie pan directly on the crust in its pan.]*

$1\frac{1}{2}$ cups sifted all-purpose flour
$1\frac{1}{2}$ tsp. granulated sugar
$\frac{1}{2}$ tsp. salt

$\frac{1}{2}$ cup canola oil
2 tbsp. cold low-fat milk

Sift dry ingredients into a 9-inch pie pan. Combine canola oil and milk in a small bowl. Whip with whisk until thickened and creamy. Sift flour, sugar and salt into a 2-quart bowl. Pour whipped oil/milk mixture over flour mixture. Mix with a fork until flour is completely dampened. Press dough evenly and firmly with fingers to line bottom of pan; then press dough to line sides of pan, to partly cover rim of pan. Press dough to uniform thickness over the pan.

To flute edge: pinch dough lightly with fingers. *(Always use a low-fluted edge, or the dough-edge will collapse upon baking.)* Makes one 9-inch crust.

Baking Directions:

1) For "Unbaked Shell": Fill as desired; bake in preheated oven at 400° for 10-15 minutes; then reduce temperature to 350° and bake until done. Good for fruit pies.

2) For "Baked Shell": Prick entire surface of pie shell; bake in preheated oven at 425° for 12-15 minutes or until golden brown. Good for ice cream pie or pre-cooked pudding pies or refrigerator-set pies.

. . . .

CREAM PUFFS

(Recipe contributed by Enid Lopes.)

1 cup boiling water
1 cup all-purpose flour, sifted
$\frac{1}{2}$ cup corn oil
$\frac{1}{2}$ tsp. salt
4 eggs, unbeaten
confectioners' sugar for garnish

Suggestions for FILLING:
1 pint heavy cream, sweetened and
    whipped stiff; 1 pint ice cream; prepared
    packaged (3 oz.) pudding or custard mix

Have ready: a large ungreased cookie sheet.

Prepare or Ready the FILLING. Refrigerate prepared pudding or custard; keep ice cream frozen; whip heavy sweetened cream in stiff peaks and refrigerate.

Prepare the PUFFS. Bring 1 cup of water to a boil in a large saucepan. Reduce heat to simmer; add oil, salt and sifted flour all at once. Cook the mixture on medium heat, stirring vigorously with a wooden spoon, until batter leaves sides of pan and forms a compact ball. Remove from heat to cool slightly.

Add eggs, one at a time, beating after each addition, until mixture is smooth and glossy. Drop batter by tablespoons, 2 inches apart on *ungreased* cookie sheet. Bake in preheated oven at 400° for 45 minutes, until puffs are light and dry. Thoroughly cool puffs before filling. Cut open and add filling of choice. If filling with ice cream, freeze filled puffs until serving; or refrigerate filled whipped cream/custard/pudding puffs until serving. Dust puffs with confectioners' sugar at serving. Makes about 8 large or 12 medium puffs.

POUND CAKE

[A Cooking Hint: Always be sure to remove even the tiniest trace of egg yolk from separated egg whites that are to be beaten. Even a smallest bit of yolk can prevent whites from beating stiffly.]

4 egg whites beaten stiff, or use 4 portions of dried egg whites and follow directions on package for egg white reconstitution
1 cup butter or Smart Balance spread
1 cup granulated sugar
4 large egg yolks or 1 cup egg substitute

1 tsp. vanilla extract
2 cups all-purpose flour
$\frac{1}{4}$ tsp. cream of tartar
$\frac{1}{4}$ tsp. salt
optional additions: 1 cup raisins, 1 cup mini chocolate chips, 1 cup chopped walnuts

Preheat oven to 325°.
Have ready: a 9x5 loaf pan, greased and floured.

Cream butter (or Smart Balance) with sugar in a large bowl. Beat in egg yolks (or egg substitute), one at a time. Blend in vanilla. Add flour mixed with cream of tartar and salt, a little at a time. Fold in whipped egg whites. Optional additions (raisins, chocolate chips, nuts), may be added at this time. Pour batter into the prepared pan. Bake in center of preheated oven at 325° for 1 hour or until top is golden and inserted toothpick removes clean. Remove from pan and cool. Serves 8.

....

ICE CREAM CAKE
(Freeze up to 2 weeks.)

1 Pound Cake (5x8x3) (See recipe above; or use packaged pound cake.)
1 quart Neapolitan ice cream (or any flavors you desire); cut into 1-inch slices,(about 6-8 slices)

$\frac{1}{2}$ cup strawberry preserves
$\frac{1}{2}$ cup chocolate syrup or 1 cup crushed Oreos
1 pt. heavy whipping cream, whipped into stiff peaks with 2 tbsp. confectioners' sugar
Shavings from 1 small bar of chocolate

Have ready: one 9x12 freezer-proof serving tray, lined with a paper doily; electric mixer to whip cream.

Whip the cream with 2 tablespoons confectioners' sugar until stiff peaks form. Set aside in refrigerator. Slice pound cake into 2 layers lengthwise. Place bottom layer on a freezer-proof serving platter lined with a paper doily. Spread layer with strawberry jam. Layer with 3-4 slices of ice cream, 1-inch thick, to fit the pound cake. Place second pound cake layer on top of ice cream and spread with chocolate syrup or crushed Oreos. Layer with 3-4 remaining slices of ice cream. Then, frost the ice cream cake with prepared whipped cream. Sprinkle with chocolate shavings. Freeze cake for several hours. Wrap frozen ice cream cake in plastic wrap and continue to freeze until needed, up to 2 weeks. Serves 8.

SPONGE CAKE

[A Cooking Hint: Use substitutes to fit health needs: use egg whites or egg substitute for whole eggs. NOTE: However, in baking some cakes or pastries, whole eggs perform better; especially sponge cake batters.]

(Makes two 8-inch layers; or one 10-inch tube cake. Layers are excellent for strawberry or berry short cakes.)

1 cup cake flour

$\frac{1}{2}$ tsp. salt

1 cup granulated sugar, divided

1 tsp. baking powder

1 tsp. water

1 tbsp. fresh lemon juice, strained

1 tbsp. grated lemon rind

6 large eggs, at room temperature, separated

confectioners' sugar for garnish, if desired

Preheat oven to 350°.

Have ready: an electric mixer; two 8-inch ungreased pans; or one 10-inch tube pan, ungreased.

Sift cake flour, salt, $\frac{1}{3}$ cup sugar and baking powder into a small bowl. Combine water, lemon juice and rind into another small bowl.

Beat egg yolks in a medium-size bowl for 7-8 minutes until pale yellow and thick. Gradually add $\frac{1}{3}$ cup sugar to egg yolks alternating with lemon juice/water mixture, beating well after each addition. Using a rubber spatula, fold sifted flour mixture into the egg yolks about 1 tablespoon at a time. Do not overbeat.

With an electric mixer, beat egg whites in a clean large bowl until foamy. Gradually add remaining $\frac{1}{3}$ cup sugar and continue beating until whites form stiff, shiny peaks. Carefully, fold the egg yolk mixture into beaten egg whites.

Pour batter into 2 ungreased 8-inch pans or a 10-inch tube pan. Bake 8-inch pans for 25-30 minutes and bake tube pan for 40-45 minutes, in center of preheated oven at 350° until top is golden brown and slightly rounded and inserted toothpick returns clean. Remove pan(s) from oven and cool cake completely in the pan and on a wire rack (before removing cake from pan). Garnish tube cake with confectioners' sugar, if desired. Serves 8.

STRAWCHERRY SHORT CAKE WITH WHIPPED CREAM

2 sponge cake layers (see recipe on page 341); or use packaged layers
1 cup cherry preserve
1 quart (2 lbs.) fresh strawberries, rinsed, drained, patted dry
    (Reserve 1 dozen strawberries with stems intact.)
1 dozen fresh cherries with stems
2 tbsp. Kirsch or Chambord (optional)
1 pt. heavy cream for whipping, 2 tbsp. confectioners' sugar;
    or 12 oz. tub of non-dairy topping (low-fat available)

Have ready: a large glass serving plate, lined with a paper doily; an electric mixer.

If using whipped cream, pour heavy cream into a large bowl. Sprinkle confectioners' sugar, 1 tablespoon at a time over cream and beat at high speed until soft peaks form and hold their shape. Set aside.

Lay one sponge cake layer on a plate with a doily. Spread layer with 1 cup cherry preserves; thinly slice 8 prepared strawberries (without stems) and arrange them over the preserves. Sprinkle with Kirsch and place the other sponge cake layer over cream and preserves. Spread entire cake with whipped cream (or non-dairy topping). Garnish top of cake with whole stemmed strawberries and stemmed cherries. Refrigerate cake until serving. Serves 8.

A Variation of this PARTY CAKE:

FOURTH-OF-JULY CREAM CAKE (Red, White & Blue)
<u>Ingredients</u>: Add 1 cup blueberries, rinsed, drained to the preserves between layers. Sprinkle ½ cup blueberries over cream-frosted cake; garnish with stemmed strawberries and cherries.

Eva Feeds Goats.

CHOCOLATE BERRY-CREAM CELEBRATION CAKE
[A Cooking Hint: Use substitutes to fit health needs. Use canola oil, Smart Balance spread in baking or cooking when recipe calls for butter, or other oils which contains trans fats.]

For 2 9-inch layers:

1 pkg. (22 oz.) devils food cake mix

$1\frac{1}{3}$ cups low-fat or fat-free milk;

    (or 1 cup low-fat or fat-free milk plus $\frac{1}{3}$ cup strawberry

    or cherry liqueur)

3 large eggs or $\frac{3}{4}$ cup egg substitute

$\frac{1}{2}$ cup canola oil

FILLING and FROSTING:

1 cup cherry (or strawberry preserves)

6 large fresh strawberries, rinsed, drained, patted dry with paper towels, sliced

1 pint heavy cream, whipped into peaks;

    (or 12-oz. container whipped topping, fat-free available)

1 doz. or more large fresh strawberries with stems, rinsed, drained, patted dry

    with paper towels

1 doz. fresh Bing cherries with stems

$\frac{1}{2}$ cup prepared chocolate Fruit Dip

Preheat oven to 350°. (If using dark-coated pans, preheat oven to 325°.)

Have ready: 2 9-inch metal or Pyrex layer cake pans, greased and lightly dusted with flour.

Prepare cake mix as directed on package. Pour cake mix in a large bowl. Beat in milk (and liqueur), $\frac{1}{2}$ cup canola oil and 3 large eggs, one at a time (or egg substitute). Beat at medium speed for 2 minutes. Pour into 2 prepared 9-inch pans and bake in center of preheated oven at 350° for 30-33 minutes, or until toothpick inserted into center of cake removes clean. Cool in pan on wire rack for 15 minutes. Frost cake when thoroughly cooled.

When ready to frost, lay bottom layer on a doily-lined cake plate. Spread top of bottom layer with 1 cup preserves; add a layer of sliced strawberries over preserves; top with second layer. Frost top and sides of cake with whipped topping. Garnish top of cake with stemmed cherries and stemmed strawberries. Dip 6-8 strawberries into chocolate Fruit Dip before using as garnish. Refrigerate until serving. This luscious cake serves 8-9.

DOUBLE CHOCOLATE CHERRY CAKE

*[A Cooking Hint: When selecting eggs for a recipe (cake, cookies, pies),
use large-size eggs, unless specified.]*

1 pkg. (22 oz.) chocolate cake mix
$\frac{1}{2}$ cup canola oil
1 cup low-fat milk
3 large eggs or $\frac{3}{4}$ cup egg substitute
$\frac{1}{3}$ cup Cherry Heering liqueur
    or cranberry-cherry juice

FROSTING:
1 can (1 lb.) prepared dark chocolate fudge
    frosting mix
$\frac{1}{2}$ cup dark chocolate, finely chopped
1 dozen fresh Bing cherries, pitted,
    chopped for filling
1 dozen fresh Bing cherries, with stems,
    for garnish

Preheat oven to 350°.

Have ready: 2 8-inch round baking pans, greased and lightly floured; a 12-inch cake plate lined with a paper doily.

In a large bowl, blend cake mix, milk, liqueur (or juice), oil and eggs (or egg substitute) at low to medium speed; then, beat for 2 additional minutes at medium speed. Pour batter into prepared pans and bake in center of preheated oven at 350° for 35-38 minutes, or until inserted toothpick at center of cake removes clean.

Cool in pan on rack for 15 minutes. Cool completely before frosting. When ready, place one layer on doily-lined serving plate. Spoon $\frac{1}{2}$ cup canned frosting into a small bowl and stir in chopped cherries. Spread over bottom layer. Place top layer over prepared bottom layer. Frost entire cake with remainder of dark chocolate frosting. With your hands, pat chopped chocolate around sides of cake. Garnish top of cake with fresh stemmed Bing cherries. Refrigerate cake if not serving within the day it was made; or wrap in plastic and freeze cake *(without cherries garnish)* up to 1 week; garnish defrosted cake just before serving. Serves 6-8.

Enjoying and performing at Mary and Lou's 50th Anniversary. Photo: B. and L. Sansone

FROSTED CHOCOLATE BRICKLAYER'S CAKE

[A Cooking Hint: Use substitutes to fit health needs; substitute low-fat or fat-free sour cream or yogurt instead of whole milk or cream.]

1 cup butter or Smart Balance spread
$3\frac{1}{2}$ oz. dark chocolate, chopped
$\frac{2}{3}$ cup water
$2\frac{1}{2}$ cups all-purpose flour
2 tsp. baking powder
$1\frac{2}{3}$ cups light brown sugar
$\frac{2}{3}$ cup low-fat sour cream
2 eggs, beaten or $\frac{1}{2}$ cup egg substitute

FROSTING:
7 ounces dark chocolate, chopped
6 tbsp. water
3 tbsp. light cream or evaporated milk
   (fat-free available)
1 tbsp. butter, chilled

Preheat oven to 375°.

Have ready: a 9x12-inch cake pan, greased; then line the base with baking parchment.

Prepare the CAKE. In a saucepan, melt butter, chocolate and water over low heat, stirring frequently. Sift the flour and baking powder into a mixing bowl and stir in the sugar. Pour the hot chocolate liquid into this bowl and beat thoroughly, until all of the ingredients are evenly blended. Stir in sour cream, followed by beaten eggs. Pour the batter into a greased and parchment-lined 9x12-inch baking pan and bake cake in preheated oven at 375° for 40-45 minutes, or until inserted toothpick remove clean. Allow cake to cool in pan before turning it out onto a wire rack. Cool completely.

Prepare the FROSTING. Melt chocolate with water in a saucepan over very low heat. Stir in cream. Remove pan from heat. Stir in chilled butter; then, pour frosting over the cooled cake, using a spatula to spread it evenly over the top of the cake. Serves 8.

Mary and Lou celebrate their 50th Anniversary Party. Photo: B. and L. Sansone

CARROT CAKE

2 cups all-purpose flour

2 tsp. baking powder

$1\frac{1}{2}$ tsp. baking soda

1 tsp. salt

2 tsp. cinnamon

2 tsp. nutmeg

$\frac{1}{2}$ tsp. cloves

2 cups granulated sugar

$1\frac{1}{2}$ cups canola oil

4 eggs or 1 cup egg substitute

2 cups carrots, pared, grated
  (about 2-3 large carrots)

1 can (8 oz.) crushed pineapple with juice

$\frac{1}{2}$ cup walnuts, chopped

$\frac{1}{2}$ cup semi-sweet chocolate morsels

CREAM CHEESE FROSTING:

2 oz. ($\frac{1}{2}$ stick) butter or Smart Balance spread, softened at room temperature

1 pkg. (8 oz.) low-fat cream cheese, softened at room temperature

1 tbsp. vanilla extract

1 box (1 lb.) confectioners' sugar, sifted

$\frac{1}{2}$ cup walnuts, finely chopped

Preheat oven to 350°.

Have ready: a 9x12-inch baking pan, greased with butter (or Smart Balance).

Prepare CAKE. In a large bowl, sift together: flour, baking powder, baking soda, salt, cinnamon, nutmeg and cloves. Set aside.

In another large bowl, mix together: sugar, oil, eggs (or egg substitute), carrots and pineapple (with juice). Add the flour mix, a little at a time, to the egg mixture and combine thoroughly. Fold in nuts and chocolate chips. Pour batter into the prepared pan and bake for 35-45 minutes, or until an inserted toothpick removes clean. Cool the cake completely before removing from pan.

After the cake has thoroughly cooled, Prepare FROSTING. Cream together in a large bowl: butter (or Smart Balance), cream cheese and vanilla, until free from lumps. Add confectioners' sugar, a little at a time and beat until smooth. Spread frosting on top of cooled carrot cake. Garnish with finely chopped walnuts. Serves 8-10.

Cats at Supper.

CHEESECAKES FOR A CROWD
(These mini-cheesecakes are a grade school party-time favorite.)

GINGER CHEESE:

18 ginger snaps

18 dark chocolate Kisses (remove foil)

2 8 oz. pkg. cream cheese, softened
    (low-fat available)

$\frac{3}{4}$ cup granulated sugar

2 eggs or $\frac{1}{2}$ cup egg substitute

1 tbsp. frozen orange juice concentrate

1 tsp. vanilla extract

1 pt. heavy cream for whipping;
    or 1 pt. non-dairy whipped topping

$2\frac{1}{2}$-inch paper liners to fit into cups
    of cupcake/muffin pans

Preheat oven at 375°.

Have ready: cupcake/muffin pan(s) with $2\frac{1}{2}$-inch cups.

Place 18 paper liners in cupcake pan(s). Fit 1 ginger snap and 1 dark chocolate Kiss at the bottom of each liner. In a bowl, beat together with an electric mixer: softened cream cheese, sugar, eggs (or egg substitute), orange juice and vanilla.

Spoon cream cheese mixture into liners. Bake cupcakes in preheated oven at 375° for 20 minutes or until set. Refrigerate until serving. At that time beat whipping cream until peaks form; garnish each cupcake with a spritz of whipped cream. Refrigerate until serving. Makes 18 ($2\frac{1}{2}$-inch) mini-cheesecakes.

....

BERRY CHEESE:

18 vanilla wafers

2 8 oz. pkg. cream cheese (low-fat available)

2 eggs or $\frac{1}{2}$ cup egg substitute

$\frac{1}{2}$ cup granulated sugar

2 tsp. vanilla extract

2 cups Cherry or Blueberry Pie Filling

1 pt. heavy cream for whipping;
    or 1 pt. non-dairy whipped topping

$2\frac{1}{2}$-inch paper liners to fit into
    cupcake/muffin pans

Preheat oven to 375°.

Have ready: cupcake/muffin pan(s) with $2\frac{1}{2}$-inch cups.

Place 18 paper liners into cupcake pan(s). Fit 1 vanilla wafer into each muffin cup. In a bowl, combine cream cheese, eggs (or egg substitute), sugar, vanilla; with electric mixer, beat at medium speed for 5 minutes, until thoroughly blended. Spoon cream cheese mixture over each wafer to $\frac{1}{4}$-inch from tops of cups. Bake cupcakes in preheated oven at 375° for 12-15 minutes. Cool. Spoon fruit pie filling over each mini cheesecake. Refrigerate until serving. At serving time, beat whipping cream into peaks; garnish each fruit-cheesecake with a small dollop of whipped cream. Makes 18 ($2\frac{1}{2}$-inch) mini Berry Cheesecakes.

PARTY CUPCAKES (with FROSTINGS)

LEMON CUPCAKES
1 pkg. (18.25 oz.) lemon cake mix
1 cup low-fat (or fat-free) milk
$\frac{1}{4}$ cup lemon juice

$\frac{1}{3}$ cup canola oil
3 large eggs or $\frac{3}{4}$ cup egg substitute
1 tbsp. grated rind of 1 lemon

CHOCOLATE CUPCAKES
1 pkg. (18.25 oz.) chocolate cake mix
$1\frac{1}{3}$ cups low-fat (or fat-free) milk
$\frac{1}{2}$ cup canola oil

3 large eggs or $\frac{3}{4}$ cup egg substitute
($\frac{1}{2}$ cup mini semi-sweet chocolate morsels)

STRAWBERRY CUPCAKES
1 pkg. (18.25 oz.) white cake mix
1 cup low-fat (or fat-free) milk
$\frac{1}{3}$ cup white grape juice

$\frac{1}{2}$ cup canola oil
3 large eggs or $\frac{3}{4}$ cup egg substitute
$\frac{1}{2}$ cup ripe strawberries, rinsed, drained, mashed

CUPCAKE DECORATIONS:
dark chocolate nonpareils, jelly beans, spice drops, chocolate morsels, M&M's,
   fresh blueberries and strawberry halves, etc.

3 dozen mini cupcake paper liners for mini cup-size pans.
(Continued on following page)

Jim and Stella Sansone and Family at the Sansone Farm, Hopewell, NJ. Photos: J. Sansone

(Continued from page 348)

FROSTINGS:
CHOCOLATE CREAM CHEESE FROSTING (Makes 2 cups)
3 oz. semi-sweet chocolate morsels, melted over hot water; use a small double boiler
    or 2 small pots
3 oz. cream cheese, softened
$\frac{1}{4}$ cup low-fat milk or evaporated milk
2 cups confectioners' sugar

Combine melted chocolate into cream cheese; stir in milk to make a smooth mixture; gradually add 2 cups confectioners' sugar. Spread on tops of cooled cupcakes. Garnish with candies.

LEMON ICING (or: ORANGE ICING) (Makes 1 cup)
2 cups sifted confectioners' sugar
1 tbsp. melted butter (or Smart Balance spread)
1 tbsp. grated lemon rind (or orange rind)
$\frac{1}{4}$ cup lemon juice (or orange juice)

Blend all ingredients in top portion of double boiler. Insert pot into lower pot of boiling water; stir and cook over heat for 10 minutes. Remove top pot from heat and beat icing with electric beater until cooled and of good spreading consistency.

OR: use packaged prepared, ready-to-use frosting.

INSTRUCTIONS:
Preheat oven to temperature as stated in directions on cake mix package, usually 350°.
Follow directions on packages of cake mixes, using ingredients as stated in recipes (on page 348); include special additional ingredients.
Follow baking temperature instructions on package of cake mixes, usually 350°.
Line mini-cupcake pans with paper cupcake liners.
Fill each cup $\frac{1}{2}$-full with batter.
Baking time differs with size of cupcakes. At 350°, mini cupcakes should ready in 10 minutes; cupcakes are baked when centers are firm and an inserted toothpick removes clean. (Or, you may bake mini cupcakes at a lower temperature of 325° for 15-18 minutes. This is the usual suggested baking time for regular size cupcakes on cake mix packages.)
Cool cupcakes completely before frosting.
Frost and garnish cupcakes as directed in recipes, above.
Transporting cupcakes will be easier if you return/insert frosted cupcakes to *cleaned* cupcake pans, after frosting (do not remove paper liners).
1 box of cake mix can serve 30-36, 2-inch "mini"- cupcakes.

LEMON POPPY SEED CUPCAKES

1 pkg. (22 oz.) yellow cake mix
3 eggs or $\frac{3}{4}$ cup egg substitute
1$\frac{1}{3}$ cups low-fat milk
$\frac{1}{2}$ cup canola oil
1 tsp. lemon extract
1 tbsp. lemon rind, gratcd
2 tbsp. poppy seeds

LEMON ICING:
1 cup sifted confectioners' sugar
a few tablespoons fresh lemon juice
> Smoothly blend 2 tablespoons (or more) lemon juice into confectioners' sugar. Consistency should be like a soft, runny paste. Drizzle and spread icing over each cupcake. Icing will harden slightly.

Preheat oven to 350°. (If using dark-coated pans, preheat to 325°.)
Have ready: greased cupcake pans (for small cupcakes); or use paper cupcake liners.
Combine cake mix with milk and oil. Beat at medium speed for 2 minutes; stir in extract, grated rind and poppy seeds until thoroughly blended. Spoon into prepared greased cupcake pans, $\frac{3}{4}$-filled. Bake at preheated oven at 350° for 10 minutes, or until toothpick inserted in center of cupcake removes clean. Frost with Lemon Icing or dust with confectioners' sugar at serving. Serves about 16-20 small cupcakes, depending on size.

PUMPKIN-CHOCOLATE CHIP CUPCAKES

1 pkg. (22 oz.) yellow or chocolate cake mix
1 cup low-fat milk
3 eggs or $\frac{3}{4}$ cup egg substitute

1 can (1 lb.) pure pumpkin
8 oz. tiny chocolate morsels
1 tsp. pumpkin pie spice

Preheat oven to 350°. (If using dark-coated pans, preheat to 325°.)
Have ready: greased cupcake pans (for small cupcakes); or use paper cupcake liners.
Combine cake mix, eggs, milk, pumpkin and spice. Stir in tiny chocolate morsels. Beat at medium speed for 2 minutes, to make a smooth batter. Spoon into prepared greased cupcake pans and bake in preheated oven at 350° for 10 minutes, or until inserted toothpick removes clean. Makes 16-20 small cupcakes, depending on size. Frost with Lemon Cream Cheese Frosting.

LEMON CREAM CHEESE FROSTING

1 cup sifted confectioners' sugar
1 tsp. grated lemon rind
$\frac{1}{4}$ tsp each: ground cinnamon, nutmeg

5 oz. low-fat cream cheese
1 tsp. lemon extract

In a small bowl, blend cream cheese with confectioners' sugar until smooth and creamy. Stir in and blend lemon extract and rind and spices. Spread over tops of cupcakes.

(Continucd on following page)

350

(Continued from page 350)

PUMPKIN CUPCAKES WITH CREAM CHEESE FROSTING

1 box (22 oz.) yellow or chocolate cake mix
1 can (1 lb.) pure pumpkin
1 cup low-fat milk

3 eggs or $\frac{3}{4}$ cup egg substitute
1 tsp. pumpkin pie spice

Preheat oven to 350°. (If using dark pans, preheat oven to 325°.)
Have ready: greased cupcake pans (for small cupcakes); or use cupcake liners.

Combine cake mix, pumpkin, eggs, milk and pumpkin pie spice. Beat at medium speed for 2 minutes, to make a smooth batter. Spoon into prepared greased cupcake pans and bake in preheated oven at 350° for 10 minutes, or until inserted toothpick removes clean. Makes 16-20 small cupcakes, depending on size. Frost with Lemon Cream Cheese Frosting, (see page 350); or Chocolate Cream Cheese Frosting (see page 349).

PECAN-PUMPKIN CHOCOLATE MARBLE LOAF

[A Cooking Hint: Use substitutes to fit health needs; substitute apple sauce or pure pumpkin for added moisture and no additional fat.]

1 pkg. (18.5 oz.) yellow cake mix
$\frac{3}{4}$ cup low-fat milk
   or low-fat evaporated milk
2 large eggs, beaten or $\frac{1}{2}$ cup egg substitute
$\frac{1}{2}$ cup canned pure pumpkin

1 tsp. pumpkin pie spice mix
   (or a blend of cinnamon, nutmeg,
   cloves, allspice)
$\frac{1}{2}$ cup semi-sweet chocolate morsels
$\frac{1}{2}$ cup pecans, chopped

Preheat oven to 350°.
Have ready: a 9x13-inch cake pan or "Edge" pan, greased with butter or Smart Balance spread and dusted with flour.
Combine cake mix, eggs (or egg substitute), milk, pumpkin and spices and beat until smoothly blended. Remove $1\frac{1}{2}$ cups of batter to a small bowl; stir in chocolate morsels. Pour and evenly spread pumpkin batter in prepared 9x13 pan. Spoon chocolate morsels-pumpkin batter over pumpkin batter in pan, in 2 vertical lines across length of the pan. With a knife or pastry spatula, cut chocolate morsel batter into pumpkin batter.
Sprinkle entire surface of batter in pan with chopped pecans. Bake in preheated oven at 350° for 28-30 minutes, or until inserted toothpick remove clean.
Do not overbake. Cool cake completely in pan before removing. To serve: cut portions when cake is completely cooled. Serves 12-15 portions.

RASPBERRY-YOGURT CAKE
[A Cooking Hint: Do not pre-sift flour unless specified in recipe.]

1 cup plain yogurt

$1\frac{1}{2}$ cups confectioners' sugar

3 large eggs or $\frac{3}{4}$ cup egg substitute

$\frac{1}{4}$ cup butter, or Smart Balance spread, melted

2 cups sifted all-purpose flour

1 tbsp. grated orange or lemon rind

1 tsp. baking powder

TOPPING:

$2\frac{1}{2}$ cups granulated sugar

$3\frac{1}{2}$ cups water

1 tbsp. lemon or orange juice

1 cup heavy cream for whipping

2 tbsp. pistachio nuts, ground

2 cups fresh raspberries, mashed

GARNISH:

whipped cream

$\frac{1}{2}$ pint fresh raspberries, gently rinsed, drained, patted dry with paper towels

Preheat oven to 350°.

Have ready: a 9x9-inch baking pan, greased with butter or Smart Balance spread; dusted with flour.

Prepare BATTER. In a large bowl, beat together: yogurt and confectioners' sugar. Gradually, beat in eggs (or egg substitute), butter (or Smart Balance spread), flour and grated rind; beat until smooth. Add baking powder; beat as gently and lightly as possible. Pour batter into prepared pan and bake in preheated oven at 350° for 40-45 minutes.

Prepare TOPPING while cake bakes. Combine sugar, water and lemon (or orange) juice in a saucepan. Boil, stirring, until sugar is dissolved. Then, simmer frosting for 10 minutes longer, without stirring. Remove pan from heat; cover.

When cake is done, remove pan from oven; cut cake into squares or diamonds. Pour hot syrup over cake a little at a time, so that all of the syrup is absorbed. Cover cake and cool for several hours.

Just before serving, whip the cream. Sprinkle ground nuts over cake. Place portions of cake on a large serving dish; top each portion with a dollop of whipped cream and a spoonful of mashed raspberries. Add a spoonful or two of whole raspberries. Serves 6.

CHOCOLATE PUMPKIN FRUITCAKE BONBONS

1 lb. chopped candied fruitcake mix

1 lb. light raisins

$\frac{1}{2}$ cup finely chopped walnuts

$\frac{1}{2}$ cup finely chopped almonds

$\frac{1}{2}$ cup finely chopped pecans

$\frac{1}{2}$ cup finely chopped dark chocolate

1$\frac{1}{2}$ cups all-purpose flour

$\frac{1}{4}$ cup dark cocoa

$\frac{1}{4}$ tsp. each: allspice, cinnamon, baking soda

3 large eggs, or $\frac{3}{4}$ cup egg substitute

1 can (1 lb.) pure pumpkin

3 tbsp. dark rum

$\frac{1}{2}$ tsp. almond extract

$\frac{1}{4}$ cup canola oil

$\frac{1}{2}$ cup granulated sugar

$\frac{1}{2}$ cup dark brown sugar

candied cherry halves, for garnish

$\frac{1}{4}$ cup brandy

Happy Birthday to Jane. Photo: C. Smaldone del Gais

Preheat oven to 275°.

Have ready: Greased mini cupcake tins with enough cups for 45-48 mini fruitcake bonbons. Insert *foil* liners into greased cups.

In a large bowl, combine chopped fruitcake mix, chopped chocolate, raisins, chopped nuts and $\frac{1}{2}$ cup flour; toss to coat fruit, nuts and chocolate. Set aside. Sift remainder of flour with allspice, cinnamon, baking soda and cocoa; set aside.

In a small bowl, beat eggs at medium speed until light and fluffy. Beat in pumpkin, rum and almond extract. In a large bowl, beat sugars with oil at medium speed until fluffy. Beat in egg mixture. Beat in flour and spices mixture until batter is well combined. Turn batter into the large bowl with fruits, nuts and chocolate. Toss to combine thoroughly.

Spoon and pack batter into mini cupcakes lined tins, about 2 tablespoons per bonbon. Garnish each bonbon with a candied cherry-half. Bake on middle rack of preheated oven at 275° for 25-30 minutes, or until firm, and inserted toothpick removes clean. Remove tins from oven. Sprinkle $\frac{1}{4}$ cup brandy over the bonbons.

Allow the bonbons to cool completely. Remove them from tins to airtight containers; or to foil-lined boxes, 9x15x3. Store in a cool place to ripen for 2 weeks. Serve with brandy. Makes about 4 dozen bonbons.

CHOCOLATE KAHLUA STRAWBERRY MOUSSE
[A Cooking Hint: Unused egg white may be kept frozen in a covered
container for 4-5 months.]
(Prepare early on serving day or on day before.)

1 pkg. ladyfingers

6 oz. semisweet chocolate morsels

1 tbsp. each: Kahlua and Chambord
   (or Cherry Heering)

6 egg yolks, beaten,
   or $1\frac{1}{2}$ cups egg substitute

6 egg whites, or 6 portions dried egg whites,
   like *Just Whites*; (follow instructions on
   package to reconstitute the egg whites)

a pinch of salt and 2 tbsp. granulated sugar

$1\frac{1}{4}$ cups heavy cream, beaten into stiff peaks,
   or 12 oz. low-fat whipped topping

1 pt. heavy cream, whipped into peaks,
   or 1 cup low-fat whipped topping,
   for garnish

12 or more fresh large strawberries, rinsed,
   drained, patted dry with paper towels

Have ready: a small double boiler, or 2 small pots to fit into each other;
or a small metal bowl to fit into a small pot. A large decorative glass bowl.

Line around the edge of a large decorative glass bowl with ladyfingers. Rounded sides of
ladyfingers should be displayed through the bowl. Set aside.

Add chocolate morsels into top half of double boiler (or small metal bowl). Fit the pot of
chocolate over a pot of simmering water; stir chocolate until melted. Remove from heat and stir
in liqueur. Set aside to slightly cool. In a separate bowl, whip heavy cream to medium stiff
peaks; set aside. In another bowl, whip egg whites (or 6 portions dried egg whites) with a dash of
salt, until soft peaks form. Gradually sprinkle sugar into the whites and continue to beat to stiff
peaks. Fold in beaten egg yolks (or egg substitute). Fold in melted chocolate until completely
incorporated; then, fold in whipped cream until evenly blended. Spoon the mousse into a large
decorative glass bowl lined with ladyfingers. Chill mousse until firm, about 2 hours. Just before
serving, garnish with whipped cream and strawberries. Keep refrigerated until serving.
Serves 6-8.

A Tea Party at the Library. Photo: Michelle Mascolo

TRIFLE WITH ME

[A Cooking Hint: Peel and individually wrap bananas that are a little too ripe, in aluminum foil, and freeze. The results resembles ice cream. You may dip frozen bananas in chocolate sauce and roll them in chopped nuts; and then, refreeze them, for a real treat.]

½-inch slices pound cake or sponge cake (see recipe for POUND CAKE page 340;
    see recipe for SPONGE CAKE page 341)
¼ cup sherry
½ lb. fresh strawberries, rinsed, drained, patted dry with paper towels
½ cup sliced almonds
4 fresh peaches (in season), halved; or 2 navel oranges, peeled,
    each cut into ½-inch slices (remove pith)
2 bananas, sliced into narrow rounds
2½ cups low-fat milk or low-fat evaporated milk
4 egg yolks from large eggs or 1 cup egg substitute
½ cup granulated sugar
¼ cup cornstarch
1½ cups heavy whipping cream or low-fat whipped topping
2 tbsp. brandy

Have ready: a large glass "trifle bowl".

Arrange 5 slices pound cake (or sponge cake) at bottom of a large glass bowl; trim corners of cake to fit neatly. Sprinkle cake with half of the sherry. Spread sliced strawberries on top. Layer remaining slices of cake over the strawberries, and sprinkle with remaining sherry. Spread almonds over the cake and top with remaining strawberries. Arrange peach halves (or orange slices) over the strawberries. Top with sliced bananas.
    In a medium-size saucepan, pour milk and bring to a boil. Remove from heat and set aside. In a bowl, whisk together: egg yolks (or egg substitute) and sugar. Add slightly cooled milk and cornstarch, whisking to thoroughly combine. Return this mixture to the saucepan and cook over low heat for about 10 minutes, stirring continuously, until the custard thickens. When the custard is thick enough to coat the back of a spoon, remove it from the heat, still stirring. Allow custard to cool slightly. Pour custard over fruit and cake. Chill the trifle in the refrigerator for several hours.
    Whip heavy cream with brandy until soft peaks form. Spread cream over top of trifle (or pipe through a pastry bag with a large tip). Chill the trifle until ready to serve. Serves 4-6.

PIGNOLA COOKIES
(Carol Colantuono Bonura's recipe is the "very best in the whole world".)

$\frac{1}{4}$ lb. pignola (pine nuts)
$1\frac{3}{4}$ cups granulated sugar
1 lb. almond paste
4 egg whites from jumbo-size eggs (Use only jumbo-size.)
confectioners' sugar for garnish (optional)
parchment paper

Preheat oven to 375°.

Have ready: 2 9x15-inch cookie sheets lined with parchment paper.

In a large bowl, with electric mixer, cream almond paste at medium speed. Gradually add sugar to the paste and beat to form small balls. Add egg whites to mixture and continue to beat batter until creamy. Drop cookie paste by the tablespoonful, 1 inch apart, on parchment paper-lined cookie sheets. Gently press pine nuts on top of each cookie. Bake cookies in center of preheated oven at 375° for 20 minutes, until slightly golden in color. Cool cookies completely before gently removing from parchment, using a very thin-edged spatula. Dust cookies with confectioners' sugar before serving (optional). Makes about 3 dozen 2-inch cookies.

Suggestions:
 1) Cookies may stick to the parchment paper and become difficult to remove. If this happens, place cookie sheets (with cookies on parchment) into the freezer. Once hardened, they will easily remove from the parchment.
 2) Pignola cookies may be frozen for 6 months, with or without confectioners' sugar. They thaw in about 30 minutes and look and taste freshly baked.
 3) Use *only fresh* Almond Paste (not from a tube) for best results.
 4) Do *not* double the recipe.

LEMON DROP COOKIES (ANGINETTI)

3 large eggs or ¾ cup egg substitute
½ cup milk
2 tsp. lemon extract
½ cup granulated sugar

½ cup canola oil
3 cups all-purpose flour
3 tsp. baking powder

LEMON ICING:
2 cups confectioners' sugar
2 tbsp. water
1-2 tbsp. lemon juice
colored candy sprinkles for garnish

Preheat oven to 350°.

Have ready: 2 9x15-inch cookie sheets, lightly greased with butter or Smart Balance spread.

With an electric mixer at medium speed, beat eggs (or egg substitute), milk, lemon extract, sugar and oil until well blended. On low speed, add flour and baking powder. Mix until just blended. Dough should be soft and sticky. Lightly dust the dough and your fingers with a little additional flour. Drop dough from a teaspoon onto lightly greased cookie sheets, spacing cookies 2 inches apart. Bake immediately in a preheated oven at 350° for 8-10 minutes or until very light brown. Remove cookies from pan onto wire racks. Cool; frost with Lemon Icing.
Prepare LEMON ICING. With an electric mixer at medium speed, beat all icing ingredients (except Sprinkles) until smooth. Using a metal spatula, frost tops of cookies. Frosting will drip down sides and coat the cookies. Garnish with candy sprinkles. Dry frosted cookies on racks; store cookies in airtight containers or freeze, unfrosted. Makes about 3 dozen cookies.

We shall always and forever remember "the Best of Friends".

SICILIAN SESAME COOKIES

3 cups all-purpose flour
$\frac{1}{4}$ tsp. salt
$2\frac{1}{2}$ tsp. baking powder
$\frac{1}{2}$ cup butter or Smart Balance spread,
    at room temperature
1 cup granulated sugar

3 large eggs or $\frac{3}{4}$ cup egg substitute,
    lightly beaten
1 tsp. vanilla extract

(extra flour for kneading dough)
1 cup milk
1 cup sesame seeds

    Preheat oven to 375°.
    Have ready: 2 9x15 cookie sheets, greased with butter or Smart Balance spread;
a floured board.
    Spread sesame seeds on a large flat plate. Set aside.
    In a bowl, mix flour, salt and baking powder. In a large bowl, cream butter (or Smart Balance spread) and sugar. Add eggs (or egg substitute) and vanilla to the sugar/butter mixture and beat thoroughly until fluffy. Add the flour mix, a $\frac{1}{2}$ cup at a time, to the egg/butter mixture. Mix well after each addition. Place dough on a floured board; knead until smooth. Using a tablespoon, form tiny loaf-like biscuits from the dough, rolling dough between your hands. Repeat with remaining dough. Dip each cookie loaf into the milk and then roll cookie(s) in sesame seeds until well-coated. Place them on greased cookie sheets and bake in preheated oven at 375° for 20 minutes or until lightly browned. Remove cookies from tray; allow to cool. This biscuit-like cookie freezes well. Makes about 4 dozen cookies.

RICOTTA COOKIES
(Marie Restaino's special Italian cookie recipe.)

$\frac{1}{2}$ lb. butter
2 cups granulated sugar
3 large eggs
1 tsp. baking soda

1 tsp. salt
2 tsp. vanilla extract
4 cups all-purpose flour
1 lb. (2 cups) ricotta

    Preheat oven to 350°.
    Have ready: 2 ungreased large cookie sheets.

    Prepare COOKIES. Cream together: butter and sugar; add eggs, one at a time, beating well after each. Beat in baking soda, salt and vanilla. Add flour and ricotta, alternately, starting and ending with flour. Drop by teaspoonful onto cookie sheets; bake in preheated oven at 350° for 12-15 minutes, or until light brown. Frost COOKIES with Butter Icing; garnish with coconut, nuts or jimmies. Makes about 3 dozen cookies.

BUTTER ICING: Cream Together: 2 cups confectioners' sugar and $\frac{1}{4}$ cup softened butter. Add, and beat until smooth: $\frac{1}{4}$ tsp. salt, 1 tsp. vanilla, 3-4 tbsp. milk. Spread on tops of cooled, baked cookies. Garnish with: shredded coconut, chopped walnuts, chocolate jimmies.

MARZIPAN BARS

*[A Cooking Hint: A large piece of citrus peel placed in a box of brown sugar
will keep sugar moist and lump free.]*

CRUST:
1/2 cup (1 stick) butter
    or Smart Balance spread, softened
1/2 cup firmly packed brown sugar
1 tsp. almond extract
1/4 tsp. salt
1 1/2 cups all-purpose flour
3/4 cup raspberry jam

FILLING:
1/2 lb. almond paste
1/2 cup granulated sugar
1 tsp. almond extract
3 large eggs or 3/4 cup egg substitute

FROSTING:
2 tbsp. butter or Smart Balance spread, softened
1 1/2 cups confectioners' sugar
2 tbsp. milk
1 tsp. almond extract
1 oz. semisweet chocolate, melted or 1 oz. pkg. "redi-melted" semisweet chocolate

Preheat oven to 350°.

Have ready: a 9x15-inch ungreased baking pan.

Prepare CRUST. In a medium-size bowl, cream together: butter (or Smart Balance spread), brown sugar, almond extract and salt; beat in flour until mixture forms a dough. Press dough on the bottom of 9x15-inch baking pan. Spread jam evenly over the crust.

Prepare FILLING. In a medium-size bowl, cream together: almond paste and granulated sugar, beating mixture until smooth. Beat in almond extract and eggs (or egg substitute), one portion at a time, beating well after each addition. Spread the filling over jam (crust); bake crust and filling in middle of preheated oven at 350° for 20-25 minutes, or until filling is pale golden. Then, allow to cool.

Prepare FROSTING. In a medium-size bowl, beat together: butter (or Smart Balance spread), confectioners' sugar, milk and almond extract until mixture is smooth. Then, beat in melted chocolate. Spread frosting over filling; chill the pastry, covered with foil or plastic wrap, for 1 hour. Then, cut into bars. Store is airtight container. Makes about 24 marzipan bars.

MARZIPAN COOKIES

1 cup butter or Smart Balance spread,
   at room temperature
$\frac{1}{2}$ cup granulated sugar
3 tsp. almond extract
$2\frac{1}{2}$ cups all-purpose flour

red, yellow, green food colors
whole cloves
cinnamon stick
green candied pineapple
   or green candied cherries

Preheat oven to 300°.

Have ready: 3 ungreased 9x15 baking sheets; a few toothpicks; a fine pebbly grater.

Mix butter (or Smart Balance spread) and sugar in a medium-size bowl. When creamy, beat in almond extract. Stir in flour, one-fourth at a time, mixing well after each addition. Divide dough into thirds. Add a few drops of red food coloring to one part of the dough and knead until color is thoroughly blended. Tint remaining dough, one part with yellow food color; the remaining section with green food color. Using a teaspoon to assist you, shape marzipan cookies as described below, and place cookies 1 inch apart on ungreased baking sheets.

1)Apples: Shape green dough into small balls, using about $1\frac{1}{2}$ teaspoons of green dough for each apple. Flatten slightly into an apple shape and insert a whole clove into top, for a stem. Using a wooden toothpick, draw a small **X** on bottom of each apple.

2) Bananas: Shape yellow dough into small 2-inch long cylinders, using about 1 1/2 teaspoons of dough for each. Taper ends and curve slightly to form a banana. Using a small knife, make a shallow slit lengthwise down each banana.

3) Pears: Shape yellow (and/or green) dough into small balls, using about $1\frac{1}{2}$ teaspoons of dough for each. Taper one end to make a pear shape. Insert a tiny piece of cinnamon stick into dough at stem end. Using a wooden toothpick, make a small **X** on bottom of each pear.

4) Strawberries: Shape red dough into strawberry shapes, using about $1\frac{1}{2}$ teaspoons of dough for each. Roll each strawberry lightly on surface of a fine pebbly grater to create a rough texture. Insert a small sliver of candied pineapple for a stem.

Bake cookies on ungreased baking sheets in preheated oven at 300° for 30 minutes, until firm but *not* brown. Transfer to wire racks to cool. These cookies freeze well. Makes about 6 dozen marzipan fruit-shaped cookies.

GREEK CLOVE CRESCENTS

1 cup butter or Smart Balance spread, softened

$1\frac{1}{2}$ cups confectioners' sugar

1 large egg or $\frac{1}{4}$ cup egg substitute

1 tsp. vanilla extract

1 tsp brandy (or brandy extract)

$2\frac{1}{2}$ cups all-purpose flour

whole cloves for garnish

confectioners' sugar for garnish

Preheat oven to 375°.
Have ready: 2-3 ungreased 9x15-inch cookie sheets.

Thoroughly mix butter (or Smart Balance spread), confectioners' sugar, egg (or egg substitute), vanilla and brandy. Blend in flour, $\frac{1}{2}$ cupful at a time until a smooth dough is formed. Shape dough by the tablespoonful to form crescents. Lay cookies on ungreased cookie sheets, 20-24 per sheet. Insert a whole clove into center of each crescent. Bake cookies in preheated oven at 375° for 10-12 minutes or until set, but not brown. Cool thoroughly. Freezes well. Dust with confectioners' sugar before serving. Makes about 5 dozen cookies.

NORWEGIAN WREATHS

1 cup butter or Smart Balance spread, softened

$1\frac{1}{2}$ cups confectioners' sugar

1 large egg or $\frac{1}{4}$ cup egg substitute

1 tsp. vanilla extract

1 tsp. grated orange peel

$2\frac{1}{2}$ cups all-purpose flour

Garnishes: beaten egg white   colored sugars, red and green
candied red and green cherries, finely chopped

Preheat oven to 375°.
Have ready: 2-3 ungreased 9x15-inch cookie sheets; a pastry brush.

Thoroughly mix butter (or Smart Balance spread), confectioners' sugar, egg (or egg substitute), vanilla and grated orange peel. Blend in flour, $\frac{1}{2}$ cupful at a time into a smooth dough. Shape dough by rounded tablespoons into pencil-like strips, about 7 inches long. Form each strip into a circle, overlapping $\frac{1}{2}$ inch at each end. Lay circles on ungreased cookie sheets, 20-24 per sheet. Beat white of 1 egg until foamy. Brush tops of cookie wreaths with beaten egg white. Sprinkle with red or green sugars. Press bits of red candied cherries onto centers of the overlap, for holly berries; add tiny leaves of green candied cherries. Bake cookie wreaths on ungreased cookie sheets in preheated oven at 375° for 8-10 minutes, or until set, but not brown. Remove cookies immediately from baking sheets. Cookies freeze well on trays with waxed paper between layers. Makes about 5 dozen wreaths.

LOVE COOKIES

1 cup butter or Smart Balance spread, softened

1½ cups confectioners' sugar

1 large egg or ¼ cup egg substitute

1 tsp. vanilla extract

½ cup dark molasses

1 tsp. grated lemon peel

1 tsp. each: cinnamon, cloves, allspice, nutmeg

¼ cup chopped walnuts

2½ cups all-purpose flour

LEMON GLAZE:

1 cup confectioners' sugar

1 tsp. lemon juice

1½ tsp. water

Preheat oven to 375°.

Have ready: 2-3 ungreased 9x15-inch cookie sheets; a 2-inch heart-shaped cookie cutter; a floured cloth-covered board; a floured rolling pin.

Thoroughly mix: butter (or Smart Balance spread), confectioners' sugar, egg (or egg substitute), vanilla, molasses, lemon peel, spices and walnuts. Blend in flour, ½ cupful at a time, until dough is smooth and workable. Cover dough with plastic wrap; chill dough in refrigerator for 2-3 hours. Then, roll dough ¼-inch thick on a well-floured cloth-covered board. With floured cookie cutter, cut dough into 2-inch hearts. Place hearts on ungreased cookie sheets, 20-24 per sheet. Bake cookies in preheated oven at 375° for 10-12 minutes or until no imprint remains when lightly touched by finger.

Prepare LEMON GLAZE while cookies are baking. In a bowl, blend confectioners' sugar, lemon juice and water until a spreadable consistency is formed. While cookies are warm, brush them with Lemon Glaze. Allow them to set. Makes about 4 dozen heart-shaped cookies.

Happy 9th Birthday.

Fondues, page 333ff

Cheese Tray One, page 325ff

Macaroni and Cheese, page 139

Cheese Tray Two, page 325

Rice Pudding with Fruit, page 214

Ricotta Cookies, page 358

Key Lime Pie, pages 264-265

Blueberry Pie, page 337

Ice Cream Torte, page 340

Ice Cream Tortoni, page 219

Orange Cranberry Cheesecake, page 239

Heavenly Orange Ricotta Cake, page 222

Party Cupcakes, page 348

Chocolate Cherry Pudgel, page 199

Strawcherry Shortcake, page 342

Panne Dolce, page 3

Chocolate-Pumpkin Fruitcake Bon Bons, page 353

APPLE-OATMEAL COOKIES

1½ cups quick-cooking rolled oats
¾ cup all-purpose flour
¾ cup whole wheat flour
½ cup firmly packed brown sugar
1 tsp. baking powder
¼ tsp. baking soda
¼ tsp. salt
1½ tsp. cinnamon

½ cup dried cranberries
1 cup peeled, finely chopped
   Granny Smith apple
½ cup finely chopped walnuts (optional)
½ cup tiny chocolate morsels (optional)
1 large egg or ¼ cup egg substitute
½ cup canola oil
⅓ cup low-fat milk
½ cup honey

Preheat oven to 375°.

Have ready: 2 ungreased 9x15-inch baking sheets.

In a medium bowl, combine oats, flour, whole wheat flour, brown sugar, baking powder, baking soda, salt and cinnamon. Stir to combine. Stir in dried cranberries, apple, nuts (optional) and chocolate morsels (optional). In a large bowl, combine egg (or egg substitute), honey, oil and milk. Stir in dry ingredients and mix thoroughly to form a smooth batter. Drop rounded teaspoons of batter onto ungreased baking sheets, leaving 2 inches between cookies. Dip fingers into water and press down on cookies to flatten them to about 1½-inch diameter.

Bake cookies in center of preheated oven at 375° for 10-12 minutes, or until lightly golden. Remove cookie sheets from oven. With a thin metal spatula, transfer cookies to a cooling rack. Cookies freeze well in layers; waxed paper between layers. Makes about 3 dozen cookies.

St. Pius X Halloween Party. Photo: L. Curro

PEANUT BUTTER DREAMS
(Recipe contributed by Enid Lopes.)

(1) Ingredients for <u>Bottom Layer</u>:

$\frac{1}{2}$ cup peanut butter

$\frac{1}{4}$ cup unsalted butter, softened

1 cup sifted all-purpose flour

$\frac{1}{3}$ cup light brown sugar, firmly packed

Preheat oven to 350°. (Maintain this oven temperature until recipe is completed.)
Have ready: a greased 8-inch square pan.
Blend peanut butter with butter. Gradually beat in sugar. Work in flour with back of a spoon. Pat dough onto bottom of greased 8-inch square pan. Bake bottom layer of cookies in preheated oven at 350° for 15 minutes.
Meanwhile, prepare the torte-like topping.

(2) <u>Topping</u>:

2 eggs, well-beaten

$1\frac{1}{2}$ cups light brown sugar, firmly packed

$\frac{1}{4}$ cup all-purpose flour

$\frac{1}{2}$ tsp. baking powder

$\frac{3}{4}$ cup flaked coconut

6 oz. semisweet chocolate morsels

1 tsp. vanilla extract

Beat eggs with brown sugar until creamy. Blend in flour and baking powder. Fold in remaining ingredients. Pour over baked bottom layer. Bake in preheated oven at 350° for 30 minutes. Cool thoroughly in pan before cutting into squares. Yields 16 bars.

YUMMY BARS

2 cups firmly packed brown sugar

2 cups all-purpose flour

$\frac{1}{2}$ cup (1 stick) butter
    or Smart Balance spread, softened

1 tsp. baking powder

$\frac{1}{4}$ tsp. salt

1 tsp. vanilla extract

1 cup low-fat milk

1 large egg or $\frac{1}{4}$ cup egg substitute

1 cup semisweet chocolate morsels

$\frac{1}{2}$ cup finely chopped walnuts

$\frac{1}{4}$ cup unsweetened flaked coconut

Preheat oven to 350°.
Have ready: a 9x15-inch baking pan, greased with butter or Smart Balance spread.
In a large bowl, mix together: brown sugar and flour. Using a pastry cutter or 2 knives, cut in the butter (or Smart Balance spread) until mixture resembles coarse crumbs. Remove 1 cup of mixture and set aside for topping. To the mixture in the large bowl, add baking powder and salt. With a fork, lightly beat in milk, vanilla and egg (or egg substitute), until a smooth batter is formed. Pour batter into prepared pan.
In a small bowl, combine chocolate morsels and walnuts. Fold in coconut. Sprinkle reserved crumb mixture over top of batter in pan. Sprinkle with chocolate morsels/walnuts mixture. Using a long flat spatula, spread topping evenly over batter in pan. Bake in center of preheated oven at 350° for 35 minutes, or until inserted toothpick removes clean. Completely cool pan on wire rack before cutting into 24 bars. Store in airtight container up to 5 days.

AMARETTOS
Reprinted from: MENU LOG: A Collection of Recipes as Coordinated Menus
by Marion O. Celenza, page 378.

<u>Unbaked Cookies</u>.

12 oz. semisweet chocolate morsels
1 cup sugar
6 tbsp. corn syrup
$\frac{1}{2}$ cup water
$\frac{1}{2}$ cup Amaretto liqueur

1 cup puréed almonds
1 cup flaked coconut
1 cup granulated sugar
7-8 cups plain chocolate wafers, finely crushed

Melt chocolate morsels over hot, not boiling, water. Remove from hot water and stir in sugar and corn syrup. Add Amaretto and water and mix thoroughly. In a large mixing bowl, combine crushed wafers, puréed almonds and coconut. Stir chocolate mix into wafer mix to blend completely. Form $1\frac{1}{2}$-inch balls with hands. Wet hands occasionally as you work. Pour granulated sugar into a small bowl. As you form Amarettos, drop them into the sugar and roll them to coat thoroughly. Transfer cookies to a prepared tin or box, lined with foil. Arrange cookies by layers, with waxed paper between layers. Pack tightly in foil and store in a tin or plastic container for several weeks to ripen. They improve with age. Yields: about 6 dozen.

SUGARPLUMS
Reprinted from: MENU LOG: A Collection of Recipes as Coordinated Menus
by Marion O. Celenza, page 377.

$4\frac{1}{2}$ oz. cream cheese, completely softened
$\frac{3}{4}$ cup butter or
   Smart Balance spread, softened
$\frac{3}{4}$ cup firmly packed brown sugar
1 tsp. salt

1 tsp. almond extract
$2\frac{1}{2}$ cups all-purpose flour
1 cup ground almonds
6 doz. chocolate kisses, unwrapped
   (with or without almonds)

FROSTING:
Blend: 1 cup confectioners' sugar
2-3 tbsp. Amaretto liqueur
a little water, if mixture is too thick

Preheat oven to 350°.
Have ready: 3 9x15 ungreased baking sheets.
Cream butter and cream cheese with brown sugar. Add salt, almond extract and flour; mix thoroughly. Dough will be heavy. Stir in nuts. With your fingers gather 1 teaspoon of dough to wrap around each chocolate kiss; form replicas of chocolate kisses, about 1 inch in diameter. Arrange cookies on ungreased cookie sheets, 24 to a pan. Bake in preheated oven at 350° for 10 minutes until light tan in color. Remove from oven and cool completely. Dip tops of cookies into frosting to resemble snow-capped mountains. Yields about 6 dozen.

FORGET-IT

Reprinted from: MENU LOG: A Collection of Recipes as Coordinated Menus
by Marion O. Celenza, page 379.
*[A Cooking Hint: Always be sure to remove even the tiniest trace of egg yolk
from separated egg whites that are to be beaten. Even the smallest bit of yolk
can prevent whites from beating stiffly.]*

6 egg whites
$1\frac{1}{2}$ cups granulated sugar

2 cups semisweet chocolate morsels
$1\frac{1}{2}$ cups chopped walnuts
1 cup flaked coconut

Preheat oven to 375° for 3 hours prior to baking the cookies; equally space racks in oven.
Have ready: 3 9x15 baking sheets lined with aluminum foil.
Beat egg whites in a large bowl with electric mixer on high. Gradually add sugar and
continue to beat until meringue is stiff and holds peaks. Do not underbeat. Fold in chocolate
morsels, walnuts and coconut. Drop by heaping teaspoons onto foil-lined cookie sheets, about
20 cookies per sheet. After all of the batter is used, open the oven door and place all of the trays
that fit into the oven; close the oven door; *turn off oven.* Allow the cookies to slowly bake in the
oven overnight, or for at least 8-9 hours. *(Do not open oven door during this baking period.)* Then,
remove trays from oven and carefully peel off cookies from foil onto serving tray. Treat the cookies
gingerly. They are very fragile. When storing, you may wish to make layers of cookies with tissue
paper between layers. (These cookies are well worth the effort!) Yields about 5 dozen.

CHOCOLATE CHIP COOKIES

Reprinted from: MENU LOG: A Collection of Recipes as Coordinated Menus
by Marion O. Celenza, page 371.

2 cups plus 4 tbsp. butter
    or Smart Balance spread
2 cups granulated sugar
$1\frac{1}{2}$ cups brown sugar
2 eggs or $\frac{1}{2}$ cup egg substitute
2 tsp. vanilla extract
5 cups all-purpose flour

1 tsp. baking soda
$\frac{1}{2}$ tsp. baking powder
1 cup chopped walnuts
1 cup semisweet chocolate morsels
1 cup semisweet chocolate morsels,
    (for topping)

Preheat oven to 325° after dough has been chilled.
Have ready: 3 greased 9x15 baking sheets.
Beat butter (or Smart Balance spread) with mixer at medium speed until very creamy.
Add sugars and blend well. Blend the eggs (or egg substitute) and vanilla and beat them into the
butter/sugar mixture. Blend flour, baking soda, baking powder and combine $\frac{1}{3}$ at a time, into
butter mixture. Stir in nuts and 1 cup chocolate morsels. Plastic wrap dough and chill until firm,
about 2-3 hours. Then, form 2-inch balls with dough; place on greased baking sheets, 2 inches
apart, 15-20 cookies per sheet. Press tops of each cookie with a tablespoon to flatten slightly.
Sprinkle and press lightly: chocolate morsels on tops of each cookie. Bake in preheated oven at
325° for 8-10 minutes. Cool before removing cookies from sheets. Yields: about 6 dozen cookies.

5 ITALIAN BISCOTTI RECIPES

APRICOT-ALMOND BISCOTTI
Reprinted from: MENU LOG: A Collection of Recipes as Coordinated Menus
by Marion O. Celenza, page 386.

4 eggs or 1 cup egg substitute	$1\frac{1}{2}$ tsp. baking powder
$\frac{1}{2}$ cup plus 4 tbsp. honey	$\frac{1}{2}$ tsp. baking soda
4 cups all-purpose flour	$1\frac{1}{2}$ cups finely chopped dried apricots
$1\frac{1}{3}$ cups brown sugar	1 cup sliced almonds with skins
$2\frac{1}{2}$ tsp. anise seeds	dash of salt

Preheat oven to 325; then. lower to 300° for second baking.

Have ready: 3 9x15 baking sheets, greased and floured; a floured board.

In a small bowl, beat eggs with honey until well blended; set aside. In a large mixing bowl, combine flour, brown sugar, anise, baking powder, soda and salt. Make a well in center and add egg mix, apricots and almonds. Mix until dough is smooth and combined, about 2 minutes. Transfer dough to floured board and divide dough in half. Cover half not used. Divide each half of the dough into 3 sections approximately 12x2 inches each, and shape them into rectangular loaves. Lay 2 rectangles, lengthwise, on cach prepared baking sheet 3 inches apart. Bake in preheated oven at 325° for 20-25 minutes or until golden brown. Bake one baking tin at a time, placing tin on rack in center of oven.

Remove from oven and cool for 2 minutes. Using 2 metal spatulas, transfer one section at a time to board. Using a sharp serrated knifc, slice each section into $\frac{1}{2}$-inch diagonal slices, about 15-18 biscotti per section. Replace biscotti on baking sheets, standing upright and slightly apart from each other. Lower temperature in oven to 300° and bake for 5 more minutes.

Remove to rack and cool completely. Then, store biscotti in airtight containers. Yields about 6 dozen. (Continued on page 368)

Hair stylist Angela, daughter Faye and son-in-law Oscar enjoy the party.
Photo: A. Arolithianakis

(Continued from page 367)

CHOCOLATE BISCOTTI COOKIES
Reprinted from: MENU LOG: A Collection of Recipes as Coordinated Menus
by Marion O. Celenza, page 375.

$1\frac{1}{2}$ cups butter or Smart Balance spread

$1\frac{1}{3}$ cups brown sugar

2 eggs or $\frac{1}{2}$ cup egg substitute

$\frac{1}{3}$ cup cocoa

2 squares bitter chocolate, melted

4 cups all-purpose flour

1 tbsp. baking powder

1 tbsp. anise extract

1 tbsp. crushed anise seed

1 tbsp. cinnamon

1 cup chopped peanuts or filberts

$\frac{1}{2}$ cup milk

Maryann and Joseph Rietschlin join the Torrisi party.
Photo: P. Torrisi

FROSTING:
1 cup confectioners' sugar
1 tbsp. anisette
1 square bitter chocolate, melted

Blend until smooth; add a little water if frosting is too thick. Dip tops of cookies into icing or spread with a butter knife.

Preheat oven to 375°.

Have ready: 3 ungreased 9x15 baking sheets.

Cream butter, sugar and eggs. Add cocoa and chocolate; mix well. Blend flour with baking powder and add to egg mixture. Add flavoring and nuts; gradually add milk, blending thoroughly. Spoon dough into round balls; shape them into the size of walnuts, onto an ungreased baking sheet and bake for 10 minutes. Remove from oven and thoroughly cool. Frost. Allow frosting to become firm before storing in tins, in a cool place. Yields about 6 dozen. (Continued on following page)

(Continued from page 368)

CHOCOLATE WALNUT BISCOTTI
Reprinted from: MENU LOG: A Collection of Recipes as Coordinated Menus
by Marion O. Celenza, page 387.

1 cup butter, or Smart Balance, softened
$\frac{1}{2}$ cup granulated sugar
4 eggs or 1 cup egg substitute
2 tsp. vanilla extract
4 cups all-purpose flour
3 tsp. baking powder
$\frac{1}{4}$ tsp. salt
2 cups semisweet chocolate morsels
2 cups chopped walnuts

FROSTING:
Combine: 4 squares semisweet baking chocolate with 1 tbsp. canola oil; melt over hot water, stirring to make a smooth frosting.

Preheat oven to 325°.
Have ready: 3 9x15 baking sheets, greased and floured; a floured board.

Beat butter and sugar until light and fluffy. Beat in eggs and vanilla. Mix in flour, baking powder and salt. Stir in chocolate morsels and walnuts. On board, divide dough into 6 sections. Cover dough while working on one section at a time. Form each section into a 2x12-inch rectangle. With spatulas, transfer recangles to baking sheets. Place 2 rectangles per sheet. Bake on rack in center of oven for 20-25 minutes or until lightly browned. Bake one tray at a time.

Remove to cutting board and cool slightly. Then, with serrated knife, cut each rectangle into diagonal slices, $\frac{3}{4}$-inch thick. You will make about 15 slices per rectangle. Place slices back on baking sheet in upright position, slightly apart. Return biscotti to oven and bake for 5 minutes. Remove to baking racks and cool thoroughly. Prepare frosting and dip ends of each biscotti into chocolate frosting. Allow to set and dry before packing in airtight containers. Store containers in a cool place. Yields about 6 dozen biscotti. (Continued on page 370)

Happy 50th Anniversary, Pat and Sal Torrisi. Photo: P. Torrisi

(Continued from page 369)

NOCELLE
Reprinted from: MENU LOG: A Collection of Recipes as Coordinated Menus
by Marion O. Celenza, page 388.

2 cups granulated sugar

1 cup butter or Smart Balance spread,
    melted; or $\frac{3}{4}$ cup canola oil

$\frac{1}{4}$ cup anise seeds

$\frac{1}{4}$ cup anisette

3 tbsp. whiskey

6 eggs or $1\frac{1}{2}$ cups egg substitute

$5\frac{1}{2}$ cups all-purpose flour

1 tbsp. baking powder

2 cups coarsely chopped hazelnuts

2 cups whole candied cherries

Albertine Griffith celebrates a glorious 100th.
Photo: C. Rodriguez

Preheat oven to 375°.

Have ready: 3 9x15 baking sheets, greased.

In a large mixing bowl, combine sugar with butter, anise seeds, anisette and whiskey.
Beat in eggs. Mix flour and baking powder, and stir thoroughly into sugar mixture. Cover
and refrigerate for 2-3 hours. Then, turn dough onto floured board and divide the dough into
6 rectangles. Work 1 rectangle at a time; cover the rest.

Form each rectangle into a 2x12-inch log, $\frac{1}{2}$-inch thick. With spatulas, transfer each log to
prepared baking sheets, 2 per pan. Bake for 15-20 minutes or until golden brown.

Remove from oven and cool for several minutes. Return each log to floured board and slice
the logs $\frac{1}{2}$-inch thick on the diagonal, about 15 to 16 pieces per log. Place the slices upright,
slightly apart on baking sheets and bake again for 5 minutes. Remove biscotti from oven and
cool thoroughly. Store in airtight containers. Yields about 6 dozen.

(Continued on following page)

(Continued from page 370)

CHOCOLATE ALMOND BISCOTTI
Reprinted from: MENU LOG: A Collection of Recipes as Coordinated Menus
by Marion O. Celenza, page 389.
*[A Cooking Hint: A large piece of citrus peel placed in a box of brown sugar will keep
sugar moist and lump-free.]*

2 cups brown sugar

1 cup butter or Smart Balance spread,
    melted; or $\frac{3}{4}$ cup canola oil

$\frac{1}{4}$ cup anise seeds

$\frac{1}{4}$ cup anisette

3 tbsp. Amaretto

1 square melted semisweet chocolate

5 eggs or $1\frac{1}{4}$ cups egg substitute

$5\frac{1}{2}$ cups all-purpose flour

1 tbsp. baking powder

1 tbsp. cinnamon

1 cup chopped almonds

$\frac{1}{2}$ cup coarsely chopped almond kisses

$\frac{1}{2}$ cup coarsely chopped chocolate
    covered almonds

FROSTING:

1 square melted semisweet chocolate

1 cup confectioners' sugar

2 tbsp. Amaretto liqueur

Preheat oven to 375°.

Have ready: 3 9x15 baking sheets, greased; a floured board.

In a 6-quart mixing bowl, combine sugar with butter, anise seed, melted chocolate, anisette and Amaretto. Beat in eggs. Mix flour with baking powder and stir thoroughly into sugar mixture. Add cinnamon, and all chocolate candy-nuts; mix by hand until well blended. Cover and refrigerate for 2-3 hours. Then, turn onto floured board and divide dough into 6 wedges. Work on 1 wedge at a time; cover the rest. Form wedges into logs, 2x12x$\frac{1}{2}$-inches thick. With spatulas, transfer logs to prepared greased pans, 2 per pan. Bake for 15-20 minutes or until golden brown.

Remove from oven and cool for several minutes. Return each log to board and slice logs $\frac{1}{2}$-inch thick on the diagonal, about 15 pieces per log. Place the slices upright and slightly apart on baking sheets and bake again for 5 minutes. Remove from oven and cool thoroughly. Prepare FROSTING. Blend all frosting ingredients thoroughly. Spread with flat knife or spatula on tops of biscotti. Allow to dry thoroughly. Then, store in airtight containers in a cool place. Yields about 6 dozen.

HOTSY-TOTSY PEANUTS
(Recipe contributed by Enid Lopez.)

1 lb. unsalted peanuts (shelled)
2 garlic cloves, minced
1 tbsp. curry powder

$\frac{1}{2}$ tsp. cayenne pepper
1 tbsp. olive oil

Have ready: a microwave oven. (*NOTE: below)

Combine all ingredients in a microwaveable bowl or tray. Cook uncovered in Microwave for 2 or 3 minutes, stirring nuts every 30 seconds. A tasty snack.

*NOTE: may be baked in conventional oven. Spread combined nut mixture over a 5x7-inch tray. Roast nuts in preheated conventional oven at 300° for about 30 minutes, stirring them occasionally.

ANNE'S CANDY IS DANDY
(Recipe contributed by Anne Carbone Recca.)

2 cups dates or apricots, chopped;
    or 1 cup of each
1 cup golden raisins and
    1 cup cranberry raisins

2 cups nuts, chopped (walnuts, almonds,
    pecans, filberts, any or a mix)
3 large eggs, beaten

Preheat oven to 350°.
Have ready: cupcake pans with 2$\frac{1}{2}$-inch cups, lined with waxed cupcake inserts.

In a large bowl thoroughly mix all of the selected ingredients. Spoon the candy mixture into lined cupcake pans and bake in preheated oven at 350° for 18-20 minutes. Remove pan from oven and cool thoroughly. Makes about 2 dozen.

ROASTED CHESTNUTS
(Score chestnuts early in the day; roast at serving time.)

1 lb. large chestnuts

Preheat oven to 475°.

With a small sharp knife, cut a cross through the center of the flat part of each chestnut. Place chestnuts in an 8-inch pie pan, cross-side up. Roast them for 20 minutes or until you see the cut skin start to curl. Cool for 5 minutes and serve. Peel off shell with fingers and enjoy while warm.

OLYMPIA'S PIZZELLE
(Contributed by Terry Cipollone Cayton.)

6 large eggs
$1\frac{1}{2}$ cups granulated sugar
1 cup Crisco vegetable oil
2 tbsp. anise extract
6 tbsp. anisette liqueur

2 tbsp. vanilla extract
2 tsp. grated lemon peel
4 tsp. baking powder
$3\frac{1}{2}$-4 cups all-purpose flour

confectioners' sugar for garnish

Have ready: a Pizzelle Iron.

Combine the first 7 ingredients in a medium-size bowl; beat batter with a mixer or by hand. Add baking powder and flour. The batter will become thick. Preheat Pizzelle Iron and proceed to cook pizzelles according to the baking iron's instructions. Usually pizzelles bake very quickly; 20 to 30 seconds should do it! Place them on a metal rack to dry. Optional: garnish with confectioners' sugar at serving. Makes about 5 dozen.

Celebrate with Dr. Alberto Cayton and Peter Ybasco. Special friends in youth, rediscovered and not forgotten.
Photo: T. Cayton

HEAVEN!
PERCOCA* IN WINE

<u>For Each Serving</u>:
1 or more fresh ripe cling peaches, with skin, rinsed, patted dry with paper towels;
    sliced into 5-6 wedges
4 oz. red table wine (from your home-processed wine cellar, if possible);
    or sweet and tawny Muscatel
a large wine goblet

    My paternal grandfather, Aniello Orlando, introduced me to "Cielo" (Heaven) when I was 5. A simple after-supper summer ritual, Nonno, would select one or two ripe peaches (Percoca) from our California cling peach tree which grew in our large Brooklyn garden. He'd run cool water over the peaches and gently patted them dry with a clean linen napkin. After pouring a hearty goblet of home-processed wine, he'd slice a pale yellow-green, fuzzy-skinned and perfume-scented peach into 5 or 6 wedges. He'd add the slices to steep in the goblet of wine to blend the flavors for several minutes. And then, he would offer his granddaughter a slice of "heaven".

    *Percoca is the Italian (Neapolitan) dialectical spelling for the cling peaches which grew in our Brooklyn garden. Peaches are thought to be native of Persia, known to the early Romans, and brought to Italy. The cling peach seeds found their way to California via our early settlers.

    We thank Teresa Cerasuola (American-Italian Historical Association) for her professional assistance in our research concerning Percoca.

Let's celebrate a "big birthday" with Nancy (the Birthday Girl) and Dr. E.J. Pesiri and their loving family.
Photo: A. Swanson

Accompaniments

Dressings

Sauces

Gravies

...and More

[A Cooking Hint: Store all homemade dressings in refrigerator. Most dressings, especially non-creamy, may be stored for several weeks in refrigerator, unless otherwise noted in recipes.]

"NO-SALT" – SALT SPICE MIX

1 tbsp. each: garlic powder, mustard powder
2 tsp. each: dried thyme leaves, onion powder, paprika, celery leaves
1 tsp. each: white pepper, black pepper, oregano
2 tbsp. grated dried lemon peel

Blend ingredients in a small bowl. Place a small funnel with a $\frac{1}{2}$-inch tube opening into a half-cup jar (with a screw-on lid). Spoon, and force the herbs through the funnel tube into the jar. Screw the lid securely. This mix stays quite potent for several months in a cool dark pantry. (Also, the spices and herbs provide a delicious scent.)

ITALIAN DRESSING (OLIVE OIL AND RED WINE VINEGAR DRESSING)

$\frac{1}{2}$ cup extra-virgin olive oil
2 tbsp. red wine vinegar
2 garlic cloves, crushed
$\frac{1}{4}$ tsp. salt
$\frac{1}{8}$ tsp. black pepper
1 tbsp. chopped basil
$\frac{1}{4}$ tsp. oregano
a few flakes hot red pepper

Combine and mix all ingredients into a 1-pint jar with a tight lid. Shake dressing thoroughly before serving. Keeps in refrigerator for 2 weeks.

BALSAMIC OLIVE OIL DRESSING

$\frac{1}{2}$ cup extra-virgin olive oil
$\frac{1}{4}$ cup balsamic vinegar
1 tbsp. mixed: dried oregano, basil, rosemary, marjoram
1 bay leaf
2 garlic cloves, minced
1 tsp. honey
1 tsp. prepared Dijon-style mustard
a few grains hot red pepper flakes

Thoroughly combine all ingredients in a 1-pint jar with a tight cap. Shake dressing before using. Keeps for about 2 weeks in refrigerator.

HONEY MUSTARD DRESSING

$\frac{1}{2}$ cup extra-virgin olive oil
$\frac{1}{4}$ cup cider vinegar
1 tsp. honey
1 tsp. dry mustard
$\frac{1}{4}$ tsp. cracked black pepper, salt to taste
1 tsp. lemon juice
$\frac{1}{4}$ tsp. dill weed

   Combine all ingredients in a 1-pint jar with a tight cover. Shake dressing thoroughly to combine. Refrigerate. Shake well to mix before serving. Keeps in refrigerator for 2 weeks.

RED WINE HONEY MUSTARD DRESSING

$\frac{1}{4}$ cup red wine vinegar
2 tbsp. extra-virgin olive oil
1 tsp. dill weed
1 tbsp. Dijon mustard
a sprinkling of salt
$\frac{1}{8}$ tsp. freshly ground black pepper
1 tbsp. honey

   In a small bowl or jar with a cover, combine dressing ingredients. Set aside if using at this time; or cover with lid and refrigerate until 1 hour prior to serving. Shake well before using.

CREAMY HONEY MUSTARD DRESSING

$\frac{3}{4}$ cup mayonnaise, low-fat available
2 tbsp. cider vinegar
2 tbsp. fresh lemon juice
2 tbsp. honey mustard spread
1 tbsp. dill weed, chopped (or use 1 tsp. dried dill weed)
$\frac{1}{4}$ tsp. freshly ground black pepper, salt to taste

   Thoroughly combine all ingredients in a 1-pint jar with a tight cap. Stir dressing before serving. Keeps in refrigerator for 1 week.

TUSCANY DRESSING

$\frac{1}{2}$ cup extra-virgin olive oil
$\frac{1}{2}$ cup red wine vinegar
$\frac{1}{2}$ tsp. fresh chopped rosemary
$\frac{1}{2}$ tsp. fresh chopped thyme leaves
1 tsp. dried oregano
$\frac{1}{2}$ tsp. dried basil
$\frac{1}{4}$ tsp. freshly ground black pepper
2 basil leaves

Thoroughly combine all ingredients in a 1-pint jar with a tight cap. Shake dressing thoroughly before serving. Keeps in refrigerator for 2 weeks.

HONEY ORANGE DRESSING

$\frac{1}{4}$ cup extra-virgin olive oil
$\frac{1}{4}$ cup orange juice
1 tbsp. honey
1 small red Chile pepper, deseeded, chopped
1 tsp. dried oregano

Combine dressing ingredients in a small bowl or a jar with a screw-on lid. When handling hot pepper varieties, wear plastic gloves. Wash your hands thoroughly; avoid touching face and eyes.

Shake jar of dressing to blend thoroughly. Refrigerate dressing until needed, up to 1 week. Remove dressing from refrigerator 1 hour prior to using. Shake dressing to blend. Drizzle dressing over salad when serving.

FRENCH DRESSING

1 cup mayonnaise, low-fat available
1 tbsp. white vinegar
1 tsp. dry mustard
$\frac{1}{2}$ tsp. Worcestershire sauce
$\frac{1}{4}$ tsp. salt, dash of black pepper
1 tsp. confectioners' sugar
$\frac{1}{2}$ tsp. paprika
$\frac{1}{4}$ tsp. garlic powder

Combine all ingredients in a small bowl. Beat with electric mixer for 2 minutes. Pour into 1-pint jar with a secure cover. Refrigerate until serving. Stir thoroughly to mix. Keeps in refrigerator for 1 week.

LEMON-OIL DRESSING

½ cup extra-virgin olive oil
¼ tsp. salt, dash of black pepper
1 garlic clove, crushed
juice of 2 lemons, strained

Combine all ingredients in a 1-pint jar with a tight cover and shake dressing thoroughly before using. Refrigerate until serving. Use over greens salads; vegetables such as broccoli, asparagus, spinach or green beans. Keeps in refrigerator for 2 weeks.

RUSSIAN DRESSING

1 cup mayonnaise, low-fat available
½ cup chili sauce
½ cup pickle relish
1 tsp. confectioners' sugar
1 tbsp. black caviar, optional

Combine all ingredients into a 1-pint jar with a tight lid. Stir to mix. Refrigerate until using. Keeps in refrigerator for 1 week.

BLEU CHEESE DRESSING

½ cup extra-virgin olive oil
¼ cup white vinegar
¼ tsp salt
⅛ tsp. cracked black pepper
1 tsp. onion powder
½ cup crumbled bleu cheese (or Roquefort or Gorgonzola)

Combine and beat all ingredients in a small bowl. Pour into a 1-pint jar with a wide mouth. When ready to serve, stir thoroughly and spoon over salad. Keeps in refrigerator for 1 week.

CAESAR DRESSING WITH BACON

½ cup extra-virgin olive oil
2 garlic cloves, minced
¼ cup egg substitute
½ cup grated Parmesan cheese
¼ tsp. salt
⅛ tsp. cracked black pepper

¼ tsp. dry mustard
juice of 1 lemon, strained
1 tbsp. chopped anchovy (optional)
2 strips cooked bacon, crumbled
1 cup toasted cubes French bread
  (or packaged croutons)

Allow minced garlic sit in olive oil for 1 hour. In a small bowl, beat the egg substitute, cheese, salt, pepper, dry mustard and lemon juice. Add oil mix. Beat with electric mixer for 30 seconds. Stir in anchovy. Refrigerate. When needed, shake dressing thoroughly. Add croutons and crumbled bacon to salad mix and pour dressing over the salad. Toss to coat thoroughly. Stores in refrigerator in a covered container for a few days.

CAESAR DRESSING

3 tbsp. white wine vinegar
3 tbsp. fresh lemon juice
1-2 garlic cloves, minced
1 tsp. Dijon mustard
1 tsp. Worcestershire sauce

4 anchovies, minced
¼ tsp. salt
¼ tsp. freshly ground black pepper,
  or more to taste
¼ cup egg substitute
½ cup extra-virgin olive oil

In a small bowl, combine olive oil, vinegar, lemon juice, garlic, mustard, Worcestershire sauce, anchovies, salt and pepper and egg substitute. Whisk dressing until frothy, then creamy. Cover bowl and refrigerate until needed. Stores in refrigerator for a few days.

MAYONNAISE

½ cup egg substitute
2 tbsp. lemon juice (1 tbsp. white wine vinegar, if necessary)
1 tbsp. mild mustard
1¼ cups extra-virgin olive oil
dash of salt, dash of white pepper

In a small bowl, whisk together: egg substitute, dash of salt and white pepper. Add 1 tablespoon of lemon juice and the mustard. Beat until thick (about a minute or two). Add the oil, a teaspoon at a time, whisking constantly. After you've added 2 tablespoons of oil, the mixture should be thick. Add the remaining oil more quickly, a tablespoon at a time, whisking constantly. Taste, and if desired, stir in the rest of the lemon juice (and 1 tablespoon of white vinegar); add more salt and pepper, if necessary. Refrigerate dressing in a covered jar. Use within 1 week.

SPICY SALAD DRESSING

1 cup Miracle Whip dressing
$\frac{1}{4}$ cup chili sauce
$\frac{1}{4}$ tsp. salt
$\frac{1}{8}$ tsp. black pepper
1 tbsp. dill weed

1 tbsp. chopped dill pickle
dash of cayenne
1 tbsp. extra-virgin olive oil
1 tbsp. Worcestershire sauce

Beat all ingredients in a small bowl. Store in a tightly covered jar in refrigerator until needed. Use within 1 week. Stir dressing thoroughly before serving.

ISLANDS SPICY DRESSING

$\frac{1}{4}$ cup extra-virgin olive oil
juice of 1 lime, strained
2 tbsp. white wine vinegar
1 large garlic clove, minced

$\frac{1}{2}$ tsp. Hungarian paprika
$\frac{1}{2}$ tsp. ground cumin
$\frac{1}{2}$ tsp. curry powder
$\frac{1}{2}$ tsp. granulated sugar
dash of salt, or to taste

Blend all ingredients in a 1-pint jar with a tight lid. Refrigerate dressing until needed; shake thoroughly before serving. Keeps in refrigerator for 2 weeks.

PARMESAN CHEESE DRESSING

$\frac{1}{2}$ cup extra-virgin olive oil
$\frac{1}{4}$ cup white wine vinegar
2 tbsp. lemon juice
1 tbsp. dried oregano

$\frac{1}{4}$ tsp. black pepper
$\frac{1}{2}$ tsp. salt
$\frac{1}{2}$ cup grated Parmesan cheese
1 bay leaf

Combine all ingredients in a 1-pint jar with lid. Refrigerate until needed. Shake dressing thoroughly before serving. Use within 1 week.

ASIAN DRESSING I

$\frac{1}{4}$ extra-virgin olive oil

2 tbsp. sesame oil

2 tbsp. rice wine vinegar

2 tbsp. *lite* soy sauce

2 tbsp. lemon juice, strained

1 tbsp. grated gingerroot

1 tbsp. grated lemon rind

$\frac{1}{4}$ tsp. salt

1 garlic clove, minced

2 tbsp. peanuts, without skin, chopped fine

Combine all ingredients in a jar with a lid. Refrigerate until needed. Shake dressing thoroughly before serving. Keeps in refrigerator for 1 week.

ASIAN DRESSING II

$\frac{1}{4}$ cup sherry

2 tbsp. *lite* soy sauce

2 tbsp. hoisin sauce

Chinese 5-spice powder, to taste

Combine all ingredients in a jar with a lid. Refrigerate until needed. Shake dressing thoroughly before serving. Keeps in refrigerator for 1 week.

CREAMY LIME-BASIL DRESSING

1 cup mayonnaise, low-fat available

$\frac{1}{4}$ cup fresh lime juice, strained

2 tbsp. cider vinegar

2 tbsp. fresh basil leaves, finely chopped

$\frac{1}{4}$ tsp. freshly ground black pepper

$\frac{1}{4}$ tsp. salt, or to taste

$\frac{1}{4}$ tsp. each: garlic powder, onion powder

$\frac{1}{4}$ tsp. granulated sugar

In a 1-pint jar with a tight lid, thoroughly blend all ingredients. Refrigerate until needed, up to 1 week. At serving, stir to mix thoroughly.

VINAIGRETTE

½ cup extra-virgin olive oil

2 tbsp. red wine vinegar

1 tbsp. lemon juice

1 tsp. prepared mustard

1 tsp. Worcestershire sauce

½ tsp. salt

¼ tsp. black pepper

1 tsp. dried basil leaves

1 garlic clove, minced

(¼ cup sour cream for creamy dressing),
    optional

Mix all ingredients in a 1-pint jar with a lid. Refrigerate until serving, up to 1 week; (for creamy vinaigrette), for a few days. Shake thoroughly before serving.

RASPBERRY VINAIGRETTE

½ cup extra-virgin olive oil

¼ cup red wine vinegar

1 tsp. dill weed

1 tbsp. honey

2 tbsp. lemon juice, strained

½ tsp. salt

⅛ tsp. black pepper

½ cup fresh raspberries, gently rinsed,
    drained, patted dry with paper towel,
    mashed

With a fork, mash raspberries at bottom of a wide-mouthed 1-pint jar with a lid. Add remainder of ingredients; whisk to blend thoroughly. Cover tightly with lid. Refrigerate until needed, up to a few days. Shake to blend thoroughly at serving.

THOUSAND ISLAND DRESSING

1 cup mayonnaise

¼ cup chili sauce, or catsup

1 hard-cooked egg, finely chopped

2 tbsp. pimiento olives, minced

1 tbsp. green pepper, minced

1 tbsp. fresh parsley, minced

"Low-Fat" THOUSAND ISLAND DRESSING

1 cup prepared tomato sauce

¼ cup tarragon vinegar

2 tbsp. extra-virgin olive oil

1 garlic clove, minced

a few dashes Tabasco

2 tbsp. dill pickle, minced

2 tbsp. celery, minced

1 tbsp. Worcestershire sauce

1 tsp. prepared honey-mustard

For *BOTH* DRESSING recipes: Thoroughly combine all ingredients for selected recipe in a large jar with a screw-top lid. Refrigerate dressing until ready to serve. Stir thoroughly at serving. THOUSAND ISLAND DRESSING keeps in refrigerator for 2 days; *"Low-Fat"* version keeps in refrigerator for 1 week.

AIOLI (GARLIC SAUCE)

1 cup mayonnaise (low-fat available) $\frac{1}{4}$ tsp. black pepper

4 garlic cloves, minced   1 tbsp. lemon juice

$\frac{1}{4}$ cup extra-virgin olive oil   dash of salt

Thoroughly blend all ingredients in small bowl. Seal bowl with plastic wrap and refrigerate until needed, up to 1 week. Stir dressing before serving.

COLE SLAW DRESSING

$\frac{1}{2}$ cup Miracle Whip dressing $\frac{1}{4}$ tsp. black pepper

$\frac{1}{4}$ cup cider vinegar   1 tsp. granulated sugar

juice of 1 lemon, strained $\frac{1}{2}$ tsp. celery seed

Thoroughly blend all ingredients in a small jar with a lid. Refrigerate until serving, up to 1 week. Shake dressing thoroughly before serving.

APPLE CIDER DRESSING

$\frac{1}{2}$ cup apple cider   dash of salt, dash of pepper, dash of cumin

$\frac{1}{4}$ cup extra-virgin olive oil   1 tbsp. lemon juice, strained

1 tbsp. brown sugar   1 tbsp. sherry

$\frac{1}{4}$ tsp. each: ground cinnamon,
     nutmeg, cloves

Thoroughly mix all ingredients in a small jar with a screw-on lid. Shake dressing vigorously before serving. Keeps in refrigerator for several weeks.

MARINADE (FOR PORK, CHICKEN, FISH)

$\frac{1}{4}$ cup extra-virgin olive oil

3 tbsp. chopped parsley

$\frac{1}{4}$ tsp. cracked black pepper

$\frac{1}{4}$ tsp. salt

1 tbsp. honey

2 tbsp. prepared mustard

juice of 1 lemon, strained

Combine all ingredients in a small bowl. Refrigerate marinade until needed. Brush marinade on both sides of meat, chicken, fish prior to their cooking; and occasionally, during the cooking. *Do not save or re-use leftover marinade.*

MORNAY SAUCE

4 tbsp. olive oil or butter

4 tbsp. all-purpose flour

1 cup evaporated milk

$\frac{1}{2}$ tsp. salt

$\frac{1}{4}$ tsp. black pepper

4 oz. grated Swiss cheese
   (or Cheddar or Parmesan)

cayenne pepper to taste

Over medium heat, in a small saucepan, melt butter (or heat oil) and stir in flour to make a smooth blend. Stir in milk, black pepper, (cayenne), salt. Blend in grated cheese, stirring constantly to make a smooth sauce. Proceed as directed in your recipe.

TARTARE SAUCE

1 cup mayonnaise

1 tsp. honey mustard

1 tbsp. lemon juice

1 tbsp. parsley, finely chopped

1 tsp. minced scallion

1 tbsp. sweet pickle, finely chopped

1 tbsp. capers, drained

$\frac{1}{4}$ tsp. freshly ground black pepper

$\frac{1}{8}$ tsp. salt, or to taste

Thoroughly combine all ingredients in a 1-pint jar with a lid. Keep refrigerated until ready to use (within 2 days). Stir well before serving. Serve with fried fish.

BARBEQUE SAUCE I

1 cup catsup

1 tbsp. white vinegar

$\frac{1}{4}$ cup orange juice

$\frac{1}{4}$ tsp. salt

$\frac{1}{8}$ tsp. Tabasco

1 tbsp. Worcestershire sauce

$\frac{1}{4}$ cup dark molasses

$\frac{1}{4}$ tsp. whole cloves

$\frac{1}{4}$ tsp. garlic powder

$\frac{1}{2}$ tsp. dry mustard

1 tbsp. olive oil

dash of black pepper

Simmer all ingredients in a small saucepan for 5 minutes. Use as directed in recipe.

BARBEQUE SAUCE II

1 tbsp. olive oil

1 onion, chopped

2 cups prepared tomato sauce

1 cup red wine vinegar

1 tbsp. garlic powder

$\frac{1}{4}$ tsp. freshly ground black pepper

$\frac{1}{4}$ tsp. cayenne pepper

$\frac{1}{4}$ tsp. sweet paprika

1 tsp. salt

$\frac{1}{2}$ cup packed brown sugar

2 tbsp. Worcestershire sauce

Combine all ingredients in a small saucepan and simmer for 5 minutes. Proceed as directed in recipe; or store in refrigerator until needed, up to several days.

BOURBON SAUCE

1 cup of Barbeque Sauce (see recipes above)

$\frac{1}{4}$ cup orange marmalade

2 tbsp. bourbon

Combine all ingredients in a small bowl. Proceed as directed in recipe; or refrigerate until needed, up to several days.

GARAM MASALA

2 tablespoons each:

cardamom powder	ground cloves	whole black peppercorns
coriander seeds, crushed	ground cinnamon	cumin

Blend spices thoroughly; pour into a $\frac{1}{2}$-pint jar with a screw-top lid. As with any spice, potency will dissipate over a prolonged time.

A PAIR OF SAUCES FROM THE VIRGIN ISLANDS
(Contributed by Enid Lopes.)

COWITCH SAUCE *(A very spicy HOT sauce for Fish.)*

2 medium-size onions, sliced	7 whole cloves
1 cup olive oil	1 tsp. grated nutmeg
$\frac{1}{2}$ cup white vinegar	$\frac{1}{2}$ tsp. mace
3 or 4 bay leaves	salt, to taste
7 whole black peppercorns	hot Bird pepper or Scotch Bonnet or cayenne, (a small piece, about $\frac{1}{4}$-inch)

Simmer all ingredients in a saucepan for 5 minutes. Pour sauce into a quart-size jar with a lid and keep refrigerated for up to 2 weeks.

NATIVE SEASONING (Also called CREOLE SEASONING or POUNDED SALT)
(Used as a seasoning to flavor all types of meat, fish, poultry. Enid uses a mortar and pestle to blend the ingredients. You may wish to use a food processor.)

1 cup sea salt, pounded to a fine texture	1 tsp. mace
$\frac{1}{2}$ tsp. ground cloves	1 tsp. ground nutmeg
4 whole garlic cloves	a sprig of parsley
4 tsp. ground black pepper (Hot red pepper may be substituted when using spice mix on fish.)	a sprig of celery leaves

Combine all ingredients in a bowl. Pour into a 1-pint jar with a lid. Store the jar of spice in a cool pantry for a month or longer.

BEARNAISE SAUCE

1 small onion, chopped fine	$\frac{1}{4}$ cup olive oil or melted butter
1 tbsp. dried tarragon, crushed	$\frac{1}{2}$ cup egg substitute
1 tbsp. chopped chervil (or parsley)	1 tbsp. cold water
$\frac{1}{4}$ cup dry white wine	$\frac{1}{2}$ tsp. salt
2 tbsp. white wine vinegar	$\frac{1}{4}$ tsp. black pepper

In top half of a quart-size double boiler, whisk egg substitute over hot water. Add cold water, herbs, onion, wine and wine vinegar, steadily whipping. Add oil (or butter) a little bit at a time; continue to whisk until sauce has thickened and is creamy. Season with salt and pepper. Should the sauce curdle, add another tablespoon of cold water. Remove sauce from heat and whip vigorously. Use as directed in recipe.

BÉCHAMEL SAUCE

2 tbsp. butter or Smart Balance spread	$\frac{1}{8}$ tsp. ground nutmeg
2 tbsp. all-purpose flour	pinch of salt
$1\frac{1}{2}$ cups evaporated milk (fat-free available)	$\frac{1}{4}$ Gruyere cheese, grated
$\frac{1}{8}$ tsp. freshly ground black pepper	$\frac{1}{4}$ cup Parmesan cheese, grated

Melt butter (or Smart Balance spread) in a small saucepan over medium-low heat until bubbles form. Whisk in flour and cook, stirring for 2 minutes, until sauce is smooth. Slowly add milk, whisking continuously, cooking until thick. Remove sauce from heat. Sir in salt, pepper, nutmeg, grated Gruyere cheese and Parmesan cheese. Proceed to use as directed in recipe.

CHILI SAUCE

$1\frac{1}{2}$ cups prepared tomato sauce	1 cup prepared beef gravy,
2 tbsp. prepared hot horseradish	(or 1 beef bouillon cube mashed
a few shakes Tabasco	into 1 cup hot water, combined with
1 small onion, minced	2 tbsp. flour, dissolved into
1 tbsp. olive oil	$\frac{1}{4}$ cup cold water)

Combine and mix all ingredients in a 1-quart saucepan. Simmer for 10 minutes. Serve with meat, fish, poultry or vegetables.

CHEESE SAUCE

3 tbsp. olive oil

$\frac{1}{4}$ cup all-purpose flour

$1\frac{1}{2}$ cups whole milk or evaporated milk

1 cup grated sharp Cheddar cheese
    or other cheese of choice

$\frac{1}{2}$ tsp. salt

$\frac{1}{4}$ tsp. black pepper

$\frac{1}{2}$ tsp. dry mustard

1 tsp. onion powder

1 tsp. Worcestershire sauce

few drops Tabasco

Heat oil over low temperature and stir in flour. Add milk and rest of ingredients. Stir constantly over low heat until mix is creamy and starts to thicken. Serve hot as directed in recipe.

BASIC CURRY SAUCE

3 tbsp. olive oil

3 tbsp. all-purpose flour

$\frac{1}{2}$ tsp. salt

$\frac{1}{4}$ tsp. black pepper

a few whole cloves

$\frac{1}{2}$ tsp. ground ginger

$\frac{1}{4}$ tsp. each: cardamom, cumin,
    curry powder, mace

1 cup whole milk or evaporated milk

1 onion, minced

$\frac{1}{2}$ cup celery, minced

$\frac{1}{2}$ cup apple, finely chopped (do not pare)

1 tsp. grated lemon rind

$\frac{1}{2}$ cup sherry

1 cup homemade chicken or vegetable stock
    (or use bouillon cubes)

In a 1-quart saucepan, warm oil over low heat. Stir in flour, salt, seasonings, spices and herbs. Sir to thoroughly mix, over low heat. Gradually add milk, stirring continuously until creamy. Add onion, celery, apple, lemon rind and stock. Stir to mix. Cook until sauce starts to simmer, and thickens. Add sherry. Stir to blend. Pour sauce over cooked chicken, lamb or seafood (from which you have gotten the stock.) Stir to combine and continue as in recipe.

CURRY SALSA

1 large onion, finely chopped

2 tbsp. olive oil

1 tsp. peeled gingerroot, minced

2 garlic cloves, minced

1 green bell pepper, deseeded, finely chopped

1 red bell pepper, deseeded, finely chopped

$\frac{1}{4}$ cup all-purpose flour

2 tbsp. curry powder

2 cups chicken both (less-salt variety)

1 can (20 oz.) chopped plum tomatoes

2 tbsp. fresh lime juice

1 tbsp. grated lime zest

salt, black pepper to taste

In a 2-quart saucepan with a lid, cook onion in olive oil over moderate heat until tender; add garlic and gingerroot, stirring and cooking for 1-2 minutes longer. Add peppers and cook for several minutes until softened. Stir in curry and flour and cook for 2 minutes. Add broth and tomatoes, mixing thoroughly; cook for 5 minutes. Stir in lime juice and zest, salt and pepper. Remove from burner.

Salsa may be prepared a couple of days in advance, covered and refrigerated. Reheat sauce when needed. For seafood, chicken, lamb. Serves 6 portions.

CHINESE BARBEQUE SAUCE

3 tbsp. olive oil

1 tbsp. peanut oil

3 scallions, chopped

2 garlic cloves, minced

1 small onion, finely chopped

1 tbsp. cornstarch stirred into
  $\frac{1}{4}$ cup cold water

1 cup stock (or 1 tbsp. Gravy Master
  dissolved in 1 cup water)

1 tbsp. *lite* soy sauce

1 tbsp. hoisin sauce (*NOTE: below)

$\frac{1}{4}$ cup plum sauce (*NOTE: below)

$\frac{1}{2}$ cup catsup

1 tsp. grated gingerroot

$\frac{1}{4}$ cup honey

3 tbsp. creamy peanut butter

1 tbsp. rice vinegar

Heat oils in a 1-quart saucepan; sauté garlic, onion and scallions. Stir in cornstarch mixed with water. Add remaining ingredients and stir over low heat until peanut butter is melted. Use sauce to baste and/or as a barbeque sauce in Chinese recipes.

*NOTE: Hoisin and plum sauces may be purchased at supermarkets (Asian food section) or at specialty food stores.

HOLLANDAISE SAUCE

½ cup olive oil
3 beaten eggs or ¾ cup egg substitute

1 tbsp. lemon juice
1 tsp. sherry
a few grains of red cayenne pepper

In top part of small double boiler, heat olive oil over hot, not boiling, water and slowly stir in beaten eggs (or egg substitute). Add lemon juice, sherry and cayenne, stirring continuously. Keep water in lower pot very warm as you prepare sauce. You may prepare sauce in advance; refrigerate up to 2-3 days. When ready to use, warm the sauce over hot, not boiling water, stirring continuously.

HAWAIIAN SWEET AND SOUR SAUCE

½ cup meat, poultry or seafood stock
1 tsp. mustard powder
¼ tsp. black pepper
½ cup dark corn syrup
1 tbsp. brown sugar
1 tbsp. *lite* soy sauce

½ cup green pepper, deseeded, sliced
1 tsp. cornstarch stirred into 2 tbsp. cold water
1 cup pineapple chunks
1 cup pineapple juice (or peach nectar)
6 maraschino cherries, crushed

Combine all ingredients in a small bowl. Pour over meat, poultry or seafood which is cooking; continue to simmer for 10-15 minutes longer. Or, to saucepan, add some stock made from ½ cup hot water and chicken bouillon (or cooked seafood liquid). Or, prepare stock by stirring 1 tablespoon Gravy Master into ½ cup hot water; add to sauce to simmer for 15 minutes as directed above.

MUSHROOM SAUCE

3 tbsp. olive oil
1 tbsp. minced onion
3 tbsp. all-purpose flour
½ tsp. salt
¼ tsp. black pepper
1 cup whole milk or evaporated milk
1 cup mushroom stock (with mushrooms)
1 tbsp. Worcestershire sauce

MUSHROOM STOCK:
5-6 small white mushrooms, rinsed, chopped
1 cup water

Simmer chopped mushrooms in boiling water for 2 minutes. Add stock to sauce.

Prepare mushroom stock as directed; set aside. In a 1-quart saucepan, lightly brown onion in hot oil. Stir in flour until smooth. Add milk and mushroom stock with mushrooms, salt, pepper and Worcestershire sauce. Stir and cook for 1 minute longer. Keep sauce warm over a pan of hot water until ready to serve.

MUSHROOM TOMATO SAUCE
(May be prepared 2-3 days in advance and refrigerated; or frozen for several weeks.)

1 lb. mushrooms, scrubbed, thinly sliced

1 large garlic clove, minced

1 small onion, chopped

3 tbsp. olive oil

3 cups tomato purée

½ tsp. salt, or to taste

½ tsp. black pepper

¼ tsp. each: fresh basil, fresh parsley, dried thyme

In a 2-quart saucepot, over medium heat, sauté onion, garlic and mushrooms in olive oil. When lightly browned (2 minutes), add purée, spices and herbs. Simmer gently for 30 minutes. Serve over pasta or rice; or use to accompany beef or fowl. Serves 4-6.

....

BEEF BOLOGNESE TOMATO SAUCE
(May be prepared 2-3 days in advance and refrigerated; or frozen for several weeks.)

¼ cup minced pancetta or bacon

1 small yellow onion, minced

1 garlic clove, minced

1 medium-size carrot, pared, finely chopped

1 celery stalk, finely chopped

2 tbsp. olive oil

1 lb. lean chopped beef, crumbled

2-3 fresh basil leaves, chopped

½ tsp. each: oregano, thyme, nutmeg

2 bay leaves

½ tsp. each: salt, black pepper (to taste)

3 cups tomato purée

½ cup white wine, like Soave Bolla

½ cup grated Pecorino Romano

In a 2-quart saucepot, over medium heat, cook crumbled chopped beef, onion, garlic, carrot, celery in pancetta and olive oil until beef is lightly browned, stirring occasionally, to maintain beef in small chunks. Add tomato sauce, herbs and spices; stir to combine. Slowly simmer for 30 minutes, with lid loosely covering pot of sauce. Stir in wine and cheese during last 5 minutes. Remove and discard bay leaves. Serve over pasta or rice. Serves 4-6.

....

PROSCIUTTO DI POMIDORO

2 tbsp. olive oil

2-3 large garlic cloves, minced

1 small yellow onion, minced

6 slices (about 3 oz.) prosciutto, shredded

1 can (35 oz.) peeled plum tomatoes, mashed

6 fresh basil leaves, chopped

¼ cup Italian parsley leaves, chopped

½ tsp. salt

¼ tsp. freshly ground black pepper

a pinch of hot red pepper flakes

1 cup dry white wine, like Pinot Grigio

In a 2-quart saucepot, over medium heat, cook onion, garlic and prosciutto in olive oil for 5 minutes, or until onion is translucent and prosciutto is lightly crisped. Add tomatoes with juices and simmer sauce, uncovered, for 30 minutes. Stir in herbs and spices and continue to low-simmer for another 30 minutes. Serve over pasta. Serves 4.

MARIONARA SAUCE (MARINARA)
(METHOD I)

*[A Cooking Hint: These sauces, as most sauces with a tomato base,
may be prepared 2-3 days in advance and refrigerated;
or frozen in containers for several weeks. Soften in refrigerator.]*

4-5 lbs. fresh ripe plum tomatoes
1 can (6 oz.) tomato paste, as needed
   (if sauce needs thickening)
3 tbsp. olive oil
1 tsp. salt
$\frac{1}{4}$ tsp. black pepper
a few grains hot red pepper flakes

1 tbsp. fresh basil, chopped
1 green pepper, deseeded, chopped
2 large garlic cloves, minced
1 small yellow onion, chopped
1 tbsp. mixed: oregano, thyme, rosemary
$\frac{1}{2}$ cup grated Parmesan cheese

    In a 4-quart saucepot, heat oil; brown garlic, onion and green pepper. Set aside. Wash tomatoes and place in a 6-quart pot with a lid. Add $\frac{1}{4}$ cup water; cover pot and bring to boil. Simmer for 5 minutes, until tomatoes are soft. Drain and strain tomatoes and liquid through a colander or a sieve with a large bowl underneath, to contain the puréed tomatoes. Or use a food mill which separates pulp from skin and seeds.

    When using a colander, use your hands to push tomatoes through. Discard the squeezed skins/seeds. Transfer purée to saucepot with cooked vegetable mix. Add remaining ingredients except cheese; stir to thoroughly blend. Gently simmer sauce with lid askew for 1 hour. As sauce simmers, stir in tomato paste to thicken sauce, if necessary. Stir in cheese upon completion. Serves 6.

MARINARA SAUCE
(METHOD II)

2 lbs. canned plum tomatoes
3 tbsp. olive oil
1 small yellow onion, finely chopped
2-3 large garlic cloves, minced
1 small green pepper, deseeded, chopped
1 can (6 oz.) tomato paste

1 tsp. salt
$\frac{1}{4}$ tsp. black pepper
a few flakes hot red pepper
2-3 fresh basil leaves
1 tbsp. mixed: oregano, thyme, rosemary
$\frac{1}{2}$ cup grated Parmesan cheese

    Strain plum tomatoes through a colander as in Method I, or use blender. In a 2-quart saucepot with a lid, lightly brown garlic, onion and green pepper in hot oil. Add puréed tomatoes, tomato paste and remaining ingredients, except cheese. Stir to thoroughly blend. Loosely cover pot of sauce; simmer gently for 1 hour, stirring occasionally. Stir in cheese during last minutes of cooking. Serves 4.

MARINARA SAUCE
(METHOD III- QUICK AND EASY)

3 cups prepared tomato purée

3 tbsp. olive oil

1 small onion, finely chopped

2-3 garlic cloves, minced

1 small green pepper, deseeded, chopped

1 tbsp. mixed: oregano, rosemary, thyme

a few leaves fresh basil

1 tsp. salt; $\frac{1}{4}$ tsp. black pepper

a few grains hot pepper flakes

$\frac{1}{2}$ cup grated Parmesan cheese

Cook onion, garlic and green pepper in hot olive oil in a 2-quart saucepot with a cover. Add and blend tomato purée and herbs/spices. Partially cover pot; simmer sauce for 1 hour. Stir in Parmesan cheese during last 5 minutes. Serves 4.

SAUSAGE AND MEATBALL TOMATO SAUCE
(May be prepared in advance and refrigerated up to 3 days; or, frozen in containers for several weeks.)

MEAT:

3 links sweet Italian fennel sausage

3 links hot Italian fennel sausage

2 lbs. chopped beef for meatballs

Add: $\frac{1}{2}$ cup fine bread crumbs,
1 tbsp. chopped parsley, $\frac{1}{4}$ tsp. salt,
$\frac{1}{4}$ tsp. black pepper, 1 egg, beaten
(or $\frac{1}{4}$ cup egg substitute)

3 tbsp. olive oil

3 large garlic cloves, minced

1 small onion, chopped

In a skillet, brown sausages on all sides, onion and garlic in olive oil at 300° for 5 minutes until sausages are cooked through, but not dry. Remove sausages to a platter. In a 2-quart bowl, combine meatball ingredients; form 3-inch meatballs. Brown them in same skillet on all sides for 4-5 minutes, until cooked through, but moist. Remove meatballs to the platter. Scrape bottom of skillet to loosen leavings. In a large bowl combine the following ingredients for sauce.

SAUCE:

4 cups Italian plum tomatoes, strained,
   or use blender

2-3 tbsp. tomato paste

$\frac{1}{2}$ tsp. salt; $\frac{1}{4}$ tsp. black pepper

1 tbsp. mixed: oregano, rosemary,
   thyme, marjoram

2-3 fresh basil leaves

$\frac{1}{2}$ cup red table wine

$\frac{1}{2}$ cup Parmesan cheese

Combine all meat and leavings in a 4-quart saucepot with a cover. Combine sauce ingredients *(except wine and cheese)* and add to saucepot to thoroughly mix. Simmer with lid askew for 1 hour, stirring occasionally. During last 5 minutes, stir in wine and cheese. Serve over pasta or rice. Serve sausages and meatballs as an accompaniment. Serves 5-6.

RAGOUT

MEAT:

2 links sweet Italian fennel sausages
2 links hot Italian fennel sausages
$\frac{1}{2}$ lb. lean pork for gravy
1 slice top round for braciola (pounded thin)
   (SPRINKLED WITH: 1 tbsp. chopped
   parsley, $\frac{1}{4}$ cup mixed: raisins/pignola,
   salt/pepper to taste)

1 lb. lean chopped beef for meatballs
   (ADD/MIX: 1 beaten egg, salt and
   pepper to taste, $\frac{1}{2}$ cup fine bread
   crumbs, 1 tbsp. minced parsley)

Prepare BRACIOLA. Lay pounded slice of top round on a sheet of waxed paper. Sprinkle with parsley, raisins mix, salt and pepper. Roll up and tie with Cook's string or knit with a thin metal skewer. Set aside. (Remember to remove string, or skewer before serving; cut braciola into sections.)

Prepare MEATBALLS. In a bowl, combine chopped beef, egg, crumbs, parsley, salt and pepper. Form 2-inch balls. Set aside.

SAUCE:

1 large can (about 2 cups) plum tomatoes, strained through colander; or use a blender
1 can (6 oz.) tomato paste stirred into $\frac{1}{4}$ cup hot water
3 tbsp. olive oil
2-3 large garlic cloves, chopped
1 small onion, chopped
$\frac{1}{4}$ cup each: red and green pepper, deseeded, chopped
1 tbsp. mixed: oregano, thyme, marjoram, rosemary
2-3 fresh basil leaves
1 tsp. salt, $\frac{1}{4}$ tsp. black pepper, a few grains hot red pepper flakes
$\frac{1}{2}$ cup red table wine
$\frac{1}{2}$ cup Pecorino Romano cheese, grated; more cheese at serving

Prepare RAGOUT SAUCE. Heat olive oil in a 4-quart saucepot. Lightly brown onion, garlic and green/red peppers. Scrape bottom of pan to remove leavings. Then, cook sausages and pork over medium-high heat on all sides, about 5-6 minutes. Transfer pork and sausages to a large bowl; set aside. (Cut sausages in half at serving.) Cook meatballs, then braciola, in same pot, to lightly brown on all sides. Do not overcook. Transfer meat to large bowl with sausages. Set aside.

Scrape leavings from bottom of saucepot. Pour strained tomatoes into saucepot; stir in creamed tomato paste, herbs and spices to thoroughly blend into sauce. Lay the cover loosely on top of pot; bring the pot of sauce to simmer for 30 minutes. Stir in the cooked meat and simmer for another 30 minutes. During last 5 minutes, blend wine and cheese into sauce. At serving, remove meat to a platter. Serve Ragout Sauce over pasta or rice, with the meats as an accompaniment. Serves 4-6.

RED PEPPER SAUCE

4 large red bell peppers, deseeded, cut into chunks

4 large garlic cloves, peeled

¼ cup olive oil

1 small onion, chopped

1-inch Chile pepper, deseeded

1 cup prepared tomato sauce, unseasoned

2 tbsp. balsamic vinegar

1 tsp. salt

¼ tsp. black pepper

1 tsp. each: oregano, basil

1-2 large bay leaves

½ cup Asiago cheese, grated

Purée prepared red peppers in a food processor or a minute or two. Add garlic and pulse for half a minute. In a medium-size saucepan with a cover, heat olive oil and lightly brown onion and Chile. (Careful handling when using hot pepper.) Cool slightly; then, add puréed red peppers/garlic. Stir in tomato sauce, vinegar, herbs, spices. Return the saucepot with cover to the stove and simmer sauce for 30 minutes, stirring occasionally. Remove bay leaves and discard. Stir in grated cheese. Serve over pasta. Garnish with more cheese, if desired. Serves 4-5.

. . . .

RED PEPPER VODKA SAUCE

RED PEPPER SAUCE (see recipe above)

To the INGREDIENTS, add:
1 cup creamy ricotta
½ cup vodka

Add and stir in ricotta and vodka to prepared RED PEPPER SAUCE during last 5 minutes of cooking the sauce. Then, stir in Asiago cheese. Serve over pasta. Add more cheese, if desired. Serves 4-5.

. . . .

VODKA MARINARA SAUCE

MARINARA SAUCE (see recipes pages 393-394)

To the INGREDIENTS, add:
1 cup creamy ricotta
½ cup Parmesan cheese

½ cup vodka
a few grains hot red pepper flakes

Add and blend ricotta, Parmesan, vodka and hot pepper during last 5 minutes of cooking the sauce. Serve over pasta. Add more cheese, if desired. Serves 4-5.

SALSA PUTTANESCA

1 can (20 oz.) plum tomatoes
   or 1 large can crushed tomatoes
6 plum tomatoes, skin removed
   (*NOTE: below)
1 large yellow onion, thinly sliced
6 garlic cloves, chopped
2 tbsp. olive oil
1 tbsp. butter or Smart Balance spread

$\frac{1}{2}$ cup pitted oil-cured olives, chopped
6 anchovy fillets, coarsely chopped
1 tbsp. capers
6 basil leaves, torn into pieces
$\frac{1}{4}$ tsp. each: salt, black pepper
hot red pepper flakes, to taste
1 tsp. dried oregano

*NOTE: Drop 6 ripe plum tomatoes into boiling water for 1 minute. Remove tomatoes from pot; peel off skin with fingers. Coarsely chop tomatoes and set aside in a 2-quart bowl.

Meanwhile, food process 1 large can plum tomatoes (or use crushed tomatoes). Add to chopped tomatoes in bowl. In a 2-quart saucepot with a lid, lightly brown onion and garlic in a mix of olive oil and butter (or Smart Balance spread). Do not burn. Scrape bottom of pot to loosen leavings. Pour tomatoes into this pot; add black pepper, salt, hot pepper flakes, anchovies, capers, chopped olives, oregano and basil. Blend thoroughly. With lid askew, simmer sauce for 30 minutes. Turn off heat under pot. Remove basil leaves and discard. Serve over 1-1$\frac{1}{2}$ lbs. spaghetti or perciatelli pasta. Serves 6.

BASIC BROWN GRAVY
(For meat and poultry; about 2 cups.)

2-3 tbsp. olive oil
1 small onion, finely chopped
2-3 tbsp. flour stirred into $\frac{1}{4}$ cup water
$\frac{1}{2}$ cup prepared tomato sauce
1 tsp. Gravy Master

$\frac{1}{4}$ tsp. each: salt, black pepper
dash of red cayenne pepper
meat or fowl drippings plus water,
   to make 1 cup stock (*NOTE below)
2 tbsp. Marsala wine (or sweet vermouth)

Lightly brown onion in heated olive oil. In a small bowl, stir flour into cold water until smooth; add stock, tomato sauce, Gravy Master, salt, pepper and cayenne. Whisk stock mix into oil/onion mix. Cook and stir gravy over low heat until it thickens. Stir wine into gravy as it thickens. Keep sauce warm over a pan of hot water.

*NOTE: If no drippings are available, use 2 beef or chicken bouillon cubes dissolved into 1 cup hot water.

SEAFOOD TOMATO SAUCE

1 large can (3 cups) Italian plum tomatoes, strained; or use blender

2 tbsp. tomato paste, stirred into $\frac{1}{4}$ cup hot water

3 tbsp. olive oil

2 large garlic cloves, minced

1 small onion, chopped

$\frac{1}{4}$ cup fresh basil

1 tbsp. mixed: oregano, thyme

$\frac{1}{2}$ tsp. salt

$\frac{1}{4}$ tsp. black pepper

a few grains of hot pepper flakes

2-3 bay leaves

$\frac{1}{2}$ cup dry white wine

2 cups raw, cleaned seafood: clams, crabs, lobsters, mussels, shrimp, squid - any of these; or a combination of several (*NOTE below)

In a 4-quart saucepot with a cover, sauté garlic and onion in olive oil until lightly browned. Add other sauce ingredients except seafood and wine. Stir and simmer covered, for 30 minutes. Add wine in last 5 minutes of cooking. Add 2 cups cleaned seafood and simmer for an additional 10 minutes. Remove bay leaves and discard. Serve sauce over spaghetti, linguini, rice. Serves 4-5.

*NOTE:

CLAMS: Use 1 cup chopped clams plus liquid; strain liquid through cheesecloth or a fine strainer.

CRABS or LOBSTERS: Use 6 small crabs; or 1 whole lobster; or 4 lobster claws.

MUSSELS: Scrub thoroughly. Add 1 dozen mussels in shell in sauce.

SQUID: Use 2 cupfuls; clean, cut into rings.

PESTO SAUCE

2 cups fresh basil leaves, rinsed, drained

6 large garlic cloves

1 oz. pignola (pine nuts)

$\frac{1}{2}$ cup grated Parmesan cheese

$\frac{1}{2}$ cup extra-virgin olive oil

salt, black pepper, to taste

Optional: $\frac{1}{4}$ cup finely chopped walnuts

Combine all ingredients in a food processor. Purée for 30 seconds or until basil leaves are creamed. Add 1-2 tablespoons of water, if sauce is too dry. Serve immediately, or pour into a 1-pint plastic container and freeze up to 1 week. If sauce has been frozen, transfer to refrigerator early on serving day. When needed, warm the container (lid removed) over a pan of hot water. Stir the sauce while warming. Serve over pasta or rice. Toss to coat. Serves 12 oz. of pasta.

HAWAIIAN TOMATO SAUCE
(May be prepared a day in advance.)

2 tbsp. olive oil

½ cup green bell pepper, deseeded, chopped

1 cup prepared tomato sauce

½ cup pineapple chunks

½ cup pineapple juice

1 tbsp. white wine vinegar

1 tbsp. Gravy Master

2 tbsp. brown sugar

1 tbsp. prepared mustard

½ tsp. salt

¼ tsp. black pepper

few dashes Tabasco

1 tbsp. cornstarch stirred into ¼ cup cold water

Combine all ingredients in a 1-quart saucepan. Simmer for 5 minutes. Serve over hot rice.

HOMEMADE CHICKEN BROTH (STOCK)

2 chicken legs, 2 chicken wings,
    rinsed in cold water

6 cups boiling water

1 celery stalk, finely chopped

1 carrot, pared, finely chopped

1 small onion, finely chopped

2 large garlic cloves, minced

1 bay leaf

salt, black pepper, to taste

Do not remove skin from chicken parts. Boil 6 cups water in a 4-quart soup pot with a cover. Add all prepared ingredients. Cover pot and lower to simmer for 35-40 minutes. Remove chicken meat from legs and wings; finely chop; set aside. Discard skin and bones and bay leaf. Either purée vegetables in the stock and return them to the pot; or, allow vegetables to remain as is. Return chopped chicken to stock pot; (or make yourself a delicious chicken salad sandwich). Proceed as directed in your recipe. Makes 6 cups chicken broth (stock).

HOMEMADE VEGETABLE STOCK

6 cups boiling water

2 tbsp. olive oil

salt, black pepper, to taste

1 bay leaf

1 small onion, finely chopped

2-3 large garlic cloves, minced

1 large celery stalk with greens, chopped

1 large carrot, pared, finely chopped

Pour 6 cups water into a 2-quart soup pot and bring to a boil. Add vegetables, salt, pepper and bay leaf. Cover pot and simmer stock for 30 minutes. Either purée vegetables and return to pot; or allow vegetables to remain as is. Proceed as directed in your recipe. Makes 6 cups vegetable stock.

WHOLE CRANBERRY ORANGE SAUCE

12 oz. fresh cranberries
1 cup orange juice with pulp

1 cup granulated sugar
$\frac{1}{4}$ cup chopped walnuts

In a medium-size saucepan with a lid, dissolve sugar into orange juice; bring to a boil and stir in cranberries. Return to boil; reduce heat and simmer for 10 minutes, stirring occasionally. Remove pot from heat; stir in walnuts. Cool sauce completely at room temperature. Then, pour sauce into a container with a screw-on cap or a tight lid. Refrigerate sauce up to 1 month. Serves 8-10.

SEASONED DIPPING OILS

(1)	(2)	(3)
$\frac{1}{2}$ cup extra-virgin olive oil	$\frac{1}{2}$ cup extra-virgin olive oil	$\frac{1}{2}$ cup extra-virgin olive oil
2 tbsp. balsamic vinegar	2 tbsp. pitted, chopped	juice of 1 lemon, strained
1 tbsp. chopped sun dried	Sicilian olives	1 tsp. grated lemon peel
tomatoes	2 garlic cloves, minced	2 garlic cloves, minced
1 tbsp. crushed, dried	1 tsp. black peppercorns	1 tsp. black peppercorns
rosemary	1 tsp. each: dried oregano,	1 tsp. capers
2 garlic cloves, minced	chopped fresh basil	1 tsp. dried oregano
$\frac{1}{2}$ tsp coarsely ground	1 bay leaf (whole)	
black pepper		

Store each recipe of seasoned dipping oils in separate glass 1-pint jars with screw-top lids. Shake well. At serving time, stir/shake the oils to blend thoroughly; pour each mix into separate serving bowls and set them around a large serving tray. Accompany with small chunks of crusty artisan bread, arranged in a basket in center of the serving tray. If not using within a few hours, refrigerate Dipping Oils. Use within 1 week.

GUACAMOLE (AVOCADO DIP)
[A Cooking Hint: Dip peeled avocado, banana or apple into lemon juice
(or other citrus juice) to prevent its discoloration.]

2 ripe Hass avocados
3 cherry tomatoes, chopped
1 tbsp. onion, minced
2 tbsp. fresh lemon juice

1 tsp. garlic powder
1 tbsp. fresh cilantro, minced
$\frac{1}{2}$ tsp. smoked Spanish paprika
2 tbsp. pignola (pine nuts) for garnish

Peel avocados. Mash them in a medium-size bowl; discard stones. Add lemon juice, chopped tomatoes, onion, garlic powder and cilantro. Pack and mound the dip into a 6-inch serving bowl. Sprinkle with paprika; insert pignola over the avocado ball (like a porcupine). Place bowl in center of a platter; scatter corn chips around the platter. Serves 4-6.

SANDWICH SPREADS AND DIPS

1) CREAM CHEESE, PEPPERS AND OLIVES

12 oz. low-fat cream cheese,
   at room temperature
2 tbsp. pitted Kalamata olives, finely chopped

1 tbsp. each: red bell pepper, green bell pepper,
   deseeded, finely chopped

Mash cream cheese with a fork and blend smoothly. Combine rest of ingredients to blend into the cream cheese. Spread on triangles of firm bread, or crackers; or on firm raw vegetables or fruit: carrots, celery, apples.

2) CREAM CHEESE, WALNUTS & CRANBERRY RAISINS

12 oz. low-fat cream cheese, at room temperature
2 tbsp. each: walnuts and cranberry raisins, finely chopped

Mash cream cheese with a fork and blend smoothly. Combine rest of ingredients, to blend into the cream cheese. Spread on triangles of firm bread, or crackers; or on firm raw vegetables or fruit: carrots, celery, apples.

3) CREAM CHEESE & SCALLION SPREAD

$\frac{1}{2}$ lb. low-fat cream cheese
$\frac{1}{2}$ lb. low-fat cream cheese
pinch of salt

$\frac{1}{4}$ cup scallions, with some greens, chopped
2 tbsp. red bell pepper, deseeded,
   finely chopped
$\frac{1}{4}$ tsp. garlic powder

Mash cream cheese with a fork and blend smoothly. Combine remainder of ingredients, to blend into the cream cheese. Spread on triangles of firm bread, or crackers; or on firm raw vegetables or fruit: carrots, celery, apples.

4) BLEU CHEESE DIP

1 cup low-fat sour cream
1 tbsp. prepared horseradish

$\frac{1}{4}$ tsp. freshly ground black pepper
1 tbsp. chives, minced
1 cup bleu cheese, finely chopped

Thoroughly blend all ingredients into a small bowl. Cover bowl and refrigerate until serving, up to 2 days. Serve with raw vegetables or crunchy crackers.

ACCOMPANIMENTS

HOW TO ROAST PEPPERS

<u>Method 1</u>) If roasting more than 2 peppers, preheat oven to 450°. Lay 4-6 peppers on a metal cookie tray lined with a sheet of foil. I remove seeds before roasting peppers, by coring them and removing the stem with the ribs and seeds. Insert a clove of peeled garlic into the cavity of each pepper. Roast peppers 5 to 15 minutes on each side, depending upon size; turn them once. The skin will char. Remove tray from oven; wrap peppers in their foil; allow peppers to steam, covered in the foil, until they are cool enough to handle. Then, peel off skin, starting at the blossom end. You may serve them (with the garlic) as a whole pepper or sliced into strips. <u>Suggestions for peppers</u>: Large red, orange, yellow, purple, green bell peppers.

<u>Method 2</u>) OR: If you're roasting 1 or 2 peppers, use a long-handled fork with a heat-proof handle. Remove core/seeds as in Method 1. Spear peppers, one at a time with long-handled fork. Char peppers over an open flame, turning them every 2-3 minutes, until skins are charred. Then, proceed to remove skin as in Method 1.

<u>Method 3</u>) OR: Broil peppers by laying them on a cookie sheet lined with foil as in Method 1. First, remove core/seeds as in Method 1. Broil in preheated broiler-oven about 3 inches from heat, using a long-handled fork with a heat-proof handle, turning peppers every 3-4 minutes, for 10-15 minutes, depending upon size of peppers. When peppers are charred, wrap them in their cooking foil; proceed as directed in Method 1 to remove skin.

If preparing Chiles, use protective gloves. ***IN ANY CASE, DO NOT LEAVE PROCEDURE UNATTENDED!!!***

. . . .

HOW TO SKIN A TOMATO

1. Wash tomato.
2. Immerse tomato in boiling water for 1 minute.
3. Remove tomato from boiling water and plunge it into cold water.
4. Peel off skin with fingers.

. . . .

HOW TO SKIN A PEACH

Follow same directions: How to Skin a Tomato. (See recipe above.)

NOTES FROM THE COOK

I The Cook's Equipment

Listed are the basic necessities to carry out the Home Cook's projects.

~ Cooking Units which include at least **4 Burners** and **1 Large Oven**. A gas-heated oven-broiler is good; and 2 ovens are even better. The luxury of an **Indoor or Outdoor Grill** further extends the home cook's domain.

~ A **Refrigerator-Freezer** of adequate size.

~ A separate **Upright Freezer**, if possible.

~ A basic set of **Heavy Pots**: 1-, 2-, 4-quart pots with covers/lids and oven-proof handles.

~ **Skillets** (with covers/lids and ovenproof handles): 5-inch, 8-inch, 12-inch.

~ 2 small **Saucepans** (with lids and ovenproof handles).

~ A heavy **Stockpot** (6 quarts) with a covers/lids and ovenproof handles.

~ A 2-quart **Double-Boiler**.

~ A 4-quart **Steamer with Basket**.

~ 1 or 2 **Grill Pans** with flat lids and ovenproof handles: 8-inch, 12-inch.

~ A **Roaster Pan** (with a cover) to fit a 15 lb. turkey.

~ A large **Dutch Oven** with cover.

~ A 15-inch square **Electric Skillet**.

~ An 8-inch oiled **Cast Iron Skillet**.

~ At least 2 or 3 **Baking Sheets**: 9x12, 9x15.

~ 1 or 2 **Baking Tins**: 9x15x2-3 inches.

~ 2 or 3 **Round/Square** 8-9-inch **Pie and Layer Cake Pans**.

~ A 10-inch **Bundt Pan**; a 9-inch **Spring-form Pan**.

~ Several 5x7-inch **Loaf Pans**.

~ **2 Muffin Tins**: 2½-inch cups and mini-cups.

~ Several heat-resistant **Pyrex Bowls**: 1-quart, 2-quart, 3-quart.

~ A large 2-3-quart **Casserole Dish**.

~ 2 sets graduated **Mixing Bowls** (aluminum and Pyrex).

~ A set of **Funnels**; a nest of **Measuring Spoons**; a nest of **Measuring Cups**.

~ A quality brand **Stationary Mixer** with bowls and dough hooks.

~ **A Food Processor; a Blender**.

~ An electric **Mini-Chopper**; portable **Electric Beaters**.

~ A **Ricer**; a nest of **Metal Strainers**; a **Colander**.

~ A 2x3-foot **Wood Pastry/Work Board**; a 10x15-inch **Glass-tempered Cutting Board**

~ An oiled **Wood Salad Bowl**, 6 **Salad Serving Bowls**, a pair of **Salad Servers**.

~ A **Glass Salad Bowl**; a 2-quart **Glass Fruit Bowl**.

~ Several 12-15-inch **Serving Platters**; **Oil/Vinegar Cruets**.

~ A set of **Spatulas**; ½-pint **Soup Ladle**; a large **Slotted Spoon**; a **Hand-Masher**.

~ A **Vegetable Peeler**; a **Can Opener**; a **Lid Flipper**; **Bottle Tongs**; **Metal Skewers**.

~ A **Cork Screw**; a **Whisk**; a **Mandoline**.

~ Asbestos-lined **Pot Rests**; **Oven-proof Mitts** and **Glove Pot Holders**.

~ **Cheese Grater**; 2 **Pepper Mills** (for black pepper and white pepper).

~ Several nests of plastic **Storage Containers** of varied sizes.

(Continued on page 404)

(Continued from page 403)
II Stocking the Pantry

"Spices on Demand":

Salt-box, Kosher salt, Sea Salt
Black Peppercorn, White Peppercorn in separate Pepper Grinders
Ground Black Pepper in a jar
No-Salt/Salt Spice Mix (Create your own mixture; or, See page 376 for recipe.)

Stock HERBS and SPICES (SEASONINGS) in small quantities, as needed. Once these spice containers are unsealed, the seasonings may dissipate quickly. Start an indoor Herb Garden in clay pots by a sunny window; or, outdoors in summer, in a window box or in a sunny corner of your garden. Dry your home-grown herbs. At the end of season, cut branches of herbs, bundle them with a soft ribbon-cord and suspend the fragrant herbs indoors, by a sunny window or skylight, to air-dry and to use.

Allspice (ground)
Basil Leaves
Bay Leaves
Cardamom (ground)
Celery Flakes, Celery Seed
Chili Powder
Cilantro Leaves
Cinnamon (ground), Cinnamon Sticks
Cloves Ground, Whole Cloves
Coriander Seed
Dill Weed, Dill Seed
Fennel Seed
Garlic Powder
Fresh Garlic (stored in vented jar)

Ginger (ground), Ginger glacé
Mace Powder
Mustard Seed, Mustard Powder
Nutmeg (ground), Whole Nutmeg
Onion Powder
Oregano Leaves
Paprika (Hungarian, Spanish)
Parsley Leaves
Rosemary Leaves
Saffron Threads in a small tin
Sage Leaves
Tarragon Leaves
Thyme Leaves
Turmeric

Extracts:.
Almond Pure Extract

Lemon Pure Extract

Vanilla Pure Extract

Bouillon:
Beef Bouillon Cubes

Chicken Bouillon Cubes

Vegetable Bouillon Cubes

(Continued on following page)

(Continued from page 404)

"Cooking Needs"

OILS: Olive Oil, Extra-Virgin Olive Oil, Canola Oil

PREPARED PACKAGED FOODS:

Beans, dried, canned: black beans, cannellini, kidney, lentils, split peas
Broth: low-sodium chicken
Evaporated Milk
Gelatin
Pasta, Noodles
Peanut Butter, Jams, Preserves
Rice: Arborio, Brown
Salmon (Wild) in cans
Soups (low-salt, low-fat)
Tomatoes in cans (whole plums, purée)
Tuna (solid, in water) in cans
Tomato Marinara Sauce (in jars)

BAKING and COOKING NEEDS:

All-purpose enriched Flour; Bisquick (low-fat) [Store in airtight containers.]
Baking Powder, Baking Soda
Breadcrumbs, plain [Store in airtight container.]
Cake Mixes: yellow, chocolate
Cereals (high fiber, low-fat, low-sugar, low-salt) [Store in airtight containers.]
Chocolate morsels, chocolate for grating, melting (dark or semi-sweet)
Coffee, Tea, Cocoa [When opened, store coffee in refrigerator.]
Cornmeal, Corn Starch [Store in airtight containers.]
Honey, Molasses
Nuts [Store in small amounts in assorted air-tight containers.]
Oatmeal [Store in air-tight container.]
Sugars: granulated, brown, confectioners' [Store in small amounts in airtight containers.]
Vinegar: red wine, white distilled, cider, balsamic

(Continued on page 406)

(Continued from page 405)

III Refrigerator Staples: (Follow directions on food labels to refrigerate product after opening. Observe "Use By" dates printed on canned goods; discard if expired.)

Fresh Milk

Butter, Smart Balance spread (in temperature-selected section of refrigerator)

Fresh large Eggs; Egg Substitute in container

Cheese (in climate-control section of refrigerator)

Catsup, Horseradish in jar, Mayonnaise, Sauces in jars

Fresh Fruit (in Bins): Oranges, Lemons, Limes, Berries, any cut fruit

Fresh Vegetables (in Bins): Carrots, Celery, Onions, Potatoes, Greens

Bottled/Filtered Water, other beverages in bottles, cans

Coffee Beans (or ground coffee) in container

Peanut Butter, Jams/Preserves, Pancake Syrup.
    (Once container is opened, refrigerate.)

"Secrets of a Fridge"

Your refrigerator holds your secrets and freezes them solidly. How old is the butter in that white plastic dish?
One, two, three __ eight large eggs. And when were they tucked so neatly into their cubbyholes? I'm talking "dates".
Have you checked the packaged cheese lately?
There are two jars of pickles: one is "Sweet Gherkins"; the other: "Kosher Dill".
Sure, they're "preserved" in a vinegar of sorts; but nothing can be preserved forever.
And, how long is "forever" when it comes to the age of foods? Evaluate _ and sanitize your refrigerator AT LEAST once a month: remove and wash trays, glass shelves, bins and drawers; move the fridge and clean behind and under it!
And we haven't even touched upon the freezer. The snow on some of those packages has formed an arctic tundra.
When it comes to observing rules for refrigeration, remember Rule #1: When in the slightest doubt, toss it out!

(Continued on following page)

(Continued from page 406)

<u>IV-A</u> EQUIVALENTS AND MEASURES

	equals		*equals*
A pinch	⅛ tsp. or less	16 oz.	1 lb.
3 tsp.	1 tbsp.	1 oz.	2 tbsp. fat/liquid
2 tbsp.	⅛ cup	1 cup liquid	½ pint
4 tbsp.	¼ cup	2 cups	1 pint
16 tbsp.	1 cup	2 pints	1 quart
5 tbsp. + 1 tsp.	⅓ cup	1 quart	4 cups
4 oz.	½ cup	4 quarts	1 gallon
8 oz.	1 cup	8 quarts	1 peck (apples, pears, etc.)

<u>IV-B</u> BAKING EQUIVALENTS

<u>Butter/Smart Balance Spread</u>	<u>Light Olive Oil/Canola Oil</u>
	USE
1 tsp.	¾ tsp.
1 tbsp.	2¼ tsp.
2 tbsp.	1½ tbsp.
¼ cup	3 tbsp.
⅓ cup	¼ cup
½ cup	¼ cup + 2 tbsp.
⅔ cup	½ cup
¾ cup	½ cup + 1 tbsp.
1 cup	¾ cup

CASSEROLES and ONE-POT SUPPERS (See pages 110-145)

KISS THE COOK
(About The Author)

Marion Orlando Celenza's Italian heritage permeates her recipes and gardening. Even as a child, she experimented with recipes and planted a garden of vegetables, herbs and fruits. Over the ensuing years, she would grow and dry herbs and peppers, process homegrown pickles and tomatoes and harvest garden fresh garlic.

Her garden has played host to many varieties of tomatoes, beets, onions, zucchini, several eggplant varieties, Brussels sprouts, rapini, beans, corn, pumpkins and butternut squash. (The latter as a result from a handful of seeds salvaged from a dinner menu.)

As a pre-teen, Marion commenced to document her family's recipes in a composition notebook. Today, she continues to document her cooking experiments on notepads which reside in a corner of her lab table: the kitchen counter.

In 2004 she published MENU LOG: A Collection of Recipes as Coordinated Menus, original recipes, arranged in 52 dinner menus, coordinated to marry appetizer to salad, to entrée, to dessert, in a seasonal ambiance. "It's easy to linger over these social dinners created for people who enjoy cooking (and eating) in a relaxed style one sees in Italy; indeed, the meal is the whole evening's entertainment." KIRKUS DISCOVERIES, March 2005, vol. 1/issue 1.

In 2009 she fulfilled her lifetime project: to record archival family recipes dating to the early 1900's. FROM THE TABLE OF PLENTY Food for the Body, Manna for the Soul is an inspirational family heirloom menu cookbook. It contains over 500 recipes, 100 menus, 75 essays and scores of photos. "The book has a homegrown scrapbook-like quality, its appeal is likely to extend well beyond even Celenza's large extended family. Recipes that will give cooks many solid and simple options for creating family-dining traditions." KIRKUS DISCOVERIES.

In 2006 she published THE POETRY OF DOGS, a delightful and whimsical, yet insightful mix of original verse and colorful photography, centered around the intricate bonds between humans and dogs. LUNCH IS IN THE BAG! A Celebration of the Midday Meal followed in 2008. "Lunch menus for the special weekend days or holidays on which readers actually have time to cook...A cookbook that provides reliable versions of old favorites." KIRKUS DISCOVERIES.

A secondary school teacher of English and Drama, Marion has spent all of her adult years on Long Island. Her husband John, was the "local dentist". Their son and daughter-in-law are research geneticists (he's in plant genetics). They and a host of relatives and friends totally enjoy the bounty from Marion's kitchen (including the family's Labrador Retrievers).

Marion invites her readers to visit her colorful and informative WEBPAGE:

http://www.MarionCooks.com

Marion O. Celenza

BOOKS BY MARION O. CELENZA

MENU LOG: A COLLECTION OF RECIPES AS COORDINATED MENUS

With Celenza's trusty MENU LOG, you could easily host a year's worth of dinner parties. Designed for the "professional home chef" (the author expects readers to know how to boil water and whip an egg white). Celenza has assembled 52 complete dinners with coordinated menus for six – from appetizers to desserts. It features an excellent index, sorted according to ingredients, name of dish, main ingredient and occasion. It's easy to linger over these social dinners created for people who enjoy cooking (and eating) in the relaxed style one sees in Italy – indeed, the meal is the whole evening's entertainment. Many à la carte dishes would also make excellent lunch fare. Bonus sections include three lavish party menus, plus recipes for brunch, sandwiches, buffets, hors d'oeuvres, cakes, pies and cookies. Celenza makes no concession to popular diets, but the foods suggested are wholesome and healthfully prepared. CAVEAT: Having pored over this excellent window into a tempting way of life (and cooking), the urge to entertain may be overwhelming. KIRKUS DISCOVERIES.

LUNCH IS IN THE BAG! A CELEBRATION OF THE MIDDAY MEAL

A no-frills cookbook arranged by seasons and menus, focused on lunch. Celenza points out that in today's workaday world, lunch is often overlooked. She therefore presents menus for those special weekend days and holidays on which readers actually have time to cook. The book is arranged in several sections and opens with complete menus – usually a salad or soup, one or more entrées and a dessert-organized by season. It's followed by sections devoted to Brunch, "Lite-Bites", Sandwiches, Heroes and finally, Dressings and Sauces. Readers may scratch their heads trying to understand why the opening section which makes up the bulk of the book, is lunch-appropriate – it contains recipes for Cassoulet, Parmesan Chicken, Beef Barley Soup and plenty of other dishes that could just as well be served for dinner. This would be more of a problem if – the recipes weren't so good! There are many reliable versions of favorites such as Jambalaya or Turkey Scallopine, plus some surprisingly successful tricks like sprinkling raw garlic on top of green bean salad. These recipes are easy to follow. Photos, drawings quietly charm. A cookbook that provides reliable versions of old favorites. KIRKUS DISCOVERIES.

FROM THE TABLE OF PLENTY FOOD FOR THE BODY, MANNA FOR THE SOUL

Spiced with memories of an Italian-American childhood in Brooklyn, this cookbook serves up a generous number of tried-and-true recipes for the family table. This culinary trove details more than 500 favorite recipes from the author, her friends and family. Divided into seasonal sections, which are supplemented by an extensive segment on pasta-centered meals and a final chapter devoted to sauces and dressings, the recipes are arranged mostly as complete menus. Typically, each of these includes a salad, an entrée and a dessert – and frequently a soup or vegetable. The emphasis is on Italian-American classics but there are nods to the melting pot. The portions are invariably generous, but the author acknowledges contemporary concerns about health by including low-salt and low-fat alternative ingredients. The recipes shouldn't exceed the capabilities of even casual cooks, as Celenza's directions are clear and helpful without being overwhelming. She's also specific, if forgiving, on measurements. Interspersed among the recipes are anecdotes and photos from Celenza's past, snippets of culinary history and reflections on how food warms, sustains and nurtures us, physically, emotionally and spiritually. She evokes a sense not merely of the dishes but of the time, place and camaraderie that Celenza associates with them, giving a warm, human context to these family feasts. While this book has a homegrown scrapbook-like quality, its appeal is likely to extend well beyond even Celenza's large extended family. Recipes that will give cooks many solid and simple options for creating family-dining traditions. KIRKUS DISCOVERIES.

THE POETRY OF DOGS

A whimsical yet insightful mix of verse and photography centered around the intricate bonds between humans and dogs. Endearing and colorful true-life photos; delightfully charming poetry. For animal lovers of all ages. Plus: Bonus Address Book.